Women's Rights to House and Land

CHINA, LAOS, VIETNAM

EDITED BY

Irene Tinker
Gale Summerfield

LYNNE
RIENNER
PUBLISHERS

BOULDER
LONDON

Published in the United States of America in 1999 by
Lynne Rienner Publishers, Inc.
1800 30th Street, Boulder, Colorado 80301

and in the United Kingdom by
Lynne Rienner Publishers, Inc.
3 Henrietta Street, Covent Garden, London WC2E 8LU

Library of Congress Cataloging-in-Publication Data
Women's rights to house and land : China, Laos, Vietnam / edited by
    Irene Tinker and Gale Summerfield.
        p.   cm.
    Includes bibliographical references and index.
    ISBN 1-55587-817-2 (hc. : alk. paper)
    1. Women's rights—China.   2. Women in development—China.
3. Women—Housing—China.   4. Women's rights—Laos.   5. Women in
development—Laos.   6. Women—Housing—Laos.   7. Women's rights—
Vietnam.   8. Women in development—Vietnam.   9. Women—Housing—
Vietnam.   I. Tinker, Irene.   II. Summerfield, Gale, 1948–   .
HQ1236.5.C6W66   1999
305.42'95—dc21   99-26774
                                                           CIP

1006568958

British Cataloguing in Publication Data
A Cataloguing in Publication record for this book
is available from the British Library.

Printed and bound in the United States of America

∞   The paper used in this publication meets the requirements
     of the American National Standard for Permanence of
     Paper for Printed Library Materials Z39.48-1984.

        5   4   3   2   1

To Ester Boserup,
whose trailblazing efforts included analysis of
women's work in both cities and agricultural production

Contents

Preface   ix

Introduction
Irene Tinker and Gale Summerfield   1

1 Women's Empowerment Through Rights to House and Land
   Irene Tinker   9

2 Economic Development, Housing, and the Family: Is the
   Singapore Approach an Appropriate Model?
   Jean Larson Pyle   27

PART 1: VIETNAM

3 Women Influencing Housing in Ho Chi Minh City
   Thai Thi Ngoc Du   55

4 Women's Access to Housing in Hanoi
   Hoang Thi Lich   77

5 Women and Rural Land in Vietnam
   Tran Thi Van Anh   95

6 Cultivating the Forest: Gendered Land Use Among the
   Tay in Northern Vietnam
   Carol Ireson-Doolittle and W. Randall Ireson   115

7 New Land Rights and Women's Access to Medicinal
   Plants in Northern Vietnam
   Jennifer Sowerwine   131

PART 2: LAOS

8   Gender and Changing Property Rights in Laos
Carol Ireson-Doolittle   145

9   Reforming Property Rights in Laos
Manivone Viravong   153

PART 3: CHINA

10   Chinese Women's Housing Rights: An International
Legal Perspective
Dia Warren   165

11   Housing Reform in Urban China
Gale Summerfield and Nahid Aslanbeigui   179

12   The Impacts of Shanghai Housing Reform
Fei Juanhong   195

13   State and Market Provision of Housing in Shanghai
Barbara Hopkins   207

14   The Housing Situation for Women in Beijing
Wei Zhangling and Bu Xin   223

15   Changes in Housing Patterns for Rural Chinese Women
Li Weisha   231

16   Changing Land and Housing Use by Rural Women in
Northern China
Li Zongmin   241

Conclusion
Irene Tinker and Gale Summerfield   265

Bibliography   273
The Contributors   297
Index   301
About the Book   305

Preface

"Women's rights are human rights" has become a celebrated declaration since the Convention on Human Rights met in Vienna in 1993. It was also a theme of the Fourth World Conference for Women in Beijing in 1995. The challenge in this statement addresses the tendency in many countries to separate family or customary law from civil law and to view human rights through a narrow lens. This volume focuses on property rights to housing and land as a significant part of women's human rights. A huge transfer of assets is under way in the privatization reforms in China, Vietnam, and Laos with almost no attention to the gender dimensions of the transfer. The chapters here examine how transition policies affect women's rights as families get use and ownership titles to state and traditionally managed land and housing.

Although virtually every country that has become independent since World War II has included equality for women and men in its constitution, customary practices have tended to prevail. The demand that women have equal rights in all matters has focused on a woman's rights to control and safeguard her body—matters relating to domestic violence and reproduction. Because a woman without any economic base lacks power to demand such rights, providing income opportunities has preoccupied those organizations that support women. Yet, working without guarantees for shelter and some access to land use is crippling for most women in lower-income countries, and the absence of these guarantees in turn limits women's income opportunities.

Seeking out information on women's rights to house and land as presented in this book entailed the efforts of many graduate students: Jennifer Sowerwine and Lan-Chi Po at the University of California (UC), Berkeley; Wendy Madrigal and Lyn Jeffrey at UC Santa Cruz; and Donna Burr, Maigee Chang, and Anne Talsma at the Monterey Institute of International Studies. The Institute for Urban and Regional Development at UC Berkeley administered the project and assisted in editing; Barbara Hadenfeldt, Chris Amado, David Van Arnam, and Jenna Loyd were all unfailingly supportive. Jody Ranck and Jennifer Sowerwine commented thoughtfully on the manuscript.

A meeting of Asian and U.S. authors was held at Berkeley and Monterey with support from the Social Science Research Council and the University of California's Pacific Rim Grant. Discussions during this initial reading of the papers benefited from comments by Diane Wolf, UC Davis; Gisele Bousquet, Fresno State University; and Chantheum Latmani, Lao Women's Union, in addition to the other contributors. Sandra Morgen, University of Oregon; Lousie Lamphere, University of New Mexico; Margaret Swain, UC Davis; Le Thi Quy, Center for Family and Women's Studies; and Hai-Ping Luo, Wright State University, added to the discussions. Thanks must go to Executive Chancellor Carol Christ, Dean of International and Area Studies (IAS) Richard Buxbaum, and Executive Director of IAS David Szanton, who graced the reception for the participants and supported the project throughout.

Kathy Martin, secretary of the Office of Women in International Development (WID) at the University of Illinois at Urbana-Champaign, and Silva Dushka and Aida Orgocka, research assistants, rendered assistance during the final stages of production when Gale became director of the WID office in 1998. The Ford Foundation regional offices and headquarters have given information and financial support throughout the project; special thanks go to Oscar Salemink in Hanoi.

The editors wish to extend particular thanks to Carol Ireson-Doolittle, whose knowledge of Laos has been of critical importance to clarifying issues in this little known country. In Hanoi, Heather Grady, Oxfam United Kingdom and Ireland, briefed us about land issues and the role of nongovernmental organizations in Vietnam. At Lynne Rienner, Bridget Julian, acquisitions editor, and Shena Redmond, senior project editor, prompted us through the intricacies of production with humor and persistence; we are deeply indebted.

Gale and Irene wish to compliment each other for their work together. Special thanks to Tai and Tommy, Gale's sons, for perseverance through the demands of research and writing. Irene's husband, Millidge Walker, provided inestimable solace as chauffeur, host, reader, and companion. Finally, we extend thanks to the contributors to this volume, who overcame language and cultural differences and heavy demands on their time to collaborate on this project.

—*Irene Tinker*
Gale Summerfield

Introduction: Women's Changing Rights to House and Land in Vietnam, Laos, and China

Irene Tinker and Gale Summerfield

This volume is the first book-length product of an ongoing collaboration among women in Vietnam, Laos, and China and colleagues in the United States based on our shared concern about the lack of attention being given to the inevitable gender disparities that accompany rapid socioeconomic change. The chapter authors document how implementation of reforms often has unplanned impacts on women that limit both their options and opportunities in comparison to men. Changes in the rights to housing and land, an integral but difficult policy area in these socialist countries moving toward market economies, are detailed for both rural and urban areas and reflect the diversity that exists in North and South Vietnam, in remote Laos, and throughout the vastness of China.

The mechanism for our collaboration is the Women's Network on Economic Transition in East/Southeast Asia (WONET), which grew out of an inspiring, week-long conference in Bangkok in June 1994. During the week, women from Laos, Vietnam, Cambodia, and China were able to discuss issues about women with their counterparts in Thailand and the United States, often for the first time.

The objectives of the Bangkok meeting were to hear the issues that most concerned the women from the former command economies and to share our experience and conclusions about ways women in many countries had tried to influence national and international policy in order to prevent economic development from unfairly impacting low-income women. Research conducted by Women In Development (WID) scholars has influenced the perspective of most practitioners of development, although implementation of projects for greater equity is still flawed. Participants were asked to list those issues in

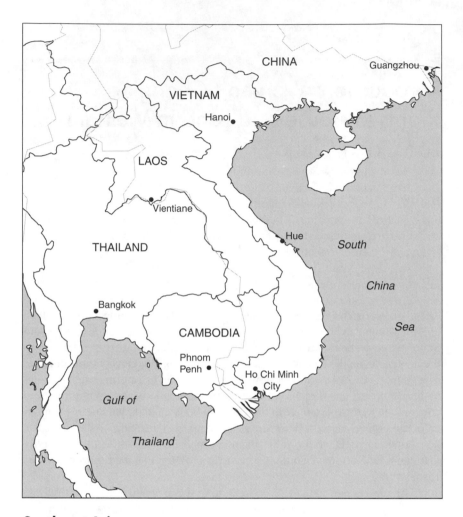

Southeast Asia

their countries that they felt might most adversely affect women and to identify key areas for collaborative research.

Difficulties in conducting team research among the diverse countries led
to a cooperative and parallel mode for studying these priorities. Seven graduate students from the University of California in Berkeley and in Santa Cruz
and from the Monterey Institute for International Studies were sent to Asia to
assist our colleagues in collecting existing data on women's condition. The
first topic selected related to the changing role of the family as a result of economic reforms. While Western women often see patriarchy, many of the
Asian women see a supportive unit of many relatives who share duties and re-

sponsibilities equitably. Some U.S. scholars are rethinking the role of the family as a counter to competitive individualism and to the regressive models presented by the right wing.

PROPERTY RIGHTS FOR WOMEN

Rapid economic change and privatization measures have begun to affect family cohesiveness, often leading to disputes over access to and use of house and land. Yet legal systems and regulations of government property are not yet in place to respond to these new social realities. Too often, the nominal equality of the former communist society gives way to remembered patriarchal dominance. The situation is in transition; the chapters in this volume indicate what is known and underscore the need for additional research in these countries and globally.

Property rights for women focus on the fundamental needs of having shelter and a base for earning income. For a rural woman, these rights mean that she can have a guaranteed share in land and house regardless of whether her husband stays with her, migrates to the city, finds another woman, or dies. She does not have to face the threat of being thrown off land she has farmed or out of a house that she maintained and possibly expanded because her husband or his relatives no longer want her there. In both rural and urban areas, housing for many poor women is not only shelter but a place to earn their income. Rural women use the house for processing materials to sell and for small-scale production or handicrafts; urban women generate income by using their housing for microenterprise, urban food production, or renting of rooms.

When the socialist governments were set up in Vietnam, Laos, and China, nominal rights were granted to women. The peasant leaders of these socialist movements realized the importance of the connection to land and granted land use titles to women as well as men; land was and is still officially owned by the state in these Asian countries. Housing in the countryside remained private, but in the city state-owned enterprises offered employees subsidized units at less than 5 percent of a worker's salary; these could be allocated to either women or men but in reality were given out through the man's work unit. Because China began its socialist phase in 1949, most urban households were living in subsidized units until recently; in Vietnam, which set up the socialist government in the North in the mid-1950s, and throughout the country in the 1970s, less than half the households were in state units in the North, fewer in the South. Laos, as a predominantly rural country, had not yet introduced subsidized housing; Russian-built apartments that were in the process of being constructed were left unfinished when the USSR government collapsed.

In practice, women in these countries seldom approached equality with men, although during the wars and civil disturbances women's work in fields and military service broke down many rigid traditional barriers. Women and men both were expected to work; in China and Vietnam a smaller family size was mandated. But household duties continued to be expected of women.

In 1976, China began its transition to a more market-oriented economy. The household responsibility system dramatically altered property rights by breaking down the communes into family farms; nonstate enterprises and self-employment were encouraged. The reforms in Vietnam (referred to as *doi moi,* or "renovation") and Laos began about a decade later, during the mid-1980s, and contain many of the elements of the Chinese model. The transition to a market economy, with its valuation of productive but not reproductive work, everywhere disadvantaged women—even in the matrilineal areas of Laos and Vietnam, where women have historically held stronger decision-making rights.

The main changes in property rights occurred with the return of family farms and private businesses. Land remains mostly under state ownership, but people may purchase the right to own a house or use the land. In Laos, a person is limited to acquiring fifteen hectares for private use; by allowing each family member to buy this amount, however, a large family can control a fairly extensive area, but a single wealthy family cannot dominate. In both China and Vietnam, some land has been set aside for people seeking to do business; how this area is allocated is less transparent than that of the main farming plots.

CONTEMPORARY LANDSCAPE

Cities in Vietnam, Laos, and China are strikingly different to a visitor. Hanoi is picturesque with its parks and lakes; its garden of scholars and single-pedestal temple in the lake decorate the heart of the city. Now slightly decaying, the European-style architecture of many buildings has earned it the nickname the "Paris of Asia" (a label shared by Shanghai). Ho Chi Minh City is larger, and its downtown is engulfed in construction; but both Hanoi and Ho Chi Minh City share a significant number of two- to three-story houses built on tiny plots approximately five by seven meters. Parents have often added the upper units to shelter their married children's families. The ground-floor access facilitates selling goods to passers-by. As officials allocate rights to build housing, more narrow houses are appearing on their tiny plots. The rectangular three- to five-story apartment buildings of the socialist planning period are already falling victim to the elements and appear old beyond their years. Squatters are also a growing part of city life in both areas. As housing permits take months to process, the poor and rich have built on and along the dikes in Hanoi; a sweep of housing from the central dikes in 1995 has left the odd sight of villas with jagged walls where rooms that were too close to the dikes were torn off.

Life in both Hanoi and Ho Chi Minh City takes place on the street. Despite occasional campaigns to drive vendors from the sidewalks, a pedestrian must look carefully to work her way through the people selling and eating noodles, mangos, and lichies; offering clothing, pots, and all variety of goods; cutting hair; playing badminton; and washing themselves on the sidewalks. The ancient guilds still leave their mark, as many streets are devoted to a single type of good: safes on one street, small hardware on another, clothing on yet another. Entrepreneurs are assertive, and a visitor's casual stroll cannot be an unbroken reverie.

Vientiane, in Laos, is quite a contrast. Although the city has a bustling center, much of it still moves at a slower pace. The plush greenery, brightly colored temples, and fairly empty streets create an atmosphere of timelessness. Single-family housing (not necessarily for nuclear families) is common. The characteristic style of housing on the outskirts of the cities is a unit built on stilts, reflecting the frequency of floods and need for a cool area under the main house; this is where young girls work at looms to produce the silk scarves and skirts that have become a major export with the reforms. Foreign-run restaurants are common in both Laos and Vietnam, NGO workers abound, and visitors arouse little curiosity. The first five-star hotel (a Chinese venture) opened in Vientiane in 1997, looking like a space capsule dropped from another world.

China entered its socialist period in 1949, much earlier than Vietnam and Laos, and its housing reflects the longer span. Most of the former private-style housing is gone, although some new units are being built. The country is so large that it cannot be contrasted with Southeast Asia in a single sweep of the hand. The major coastal cities are Beijing, Shanghai, Guangzhou, and Tianjin. Chongqing, Xi'an, and Wuhan dominate interior provinces. All have been growing rapidly since the reforms began in the late 1970s. High-rise buildings and multistory apartment buildings give the coastal cities the look of the modern metropolis. Everywhere, construction crews work on bamboo scaffolding. The traditional large boulevards near city centers add to the modern look. Traffic is dense and so is pollution. Remnants of traditional single-story courtyard housing can still be found, but modernization threatens them. Instead of building upward as in Vietnam, growing families and squatters have filled in many of the old courtyards.

In the countryside, the landscape is once again dotted with the patchwork of individual farms. Instead of teams of women weeding communal fields, one or two women can be seen tending to projects in the fields. Increasingly, women do most of the farming as husbands and sons migrate to the cities to look for work. Housing, however, in the more successful communes is a spacious contrast to the cities. In one village near Shanghai, every family has a roomy two-story house that would be the envy of people in much richer countries. The typical family still lives in difficult circumstances, as somewhere between 10 and 30 percent of the population is below the poverty line (depending on whether domestic or international standards are used), and most of these are in the countryside. Poverty is even higher in Vietnam and Laos.

CHAPTER TOPICS

Stressing that women's rights to house and land have only recently become a priority within the global women's movement, Irene Tinker surveys the literature to show how women around the world are addressing their needs for house and access to farmland. She argues that shelter empowers women and that women heads of households, until they possess a safe place for themselves and their families, will continue to be among the world's poorest people.

Jean Pyle explores the widely admired housing policy in Singapore to identify its implications for women, minorities, and employment. Understanding this experience is critical, because the Singapore model is respected and has in fact been copied explicitly in Shanghai and implicitly in Vietnam and elsewhere in China for housing and for the savings scheme.

The three chapters by Vietnamese scholars provide the reader with an insight to recent history in the country and address the ways in which the specific laws and regulations on land use and house plots affect women and men in distinct ways. Tran Thi Ngoc Du discusses reasons for the rapid urbanization of Ho Chi Minh City and details the growth of land speculation in the informal land market. She then utilizes a series of case studies of squatter areas to explore the extent of community participation in environmental improvement and housing decisions that is organized by national and international organizations. The environmental impact of tiny houses crowded along canals is detailed, and women's perceptions of their housing problems are also described.

Hoang Thi Lich first presents a history of urban settlements in Vietnam. She then analyzes recent studies of slum and squatter areas in Hanoi to outline the problems and needs of women living there and to discuss how limited sanitation and space affect women's quality of life. Tran Thi Van Anh reviews how the series of laws regulating rural cultivated land have moved from a communal system to household control, how the 1993 Land Law encouraged youthful marriage and new households, and how women tend to disregard, if they even know about, their rights for joint registration.

Two additional chapters on the upland areas of Vietnam discuss how traditional ethnic minorities utilize field and forest. Carol Ireson-Doolittle and Randall Ireson show how the balances within their system of agroforestry are changing under population pressure and new land regulations. They trace the gender dimensions of their work growing paddy, dry farming, and harvesting forest products. The growing trade in medicinal plants is the focus of Jennifer Sowerwine's study, in which she delineates the role of women and shows how the income from this activity empowers the women traders.

Manivone Viravong, an adviser both to the government of the People's Democratic Republic of Laos and to the Swedish International Development Agency (SIDA) at the time of writing, has become a pioneering entrepreneur. She reviews the new laws on land and forest use and shows how the process of privatization is likely inadvertently to transfer control of land from the traditional matrilineal inheritance patterns to male control. Carol Ireson-Doolittle spent more than a decade in Laos and provides a brief context for this little known country.

The chapters on China stress housing reform because that has become a significant part of the reform policies of the 1990s and because gender has not been addressed by those designing and implementing these policies. The section opens with an analysis by Dia Warren of housing laws in China in comparison with international legal standards. The chapter addresses how reality differs from theory, with practice tending to disadvantage women. Warren further discusses the need for institutional reform and education about legal rights.

Gale Summerfield and Nahid Aslanbeigui focus on gender aspects of housing policy as part of the overall economic transition policies. Because most urban residents in China lived in state housing before the reforms (in contrast to Vietnam and Laos), housing reform is tied to the changing role of the work unit as state-owned enterprises attempt to cut costs or face bankruptcy—a theme that reappears throughout the China section. This chapter discusses the links between housing reform and the labor market, social security, and other reforms. Issues of rental prices, home ownership, and the environment are also addressed.

Although China has been experimenting with different versions of housing reform, the model in Shanghai (drawing on the experience of Singapore as presented in Pyle's chapter) has been especially influential in molding national policy in the mid-1990s. Because of the significance of housing reform, two chapters discuss housing reform in this city—by Fei Juanhong and Barbara Hopkins. In the chapter on Beijing, Wei Zhangling and Bu Xin point out that housing in the city is affected by inequality between city and countryside as rural-urban migration is growing. That chapter and the one by Li Weisha discuss the influence of historic patterns in China on women's access to housing.

In the final chapter of the China section, Li Zongmin documents the changes in use and control of land and housing in the small village of Dongyao near Beijing and Tianjin (northern China). The chapter discusses several land redistributions and changes in women's work responsibilities in this village. These chapters together provide a view of the complexity of housing reform in the diverse areas of China.

1

Women's Empowerment Through Rights to House and Land

Irene Tinker

Women's rights to house and land in rural and urban situations have not, until recently, been deemed a critical problem by scholars or practitioners concerned with development issues. For too long, women were denied agency, glorified for their selfless devotion to their children, and embedded in kinship systems that provided some sort of shelter. Development projects focused on rural areas and sought to relieve the drudgery of subsistence living, improve income, provide credit, and increase agricultural production—all as part of a family. Today, families everywhere are disintegrating; cultural traditions that protected women, as they also constrained them, are collapsing. To survive in this rapidly changing socioeconomic milieu, women need the security of land and house to provide income and shelter for their children, and they need the power to control who shares the house.

As long as customary law governed the use of agricultural land, women had access to farmland through fathers or husbands. Such practice was based on deeply entrenched sexual divisions of labor that differed from one culture to another but generally reflected women's rights where women were subsistence farmers. Even in communist countries, where women and men in theory equally shared farming tasks on land that belonged to the commune or state, the gendered nature of household tasks was resistant to change. Assumed, along with the family unit, was a family homestead. Rural housing was self-built in most cases, by women as well as men, and belonged to the family unit.

Urban land seldom has had the clarity of customary rural land use with its communal ownership. European colonial powers, steeped in concepts of individual landownership and leasehold rights, usually established specific areas for their commercial and residential centers that were registered as foreign or private land; preexisting cities were surveyed and land adapted to Western legal systems. Surrounding lands usually remained under local customary traditions for use as agriculture and living space and were largely unmapped. Colonial administrators lived apart from indigenous cities. Servants' quarters were provided in these European settlements, but migration to cities was generally discouraged, especially for women. Indigenous women of high status were frequently secluded within the home; working women moved freely, often at personal risk, but were less restricted by cultural practices than were their rural kin. Cities continue to attract women and men seeking greater choices of life and work than exist in the countryside.

Today, as such customary land near cities is engulfed by rapid urbanization, rights to these lands are often challenged. Relatives move in to share kampongs in Indonesia, or government housing in Dar es Salaam (Sawio, 1994), or bachelor quarters in South Africa. Older housing becomes crowded urban slums. But in many countries only men can sign rental contracts (Grant, 1996). Even in squatter settlements men are presumed to be the head of household when titles for self-built shelters are provided (Sagot, 1993). In rural areas, commercial agriculture penetrates field and forest, putting pressure on farmers to sell land rights. Housing is separated from farmland, especially where land shortages and population increases result in rural landlessness. Family ties are loosened, women and men migrate together or separately, but children stay with the mother, increasing her need for shelter.

Trends toward globalization of the economy and predominance of market forces are propelling demands for clarity of land titles by indigenous as well as foreign investors. Most countries have instituted cadastral surveys; land is registered by household head, who is almost always presumed to be male. Such land rights preempt traditional claims to land use, whether by women farmers, nomadic herders, or poor gleaners. Accompanying this dislocation of traditional practices is the disintegration of family, as modernization reduces kinship ties and sanctions that bound families together. Too often, women are losing their customary rights to the use of land and house while being left by their partners to raise their children alone. This double-bind has pushed the demand for women's own rights to land and housing to the top of crucial issues for women during the twenty-first century.

Critical support for this effort has come from the 1993 Convention of Human Rights, which declared that "women's rights are human rights." Enthusiastically endorsed at the 1995 UN World Conference for Women in Beijing, this revolutionary concept sweeps away customary patriarchal control of women enshrined in customary law and allows women to demand civil rights on an equal basis with men. Where this concept is made into law, women can charge men for violence within the house as men might charge a robber on the street; bride price, which purchases the right to women's fertility and labor, would be outlawed. Going from convention to law to implementation is a long and difficult process: Nonetheless, international recognition of women's human rights is a marvelous and truly significant first step.

This chapter surveys the current state of women's rights to land and housing in developing countries, drawing on the sparse literature and on personal research. The first section reviews efforts to recognize women's economic rights through development programming, discusses the issues of poverty and women-headed households, and presents the debate about what factors empower women in household bargaining. The second section provides a geographic examination of land and housing problems and presents some of the proffered solutions. The final section begins with an analysis of suggested laws and practices that could provide women with some claim to land and housing and to existing laws that could be enforced to protect women's rights. This discussion provides the context for the ensuing chapters on Singapore, Vietnam, Laos, and China that show how changes in access to housing and land have altered women's lives, both enhancing and undercutting their household bargaining power.

WOMEN'S CHANGING ROLES IN THE HOUSEHOLD

During the first two-thirds of this century, women as individual actors were little studied in developing countries. When a Yale librarian in the 1970s searched the collection of Blue Ribbon Anthropology studies conducted before World War II, she found almost no references to women as a category; rather they were wives and mothers, part of a family or kinship system. Most sources for Ester Boserup's 1970 pathbreaking *Woman's Role in Economic Development* came from post-1950 sources; the major exceptions were studies of West African trading women that celebrated their market strengths and led many Western scholars to romanticize their independence and underestimate the persistence of a patriarchy rooted in land control (Afonja, 1990).

Postwar economists, theorizing about development in the Global South, saw women as possible impediments to change because of their conservative religious predilections. As the second wave of the women's movement took hold, women began to contest this dismissal of women and to document women's economic roles in subsistence activities and in remunerated enterprises that exist outside the formal sector. Time-budget studies and ethnographies of women's economic activities attest not only to women's essential economic contributions to family survival but to the longer hours of work women typically do when compared to men. As scholars were making women's invisible work in subsistence activities visible, activists sought to affect economic development policies whose premise was that women did not work (Tinker, 1990).

WOMEN HEADING POOR HOUSEHOLDS

Rapid economic change affected these subsistence activities even as they were being described. Migration increased, alternative forms of income freed men and women from traditional constraints, and the weakened ability of elders and society to enforce conformity to customary rules on marriage and family all contributed to new patterns of household structure, especially to the rise of women-headed households. Most such households lacked access to resources, whether rural land or urban housing, that typically were allocated through the male inheritance or male employment. The traditional solution for women rejected or abandoned by husbands was to return to their natal home. But poverty too often precludes that possibility. Many women migrated to towns, sometimes leaving their children with relatives; but the rise of women-headed households in rural areas should not be overlooked (Lee-Smith, 1993). In cities, women often moved in with kin, assisting the wife with her home and income tasks.

In Nigeria, young women worked in another woman's street–food vending stall, often in return for room and board; students flocking to a provincial capital for higher education sought out relatives for similar work, often sleeping in the vending stalls at night. In Senegal, younger women often became second or third wives in polygamous households, where they were charged with family support while older women earned income in street food-vending (Tinker, 1997a). Where housing was tied to employment on plantations or in industry, women had the choice of circulating as companions among men with such rights, seeking out rental rooms, or becoming squatters. Even minimal control of their own housing allows women to control their liaisons: In Guadalajara, women renting units with shared facilities were empowered to end abusive relationships or those in which the companion did not contribute to household expenses (Miraftab, 1997).

When women cannot find succor with kin but must earn their own income, they are greatly disadvantaged economically, especially when their children are small. Formal-sector wages are typically lower for women than they are for men; self-employed or vending women usually earn less than their male counterparts largely because they must split their working hours between income activities and family support. In rural areas, women agricultural laborers also are paid less than are men; food-for-work projects usually pay the same, but women tend to work shorter hours in order to care for their families. The presumption has been that most women-headed households are among the poorest.

Counting households headed by women and measuring their poverty present major methodological problems (Varley, 1996). Even today, with more determined counting techniques, accuracy in counting such households is elusive. Women whose husbands have migrated to urban areas or abroad are seldom willing to assume desertion. Adult men in present households are still considered the heads, even though they may be father, son, or son-in-law. Furthermore, visible males in the house through visiting unions (Massiah, 1990) or resident lovers (Miraftab, 1995) temporarily alter household structure but not control. Daughters with children move into their parents' house and maintain their own identity (Buvinic and Gupta, 1997), yet they lose their classification as household heads in the census. The original educated estimates—that 30 percent of all households are women-headed—remain a useful guideline. This estimate was made prior to the 1975 World Conference for Women in Mexico City as a heuristic device to call attention to a trend that was widespread globally but largely unnoticed by development planners.[1] By noting this high proportion of all households in many developing countries headed by women, Women In Development (WID) proponents hoped to ensure that women's concerns were included in programs designed to afford basic human needs to the poor in developing countries. The conflation of this approach with similar scholarship on poor women in the United States who are on welfare resulted in the widespread use of the term "feminization of poverty."

Because defining households, much less women-headed households, is problematic, assuming that women in such households are the "poorest of the poor" varies by culture, marriage patterns, and kin and government support, among other factors (Chant, 1996a, b). Ann Varley has assembled recent studies to question whether all women-headed households are poor and to stress the diversity of women-headed households; although she notes the often contradictory research findings, she nonetheless concludes that such households have lower dependency ratios (1997). In contrast, Claire Robertson identifies higher dependency ratios as one of several reasons that women in Kenya are poor (1996). Studies on the nutritional status of children generally find it higher in households headed by women, although this reflects priorities as much as income. Faranak Miraftab found that in Guadalajara, Mexico, women-headed households living in centrally located shared housing had total incomes equal to intact households in peripheral settlements headed by men; but most household members worked, precluding schooling for older children and thus replicating poverty in the next generation, while children in intact households did continue at school (1997).

Household poverty levels are, if anything, more difficult to measure, involving as they do concepts of household as well as monetary values that are strongly affected by cultural practices, local entitlements to rationing and housing, and access to land for self-provisioning. Kin ties that provide exchange of food and goods between urban and rural residents also complicate the accuracy of a "poverty line." Vietnamese economist Vo Tran Ang challenged the World Bank poverty studies based on caloric intake that declared 51 percent of all Vietnamese as poor, as compared to government research that produced a 20 percent figure (1996).

HOUSEHOLD BARGAINING

Development programs sought to alleviate poverty among poor women through income activities and then through microlending programs. Still, donor governments avoided targeting women heads for economic projects, fearing accusations of encouraging family dissolution or immorality. As a result, most such programs focused on women with partners. However, women's difficulties in controlling their income within patriarchal households have raised many questions about the effectiveness of such programs. Men often reduce their household contributions once women's income rises, producing a zero-sum game. Recent criticisms of the Grameen Bank complain that women's loans were largely used by their husbands; an eight-village, two-year study notes that while only 9 percent of the women used all their funds for their own activities, 70 percent used at least some of the money themselves. The study concluded that although the economic contribution of these activities was small the empowerment of women was significant (Hashemi et al., 1996)

Economists have argued that outside income is a dominating factor in household bargaining (Sen, 1990). Even unremunerated agricultural labor appears to increase the patriarchal bargaining where women are the primary subsistence farmers (Kandiyoti, 1988), but not in countries where women's labor is assumed to be an extension of household responsibilities (Agarwal, 1996). Similarly, women working within family enterprises have power that is related both to culture and to their importance to the enterprise. Thus, women in Taiwan gained little from their work in small family enterprises (Gallin, 1995), while women involved in street food preparation in Bangladesh—but who did not sell on the streets—were seen as integral to this income activity (Tinker, 1997a).

Most efforts to assist poor women in earning income involve membership in some sort of organization. The collective is everywhere stronger than the individual; it provides information and insight into issues beyond the household, but it also shows the isolated woman that she has similar problems to those of her neighbors. From Korean Mothers' Clubs to the Grameen Bank, organized women gain greater self-esteem that quickly translates into other forms of empowerment. Indeed, these many small units have swelled to the global women's movement that is causing a paradigm shift unparalleled in history (Castells, 1997). As women become empowered within and outside the household, they begin to question a basic element in the maintenance of patriarchal dominance: access to land and house.

Our concern with these data is to show the need women have for permanent shelter, whether they are poor or not, with dependents or not. Because women, even those with means, are disadvantaged when considering rights to land and housing. These rights vary by custom and history and affect any contemporary efforts to ensure use or ownership rights to women. Their ability to demand these rights is often related to available work alternatives and opportunities. Guaranteeing women's equal rights to housing, however, allows women a secure base from which to build a future for her family and enhances her bargaining power with her partner.

LAND AND HOUSING RIGHTS

In 1900, only one in eight persons lived in cities. The perception of the development community that rural poverty and underemployment were the primary issues in Asia and Africa has persisted long after migration trends have altered the rural-urban balance. By 2000, half of the global population will live in urban areas. Of these, 20 percent will live in cities of 4 million or more. Seventeen of the twenty-three megacities with more than 10 million people will be located in the Global South. The rapidity of change is greatest in Africa; but in Bangladesh, Dhaka has grown from a provincial backwater to a megalopolis expected to reach 19 million by 2015. These population changes are accompanied by the globalization of industry and a new emphasis on individual self-sufficiency over community and kinship support. Laws and practices of the market economy are based on patriarchal Western law that reinforces traditional customs and dominant religions that similarly privilege men. Yet women everywhere are still expected, and expect themselves, to be the primary caretaker of children. And as life expectancy increases, they care for the elderly as well. Without a place to call home, how can women possibly carry out these social roles?

RURAL PATTERNS

Women's access to farmland is critical in Africa, where culture dictates that women grow food to feed their families. Historically, a woman's labor, along with her fertility, was a major investment by the husband that called for a significant bride price to be paid to the bride's family, resulting in the "persistent low status of women in the domestic domain" (Afonja, 1990: 199). As a commodity, women became the property of the man's family, to be inherited by another family member should the husband die, along with the material goods accumulated by the couple. Although this arrangement used to guarantee a woman's continued access to land so that she could feed her children, the safety-net aspects of this practice are weakening; women too often lose both access to land and their material possessions, including shelter, upon the death of her husband (Lee-Smith, 1997).

The pervasive control of men over women in Africa has been documented in studies in Uganda (Obbo, 1990), Kenya (Robertson, 1996; Lee-

Smith, 1997), Zambia (Hansen, 1996), and Morocco (Maher, 1981), among others, which further indicate that women's "position tends to worsen as the part of the household income which consists of money increases" (Maher, 1981: 85). An indication of this continued low status is revealed by figures on polygamy, which today has become predominantly an African phenomenon even in countries that are not necessarily primarily Muslim: Nearly half of all women in Togo, Senegal, and Guinea, and more than 40 percent in Liberia, Cameroon, and Nigeria, live in polygamous unions (Antoine and Nanite-lamio, 1996: 132).

The introduction of modern farming methods and of commercial crops has, if anything, made the work of African women farmers more onerous. Expected to continue supplying food for the family, women's fields were too often relegated to marginal lands while the prime land was taken for commercial use by husbands who were still able to require women to work those plots; fertilizer may increase weeds, and tractors enlarge farm sizes. In recent years, economic development programs have recognized these issues and sought ways to improve women's productivity by insisting that women have access to cooperatives, extension services, and appropriate technology. Yet even when men migrate and leave their wives to work on their fields, men's control of land continues to undermine women's ability to make independent decisions about the farm. Thus, programs meant to aid women may have only added to their burdens. So also did such heralded land-reform schemes as Julius Nyerere's Ujamaa village efforts, which increased women's workload but did not result in their receiving monetary compensation because men controlled the sale of crops. Women tried to save their access to land by appealing to customary rights, which were locally considered stronger than land titles. Jana Patterson Bakari found these rights malleable and responsive to power. If they accumulate money through trade or enterprise, women often try to buy land in another woman's name (1995).

Changes in land tenure rights generally privilege men and allow them to abrogate women's land rights. Local officials in Cameroon were concerned that new laws on land registration were being abused by educated young men of the region who filed their names for titles, presumably expecting to claim these rights once the older tribal members, who knew who had what rights, had died (personal field notes, 1985). Sean Redding has documented land allocations in the Transkei in the 1920s and found that custom required men to be married in order to qualify for land. Once land was surveyed to provide for white settlers, only a finite number of arable allotments remained; these were to be inherited by the oldest son of the first wife. As a result of these changes, the value of rural wives decreased, and women without access to land were forced to migrate; this influx led authorities to prevent women from living in towns (1996).

In contrast, recent studies in Namibia show that those areas that remained under the control of local chiefs, through a sort of reservation system, preserved women's traditional rights to land. Their access continues and, due to matrilineal patterns, women heading households are able to acquire land use rights: These households held 6.38 hectares of land on average as compared to 7.19 hectares held by male households (Wamukonya, 1997).

Customary landholding brings with it the dominance of bride price as well. In South Africa, the conflict between customary rights over women and civil rights giving women equality with men raged throughout the constitutional discussions. Until 1990, women's issues were subordinated to the national struggle, but drafts of the constitution reinstated power to tribal chiefs, a move women feared would legitimize women's subordination. In 1992, the Women's National Coalition was formed from eighty-one groups and thirteen regional alliances of women's groups, plus the women's caucuses or "gender desks" of all major parties; within two years, this group issued the Women's Charter for Effective Equality, which stipulated that customary law would be subordinate to the Bill of Rights. The amended constitution, passed on February 7, 1997, gives women equal legal rights with men to land and housing.

However, progress in allowing tenant families rights to remain on land where they have lived and work for decades is slow. Because of frequent postponement of the effective date of tenancy, landowners are kicking off residents before the laws on land tenure and redistribution are implemented. Teresa Yates documents her letter with the story of Mrs. Moko, who has lived on a farm for thirty-eight years and worked there for twenty-nine years. Because she stopped working to care for her grandchildren, she was told to leave. She has filed a claim for unfair dismissal, but the best outcome she can hope for is some compensation. She will still have to leave her home (Yates, 1997).

Kenya proclaims equality of gender in its constitution but "rescinds its own nondiscrimination clause specifically in regard to personal law, which has far-reaching effects on the lives of women and their access to property" (Lee-Smith 1997). Even houses that are traditionally constructed on their farmland by women and men together are now presumed to be the property only of the husband. Some women convert to Islam, which does allow women to inherit land under personal law, but Lee-Smith notes that civil law may not be supported in practice. What is fascinating in Kenya, however, is the distinction between rural and urban land, the result of British colonial law. According to prevailing cultural assumptions, "women are assigned to rural life and work, but to the ownership of urban property. Men, on the other hand, are assigned to urban life and work but to the ownership of rural property, from which women are generally excluded" (Lee-Smith, 1997: 89). Women can purchase urban land, but few have sufficient funds to do so.

To address the growing problem of Kenyan women for access to land and housing, Lee-Smith suggests that the 28,000 women's organizations throughout the country be mobilized for this purpose. These community organizations have been alienated by the elite leadership of Nairobi-based women's organizations; they are rotating savings groups, burial societies, income-producing enterprises, and agricultural support groups. Many have been allocated land by local authorities for crops and schools. Asks Lee-Smith: Why not for rural housing clusters near urban settlements? Because an organization would hold the use rights to the land, individual women would be protected from demands of their kin just as organizations have allowed women earning money from enterprises to save in face of demands from husbands for access to their earnings.

Issues of women's access to land, both arable farmland and communal resources such as forests and commons, are equally critical in India. Bina Agarwal contends that land is the major source of power within rural households, and without access to or ownership of land, women cannot alter the fundamental gender relationships embedded in current family structures: "Command over private land could strengthen rural women's bargaining power in ways that merely enhancing wage employment opportunities . . . could not" (Agarwal, 1997: 13).

In order to extend household bargaining models beyond reliance on economic factors along, Agarwal argues for broadening and prioritizing the factors that contribute to and inhibit women's ability to bargain by considering a wide range of social norms and perceptions that operate not only within the household but beyond it as well. Extrahousehold influences include, among others, laws on land-owning and inheritance, and access to bureaucrats adjudicating land claims. She also stresses organizational support, noting that women acting collectively have far greater power than individual women (Agarwal, 1997).

To illustrate, tribal women in the Panchmahals of Gujerat State, India, have traditionally collected fuelwood and fodder in nearby state forests. Increased degradation of these forests meant greater restrictions on access; so a local nongovernmental organization (NGO) worked with local women to rehabilitate wastelands and plant their own plantations. Organizing women and so empowering them was central to the effort; women's new assertiveness allowed them to take on men who were illegally cutting grass on their plantation (Sarin, 1995).

Such organizations are widely perceived as critical to women's empowerment and have been encouraged by NGOs, local action groups, and most development projects. These positive factors may be countered by women's lack of knowledge about their rights under new laws and regulations. More problematic are prevailing social norms that discourage women from invoking their rights because social acceptance for utilizing them is absent.

As a result of rapid socioeconomic change, the plight of women alone, whether widows or mothers who have been divorced or discarded by their partners, becomes more difficult. Men abdicate their responsibilities to help support their children, an action that would have been constrained in most traditional cultures. Even widows were offered greater protection than they now receive. In India, widows in most communities are legally entitled to inherit at least some land, though Martha Chen found that "less than half exercise even use rights over what ought to be their land" (quoted in Nussbaum, 1995: 15). Once again, women were not always aware of their rights.

Women's reluctance to challenge the new laws when they conflict with traditional landholding patterns is evident in Laos, according to Viravong and Ireson. In Vietnam, land that had been consolidated into communes is currently being redistributed to families and may be registered in the names of both husband and wife. Note that while technically all land belongs to the state, land use rights may be bought and sold as though they were ownership rights. In one district in the Mekong Delta, the Vietnam office of Oxfam (United Kingdom and Ireland) has been encouraging district officers to put both names on the documents. Heather Grady reports, however, that women knew little about the process and thought that registration of both spouses was routine. "Without a sense of the potential impacts that this [having the land registered in their names] could have on their lives, women also have no interest or ability to exercise their rights." Grady recommends that the government "hold meetings exclusively for women in the communes to educate them about their rights and privileges attached to a Land Use Certificate" (1997: 7).

In Laos, the new Land Law (1996) and Forest Law (1997) show how easily women's land rights can be undermined, according to Viravong (see Chapter 9). Lowland Lao women live in matrifocal family units; a daughter, usually the youngest, inherits the parents' land and housing along with the obligation to care for them. Viravong notes that even though the law is gender-neutral, forms require the land to be registered in the name of the head of household instead of in the name of the owner of the land. Furthermore, she asserts, "since husbands are responsible for official activities outside of the household, they commonly handle the registration of household land. Men sometimes register property under their own name even though it belongs to their wives." The Lao Women's Union has been holding seminars for district staff and for women throughout the country to inform them about women's rights and the registration procedures.

Islamic conventions allow women to inherit land, a right that was extremely progressive when it was proclaimed. Once women have some land, accumulating more is not seen as unusual. Bangladeshi women have been using their loans from Grameen Bank to accumulate agricultural land, according to a fascinating study by Helen Todd (1996). Living for a year in two villages in daily contact with women members, Todd's conclusions about the use of credit by these women challenge the statistics that show women utilizing loans for various traditional women's income activities have a low return. In fact, the women lease land so that their husbands and sons can cultivate it, and when she is able, she buys the land, often in her own name. One woman, under pressure to marry her fifteen-year-old daughter, gave land as dowry to the prospective groom from another village but registered the land in her daughter's name (Todd, 1996: 228). Todd concludes that landownership effectively raises these women and their families out of poverty.

Protecting women's traditional land use rights is a problem in Mexico as well, even among the Zapatistas. A review of the thirty-four points that constitute the Zapatistas' Commitments for Peace show that although land is the dominant demand of this resistance effort, women's right to possess land is not mentioned, even though a majority of those expelled from the land, largely because they are Protestants, are women. The Commitments for Peace include support for women's health and for artisan centers. But the women themselves do not raise the issue of land, even for widows or single women (1991).

Rural housing tends to remain under family control. When catastrophes such as earthquakes devastate homes, new designs are introduced without regard to use rights. In October 1993, a devastating earthquake in central India killed thousands of farmers sleeping in their houses—piles of stone with little or no mortar; more wealthy citizens survived in their reinforced concrete homes. Some years earlier, Nepal's rural housing was crumbled by strong quakes. In both cases, funding through the United Nations Centre on Human Settlements (UNCHS) assisted the countries to rebuild. Customary inheritance through the male kinship was not questioned.

Through the intervention of the Grameen Bank, the story was different in Bangladesh after rural houses were swept away by abnormally severe floods. Loans for rebuilding to build tiny rural homes that measure roughly ten feet by twenty feet were offered only to Grameen Bank members of several years' standing; an evaluation in 1989 showed that nearly 95 percent of all housing loans went to women. However, a home loan would not be granted if the woman did not own title to the land under the house; if her husband's family or other owner would not grant her title, the bank would give her a loan to buy the land first (Tinker, 1993a).

URBAN HOUSING

Some sort of shelter is essential for human survival; for poor urban families, shelter may be a temporary shack erected on sidewalks or on marginal land. In 2000, 2 billion of the 3 billion people living in urban areas will be in developing countries: A majority of the absolute poor in the Global South will be urban. In Latin America and the Caribbean, where three-quarters of the people already live in towns and cities, women outnumber men 108 to 100. Informal housing predominates in many urban areas: two-thirds of the people in Nouakchott, Mauritania, and in San Salvador, El Salvador; more than half in Guayaquil, Ecuador, and Delhi, India; between 40 and 50 percent in Mexico City, Lima, Peru, Nairobi, Kenya, and Manila, the Philippines; and as much as 25 percent in Bangkok, Thailand. And as the populations of these cities grow, marginal spaces within the urban areas fill, leading both to increased density in squatter areas and to urban sprawl.

Squatters resist resettlement outside town because of the high costs in money and commute time. Furthermore, expenses for maintaining improved services are often beyond their household budgets (Tinker, 1993b). Throughout India, half the families offered housing in the periphery move back into town because they cannot afford costs of the shelter with its higher-grade services and cannot afford either the money or the time required to commute to work. Moreover, the move destroys their community networks, through which they learn of jobs (Bapat, 1987; Schylter, 1990)

So squatters contrive to remain where they are despite the lack of water and sewerage. A 1992 survey of squatters in the Juhu beach area of Bombay City, India, enumerated 93,000 people from fourteen Indian states living on about 175 acres in seventeen different, and not always contiguous, pockets of land along the ocean beaches and up into nearby marshland. Settlement began more than forty years ago, and little space is left on government land, so that some families have pushed into neighboring private land. In 1974, the area was officially declared a slum by the municipality, a designation that provides a minimal degree of protection against eviction, but only for those on government land. About half the families live in houses constructed of brick and cement with a permanent, fireproof roof; but almost no houses include a private latrine. Most houses have electricity illegally, but half of the families pay more for this illegal use than they would if they had legal connections. Party organizers, local NGOs, and an outreach project of the Women's University in Bombay have been able to pressure the city to improve toilet facilities, increase health and education services, and introduce training in income activities for the women (Varghese, 1993).

Pavement dwellers are the poorest and most vulnerable squatters: They erect temporary shelters on pathways and sidewalks. In Bombay the women of this community were organized by the Society for Promotion of Area Resource Centres (SPARC) to resist the threatened demolition of their shacks in 1985 (Bapat, 1987). The women's own organization, Mahila Milan, has, after a decade, begun construction for 560 families on municipal land near their pavement site. To keep costs down, the women are manufacturing their own wall blocks and precast beams and are providing all unskilled labor for the fifty-six–unit, two-story building, which incorporates many of the design features tried and tested in other housing projects. A similar group in Pune was recently allocated land where the women have helped build two-story apartments with the help of the Bombay group. The project has been receiving much media attention and has generated so much excitement that Pune has now committed to finding land for two other Mahila Milan collectives under threat of eviction (ACHR, 1998).

Because urbanization began earlier in Latin America, most squatter areas have been upgraded and provided with basic services. Women in these settlements often took the lead in demanding improved local services, leading Moser to add to women's double day a third role as community manager. This leadership was possible because women in Latin America are less likely to work outside the house than are women in Africa and much of Asia; even under structural adjustment policies, the labor participation rates for women in a squatter area of Guayaquil, Ecuador, rose from 40 percent in 1978 to only 52 percent in 1988 (Moser, 1993).

Elsewhere in Latin America, worker-priests began organizing these popular sectors after World War II; many base and community organizations continue to receive funds from abroad through the Catholic Church and NGOs. The Pope opposes political activities by priests, so links with the church are being obscured. In Caracas, Padre Armando Janssens founded the Centro al Servicio de la Accion Popular (CESAP) in 1974; it is now the largest NGO in the country. Janssens comments that homelessness, especially of children, was not a problem until recently because of the high birthrate (1997).

The numbers of street children are not as critical as in Brazil, for example. Less than half of children on the street claim to have no family. The majority live in two-parent households "although not necessarily their own parents" (Rizzini et al., 1994: 62). Reasons for working on the street relate to family violence and stepfathers as well as inadequate educational and employment opportunities. Crowded living conditions clearly contribute: Half of urban Indian families consist of 4.4 persons living in a single room (Blanc et al., 1994).

Women in cities lose the kin support that is common in rural villages; they also must earn more money to feed their children. Lee-Smith shows that urban households have a lower sense of well-being than their rural counterparts, whose monetary income may be lower because opportunities for subsistence agriculture are limited (1996). Nonetheless, urban poor, especially in Africa, engage in many types of urban agriculture, from animal, fish, and poultry-raising to vegetable production (Egziabher et al., 1994; Smit, 1996). As money plays a larger role in the family budget, men, by virtue of their ability to earn more, come to dominate women more (Thorbek, 1991). Lack of restraint from extended-family members allows men to indulge in domestic violence and to walk out on their children, resulting in the worldwide increase of women-headed households noted above.

Critical is the ability of these women heads of households to provide shelter for their families. In the 1970s, development projects were initiated by governments and NGOs to assist the poor in building their own houses. These efforts, which offered credit to household heads and required sweat equity to reduce the costs, assumed an intact family—that is, one with a male head. Even self-help housing that required sweat equity disadvantaged women who had less time to work and lacked money to pay for a replacement. As a result, most urban women remained dependent for shelter on the men with whom they lived and who could throw them out should he fancy another woman. Married or not, women in most countries do not, and often cannot, have title to their homes in their own names or with their spouse.

Costa Rica offers perhaps the most exciting home ownership program. The housing organization Comite Patriotico Nacional (COPAN) found that more women than men participated in their housing programs, both in the political action to obtain housing resources and in the actual design and construction of their homes. Once the houses were completed, men from whom the women had been separated frequently decided to move in and tried to claim title. In reaction, COPAN pressured the government to pass the Real Equality Bill in 1990. This exemplary legislation granted women household heads the right to register government-supported housing in their own names; if the woman were married, the house was registered in the names of both wife and husband (Sagot, 1993).

Women alone also need the right to rent places to live. In many countries, women are considered minors, unable to sign binding contracts. In Zimbabwe, female-headed households comprise between 43 percent and 48 percent of all households, and 42 percent of these women-headed households are women living alone, according to Miriam Grant (1996). Although many of these women are widows or come from broken marriages, many middle-class professional women remain single by choice, as they do elsewhere in Africa (Obbo, 1990). Rental housing is in short supply. After independence, houses were sold to sitting tenants who were overwhelmingly male: Women were considered illegal lodgers in single-male quarters, and only males qualified for married quarters. As a result, children are usually sent back to rural areas, since women lack space to bring in relatives to help out and, as they are lodgers in overcrowded quarters, there is no space to grow food (Grant, 1996).

Customary law in many parts of Africa provided for widows by marrying them to a brother of her husband, thus providing the widow with continued access to land while keeping the family investment in the woman's labor intact. Under these circumstances, all property in the house and the house itself belonged to the male lineage. Many urban women heading households are widows who have been chased away by kin of her dead husband or are women who ran away rather than marry the brother (Lee-Smith 1993). In many African urban areas today, the male lineage still tries to appropriate property but does not wish to be responsible for the woman. Besides the famous Otieno case in Nairobi, where the lineage eventually obtained only the body of their kinsman (Stamp, 1991), many studies record the devastation such practices wreak on women. Karen Tranberg Hansen notes the problems traders have in securing money against the day their husbands die (1996). In Dar es Salaam, groups of women are purchasing urban homes together, thereby preventing any one lineage from trying to seize the property. Such practices continue, even though in many countries laws now secure women's rights to inherit their own and often their husband's property. For example, in Zimbabwe, laws were passed in 1981 that give women property rights in the case of divorce and rights to the home on death of the husband; but the laws are seldom implemented (Grant, 1996).

In cities, rights to the house are paramount because they are more than places to sleep. Neither governments nor NGOs involved in urban housing projects have sufficiently acknowledged the extent to which houses are sites of production as well as residents. For example, squatters who had been relocated in desirable downtown walk-up apartments in Jakarta built with help from UNCHS sold out to middle-class tenants because they could not continue their productive enterprises in cramped space above the streets (Tinker, 1994). More dramatic, in 1994, police burned corn crops in urban backyards in Harare, Zimbabwe, despite near-famine conditions in that country. Family enterprises are more competitive than small enterprises because they pay no rent and are often closer to markets (Miraftab, 1994; Strassmann, 1987).

Conflict between tribal or customary laws and modern legal systems adopted in most countries makes urban planning almost impossible.[2] The lack of cadastral surveys and clear land rights inhibits foreign investment and the construction of modern buildings. If women seldom hold title to their urban dwellings, neither do men. Recent studies on urban land policies indicate that only 22 percent of barrio dwellers in Venezuela owned their land; in Cameroon only 20 percent of all urban land had been surveyed and titled, a higher figure than the 6 percent of all lands in the country that are registered. Indonesia incorporated traditional land tenure systems into a new agrarian law, but adherence to traditional *adat* continues in about one-third of Jakarta (Dowall and Clark 1991; Farvacque and McAuslan 1991). But as titles replace customary land control, men generally receive these new and stronger land rights.

EMPOWERING WOMEN THROUGH PROPERTY RIGHTS

Rapid economic transformation of developing countries is causing an acceleration of Western laws governing property ownership, both in near-subsistence societies and in former command economies. Pressures from population growth on agricultural land, as well as land consolidation by wealthy landowners and agribusinesses, are causing land shortages and increasing landlessness. Women are particularly vulnerable because land they farm is seldom regarded as their own either under customary or civil law. Frequently, women are even losing rights to homes where they have lived for years and to house plots where they can grow some of their food. Subsequent migration to urban centers by both women and men adds to the creation of megacities and their formidable housing problems.

To some extent, the privatization of state-held property in communist countries has distinctive features: Former landowners are claiming property confiscated at the time of the countries' communist revolutions. Even in these countries, however, traditional rights and customs have not been totally erased, particularly in Laos, Vietnam, and China; evidence of customary procedures and rights is seeping back into property transactions, with unpredictable results.

To counter these negative trends, a growing number of NGOs are working with poor women in both rural and urban areas to defend their access to land and housing, understand their legal rights, and organize for self-protection. These NGOs act as intermediaries between the community-based organizations and the funders, who are often from outside the country. The growing power of NGOs reflects both the broadening of civil society and the inability of the state to address critical societal problems. Both Vietnam and Laos now allow foreign NGOs to operate in their countries but require that implementation be through mass organizations such as the Women's Unions that were originally set up by the Communist Party. China has resisted foreign NGOs but has allowed a few women's organizations, such as a domestic violence hotline, to operate outside the All China Women's Federation.

The belief that women are more likely to influence decisions of importance to their lives through their own organizations is becoming more recognized (Tinker, 1999). Early development programs concentrated on economic empowerment, but women's lack of power within the household has often limited the impact of women's economic advances on their lives. If household bargaining results in a breakdown, it is essential that the woman with her children does not lose her shelter. Hence, using the power of women's organizations to change laws on titling processes for land or housing is critical.

Throughout this chapter, we have cheered the imaginative examples of such actions that are drawn from widely diverse countries: Costa Rica and its Real Equality Law, Laos where national education programs are presented, and the Grameen housing loans in Bangladesh. Pavement dwellers in India have obtained tiny urban land allocations through the Mahila Milan organizations. In Kenya, Diana Lee-Smith is urging women's community organizations to use their legitimacy to petition for communal housing plots. Questioning customary law and its control of women and their rights is widespread throughout the world; the United Nations Convention for the Elimination of all Forms of Discrimination against Women has been ratified by 167 countries and is becoming a powerful moral tool to enhance women's rights around the globe. Women's growing political power, as manifested in these many organizations on all tiers of government, needs to be extended to the household by initiating ways for women to obtain rights to their own land and housing.

NOTES

1. During the planning of the international Women in Development conference that was held in Mexico City prior to the United Nations conference under the sponsorship of the American Association for the Advancement of Science and its international office (of which I was director), I polled the women present to arrive at the received wisdom of the group. The figure of 30 percent of all households headed by women was subsequently quoted as proven, rather than as an estimate. One of the first studies completed by the International Center for Research on Women, which I founded in 1976 (for history, see Tinker, 1983) to undertake international policy studies, used census data to establish more empirical information (Buvinic et al., 1978).

2. An extreme example exists in Papua New Guinea, where indigenous tribal elders are forcibly taking back the land along with the schools and hospitals erected on them that they had sold or leased to Germans or Australians (see Tinker, 1993a).

2

Economic Development, Housing, and the Family: Is the Singapore Approach an Appropriate Model?

Jean Larson Pyle

Singapore is widely cited as an economic success story in the development literature and by international institutions (World Bank, 1993b). It is considered a model of economic development by many countries worldwide, particularly by its Asian neighbors. In a relatively short period of time, from 1965 to the present, it has achieved very high levels of per capita income and low levels of unemployment and has rehoused virtually all of the population. Because it has been based substantially on production by multinational corporations for export, it has typically been described as a market-oriented economy and has been cited as validating the export-oriented "free market policies" that the World Bank has been promoting worldwide. Its housing policy, as well as its industrial development policy, has been influential in the reforms in China, especially Shanghai, and in Vietnam.

Singapore has developed various relationships with formerly socialist economies in the region that have begun the transition toward more market involvement in their economies—Vietnam, Laos, Myanmar/Burma, and China. It acts in advisory capacities in different aspects of their development processes, has established commercial ventures in them, and seeks to promote its overall leadership role in the greater region—as a financial hub, a transportation hub, and a strong promoter of Asian values. The Singapore model can be attractive to these transitional economics because of Singapore's impressive economic statistics in terms of income and growth, its success in providing modern housing and jobs for its people, the presence of a strong state (one that is familiar to these transitional countries), and many elements of the Asian ideology (such as the importance of family, the community, hard work, and respect for authority).

More recently, however, the nature of the economic underpinnings of the Singapore model has been significantly reassessed, and its political and ideological dimensions have become more prominent and controversial. What is necessary to achieve anything close to Singapore's results may be quite different than the picture typically painted of Singapore. The Singapore model must be seen as a complex of ideological, political, and institutional factors rather than simply as an economic approach. For example, it is now acknowledged that, although Singapore has been widely cited as an example of economic liberalism, the Singaporean economy has involved much more planning than formerly recognized (Huff, 1995). In addition, although the country has democratic institutions such as a parliament and general elections, Singapore has been governed since independence in 1965 as a one-party state (the People's Action Party, or PAP) that has maintained authoritarian control over widespread dimensions of Singaporeans' lives, personal as well as political and economic. Furthermore, since the mid-1990s, Singapore has become very vocal regarding the importance of Asian values, as opposed to Western values, as a key component of a successful development model. Whether it consistently adheres to these values in its development process is now being questioned (Pyle, 1997).

This chapter provides a framework to consider the possible relevance the Singapore model may or may not have for housing policy in these transitional economies. It does not claim to be a full investigation of the Singapore model, which has been examined elsewhere (Huff, 1995). Rather, it provides some background on Singapore's development experience, its particular views of human rights, and its recent relationships with the regional transitional countries. In accordance with the theme of this volume, it then focuses on housing policy—the approaches taken, how they have changed, and what the achievements have been. Housing policy in Singapore is not simply about providing adequate shelter—it is also about reinforcing other social values and priorities the Singaporean government has. We will examine the role of housing in the development process, the substantial effects changes in housing have had on Singaporean women's activities, and its use to influence family structure. Although Singapore asserts that a core value is traditional family values, its housing policy appears inconsistent in support of these values. In this chapter I argue that the full ramifications of the economic, political, and ideological institutions of the Singaporean model should be fully understood by countries considering it an approach to emulate.

SINGAPORE'S APPROACH AND RELATIONS WITH TRANSITIONAL ASIAN COUNTRIES

At independence in 1965, Singapore was a country whose economy was based largely on entrepôt trade (providing services for transshipment of goods in and out of Southeast Asia), some naval shipbuilding and repair, petroleum refining, and many types of informal sector activities. There was an urban housing shortage, and most people lived in kampong housing (traditional village communities) that often lacked sanitary facilities and electricity. The official unemployment rate was 9 percent, with actual unemployment considerably higher when the underemployed were included. There was considerable concern regarding the pressures high population growth rates (5 percent) were putting on education, housing, and employment (Saw, 1980). Political unrest, ethnic fighting, and labor dissent were prevalent.

Subsequent to independence, the Singaporean government, led by Prime Minister Lee Kuan Yew of the People's Action Party until 1990, established carefully planned policies regarding housing and urban renewal, transportation and communications infrastructure, savings, labor and wages, fertility, health, and education.[1] It adopted an export-oriented development strategy with a wide variety of incentives to attract multinational corporations (MNCs). Labor and political unrest was suppressed in the mid- to late 1960s to ensure political and worker stability. As a result, Singapore has been transformed into a modern economy, based on production by MNCs for export, the presence of state-operated enterprises in key sectors, an up-to-date infrastructure, and, more recently, provision of services throughout the region. In 1994, 86 percent of the population lived in subsidized updated housing provided by the government; 80 percent of them owned their own flats. Unemployment levels fell so low, to 2 percent in 1990 (Department of Statistics, 1991), that officials have been concerned about the shortage of labor and its negative effects on sustainable economic development (Pyle, 1997).

The economic results are particularly noteworthy. Singapore is now categorized as a high-income country by the World Bank (World Bank, 1996).[2] Its income per capita in 1993 was $19,350, the thirteenth highest globally, putting it on a par with France, Belgium, and Austria (UNDP, 1996).[3] Its annual growth rates of gross national product per capita of 8.3 percent (1965–1980) and 6.1 percent (1980–1993) are among the very highest in the world. Singapore's provision of modern housing for such a large proportion of the populace and the continual upgrading to larger flats are unmatched in the nonsocialist world.[4] Its multiethnic population (78 percent Chinese, 14 percent Malay, and 7 percent Indian) appears to live together peaceably. It has been considered an economic success story for nearly two decades. As early as 1981, Aline Wong said neighboring countries in Southeast Asia looked to it as a model of development (Wong, 1981).

Singapore is considered a very competitive and desirable location for doing business. It has been classified as one of the world's most competitive economies in the *World Competitiveness Report* compiled by the International Institute for Management Development and the World Economic Forum of Switzerland. Singapore was listed as second, behind only the United States from 1994 to 1997 (Aggarwal, 1998; Singapore, 1995; Tan Kim Song,

1994; Tan Kim Song, 1995).[5] It has also been cited by *Fortune* magazine as the best city in 1995 and second-best city in 1996 in the world for doing business (Sim Wei Chew, 1995). A survey of 6,000 Asian executives ranks Singapore as the best place in Asia to locate a regional headquarters, surpassing Hong Kong (*Straits Times Weekly Edition,* December 21, 1996).

Since the mid-1990s, the leaders of Singapore, particularly Lee Kuan Yew, now senior minister, have become self-appointed spokespersons for an Asian model of development. They refer to Singapore's high per capita income and growth rates and its stable, though ethnically diverse, society. In regional conferences, visits to other economies, and national pronouncements, Singaporean officials say their approach differs dramatically from the Western democratic model of economic development because of its basis in Asian values, particularly the Asian model of the family and community. The current prime minister, Goh Chok Tong, cites two key factors in continuing Singapore's economic success: Singaporeans' acceptance of community over individual liberties, and their belief in strong government (Ibrahim, 1995).

Senior Minister Lee Kuan Yew, who still retains a position of substantial power within Singapore and has considerable stature internationally, speaks of the importance of Confucian values: reverence for scholarship and a strong work ethic, respect for government leaders, and a willingness to place the interests of society above those of the individual. He says these values enabled Singapore to establish its form of government, a meritocratic civil service, and to limit trade union powers (Fernandez, 1994). He asserts that Confucian values helped industrialization in Singapore, Hong Kong, South Korea, and Taiwan (often called the "four tigers" because of their dynamic growth rates). He argues that differences in family values between the East and the West are key to explaining the rise of the East (where sons and daughters want to become educated, work hard, and bring honor to the family) and problems in the West (Goh, 1994). Many key Singaporean officials believe that the form of capitalism fostered in the United States is accompanied by crime and violence, welfare dependency, and disintegration of the family.[6]

All these economic, political, and ideological aspects, taken together, reflect a particular view of what the important concerns and human rights have been throughout the development process in Singapore and what is needed to attain them. Singapore has considered increasing per capita income levels, rapid economic growth rates, and provision of jobs and housing of primary importance. Health care and education have received attention but have not been first-tier priorities. This is somewhat more of a "basic needs" approach to development than in countries that focus strictly on growth.[7] The government believes the achievements Singapore has made required a strong government and emphasis on community versus the individual. This contrasts to prioritization in the United States, often taken as the prototype Western model, where individual rights and a limited role for the government are considered of primary importance. The United States does not have the provision of housing, health care, and jobs for its citizens as fundamental goals.

Singaporean officials have particularly targeted transitional countries in the Asian region that are moving to more market-oriented economies for their message about the importance of an Asian model of development. Getting their viewpoint across has been facilitated because Singapore has established relationships with the formerly socialist economies, such as China, Vietnam, Cambodia, and Myanmar (formerly Burma). Singapore is engaged in many commercial ventures in these nations, many of them joint, and also operates in an advisory capacity.

The Chinese are interested in the Singapore approach to housing and urban development in several different contexts. Singaporean consortiums have been hired to establish turnkey industrial communities in China, similar to what Singapore has done in its own redevelopment. For example, the Singapore Suzhou Township Project was established as a joint venture between Jiangsu and Suzhou (China) firms and the Singapore Suzhou Township Development, a consortium of nineteen Singapore companies. The project involves establishing a community consisting of housing, schools, recreational facilities, commercial centers, and industrial parks (Tan Tarn How, 1994). In addition, Singaporean groups are working with the government of Qingdao (China), one of the ten fastest growing cities in the world. Singaporeans will plan, design, and build a new city, modeled on Singapore, next to old Qingdao (Patrick Tan, 1996). Furthermore, a former chief planner in Singapore has been appointed an adviser to Tianjin (China) to help solve its massive housing problem by building affordable high-rise residences for thousands of people living in one-story homes that are dilapidated. Residents would pay less than market rents for the new apartments (*Straits Times Weekly Edition,* March 5, 1994). (As we will see below, what the chief planner has been asked to do parallels what was done in Singapore in the past.)

In Vietnam, Singapore is the third largest foreign investor as of 1996, behind Taiwan and Japan (FYI Financial Statistics, 1996); Singapore is also one of its major trading partners. When visiting Vietnam, Singapore Prime Minister Goh Chok Tong observed that Hanoi reminded him of Singapore in the 1950s and appeared to be thirty to forty years behind Singapore in economic development. Dr. Goh stated that Singapore could help Vietnam in its industrialization program and in developing tourism (Sumiko Tan, 1994). Singaporean Senior Minister Lee Kuan Yew's book of speeches on nation-building has been translated into Vietnamese to enable Vietnamese leaders to understand Mr. Lee's approach to managing a country and its economic development (*Straits Times Weekly Edition,* December 3, 1994).

Singapore has long been particularly noted for its solutions, as a developing country, to the problems of urban housing shortages. Two decades ago, Singapore and Hong Kong were cited as examples of successful government efforts to address urban housing shortages in the Third World, as both were building publicly provided flats to house large numbers of people and were upgrading them steadily (Drakakis-Smith and Yeung, 1977). Even then, however, the Singapore model was considered more successful in terms of the numbers of housing units publicly provided (versus privately built), size of units and standards of living, the owner-occupied program, the administration of the program, the provision of industrial employment opportunities in the housing estates, and the satisfaction of residents (Drakakis-Smith and Yeung, 1977).

More recently, a World Bank report (1993a) on urban land management in China examined the experiences of Singapore and Hong Kong with large-scale redevelopment, finding them even more polar opposites: the former compulsory with aggressive redevelopment over the years, the latter with such limited outcomes that it is essentially inoperative. It concludes that, in comparison to Hong Kong and Seoul, Singapore's practices are the most relevant for adaptation in China and that Singapore has had the most effective program of resettlement of its population into upgraded housing. The Singapore case is particularly of interest for redevelopment in Shanghai, often considered a competitor to Singapore, and other large cities in China and Vietnam.

In considering Singapore as a model of development, these other nations must be aware, however, that although Singapore has achieved remarkably high levels of economic growth, per capita income, and upgraded housing, its accomplishments fall somewhat short in other broader measures of "human rights" or "development" such as educational attainment, literacy, income inequality, and personal freedoms. For example, Singapore is ranked thirty-fourth globally in the Human Development Index (HDI), a more "human centered" quality-of-life measure that includes life expectancy and education as well as per capita income (UNDP, 1996). Singapore has a lower standing in the education component than many other developing countries, ranking below seventy-two other nations in the world (UNDP, 1996). The Singapore government does speak of the need for citizens to upgrade their knowledge and training, but surveys of attitudes in Asian countries reveal that Singapore, Japan, and Hong Kong place less emphasis on respect for learning than do other Asian countries in their survey (Wirthlin Worldwide, 1996). In addition, the most recent data available regarding income inequality suggest that Singaporean society in 1982–1983 was less equal than most other growing economies in the region. Inequality, measured in terms of the ratio of the income share of the wealthiest 20 percent of the population to that of the poorest 20 percent, was greater in Singapore than in Hong Kong, Indonesia, Japan, Republic of Korea, Taiwan, or Thailand. Only Malaysia and the Philippines were more unequal (World Bank, 1993b; UNDP, 1996).

Social planning has been part of Singapore's development from the beginning, so much so that it is often referred to as social engineering.[8] Social policies have been pervasive—not only relocating low-income populations into high-rise housing and reshaping education but also policies to promote marriage and extensive fertility policies to change population growth rates. Social control is far-reaching on issues, both major and minor, and considerably constrains or shapes personal rights and freedoms. For example, on the one hand, opponents of the government have very restricted freedom to speak in opposition,[9] the freedom of the press is restricted,[10] there are severe penalties for drug possession and use of preventive detention, and access to information through the Internet is censored. On the other hand, chewing gum is prohibited in the subway, and there are fines for not flushing public toilets.

The government continually tells Singaporeans what values it considers important for continued economic success and therefore wants the citizens to foster and hold. The notion of "values" permeates public pronouncements. People are exhorted to pass traditional values (such as hard work, thrift, family, and community ties) on to their children (Fernandez, 1996a), work hard to maintain economic competitiveness in the fast-changing global economy (*Straits Times Weekly Edition,* October 21, 1995), and upgrade their social behavior to be considerate and to treat public and common areas as their own (*Straits Times Weekly Edition,* January 6, 1996). They are even encouraged to smile ("simply smile and be gracious") because of the importance of tourism to the economy (McDermott, 1996). The National Day speech by Prime Minister Goh Chok Tong on August 21, 1994, focused on preserving traditional moral and family values. A patriarchal understanding of the family was shown to exist when he declared that the policy of denying female civil servants family medical coverage would be upheld because benefits would continue to be channeled to the family through the fathers (Ibrahim, 1994).[11]

Beneath the surface of these conceptualizations of Asian values and underlying the political debates that emphasize harmony, accountability, and order, one often finds quite another reality that does not conform to the idealized Asian values that the Singaporean government says it upholds. It is important to examine the politics underlying the conceptualizations and the debates rather than accepting them at face value.

With these economic, political, and ideological components of the Singapore model in mind, this chapter will examine one of the major successes of Singapore's development strategy—provision of affordable housing. It describes the major features of housing policy in Singapore and changes over time. The chapter then analyzes the relationship of housing policy to the development strategy and its profound and complicated impact on women's economic and family lives. It examines whether housing policies reflected Singapore's commitment to and its roots in Asian family values.

HOUSING AND DEVELOPMENT BOARD: PROGRAMS, STRATEGIES, AND ACHIEVEMENTS

Strategies regarding housing have been a central part of Singapore's economic development strategy since the period of self-government (1959–1965) preceding independence. Most residents then lived in private housing that could be characterized in several ways (Chua, 1997): as traditional Malay kampong housing with *atap* (palm-leaf thatch) or zinc roofs or in Chinese urban squatter communities. Both of these were clusters of buildings without electricity or modern sanitation. Some others lived in shophouses, where the family business was on the first floor, with living quarters above.

The Housing and Development Board (HDB) was established in 1960 to (1) provide homes with sanitary facilities for low-income families then living in the kampong or squatter communities, and (2) proceed with urban renewal, remove slums, and alleviate crowding in the central city of Singapore, which was then surrounded by more rural areas. The HDB established the Home Ownership Scheme in 1964 so that families could purchase their flats (Wong and Wong, 1979).

As a result, the island was transformed rapidly (Chua, 1997). Whole new towns and industrial estates were planned and established to distribute the population more evenly throughout the city-state. Each planned community included light industry mixed with housing estates as well as recreational sites, educational and religious institutions, and shopping facilities (markets, hawker centers for prepared foods, and general shopping centers). The original focus on low-income families was broadened. By the 1970s, the HDB was considered a source of housing for middle-income people (Chen, 1979; World Bank, 1993b). Chiu, Ho, and Lui (1997) believe that in turn the dominant political party, the PAP, gained much popular support of the people by putting the housing program into place. The government used housing policy as a way to stabilize the social order and to solidify and maintain its political power (Chua, 1997).

All HDB housing was high-rise in design, with buildings reaching at least twelve to eighteen stories, possibly twenty-five. Both rents and purchase prices were subsidized. Rents did not exceed 15 percent of the household incomes of families in smaller flats, and these high-rises provided a much higher standard of accommodation than the former private tenement housing in slums and squatter areas (Wong and Wong, 1979). The buildings were equipped with workable plumbing systems and refuse pickup service.

Singapore's accomplishments in housing were even more dramatic in terms of space per person and price per square meter than in Hong Kong and Japan. In Singapore in 1980 (latest data found), housing space (ranging from 7.7 to 50 square meters per person) was greater than in Hong Kong (ranging from 2.2 to 5.7 square meters per person) and Japan (ranging from 8 to 35 square meters per person). In addition, the selling price per square meter in Singapore (S$400–S$650 in 1983) was significantly lower than in Hong Kong (S$650–S$1,400 in 1983) and Japan (S$2,900–S$3,100 in 1985) (Tan and Phang, 1991).

The HDB established a policy, early on, of integrating different ethnic groups within the same estate to avoid a recurrence of the race riots of the early 1960s (Chua, 1997). The importance placed on this ethnic integration has continued. The rationale given for this policy was to cultivate social cohesion and avoid having homogeneous groups become insular, parochial in their thinking, and form negative attitudes about members of other groups. If housing estates were homogeneous, society could be splintered along ethnic or religious lines (*Straits Times Weekly Edition,* May 4, 1996). As illustrated in many areas of the world, this divisiveness can undermine the social stability that is needed for economic and social development.

All Singaporean women have been able to own property since 1961. At about the same time the HDB was established, the system of colonial laws was rationalized. Rather than allowing different laws to exist for separate ethnic groups, the passage of the Women's Charter in 1961 guaranteed that a woman can own all types of property and can dispose of it any way she chooses (*Legal Status of Singapore Women,* 1986). Only limited data on property ownership and changes in it over time are available by gender (Shantakumar, 1993 traces ownership for older women between 1980 and 1990). As we will see below, single people and, after 1994, unmarried parents were not allowed to apply for HDB flats.

The program was rapidly adopted by Singaporeans. As Table 2.1 indicates, within fifteen years, one-half of the total population lived in HDB flats. There were lengthy waiting lists for these flats. For example, in 1978, when almost 70 percent of the population lived in public housing, there were 61,696 applicants on the waiting list (Saw, 1980). Waits of five years were not uncommon. The shift to HDB housing continued and, in just more than twenty years, three-quarters of the people lived in publicly provided flats. By 1994, the percentage had risen to 86 percent.

In addition, as a result of the HDB's Home Ownership Scheme of 1964, one-half of the populace lived in owner-occupied flats by 1982. The percentage owning rose to 80 percent in 1994. Ownership of HDB flats has been facilitated by the existence, since 1968, of the Central Provident Fund (CPF) and rules governing use of the funds. The CPF is a compulsory savings fund for all employees in Singapore. It is designed to provide for workers' retirement, since Singapore does not have a government-subsidized social security program. Workers and employers each pay one-half of the required percentage, which has been a variable but substantial share of wages. (For example, it was 31 percent of salary in 1979, earning 6.5 percent interest [Wee, 1979]; it rose to 50 percent of a worker's salary in 1985 [Ministry of Trade and Indus-

Table 2.1   Total Population in Singapore Living in Publicly Provided Housing,
1960–1994 (in percent)

Year	Public Flats	Owner-Occupied Public Flats
1960	9.0	
1961	11.4	
1962	15.3	
1963	18.3	
1964	22.0	
1965	23.0	
1966	24.0	
1967	26.0	
1968	29.6	
1969	32.6	
1970	35.9	
1971	38.1	
1972	43.7	
1973	45.1	
1974	50.0	
1975	54.8	
1976	60.2	
1977	64.7	
1978	69.0	
1979	71.9	
1980	74.1	
1981	74.1	
1982	75.0	50.0
1983	77.0	54.0
1984	81.0	60.0
1985	84.0	64.0
1986	85.0	66.0
1987	86.0	69.0
1988	87.0	71.0
1989	88.0	79.0
1990	87.0	80.0
1991	87.0	82.0
1992	87.0	82.0
1993	87.0	81.0
1994	86.0	80.0

Sources: Economic and Social Statistics, Singapore, 1960–1982 (Singapore: Department of Statistics, 1983), Table 8.10 (p. 118); *Yearbook of Statistics, Singapore, 1992 and 1994* (Singapore: Department of Statistics, 1992 and 1994), Table 18, p. 18.

try, 1986].) A contributor's accumulated monthly payments and interest may be used for the down payment or monthly payments for purchasing an HDB flat.[12] This innovative compulsory savings scheme has been a key influence on housing policy in Shanghai specifically and in China generally (see Fei and Hopkins, Chapters 12 and 13).

Changes in the housing program occurred over time. One, the policy of ethnic integration notwithstanding, some differentiation in types of housing

Table 2.2   Percentage of Properties Under Housing Development Board Management (Singapore) by Number of Rooms, 1960–1992

Year	1	2	3	4	5[a]	Executive[b]
1960	6.4	31.5	52.7	9.3	.2	0
1965	24.2	30.0	42.6	3.1	.06	0
1970	34.8	24.8	38.0	2.3	.03	0
1975	30.9	16.3	42.6	7.7	2.5	0
1980	18.4	13.0	47.3	15.1	6.2	0
1985	10.9	8.8	44.0	25.2	5.2	1.5
1990	4.6	6.8	40.4	32.4	11.5	3.5
1992	4.3	5.7	38.5	33.0	13.0	4.6

Sources: Calculated from *Economic and Social Statistics Singapore, 1960–1982* (Singapore: Department of Statistics, 1983), Table 8.9 (p. 117); *Yearbook of Statistics, Singapore, 1992* (Singapore: Department of Statistics, 1992), Table 8.16 (p. 151).

a. There were 44 five-room flats from 1960-1971. They started building additional units in 1972.

b. Information in this category was collected from 1983 on.

emerged in the mid-1970s and has continued to the present. Beginning in 1975, Singaporeans could apply for HUDC (Housing and Urban Development Company) flats that were exclusive estates separated from the HDB high-rise look-alikes (Drakakis-Smith and Yeung, 1977). This was a form of public housing for higher income earners who could not quite afford private housing and preferred not to live with the masses in HDB flats. This type of housing was discontinued in 1991. In the 1990s, however, upper-end buyers can purchase executive flats or the newly created "executive condominiums." Although these are publicly provided forms of housing, the executive condos are moving in a private direction (Han, 1995; Chua, 1995; Chua, 1997). Upper-end buyers can also purchase private housing, but it remains the most expensive form of abode and is very limited in availability.

Second, as new, larger flats were built in subsequent years, families were permitted to upgrade, subject to certain stipulations. Table 2.2 shows that the size of public housing was upgraded substantially. While 90.6 percent of HDB flats were three rooms *and smaller* in 1960, by 1992, 89.1 percent of the flats were three rooms *and larger.*

Housing continues to be upgraded. Since 1991, the HDB has offered Design and Build flats designed by architects and incorporating higher-quality finishes. They constituted 10 percent of new building by the HDB and ran about 10 percent higher in price than normal flats. They have been so popular that the HDB announced in 1996 that it would offer Design Plus flats that it, rather than private architects, designs. They feature tile flooring throughout and special fixtures (Tan Hsueh Yun, 1996a). In addition, in 1996 the government announced plans to establish Singapore ONE—One Network for Everyone. This will link all homes electronically with government agencies and commercial organizations, so that residents can access teleshopping, electronic libraries, entertainment, and video conferencing (Tammy Tan, 1996). It will provide censored access to the Internet.

Housing blocks are selectively being upgraded. Among the four factors said to be used by the HDB in determining which blocks of flats will be upgraded is the amount of "community spirit" the area exhibits.[13] Community spirit is, in turn, characterized partly by how residents respond to grassroots activities, national campaigns, and National Day celebrations (i.e., how many attend block parties or cleanup events, or how many fly the flag in August, the independence month [Yeoh, 1996]).[14]

Even whole towns have been selected for renewal. Renewal will proceed according to a master plan and will include revamping the town center, parks, and school system; upgrading the neighborhood centers and upgrading flats; and a mix of new public and private housing, including possible executive condos (Tan Hsueh Yun, 1996b). Further, a model has been created for the development of additional new towns in the twenty-first century. Called Punggol 21, the new towns will include private houses, executive condos, and high-grade HDB flats in smaller communities (Fernandez, 1996b).

The changes in housing in Singapore over the past thirty-five years have been unprecedented. On the one hand, residents seem pleased. In a recent survey commissioned by the *Straits Times* (Singapore), 93 percent of residents polled expressed satisfaction with their HDB flats and housing estates (Wang, 1996). On the other hand, Christopher Tremewan (1994) cites studies from the 1970s that reveal a sense of isolation in the high-rises, a loss of community, fear and insecurity, feelings of being constrained to the flat, high levels of stress and anxiety, and even elevated levels of suicide.

However, there is another aspect to housing policy besides simply providing Singaporeans with adequate and upgraded housing. The proposed changes and upgrades in housing estates (and increased benefits in other areas) are linked to the political process and the reelection of the PAP candidate in each voting district. A blatant example of this came prior to the general election on January 2, 1997. The PAP had already won the election before any voting, because the number of uncontested seats was more than the number needed for victory. Nonetheless, the PAP was determined to win in the remaining seats, referred to the contests as battles, and utilized the following tactic (threat) to gain more votes. Sumiko Tan, writing in the *Straits Times Weekly Edition* before the General Election, reported that Prime Minister Goh Chok Tong said

> If they [the voters in each district] choose the People's Action Party, their neighborhoods will be improved. Their children will benefit from schemes, like Edusave merit bursaries and scholarships, and their elderly parents will be taken care of. If they do not vote for the PAP, they will not get these pro-

grammes and their families and estates will be left behind while others progress (Sumiko Tan, 1996: 1).

Not surprisingly, the PAP won 34 of the 36 seats that were contested (Fernandez, 1997). Opposition leaders charged that such tactics were unethical, but Senior Minister Lee Kuan Yew defended them, saying parties reward their supporters, not those who did not back them (Chua, 1996). This contrasts sharply with the PAP leaders' claims that they take care of the people. In speaking at Williams College in the United States, Prime Minister Goh Chok Tong said, "In Singapore, government acts more like a trustee. As a custodian of the people's welfare, it exercises independent judgment on what is in the long-term interest of the people and acts on that basis" (Ibrahim, 1995: 1). Speaking in Boston on that same trip, Prime Minister Goh said, "In our case, we start on the basis that the government is there to lead, to govern in the interest of the people. It has a duty to build up trust between the people and itself. So long as that trust is maintained, the people will reelect the government again and again" (*Straits Times Weekly Edition,* September 16, 1995: 2).

The PAP's use of housing policy to maintain political control is not a new phenomenon. Tremewan (1994) reviews the history of housing redevelopment in Singapore from the early 1960s and discusses how the PAP used forced resettlement to undermine opposition that existed in both the rural areas and in the center city. Communities that were based on ethnicity, language, or religion were broken up, making it harder for them to oppose the moves of the PAP to solidify its control over Singapore. He cites the outbreaks of fires in many areas, and the coincidental absence of firefighters. He discusses how the forms of social organization imposed on the new towns and housing estates were developed to be a way for the party to maintain control over the state.

Most public agencies in Singapore maintain a high level of confidentiality (Chua, 1997), so there have been very few publications about the HDB. One volume, published as part of the HDB's twenty-fifth anniversary celebration, does, however, provide a great deal of information about the development and actual operation of the housing program. *Housing a Nation: 25 Years of Public Housing in Singapore,* edited by Aline K. Wong and Stephen H. K. Yeh (1985) and published by the HDB, provides considerable detail regarding "changes and improvements in policy, programme, administrative and technical inputs of the HDB since its inception in 1960" (preface). It provides information on construction (resource planning, physical planning and design, infrastructure, building standards and technology, contracts management), management of people and maintenance of their living environment (the policies and procedures of the housing schemes, i.e., eligibility, allocation, ownership, resale and transfer, family cohesion), estate management (i.e., the system and its philosophy, the physical and social dimensions of its policies), and resettlement and evaluation (study of resettlement of a village, satisfaction of residents, differing family lifestyles, the social networks and community structures in high-rise structures). Other detailed, and more recent, information is provided in *The Singapore Experience in Public Housing* (Tan and Phang, 1991), *Profile of Residents Living in HDB Flats* (Research and Planning Department, Housing and Development Board, 1995), and *Political Legitimacy and Housing: Stakeholding in Singapore* (Chua, 1997).

THE HOUSING AND DEVELOPMENT BOARD'S ROLE IN THE EXPORT-ORIENTED DEVELOPMENT STRATEGY

Housing policy and the politics surrounding it are also integrally linked to the development process and to effects on women's economic and family lives. We will look at each aspect in turn. First, the HDB and housing policy have been an important component of Singapore's development strategy and served to facilitate the development process in many different ways: by upgrading low-income housing, alleviating overcrowding, and thereby increasing the standard of living; by lessening social discontent and providing a stable environment for foreign investors; by providing employment in the construction industry; and by providing a lower-wage workforce for MNCs (due to the subsidized rents or prices) than otherwise possible. Second, as will be discussed in the next part of this chapter, the estates geographically altered the nature of women's economic activities and facilitated women's entry into the paid labor force of MNCs. The last major section in this chapter examines how, in spite of pronouncements about maintaining traditional family values, housing policy assisted in promoting whatever notion of desired family size the government chose to encourage according to the needs of the development strategy.

Several of the key ways in which housing policy greatly assisted the export-oriented development strategy are cited in a World Bank report examining the East Asian miracle. It reports approvingly that

> Hong Kong and Singapore intervened heavily in housing markets to win the support and cooperation of nonelites. By providing low-cost housing for the majority of residents, both programs have helped to decrease inequality and minimize social unrest, thus providing the long-term stability attractive to investors. Moreover, the massive construction effort created jobs when both economies faced high unemployment; subsequently, the wide availability of low-cost housing for workers helped to hold down wage demands, subsidizing labor-intensive manufacturing (World Bank, 1993b: 163).

Lee Soo Ann adds that "the pressure for higher wages was lessened while the commitment of the immigration-based population to the island was further strengthened" (1979: 233).

Others do not cast this phenomenon in the same light. Tremewan (1994) argues that the effect of this housing policy on the political economy of Singapore was to provide a working class that was dependent on the PAP for housing (because of the forced destruction of former housing) and for employment (often in MNCs) to pay for their housing. This worked well for a development strategy involving influx of multinational corporations.

EFFECTS OF CHANGES IN HOUSING ON WOMEN'S ECONOMIC ROLES

The transformation in the predominant form of housing and urban renewal had profound impacts on the nature of women's income-earning or economic activities, in several types of informal sector endeavors, and in terms of participation in the formal sector. First, there was a decrease in informal sector activities that women participated in such as trading, hawking, providing petty services, and working on small farms. Urban renewal and relocation programs displaced farming and agricultural activities and disrupted former trading networks. Increased regulation of informal sector activities discouraged much of their reestablishment in the new neighborhoods (Wong, 1981). These types of activities are characterized by low capital requirements, ease of entry, and flexible hours and typically involve little training—all favorable for women's participation. Their decline meant a loss of income-earning possibilities for those women who could not work in the formal sector because of their age, lack of education, or family responsibilities (Wong, 1981).

Tinker (1997a) describes changes in one of these areas, street food vending. One aspect of Singapore's drive to modernize since the early 1960s has been to remove the traditional food vendors from the streets and prohibit such endeavors. Instead, Singapore built food stalls over parking garages and in malls. It permitted some controlled food markets, including a few night markets at parking lots. The number of registered vendors was cut in half. Because the new food stalls required much more capital and were essentially different types of businesses, it is believed that they involved a wealthier group of businesspersons than the traditional street vendors. Based on her detailed research in seven other countries in Asia and Africa, she observes that typically men are attracted to enter this more lucrative and institutionalized form of food vending; it becomes problematic whether women will be able to compete, given their responsibilities for home duties and childcare.

Second, as the Singaporean government implemented its housing and urban redevelopment programs and shifted people from the center city to the new towns established in the less developed areas of the island, there was a big impact on the roles of women in small family businesses. Sullivan (1990) interviewed people in more than a hundred small traditional family businesses or cottage industries that coexisted in Singapore with a modern manufacturing and service economy. These small businesses were typically family-run, headed by a male boss, and involved the labor of various unpaid family members and paid employees. These businesses cover a great variety of activities, including food processing; making clothing, shoes, or items for various types of celebrations; metalworking (gold, silver, tin, iron); stone-carving; printing; electroplating; or rewinding small motors. Sullivan noted the persistence of these businesses: According to government data, small manufacturers, those with fewer than twenty employees, were *not* declining relative to the overall manufacturing sector from 1970 to 1982, in spite of the rapid inflow of foreign investment and resultant growth of the larger-scale manufacturing sector. However, such official data may not accurately reflect the demise of very small businesses.[15]

Before urban redevelopment, family enterprises and living quarters typically were located in the same or a nearby building. The shophouse—a three-story building with a shop on the first level and living quarters on the upper levels—was one form of this arrangement. This overlapping of production and living space provided the flexibility that allowed many women to manage the household, attend to childcare duties, and also contribute labor time to the family enterprise. When a central city area was targeted for urban development by the Urban Redevelopment Authority (URA), these businesses were forced to relocate to factory space in the outlying areas (which were subsidized for five years) or to accept a cash buyout and close. If the business closed, it put women in the same situation as above. Many would lose economic opportunities; some could possibly move into formal sector employment.

If the business did indeed relocate, work and living spaces were then in different locations, although they could be in the same housing estate. Many women who could formerly be casual workers in the family business now had to remain in the HDB flat to attend to child and home duties. Others could work part-time at the enterprise but often faced a longer workday and the problem of childcare. This changed the nature of women's economic participation. In addition, in many cases, it was problematic for the viability of the business, which faced even more severe labor shortages than the Singaporean economy as a whole. Children who became educated did not, for the most part, seek to continue in the family business.

Women who remained in the home in the HDB flat but who wanted some way to augment the family's economic resources that allowed flexibility in time on the job could do piecework such as seaming (Salaff, 1986; Sullivan, 1990) or work for others in the housing estate. Nirmala PuruShotam and Chung Yuen Kay (1992) describe how women working outside their homes in the formal sector can purchase the housekeeping or child-minding services of other women living in the estates at affordable rates, often hourly. The women can do this informal child-minding in their homes or can perform household tasks in the former's home at hours convenient to the needs of their own families. Such services are widely available. Unfortunately, although it has been well known these alternatives exist, there have been no surveys taken to assess the extent to which women pursued each of these options.

In terms of trends in small businesses, Sullivan found in 1982 that small family businesses were located in both traditional places and the newer locations. Traditional locations included the five-foot ways (covered sidewalks that were part of the heritage of the British architectural design), unrenovated shophouses, and alleyways. Others were formally relocated in the newer terrace factory buildings or informally, into the "cottages" of the early 1980s—the flats in the HDB estates. By 1990, in updating the interviews, Sullivan found that some areas of shophouses were targeted for restoration to preserve and illustrate the architectural heritage of Singapore's past. Unfortunately, bid prices for these properties were very high, and only one of the former enterprises she interviewed was able to afford to return. The properties were purchased by wealthier businesspersons to establish shops for attracting tourists.

Another major way in which the establishment of housing estates affected women was that the design of the new towns included locating light industry in the housing estates. The HDB typically allocated 10 to 15 percent of land within the housing estates for industrial use by labor-intensive employers (Drakakis-Smith and Yeung, 1977). This shaped both the demand for labor and the available supply of labor. On the demand side, much of this light industry consisted of plants established by incoming MNCs. These were often in industries that typically sought significant percentages of female workers, such as textile and garment firms in the 1960s and electronics firms from the 1960s to present (Pang, 1979; Pang, 1988; Salaff, 1986). Therefore, there was a strong demand for female workers. Simultaneously, as discussed above, with the burgeoning of high-rise housing estates, some types of informal sector economic opportunities contracted, and so women workers were displaced. This added to the available supply of labor. In addition, some have pointed out that the supply of female labor was increased because people now had to spend more than before on housing and needed additional income (Salaff, 1986; Tremewan, 1994).[16] The location of employment within housing estates—therefore accessible for many from their homes—facilitated their entry into paid employment in MNCs.[17] This was particularly important for the continuity of Singapore's development strategy, because labor shortages were beginning to be felt in the early to mid-1970s. Locating light industries in the housing estates and encouraging women residents to work in them was a way to ameliorate the shortages (Pang, 1979; Wong, 1980).[18]

The reconfiguration of housing and the export-oriented development strategy were accompanied by substantial increases in women's labor force participation rates. Table 2.3 shows that the female labor force participation rate increased dramatically from the time of self-government. As Table 2.4 indicates,

Table 2.3   Labor Force Participation Rate by Sex (Singapore), 1957–1994

	1957	1970	1975	1980	1985	1990	1994
Economically active women as % total female population aged 15+	21.6	29.5	35.2	44.3	44.9	48.4	51.5
Economically active men as % total male population aged 15+	87.6	82.3	79.3	81.5	79.9	78.6	78.7
Economically active persons as % total population aged 15+	57.0	56.5	58.2	63.2	62.2	63.1	64.4

Sources: Economic and Social Statistics, Singapore, 1960–1982 (Singapore: Department of Statistics, 1983); Census, 1980; Report on Labour Force Survey of Singapore, various years (1975, 1985, 1990, 1994).

the female share of manufacturing grew strikingly during the initial two decades of the life of the HDB and the export-oriented development strategy.

As discussed elsewhere, women have been a critical component of Singapore's economic growth—as workers (Pang, 1979; Pyle, 1994; Wong, 1980) and as the reproducers of the labor force of the next generation (Pyle, 1994; Pyle, 1997). However, even though the planning for the new towns incorporated light industrial activities, shops, and recreational sites, along with housing estates, it did not include adequate provision for childcare. This was a

Table 2.4   Female Share of Those Employed by Industry (Singapore), 1957–1990

	1957	1970	1980	1990
Manufacturing	17.1	33.6	46.3	44.6
Construction	3.7	6.6	7.4	5.7
Commerce	6.7	19.0	34.2	39.4
Transport, storage, and communication	NA	5.0	15.7	21.1
Finance, insurance, real estate, and business services	NA	23.0	41.6	46.7
Community, social, and personal services	25.7	33.2	35.8	49.5
Other[a]	46.8	17.2	16.4	11.6

Sources: Wong (1981); Census of Population, Singapore, various years (1970, 1980); Report on the Labour Force Survey of Singapore, various years (1975, 1985, 1990).
    NA = Not Available
    a. Other includes agriculture, forestry, and fishing, mining and quarrying, utilities, and other.

constraint on the economic activity of married women with small children. Aline K. Wong (1980) reports the developments included crèches; but she also states (Kuo and Wong, 1979) that Singapore had not yet developed an adequate statewide system of childcare. A study by the Singapore Council of Women's Organizations (1989) of women in public housing who had never had a paid occupation revealed that the most prominent reason for this was their obligation to perform childcare/household duties.[19]

The structuring of housing policy affected women's economic roles in the informal and formal sectors of the economy in the ways discussed in this section. In addition, the manner in which it changed women's participation in the labor force was also related to family policies, such as those examined in the following section.

RELATIONSHIP OF HOUSING POLICIES TO FAMILY POLICIES AND FAMILY VALUES

Over the years, housing policy has been related in a number of ways to the government's view of the "family." Housing policy has been used to reinforce the form, size, and location decisions of families in ways the government deems appropriate. This too has had a dramatic, although perhaps more subtle, effect on women's lives.

One of the most fundamental ways housing policy has related to the family has been via the government's vision of appropriate family size. Housing policy has been used to influence fertility since the early years of the independent nation, according to the needs of the development process and the nature of the society Singapore wanted to maintain. This has impacted women. When the HDB was initially established, larger families were given priority in access to publicly built housing. The minimum household size was five to qualify for a flat (families with one or two children would therefore be ineligible). The government recognized that this prioritization could be an incentive for families to have additional children more rapidly in order to qualify for this type of housing. This would be problematic, because an increased birthrate conflicted with the desire of the government to reduce population pressures and unemployment. Any desire to hold the birthrate down, however, conflicted with prevailing notions regarding appropriate family size.

Prime Minister Lee Kuan Yew saw these conflicts clearly. His comments shed light on the commitment of the state to traditional Asian values regarding family size:

> Even we, as a Government, find ourselves pursuing contradictory policies. On the one hand, we want to discourage large families. . . . On the other, we have inherited and are still practicing a system of values which gives the ad-

vantage to a man with a larger family. For instance, in public housing the number of points a man scores for priority in getting accommodation increases with the number of children he has got (February 10, 1963, at the opening address to the Seventh Conference of the International Planned Parenthood Federation, quoted in Saw, 1980: 116).

Two years later, Prime Minister Lee specified a course of action in his National Day address of August 9, 1965: "We have to revise all our social values so that no one is required to have a large family in order to qualify for a Housing Board flat" (Saw, 1980: 117). In 1968, the ruling regarding prioritization was changed so that smaller families could also apply for HDB flats. However, it was not until 1973 that families of any size would have equal priority in renting or buying HDB flats.

These changes in rules regarding access to housing were part of a larger set of social policies the government developed to reduce the adverse impact of population pressures on the provision of adequate levels of education, employment, and housing. To reduce the population growth rate, the government established family planning clinics throughout the island, legalized abortion, and liberalized sterilization. In the early 1970s, the government sought to strengthen this antinatalist program and established new sets of incentives and disincentives—all designed to reduce fertility. A two-child family became the goal, so that Singaporeans would approximately replace themselves. Those who had more than the targeted number of children lost income tax deductions, had lower priority in education, and faced both loss of maternity leave and higher delivery fees (Wong, 1979; Fawcett, 1979; Saw, 1980; Saw, 1990).

Housing policy was also involved in these antinatalist measures. Previously, subletting a room in a flat had been forbidden, under penalty of eviction. A ruling in 1973 allowed families with three or fewer children to sublet a room. The rationale was that the possibility of earning income by subletting might encourage families to have three or fewer children (Saw, 1980). The government had apparently wanted to take a stronger antinatalist stand. The minister of health had specified in 1972 that priority in access to HDB flats would go to smaller families (Wee, 1979). However, the minister of law and national development reported a year later that the government was unable to develop an equitable plan to do this.

The antinatalist policies were associated with decreases in fertility (Saw, 1990) and reduction in what was considered the appropriate family size. Although this facilitated increases in the female labor force participation rate and provided an immediate source of workers by reducing women's home and childcare duties, these antinatalist policies had the contradictory effect of lowering the stream of labor supplied in future years by reducing the natural rate of increase of the population. This had potentially serious implications for maintenance of Singapore's development strategy because labor shortages, such as Singapore was beginning to experience in the 1970s, can be a serious constraint on continued rapid rates of economic growth (Pyle, 1997).[20]

The government recognized this dilemma regarding the supply of workers in the early 1980s and moved to reverse incentives regarding fertility. It did so selectively, though, because it recognized that fertility reduction differed among Singaporeans by ethnic group, educational level, and income. The more educated, higher-income groups (largely the majority ethnic group, the Chinese) had substantially reduced their fertility rates, while the less well-educated, lower-income groups (chiefly the minority Malay) were reproducing at relatively rapid rates. These results did not fulfill Singapore's desire to move toward a more educated, higher-skilled workforce, and they potentially undermined the ethnic "balance," meaning the current proportions of each ethnic group in the society.[21]

Therefore, antinatalist fertility policies were reversed for the more well educated. Better-educated women were encouraged to have more than two children; less educated women were urged to bear fewer. Policy incentives to encourage the more educated to have *more* children included tax rebates for third and fourth children, with more sizable rebates given to those bearing the second child at an earlier age.[22]

Housing policies were used both as incentives to lower birthrates for certain groups and as inducements to increase family size in others. On the one hand, S$10,000 cash grants were offered beginning in 1984 to less educated and lower-income Singaporean women under thirty who are sterilized after the birth of the first or second child. This money would be paid into a woman's Central Provident Fund or she could use the cash toward the purchase of an HDB flat (Saw, 1990). This amount would be more than needed for the down payment on a typical three-room flat, which would sell for S$30,000. On the other hand, in 1987, priority was given to higher-income, better-educated families in three-room or larger flats wanting to upgrade upon the birth of a third child (Training and Health Education Department brochure).[23]

Housing policy therefore affected women's lives as it influenced family size—at first, the trend toward fewer children, then the trend toward higher fertility for the educated segment of the population. Housing policy also affected women's lives via the forms of the family that the government favored and supported. Access to HDB flats went to the married. The unmarried could not rent and buy flats except under unusual circumstances (Chua, 1997; Wee, 1979). Furthermore, in 1994, the prime minister announced in his National Day speech, as part of the plan to strengthen the family, that unmarried mothers would no longer be permitted to buy flats directly from the HDB (Ibrahim, 1994). This was extended to unmarried fathers shortly thereafter, to be "fair." The government did not want its status to appear respectable, and it clearly opposed single parenthood.

Because the government was anxious for young people to marry and begin having children (to augment the future supply of workers), it developed two housing programs in 1995 to allow younger couples "to own their own homes and start their families earlier" (*Straits Times Weekly Edition,* September 2, 1995: 1). One plan made it easier for couples to rent a flat while waiting for their first flat to be ready. Another gave first-time buyers priority over people wishing to upgrade in flat selection and provided their flats with better basic amenities.[24]

In addition, the government has encouraged married children to live near their parents. In 1994, it revised HDB rules to make this easier by giving priority in allocation to married couples who apply to stay with their parents in the same flat (reducing the wait time by up to two years), by allowing parents and their married children to apply for flats in the same estate, and by providing grants of S$30,000 to help children buy resale flats within two kilometers of their parents (Chua, 1997; Ibrahim, 1994; Research and Planning Department, 1995; *Straits Times Weekly Edition,* September 3, 1994). This serves several purposes. It keeps nuclear families more in touch with their extended family networks, and it enables grandparents to care for the grandchildren while the parents work. This is helpful because the government soon recognized the conflicts inherent in policies from the mid-1980s. These policies urged women to participate more in the workforce *and* to increase their fertility in order to alleviate the labor shortage in the 1980s and to provide a supply of future workers. Women had constraints on their time and needed childcare options.

We have examined housing policies since independence and can assess whether the Singaporean government's claim that development is based on traditional family values is validated. We find that in the late 1960s family policies were rapidly constructed to alter traditional family size to spur the development process. As the perceived needs of the development process changed, these policies regarding appropriate family size and fertility were then later selectively reversed. Some housing policies have become part of the package of the newer, selectively pronatalist fertility policies that have been criticized for their social engineering approach to the different socioeconomic and ethnic groups that is classist and racist (Deyo, 1991; Rajakru, 1996).

CONCLUSIONS

Singapore has received widespread attention as a development success story and as a possible model of development—an Asian model, different from Western approaches. Singaporean officials have been outspoken about the value of basing development on Asian values, particularly regarding the family and community. This approach may appear attractive to transitional economies such as China and Vietnam, because Singapore has raised per capita income to the thirteenth highest in the world, reduced unemployment to very low levels, and virtually relocated all the population into housing with modern amenities. However, the reality differs from what is said about Singapore.

Singapore is often described as a country that embraces economic liberalism. It likes to present itself as a country that honors democratic institutions and procedures (such as the parliament and elections) and Asian values, particularly regarding the family. In reality, however, the economy has been highly planned and the state has been ruled since independence by a strong man (either Lee Kuan Yew, prime minister from 1965 to 1990, now senior minister, or Goh Chok Tong, prime minister since 1990) and a few key others on interlocking directorates (Huff, 1995).

Singapore leaders promote Asian values as the basis of their development model. This chapter has examined housing policy as it intersects with these values, particularly Asian family values. It has outlined the housing programs established, changes over time, and the results in terms of the percentages of the population living in HDB flats and the proportion owning their flats. It has particularly focused on the effects of changes in housing on women's economic activities and family lives. This chapter shows that, although the achievements in housing have been remarkable, housing policy was not simply designed to provide Singaporeans with better housing. Housing policy has been politicized as one way of keeping the PAP in power. It was also fundamentally shaped in accordance with the needs of the development process. Therefore, its impact on women's economic and family lives reflected that prioritization. Women's roles in the informal sectors were altered as certain sectors such as trading, hawking, providing petty services, and small farming declined and small family businesses were relocated, making some women's continued participation in these activities difficult. The design of the housing estates, incorporating light industry and production for multinational corporations, facilitated women becoming a wage labor force for these institutions.

In addition, in spite of Singaporean leaders' assertions that the Singapore approach is fundamentally and centrally based on traditional Asian family values, this chapter reveals that, although great value is placed on the family, policies, including housing, have been shaped to encourage a form and size of family that benefit the economic development process and those in political power rather than perpetuating the traditional Asian family. Instead of adhering consistently to values regarding traditional family size, the government, using incentives that included housing policies, adopted strikingly different policies toward fertility and family size over the past three decades as it attempted to affect the supply of labor in both the short and long run and thereby maintain growth rates.

It can indeed be useful for other countries to examine the Singapore experience, but it must be examined carefully and completely. Countries considering the Singapore model or wishing to emulate its approach to housing would do well to carefully examine the Singapore government's motivations for the policies they established and to identify the effects of housing policy on people, particularly women. They should also consider all the economic, political, and ideological characteristics and implications of the approach. Before accepting the notion that Singapore can be a useful model for other transitional Asian economies, particularly based on its values regarding family and community, it is important to consider a variety of other factors. As mentioned earlier, in spite of its high rates of growth in GDP, Singapore does not have as high a rating on the Human Development Index as most other high-income nations. It has considerable inequality, there are many restrictions on personal freedoms, and the government is very interventionist, even under the mantra of free-market capitalism. The approach that transitional economies take will have a significant impact on the lives of all their people for years to come. An "approach" must not be chosen without careful examination of many indicators of "development." The high growth rates or large proportions of the populace in upgraded housing may be necessary for development, but they are not sufficient.

NOTES

1. Please note that in keeping with traditional Chinese custom the individual's surname comes first, the given names next. This convention will be followed throughout this chapter. Prime Minister Lee Kuan Yew will be referred to as Prime Minister Lee. Citations for authors will be treated accordingly. For example, soon to follow is a cite for Tan Kim Song. This will be listed under the surname Tan.

2. Singapore is not a member of the OECD. It has never asked to join. It is, however, categorized as a "more advanced developing country" in OECD publications (*Straits Times Weekly Edition,* January 20, 1996: 2).

3. In economic terminology, income per capita is referred to as real gross domestic product per capita (or GDP per capita). These are Purchasing Power Parity Dollars (PPP$).

4. Only Hong Kong has made similar massive efforts; however, as of 1987, only 40 percent of its population lived in government-provided housing.

5. The World Competitiveness Report, compiled by the International Institute for Management Development and the World Economic Forum based in Switzerland, rated forty-eight economies in eight areas: government, people, finance, domestic economic strength, internationalization, infrastructure, science, and technology.

6. See, for example, *Straits Times Weekly Edition,* September 3, 1994, which refers to the rise in divorce, out-of-wedlock births, and drug use in the West.

7. "Basic needs" is a term used by the International Labor Organization to characterize the basic goods and services necessary for a minimum standard of living—food, shelter, clothing, water and sanitation, education, and health care.

8. Singapore has been a one-party state. The People's Action Party (PAP) has been the single party controlling Singapore since independence in 1965 (it achieved self-government from Great Britain in 1959). Singapore was headed by Prime Minis-

ter Lee Kuan Yew from before independence until he stepped aside in 1990—over one-quarter of a century. His was a government characterized by paternalism and corporatism with agreement between government, unions, and business (Brown, 1993). However, in his present role as senior minister, Lee Kuan Yew still takes an aggressive and outspoken role in internal pronouncements and in representing Singapore abroad. Goh Chok Tong has been prime minister since 1990.

9. There have been several cases in the 1990s that received international attention. One, for example, is the case of Dr. Chris Lingle, a U.S. citizen serving as a visiting faculty member in Singapore. He wrote an opinion piece published in the *International Herald Tribune* that "referred to unnamed 'intolerant regimes in the region' which among other techniques used to suppress dissent, relied on 'a compliant judiciary' to bankrupt opposition politicians." *Straits Times Weekly Edition,* October 29, 1994: 3). Refer to various issues of *Straits Times Weekly Edition* from October 1994 until March 11, 1995, particularly October 29, 1994, and March 11, 1995.

The National University of Singapore even scrapped a midyear issue of one of its journals, fearing that an article on culture might offend the government (*Straits Times Weekly Edition,* November 5, 1994: 8).

10. The worst-case scenario for Singapore, recently described by Prime Minister Goh Chok Tong, included a very free press (*Straits Times Weekly Edition,* December 2, 1995). It also included Singapore being overtaken economically by other countries and a weakening of social values.

11. On August 21, 1994, he said, "Changing the rule will alter the balance of responsibility between man and woman in the family. Asian society has always held the man responsible for the child he has fathered" (Ibrahim, 1994: 5).

In the October 29, 1994, *Straits Times Weekly Edition,* Prime Minister Goh tried to rewrite what had been said. In direct contradiction to what was reported he said at the National Day speech, it is now reported that he did not say it should be the male and that he believes whether the head of the household should be the father or the mother is for the families themselves to decide.

12. CPF funds, borrowed by the government, were also used to pay for the building of the Singaporean infrastructure—airports, a container port, roads and bridges, the subway system, and the telecommunications system (from a statement made by Senior Minister Lee Kuan Yew in *Straits Times Weekly Edition,* November 5, 1994: 4). This innovative compulsory savings scheme has been a key influence on housing pol icy in Shanghai specifically and in China generally (see Fei and Hopkins, Chapters 12 and 13).

13. The other three main criteria are age of the area, geographical spread, and cleanliness.

14. Other criteria for "community spirit" are the strength of community leadership, the quality and quantity of grassroots activities organized by the local residents' committee, and the level of communication between grassroots leaders and their residents.

15. Completely accurate data on the extent of these types of business organizations and changes in them over time are impossible to obtain because many very small businesses may not have registered in earlier years and do not appear in official data.

16. As we see below, the government also sought to reduce fertility rates to facilitate increases in the female supply of labor, via reducing the amount of childcare duties. Housing policies were part of the policy package they developed to alter fertility rates.

17. Although housing policy was complementary with goals of the development strategy for the first two decades, a conflict arose over time. There was a contradiction

between the CPF and an export-oriented development strategy based on attracting multinational corporations because CPF contributions added to the cost of labor. This was cited as a problem when Singapore experienced its first serious recession in 1985, with 2 percent negative growth in GDP. In a major reassessment of national economic policy, *The Singapore Economy: New Directions* (Ministry of Trade and Industry, 1986), the government recommended that the CPF contribution of 50 percent be cut at least temporarily as part of a wage restraint strategy to keep labor costs in Singapore competitive.

18. In addition, the country could allow additional immigrants to work in Singapore. However, although Singapore has, in fact, utilized immigrants in the labor force, the country is extremely reluctant to do so and has a very xenophobic attitude toward them.

19. Before 1984, childcare in Singapore was chiefly thought to be for low-income welfare women. Since 1984, the government has been trying to change the image. There were 240 centers in Singapore (1992), and it was projected that Singapore would need 330 centers or 20,000 childcare places by 1995 (PuruShotam and Chung, 1992).

20. This effect is mitigated if substantially increased immigration is permitted. But, as mentioned, Singapore has tried to keep immigration rates as low as possible.

21. This also did not correspond with the government's vision of an ethnically stable society because the minority Malay would increase their share of the population over time.

22. For example, if the mother bears the second child before she is twenty-nine, the family receives a S$20,000 rebate, while the amount is reduced by S$5,000 for every year older the mother is when the second child is born (Ministry of Trade and Industry, 1991). (S$ refers to the Singapore dollar.)

23. For more detail on all the privileges associated with the Third Child Scheme of 1987 and their subsequent revisions phased in from December 1994 to April 1, 1996, see *Straits Times Weekly Edition,* December 3, 1994: 1. The priority in allocation, as discussed in this chapter, was retained.

24. For an outline of the queuing system for HDB flats, in effect October 1, 1994, on, see *Straits Times Weekly Edition,* September 3, 1994: 4.

PART ONE

Vietnam

3

Women Influencing Housing in Ho Chi Minh City

Thai Thi Ngoc Du

Since the socioeconomic reforms, or *doi moi,* began in 1986, cities and towns have revived their activities, particularly in trade and service sectors. Ho Chi Minh City has many advantages in this economic expansion because its population, infrastructure, economic activities, and growth potential greatly exceed other cities in the region. As a result the city has become a magnet for rural-urban migration; this influx has overflowed all available housing and expanded into squatter areas throughout the urban area. This migration flow has intensified as government control of a family's residence has become less strict, because a residency permit is not only needed to obtain shelter but also to enroll a child in school. Relaxation of controls has allowed poor rural families to seek employment and education in the city where many erected houses under bridges, along canals, and in graveyards. As many waterways became extremely polluted and others began to silt up, the government began a housing reform project to upgrade existing houses or relocate the entire settlement.

This chapter explores how housing reform affects poor people, especially women who are living in the squatter areas of the city. The first section discusses the impact of economic reform on urbanization and housing policy; this is followed by a section discusses women's use of and rights to housing. The third section examines several case studies of housing reforms in squatter areas located throughout the city; the focus of the analysis is on the differential impacts these reforms have on women and men. The final section discusses the main lessons learned from the cases and presents some conclusions and recommendations.

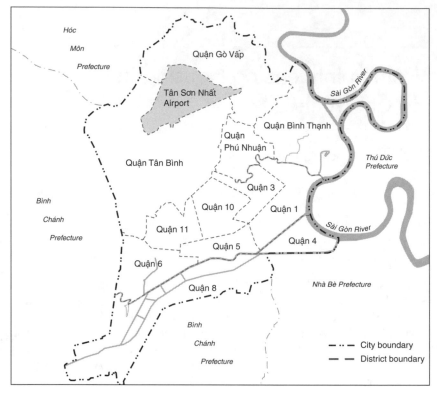

Ho Chi Minh City

IMPACT OF ECONOMIC REFORMS ON URBANIZATION AND HOUSING

As a result of the economic reforms and the open-door policy, the economic growth rate in Vietnam from 1986 to 1992 was 7 percent. This means that with a national population growth rate of 2.3 percent the per capita GDP has increased 4.6 percent per year, or more than one-third over the five-year period. Assuming this growth rate continues, Vietnam's GDP could double in the next fifteen years. Inflation has been reduced, agricultural production has increased, the average living standard of people has been improved. Even though Vietnam is ranked among the twenty poorest countries in terms of per capita GDP (US$240), its social indicators are surprisingly high, with life expectancies of sixty-four years for males and sixty-nine years for females—the same as for many middle-income countries. The infant mortality rate is merely 4 percent, while Vietnam's literacy rate is high at 88 percent (Office of Statistics, 1995). These social indicators have increased slightly since *doi moi*.

The economic growth has privileged big cities and agricultural regions rich with natural resources and contributed to a broadening gap between rich and poor, with accompanying social problems and tensions. According to the 1994 UNICEF Report, out of 14.5 million households in Vietnam, 45 percent are poor, meaning they experience a food deficit for a part of the year. If one were to classify social categories according to living standard, it would look like this:

- 5–15 percent are rich; they live mainly in urban areas, in particular in three big cities: Hanoi, Ho Chi Minh City, Hai Phong;
- 50–60 percent are in the middle class; they live in small towns and cities and in rich agricultural regions (the Mekong Delta); and
- 35–60 percent are poor; a small part of them live in cities, but the majority live in rural areas with very low average cultivated land per person.

Although a majority of the poor live in rural areas, regional income differences exist between northern and southern Vietnam. For example, although per capita agricultural production in the Red River Delta is equal to two-thirds of that of the Mekong Delta, the average income per worker in the North is only one-third to one-half of the income of agricultural workers in the South.

This disparity of income has encouraged migration to all major cities. In Ho Chi Minh City, after a period of low demographic growth between 1975 and 1985, the population growth rate is increasing at more than 3.5 percent per year. Statistics show that since 1989 immigration rates have exceeded those of natural increase. Immigration has thus neutralized efforts in family planning that have succeeded in lowering natural increase rates to 1.6 percent per year (see Table 3.1).

Various studies on migration have identified three principal migration flows directed to Ho Chi Minh City:

1. From bordering provinces such as Don Nai, Song Be, Tay Ninh (Eastern Region), Long Ann, Tien Giang (the Mekong Delta)
2. From northern provinces
3. From highlands and coastal plains of the central part of Vietnam

Although the economic growth in Ho Chi Minh City has created a need for skilled labor, only a small proportion of migrants hold some degree of professional qualifications. The Institute of Economic Research found that 65 percent are unskilled migrants from poor rural areas. As a result, Ho Chi Minh City continues to face the contradiction between lack of skilled labor and the increasing number of unemployed, which deepens the gap between rich and poor.

Table 3.1   Population Growth in Ho Chi Minh City, 1986–1993

	Total Rate	Natural Growth	Migration Rate
1986	3.97	1.63	2.34
1987	1.81	1.64	0.17
1988	1.83	1.53	0.30
1989	3.89	1.53	2.36
1990	3.55	1.52	2.03
1991	3.55	1.60	1.95
1992	3.92	1.58	2.34
1993	3.53	1.58	1.95

Source: Nguyen Thi Canh, 1994.

The urban pattern in the south continues to be dominated by Ho Chi Minh City. This area consists of the Nam Bo Plain, the Mekong Delta, the region of ancient alluvial soil usually called the Eastern Region of Nam Bo, and the highlands and plains of south-central Vietnam. In this region are seven cities with more than 150,000 people and a dozen smaller towns of between 20,000 and 80,000 inhabitants that function as district centers (see Table 3.2).

The dominance of Ho Chi Minh City in the region is reflected by its population size, which is fifteen times greater than the second-ranking city, Can Tho. Besides these two cities, only Vung Tau and Bien Hoa, which are part of the growth triangle with Ho Chi Minh City, offer opportunities for jobs, train-

Table 3.2   The Urban Pattern in Southern Vietnam, 1995

	Population	Remarks
Ho Chi Minh City	4.5 million	First-rank city; nationwide economic and cultural center.
Can Tho	285,000	Second-rank city; regional capital of the Mekong Delta.
Bien Hoa	310,000	Industrial city in the "growth triangle" of southern Vietnam.
Vung Tau	135,000	Petroleum harbor and touristic coastal city; pole of the growth triangle.
Thu Dau Mot	115,000	Traditional handicraft (pottery), located within sphere of influence of Ho Chi Minh City (20 km from Ho Chi Minh City).
Da Lat	120,000	Tourist town on the Highlands.
Nha Trang	260,000	Tourist coastal city, fishing harbor.
Rach Gia	152,000	Domestic and international trade harbor.
Buon Me Thuot	70,000	Small, regional city of the western Highlands, in the middle of minority ethnic region; rich in tropical cash crops.

Sources: Ho Chi Minh City Statistical Office, 1995; author's observations.

ing, and social promotion. Rapid economic growth and changes in residency permits have contributed to urbanization in and around Ho Chi Minh City.

NATIONAL HOUSING STRATEGY

In October 1993, the Ministry of Construction drafted the National Housing Strategy with goals for the year 2000. This strategy stated that improving housing conditions is an urgent need: Housing conditions include housing and equipment, infrastructure, and environmental conditions in the area. The National Housing Strategy has two primary emphases: facilitating low-income people to obtain convenient housing so that they would be able to organize and improve their living standards; and using poverty alleviation programs to increase employment and income of the poor as well as to improve their housing conditions.

The housing strategy projects that the total urban population in Vietnam will be more than 17 million. To respond to housing needs, housing assets in urban areas should total 135 million square meters of housing; that means an addition of 55 million square meters to existing stock. Although this represents a challenge, creating this much housing is feasible given the resources.

The housing programs for Ho Chi Minh City, announced by the Department of Land and Housing in 1995, stress four areas:

1. construction of new housing in the new urban districts and suburban areas;
2. provision of more housing for government employees, other workers, and low-income people;
3. slum clearance and resettlement of inhabitants; and
4. rehabilitation of precarious housing in slum areas during the interim.

According to this plan, spontaneous and precarious structures and squatter houses will either be upgraded according to their specific conditions or gradually eradicated. Because the government is always under pressure to provide housing for newcomers who do not yet have housing and for those forced to move by urban renovation projects, this author believes that squatter houses should be eradicated only where they become impossible to endure both for squatter-house inhabitants and for the urban management. For other squatter houses, which represent the majority, the government should accept their existence for the long term during the transition period. From 1984 to 1986, elimination of the worst squatter housing was part of official Ho Chi Minh City policy. This policy approach is still contained in official documents but is not implemented. Contradictions between official policy and actual government action contribute to confusion over actual property rights. If this viewpoint were accepted, the government would be able to invest more on upgrading the infrastructure and environmental conditions of squatter-house areas and thereby encourage people to improve their housing conditions. In the future, when the country is more developed and people's living standards have improved, urban planning operations will actually be reduced and squatter areas will be eliminated.

Ho Chi Minh City has set up the project for selling housing on credit to low-income people. Two thousand seventy-eight units will be built and sold on credit to low-income people. The total investment for this project is 34 million Vietnamese dong. However, the number of low-income people who need shelter and who are not able to buy housing on credit remains high. According to Vietnamese academic researchers, the government has to establish a policy that is able to mobilize all sources of savings from the people and from enterprises for investment in building houses. The government would no longer build houses but would provide urban plans and build necessary infrastructure.

WOMEN'S RIGHTS TO HOUSING

The constitution of Vietnam guarantees equal rights for women in all aspects of life. The basic law addressing the issue of women and housing is the Marriage and Family Law, passed in 1986, on the basis of modifications brought to the first such law passed in 1959. This law is complemented by the 1993 Land Law and the 1995 Civil Law. Taken together, these laws stipulate that husband and wife have equal rights and duties toward their common property. All acts of trade related to land and housing should have the agreement of both husband and wife. They also guarantee equal rights of inheritance to daughters and sons without any discrimination. First-rank inheritors comprise husband/wife and children. Thus, when the husband dies, the value of housing as common property is divided into two equal parts. The wife, while alive, still retains one-half; the other half (belonging to the dead husband) is divided for inheritance into equal parts among the wife and each of the children.

In order to protect the rights of property of the daughter-in-law, the Supreme Court has passed Decision No. 2/HDTP, which takes into account the current situation in rural areas of Vietnam where the extended family is a common model. Once married, the wife lives with her husband's family and participates in economic activities of the extended family. Since the economic reforms, the family enterprise is prevailing in agricultural production. All active members of the family participate in the family enterprise; the total income and budget of the family are managed by the husband or by his mother. The daughter-in-law does not get any distinct income for her work.

To prevent exploitation from the husband family, Decision No. 2 states that "in case the daughter-in-law participates in economic activities in the husband's family, has contributed to preserve or enrich the patrimony of the husband's family, the Court should consider her co-owner of the family property or patrimony, and just a simple inheritor." Should the husband die before his parents, if the daughter-in-law remains with the husband's family and takes care of his parents, the Court should decide to subtract a part of the parents' property to reimburse the daughter-in-law, if the latter requests it.

Clarification and guidance for the application of the Marriage and Family Law in favor of women are provided in Directive No. 69/TATC, issued by the Supreme Court regarding housing security for petitioners after divorce. Article 42 stipulates that the husband and wife each receive half of the common property after divorce. In case the couple lives with the extended family, the wife or the husband receives some part of the family property according to her/his contribution.

Although the Marriage and Family Law stipulates in an equitable way the division of property at divorce, in fact the rights of women and children have not been protected by many decisions from the court. It has happened often that a wife who has been working for the husband's family all her life receives only a small compensation when she is divorced. Unable to afford adequate housing, some become homeless; they have to sleep at the market, in the schoolyard, or the cooperative yard. There are cases where the parents help their married son get housing, but when the son gets a divorce, the parents request the housing back, and the divorced wife leaves the house without compensation. In southern Vietnamese provinces almost all the divorced women are expected to return to their parents' house, where they have many difficulties in finding housing. Moreover, women generally keep and feed all the children after divorce; this situation increases their difficulties. In some cases, this tension has led to serious conflicts. Because housing is a basic need for everyone's well-being, it is also the most important common property in marriage.

For the above reasons, Directive No. 69/TATC strongly urges the Court to examine carefully every case in order to secure housing for all actors involved in divorce and to protect the rights of women and children. If the house is the common property of both husband and wife, priority should be reserved to the person who feeds the children after divorce and to the person who has more difficulty in obtaining alternative housing. In cases where the husband has been working away and the wife stays alone at home with the children, the house should be awarded to the wife; the husband can take property other than the house. If other property is not of great value, the wife can give to the husband some amount of compensation. If the house is the husband's property, the court has to find a suitable solution to secure housing for the wife, perhaps assigning her a part of the house or giving her some land and compensation to build a new house. Because of the tremendous pressure on urban housing, the directive recommends that the whole house not be granted to one party, unless both parties have negotiated and agreed among themselves, or the house is too small and one of the parties can find housing elsewhere.

RIGHTS TO HOME OWNERSHIP

A significant change occurred during economic transition in the land and housing markets of Ho Chi Minh City. Not only is individual ownership of housing allowed; one person can own several houses if he/she can afford to do so. Both women and men can hold the title of ownership after purchasing a house. The new owner, if married, may register the name of the spouse as co-owner. It is only for selling the house that the agreement of both husband and wife is required by the registration service of the Department of Land and Housing.

In order to know whether there are more men or more women who register as owners in the housing trade, we have reviewed all registration sheets for 1995 at the Ho Chi Minh City Department of Land and Housing (see Table 3.3).

The general trend is for both husband and wife to be registered as owners. This trend shows that in Ho Chi Minh City people are used to legislative regulations of co-ownership that has long been practiced. What is noticeable is that the percentage of women owners is higher than men. Many of them are women heads of household, while others are married. Some preliminary explanations:

- In transition, women may have more opportunities than men to succeed in business, so they can afford housing not only for living there but also as a means of doing business.
- Businessmen or even government cadres in business sections have the possibility of purchasing several houses, so the wives can register as owners of some of them.
- From the husband's side, to let his wife register ownership is an act of honoring her.
- In the viewpoint of some people, it seems that women can deal with the authorities more smoothly in case of complication; women can be treated more generously, too.

URBAN HOUSING POLICY

Before 1989, government controls on housing purchases and construction were fairly stringent. Applicants for house purchase and construction had to

Table 3.3   Sex of Home Owners for Home Purchases Registered in 1995,
            Ho Chi Minh City

	Number	Percent
Men owners	425	13
Women owners	839	25.7
Both husband and wife	1,995	61.3
Total	3,259	

Source: Compiled by the author, 1996.

justify the purchase and construction of a new home. If they already owned a home, the government could refuse their application. There are still city procedures required of developers. Construction applications must be filed at the district construction service office and must include proof of land use title and architectural plans for the proposed construction. Some procedures are waived for construction companies building housing for relocated squatters.

From 1989 to 1993, speculation in land and housing was rife. The prices of houses and of rights to use land tremendously increased in the early 1990s. When the country was opened to foreign investment, and the government was liberalizing the economy and approved housing ownership rights to the citizens, numerous businessmen anticipated that needs for housing and land would be increasing due to immigration, development of enterprises, and greater income. Many engaged in housing and land transactions and construction of new houses. Numbers of people have become very rich in a very short time.

Soon, housing and land speculation was out of the government's control—to the extent that in 1993–1994 the government had to take stern measures by imposing fiscal regulations on housing transactions. Speculation has been mostly stopped, but housing is still very expensive. For example, sellers must now pay as tax a substantial portion of sale profits from each housing transaction. One of the consequences is that the poor encounter greater difficulty in accessing housing, resulting in illegal construction, precarious housing, and the expansion of slums.

SQUATTER AREAS

The phenomenon of slums is not new in Ho Chi Minh City. In the 1960s, because of war, people from the countryside migrated to Saigon (the pre-1975 name of Ho Chi Minh City) and contributed to the expansion of slums, which were located along canals and in swampy areas. They were all illegally constructed. According to 1977 statistics, Ho Chi Minh City counted 43,000 very precarious houses, of which 18,000 were located on and along canals that were highly polluted.

From 1975 to 1994, the city government provided housing to more than 100,000 households, mainly through work units. Ho Chi Minh City in 1994 had about 800,000 households. Further, the city eradicated thirty squatter areas comprising 5,000 housing units, built more than 12,000 new housing units for family beneficiaries of social welfare and another 86,000 units (Department of Land and Housing, 1995). However, the number of precarious houses in Ho Chi Minh City has increased to 67,000 units today. Twenty-four thousand of them are on canals, where they contribute to pollution and often obstruct the waterways. New squatter areas have emerged, and in older areas the population density has increased. For instance, the squatter area of Subdistrict 6/District 4 (the Hiep Thanh area) contained only 197 households in 1988, but at the end of 1989, when the upgrading project started, there were already 308 households. In District 11, the number of squatter housing units has increased from 3,025 to 5,046 between 1977 and 1991 (Department of Land and Housing, 1995).

Right after its establishment in 1975, the government became very concerned with the problem of slums and housing of low-income people. The government policy regarding this issue changed several times, resulting in both good and bad lessons. From 1975 to 1985, alongside the policy of strict control over immigration to the city, the government established programs of moving people from slum areas to so-called new economic zones (NEAs). These were the result of policies developed from 1975 to 1979 to limit the expansion of large cities. The government wanted to relocate unemployed urban residents to rural areas to reclaim wasteland through agriculture. Families received government assistance in relocating and in establishing themselves in NEAs, but the NEAs were not very successful. Beginning in 1979, relocated people began to return to the cities, in surrounding provinces, and to "new settlements" in suburban districts. The purpose of these projects was to reduce the number of slums and the population density in the city and to provide jobs in agriculture to nonskilled workers. Of the 5,000 households moved from the slums, roughly 3,000 households, according to government estimates, stayed in new settlements in suburban districts, while the rest dispersed, resettling in other housing.

The goodwill of the government was recognized, but implementation of such projects was not successful due to lack of funding and the difficulties urban people face in adapting to harder living conditions in the countryside. Therefore, little by little people returned to the city and settled in very crowded areas wherever space was available—even graveyards. The result was a further expansion of slum areas. The government has built a very small amount of housing at moderate cost to relocate people moved from very deteriorated slums in the city center.

From 1986 to 1989, the city's housing department undertook a few large-scale projects of slum clearance at enormous expense, spending millions in U.S. dollars to eradicate only 1,000 houses in slum areas. The high expense was due to the costs of clearing existing slum areas before new low-cost housing could be built. Those projects were not feasible unless they received international assistance.

As a result of the open-door policy (1986–1990), information exchanges with other Third World countries increased, especially with Southeast Asian countries such as Thailand, Indonesia, and the Philippines. Regional international organizations provided successful lessons concerning solutions to the problem of slums. New experiments, with focus on slum upgrading based on a community development viewpoint, were carried out. Representative of this tendency was the case of the Hiep Thanh community, which will be discussed in the fourth section of this chapter.

Recently, concerned with appearing too backward compared to its prosperous neighbors in Southeast Asia, the city government decided to conduct big urban renovation projects to improve the city's image. In this image—that is, of Ho Chi Minh City in the year 2000—there will be no place for slums and polluted areas. Since 1993, the city government has been undertaking slum clearance and drainage along Nhieu Loc-Thi Nigh Canal, which runs throughout the city and is very polluted.[1] This clearance operation includes 4,000 housing units along the canal, the goal being for inhabitants to move by April 30, 1994, to new buildings being constructed. Yet by November 1996 only 1,608 households had moved. Not all families resettled in the new units even when they were completed, as they were unable to afford the cost; instead, they relocated in other squatter areas. New low-cost housing entails a number of additional expenses for these poor squatters, including charges for rent or loan repayment, water, electricity, garbage collection, and parking.

The deadline for resettlement of the remaining canal squatters has been extended; those in Tan Binh, Phu Nhuan, and Bin Thanh were to move by the end of 1997. Squatters in the two central districts will not be resettled until the end of 1998, since the government must obtain land outside these districts before it can begin building low-cost housing there.

Public opinion and even some professionals remain skeptical about the feasibility of this project, because it needs a very large budget (US$30 million) to pay compensation to the inhabitants and to invest in housing construction for selling on credit to the people to be relocated. Also important is the social dimension: What do people in slum areas think or aspire to for their well-being in terms of housing? What solutions are convenient for their very limited means? Sociological studies and discussions with the inhabitants should be carried out in depth in order to get people's collaboration in finding sustainable solutions.

CASE STUDIES OF HOUSING PROJECTS

An important lesson from the 1995 report by the Department of Land and Housing of Ho Chi Minh City is that the subsidy system cannot solve housing problems or provide housing in good condition to everybody. Slum problems cannot be only a governmental issue; there must also be a popular participation process. Top-down projects are rarely successful despite their good intentions. To promote participation we need to understand people's aspirations, opinions, and propositions.

This section reviews three groups of housing projects. The first set, illustrating people's participation, includes upgrading in Hiep Thanh, a multipurpose project in District 3, and mixed-income housing in District 11. The second group utilizes a study by the Environment Committee of Ho Chi Minh City and the École Polytechniques Fédérale de Lausanne that focused on issues of water pollution and degraded urban environment in areas of precarious housing in Binh Thang and in District 8, both outer urban districts (ENCO, 1996). The third group of studies is drawn from research by the Environnement et Développement du Tiers-Monde-Vietnam on women's perceptions of housing needs that includes the use of the house for income activities (ENDA, 1996). Sites for this study included the city center, outer urban, and suburban areas.

In recent years, adhering to the line of thinking of "people and government collaborating together," with the assistance of community development workers, several projects of slum upgrading based on a community development approach have been undertaken. These three projects have all been assisted by international agencies and nongovernmental organizations.

Hiep Thanh Community

Hiep Thanh community consists of four poor neighborhood units in Ward 6/District 4. It is south of the town center and near the port, so the land is valuable. This area is known for containing social problems such as alcoholism, gambling, and crime. The 23,800 square meters are in part surrounded by two small canals; almost all houses are built on pillars over the canals. Three hundred and twenty-one households are living there, with 1,552 persons, among whom ninety-three households do not have official registration. The majority of inhabitants are returnees from the new economic zones. They are very poor, working in the informal sector as cyclo drivers, street vendors, and mobile vendors. The local government has made efforts to improve the housing situation and to strengthen solidarity among inhabitants who are in similar situations and suffer poverty. Recently, assisted by specialists and funds from the Environmental and Socio-economic Aspects of Tropical Deforestation in Asia and the Pacific (ESCAP), the Land and Housing Department set up a community development project for squatters in Hiep Thanh aimed at improving their income, housing, and environmental conditions.

These priorities are those expressed by the community itself. Community development workers conducted large meetings and small-group discussions to raise awareness of the issues. The community then elected a representative board that was recognized by the local government and that worked in close collaboration with other mass organizations in the community. The people organized meetings and discussed their needs; the community board then established projects to be implemented. The first goal was to improve electricity and the water supply, then to improve the environment (roads and sewage system), and finally to set up projects for credit and income generation.

Two years after the project began in 1993 with very low investment, the living conditions in the community had been very much improved, in material as well as moral aspects. People's sense of responsibility toward their own lives and those of their families had been strengthened. Improvements include a community-managed public water tap, cement lanes, evening classes for school dropouts, credit for poor women, improved community security, reduced gambling, and reduced conflict. Women were active participants in all of these activities and on the community board—but were not yet leaders.

Unfortunately, this experience did not protect the area from the urban land market. In the current rapid urbanization process, land in the central districts of Ho Chi Minh City is very valuable. The district authorities try to find land available for new urban planning operations. Slum clearance is becoming a general trend. So by the end of 1995 Hiep Thanh was slated for urban renovation, and precarious housing would be eradicated. Community development efforts begun in 1991–1992 were achieving good results by 1994, but since then an atmosphere of uncertainty has prevailed. People no longer made any effort for the improvement of the community. Changing government policy led to the loss of government credibility in this community.

Ward 9/District 3

This multipurpose project aimed at integrating credit schemes for income generation with housing and environment improvement activities. In Ward 9 in 1995, 1,560 houses were situated on or near Nhieu Loc Canal. This is the most polluted canal; many small lanes are flooded during the rainy season. People living in slum areas consisted of 1,748 households containing 8,237 people who hold a regular residence status and 318 households containing 1,213 people who do not hold regular residence status. Most of them are street vendors at Hoa Hung railway station, waste traders, and occasional workers.

Sponsored by the Department of Land and Housing and a European nongovernmental organization, the Coopération Internationale pour le Développement et la Solidarité (CIDSE), the project was begun in March 1992.

Methods of community development were applied throughout all phases of the project: preparation, implementation, management, and maintenance of the works after completion. During project implementation, the people's sense of responsibility for environmental protection and for work maintenance was strengthened because of their contributions: digging a well for water, draining the sewage network, and repairing ten lanes in the slum.

The project is characterized by the strong role played by women in the credit schemes, both as organizers and as beneficiaries. The Women's Union of the ward managed the project and mobilized the participation of the people in project implementation, organizing credit for women as well as housing improvements for all. Loans for families are available through the National Fund for Poverty Alleviation. The woman who headed the local people's committee of District 3, Ward 9, led resettlement efforts. She used to be the women's union representative for the ward but was promoted. This is an indication of the importance of Women's Union involvement in the ward.

The savings and credit program for women was modeled on the Grameen Bank approach. It started with a pilot group of six women who practiced saving for four weeks. Afterward they can borrow 200,000 VN dong (US$20) and repay 4,000 VN dong in daily installments. In such a way, the borrower is able to repay the loan plus 40,000 dong after sixty days; 6,000 dong go for interest interest and 34,000 dong are added to the savings pool. Between 1992 and 1994, nineteen groups consisting of 118 members were established.

The positive effects of the project are measured by the visible improvement of their income and the reduction of debt burden. The long-term effects are the changes in their perceptions of saving: They recognize the benefit of saving and learn that even the poor are able to practice saving. The group activities strengthen the solidarity among poor women. Once their lives improved, the women participated more actively in programs of housing and environment improvement.

The same method of savings and credit was also available to improve the house itself, including improvement of the floor, the bathroom, and the toilet. People were able to borrow greater amounts of money than they were for income activities, up to 2 million VN dong (US$200); the time for reimbursement was longer—up to 20 months.

However, like Hiep Thanh community, Ward 9/District 3 is also located in the slum clearance area, according to the new policy of the city government. As a result, all the efforts and investment of the inhabitants might be dissipated. In 1994, ninety-six precarious houses were removed; the owners received compensation and had priority to purchase or to rent new housing built by the city or district in the resettlement program. However, because their houses were illegal construction in poor condition, the compensation they received was so small that they could not afford new housing, even that built for low-income people.

Binh Thoi

Since the late 1970s, this former cemetery of 19.5 hectares has been occupied by poor people returning from NEAs. Area 7 was facing serious problems of insecurity. In 1993, the district authorities announced an urban renovation plan to clear the slum and build three-story housing. The problem is that this project requires substantial funding (US$500,000) that the city and the district are not able to afford.

Finally, the district authorities decided to reserve a part of the area for the construction of substantial housing that will be sold to institutions and individuals at a price fixed at 75–100 luong of gold (1 luong equals 37.5 grams) per flat. To obtain a flat, institutions and individuals must pay an advance to the housing construction company of the district. In exchange, the company is required to respect the design ordered by the clients. With the advances, the company has built fifty-six houses in the first phase. With the profits earned from selling those houses, the company builds new low-income housing as well as public service buildings such as a shopping center, schools, a sports complex, and a culture center. This process reflects the influence of the Singapore model of the National Saving Fund, but it should be conducted with more financial constraints (see Chapter 2).

WOMEN AND THE HOUSING ENVIRONMENT

A survey of women's attitudes toward polluting the environment in their communities was taken in two slum areas, District 8 and Binh Thanh (ENCO, 1996). Although women even in very precarious housing know how to keep their house clean, many do not consider it their responsibility to keep the area clean. Rather, they assign the task of keeping the slum clean to the government. In their view, personal efforts cannot change the situation in any meaningful manner.

In-depth interviews bring to light more evidence of this general attitude: Even when their house is equipped with toilets, they continue to use public toilets located on the canal. They use their own toilets only in an emergency, or reserve them for the elderly members in the family. The use of public toilets on the canal facilitates keeping their private toilets clean! Many responded that they prefer public toilets on the canal because "they are cleaner than other types of toilets." These respondents often feel that private toilets can "infect" the house. These toilets are of lower quality. Some are outhouses; others, with insufficient water, do not flush adequately. Toilets on the canal and the habit of placing all waste in the canal are two main factors of pollution; however, because of their perception, the women do not give priority to those problems.

The women do wish to improve the water supply and improve the waste-water drainage. Those needs are daily, immediate, and short-term, so the women feel more pressure. With a high percentage of women working at home (housewives, the jobless, home-based workers), women have lived in this polluted environment for many years. Do they have any urgent need to change or to move to a better environment? Women's responses reflect an attitude of endurance because they know their limited financial resources, which do not allow them to aspire to a better environment.

Health Concerns

As a result of these practices, according to the authorities, the environment in the slums is deteriorating rapidly. Furthermore, the atmosphere of uncertainty about slum clearance does not encourage efforts to keep the environment clear. The impact of these slum conditions on the health of women and their families is serious. Swampy areas become sources of disease contamination; tuberculosis has reappeared among women who sell charcoal; women working informally with waste recycling do not have protection such as protective masks and gloves.

Women lack knowledge of health care for themselves and for their children. No research has been done yet on the health impact of poor sanitation in canal areas. Disease vectors such as rats and insects are present, however. The shortage of water is a regular problem for most residents. Factory-bottled water is used for drinking. If canal water were clean, it could be used for washing. Instead, most squatters must rely on piped water, but sometimes squatter areas are not included in the water-supply network or are at the very end of the network, so water pressure is very low. Only one area has a well. As a result, most squatters use little water for drinking, washing, and cleaning. The proportion of malnourished children is high in slum areas. They do not send the children to kindergarten, so the children do not have a chance to benefit from health care provided in those institutions.

WORKING AND HOUSING CONDITIONS

In Ho Chi Minh City, at least 40 percent of women are in the informal sector. They are mostly street or itinerant vendors; a small number are home-based workers. Those activities are suitable to poor women because they require minimal skill and capital and provide women with flexible working hours and allow them to stay at home. In such a way, they can combine their productive work with their reproductive tasks. Even in small lanes of slums, women open small businesses in front of their houses (ENCO, 1996; Trinh, 1996).

Table 3.4   Occupational Structure of Active Population by Sex
in District Binh Thanh, Ward 15 and District 8, Ward 10, 1995 (in percent)

	District Binh Thanh, Ward 15		District 8, Ward 10	
	Men	Women	Men	Women
Handicraft, sewing, painting on fabric, embroidery	27.5	13.1	17.8	08.3
Housework	01.5	29.7	00.2	32.8
Small or street business	13.2	33.1	12.0	30.6
Daily hired worker, docker	04.9	03.0	21.5	11.4
Cyclo, tricycle	11.9	00.4	10.5	00.0
Government employee, accountant, nurse	09.1	06.9	06.7	04.5
Teacher, physician, engineer	01.0	01.9	02.4	00.9
Worker, mechanic, electronic, electric	06.9	04.3	07.1	06.1
Service, taxi driver, beauty salon	11.3	03.0	08.4	01.3
Food cooking	00.7	01.1	01.1	00.5
Cadre, political cadre, responsible for neighborhood unit	01.5	00.0	01.7	00.0
Farmer	02.0	00.2	01.1	01.4
Jobless	08.6	03.2	09.7	02.3

Source: ENCO, 1996.

A survey of seventy-five women in three wards of Ho Chi Minh City—Ward 9/District 3 (central), Ward 8/District 8 (urban periphery), and several wards in District Go Vap (newly urbanized)—found that 36 percent were microentrepreneurs or vendors; 12 percent sewed at home; 20 percent were hired as daily workers; and 8 percent did other work; 24 percent replied that they were housewives (ENDA, 1996). A more detailed breakdown of informal work done by women or men in low-income areas of the city was provided in the Environment Committee of Ho Chi Minh City and École Polytechnique Fédérale de Lausanne study (ENCO, 1996; see Table 3.4).

Income for poor families is essential in order to obtain a house title from the government. Most slum housing is at the outset illegal constructions on wasteland and unused land. Gradually, the occupants improve their houses, and the area becomes more stable. At this point the city administration accepts applications for title of housing ownership based on documentation that shows the occupant built or bought the house. Since all land in Vietnam belongs to the state, people can own their houses but not the land upon which the house is built. House title allows residents to obtain the rights of land utilization and to pay an annual tax to the government.

Table 3.5   Housing Status (in percent)

	D.8/Ward 10	D.BT/Ward 15
Rent (state ownership)	1.1	2.2
Rent (private ownership)	0.7	0.1
Owner		
Housing has been built	13.6	14.3
Housing has been purchased	30.0	23.5
Total owner	43.6	37.8
With title		
Housing has been built	26.7	42.7
Housing has been purchased	22.6	14.6
Total with title	49.3	57.3
Free shelter	3.2	1.6
Other	2.1	1.0

Source: ENCO, 1996.

The title of housing ownership is documentation of the greatest value to the resident's rights. Thus, in Ward 10/District 8, 45 percent of the households hold title; the proportion is 37.51 percent in Ward 15/Binh Thanh District, because the settlement in that ward is more recent. Ninety-five percent of households do not have to pay for housing. This point is worth being considered by planners of resettlement programs. Any additional expenses such as housing rental or installments represent new pressures for these poor women (see Table 3.5).

The average number of rooms in the house is 1.3 in Ward 10/District 8, 1.6 in Ward 15/Binh Thanh District. The average area of housing is 35–35.5 square meters, equal to 6.1–6.2 square meters per person. If the 3 square meters for kitchen and toilet are not included, the average area per person is only 5.5 square meters. The average figure for the entire city is 5.8 square meters per person.

Possessing a house title does not protect families from resettlement; it only assures them of compensation and a claim to new housing. The Environment et Développement du Tiers-Monde-Vietnam (ENDA) study found that 48 percent of the women stated that the government should have projects of building housing for low-income people. More than half of them specified that the construction of housing for low-income people should be combined with a long-term credit system that would enable poor people to purchase and own housing. They also insisted on quality in this kind of housing. Most wished to be resettled in their present ward because they are attached to their living environment.

Vietnam's goal of development in the next decades is industrialization and modernization. In Ho Chi Minh City, media coverage on this trend is widespread. In the thinking of some urban planners and people, modernization means that the city should have high-rises in the center and highways to

Table 3.6   Women's Preference of Type of Housing in the Future in Three Vietnam Districts (in percent)

	District 3 (central)	District 8 (urban periphery)	District Go Vap (newly urbanized)
An apartment in a housing block consisting of many floors	–	4	2
An apartment in a housing block with few floors and long corridors where residents can do cooking, laundry, microbusiness, or just talk	72	56	6
A separate small house with no floor and few facilities	12	40	92
A modern collective block where people have to pass by the neighbor's house before getting in their own house	16	–	–

Source: ENDA, 1996.

respond to the needs of increasing automobile traffic, and people should live in high-rises in order to reserve space for other activities, like roads and parks.

The understanding of the women surveyed about modernization, their perception of the future image of Ho Chi Minh City, and their housing preferences are not consistent with this vision. They prefer a low-rise city that preserves traditional housing, one that is beautiful, clean, and includes green spaces. Overwhelmingly they seek a quiet place to live (see Table 3.6).

Housing Issues in Resettlement Areas

Most new housing in resettlement areas is situated in four- or five-story buildings; the subsidized price of the unit is very reasonable in comparison with the market. The ENCO survey (1996) found that the women agree that new housing is more spacious and cleaner; the access to water, electricity, and toilets saves them time. Some women have been able to improve their income from baby-sitting or sewing. They also feel more secure and so can concentrate on developing their economic activity (unpublished student study). Overall, 70 percent of the interviewees stated that resettlement did not interfere with their income activities. But the other 30 percent was unable to continue as street vendors and handicraft workers.

A crucial concern is the title of housing ownership. Even those who have fully paid for the house have not received title. The Department of Land and Housing explains that the construction companies are under pressure to build housing for resettlement in a very short time. Overwhelmed by the task, they have not had time to consider how to share the expenses for land utilization rights among residents. As a result, the registration service has not received any applications for housing ownership title from the newly resettled people.

Women often find it difficult to afford the cost of new housing and its many new expenses. Indeed, many are in debt before they are ever asked to move. Thus, many prefer to use their compensation to pay off the lender and buy new slum housing elsewhere. Some move to new housing just to sell it: One study showed that after three years 20 percent of households had sold their apartments and moved out (unpublished student study).[2]

Residents are not used to the high-rise way of life. Accustomed to throwing all wastes into the canal, they continue to throw waste in common spaces or, worse, into neighbors' houses. Street vendors and cyclo drivers have no place to park cars and vehicles. Microenterprises that depend on customers cannot operate on the upper floors, which is the area reserved for subsidized housing. The ground floor is sold at market price; the construction companies use this profit to build more housing and amenities for low-income people.

CONCLUSION

Two major lessons emerge from the case studies and other examples presented in this chapter. First, residents of the squatter and slum areas, especially poor women, can and will participate in programs to improve their neighborhoods; moreover, the projects will be both cheaper and more effective if the community is involved. Second, the success of projects requires some government support in promoting community services, offering assistance for income activities, and guaranteeing property rights.

The case studies clearly illustrate the benefit of having members of the community involved in all stages of a project. In Ward 10/District 8, with the help of community development workers, women manage the maintenance of the sewer system. In Ward 15/Binh Thanh District, they organize garbage collection; this type of program is being promoted by the Women's Union and can be observed throughout the city. Participation in the earliest stages of design can lead to buildings with fewer complaints about their poor construction. Poor women are the most actively involved; they do more than poor men as well as middle-class women and men in the area. The process increases the agency of the women by improving their skills and providing experience in management.

The lack of a long-term, stable government policy can undermine these efforts to improve living environments. When residents learn they may lose housing, as in District 4 (Hiep Thanh), they stop putting energy into maintenance and improvements and allow the properties to degrade. Clear policies for slum upgrading and timetables for resettlement would allow residents of the communities affected to plan more carefully.

Resettlement itself is a concern for many households because of the type of housing available. Moving into multistory collective buildings changes their way of life both in terms of sanitary practices and for many income activities. Most residents of Ho Chi Minh City prefer to live in houses rather than in flats. Housing rights are clearer for this type of dwelling and provide a ground floor that can easily be transformed into a storefront. Additional stories can be added as children grow up and marry. In contrast, government housing for those relocated from squatter settlements is usually in the upper floors of apartment buildings.

Relocating poor people to multistory buildings is a problem in cities everywhere. Alternative styles of housing that include lower buildings and community space for working and for parking areas might be considered. Meanwhile, community organizations help the residents address some of the major problems encountered in the relocation. These organizations offer credit and training in new income activities and broadcast the negative health aspects of a polluted environment.

Residents in squatter areas and in new housing benefit from community activism organized through the Women's Union and similar governmental organizations and assisted by international agencies and nongovernmental organizations. Savings and credit programs assist women in improving income through microenterprises and help families upgrade their houses. Additional income allows households to pay the taxes for improved amenities. Community effort can stimulate improved awareness of the negative health impact, especially on children, of a polluted environment.

In sum, community participation is essential in the improvement of housing conditions in upgraded areas as well as in the resettlement areas. However, the poor lack resources for making this transition. Therefore, the government needs to assist residents during this transition beyond the provision of new housing stock. It should inform the people about future plans for their areas. Once housing is upgraded or residents are resettled, the government should ensure timely registration for house titles. Government also needs to support and encourage organizations that offer assistance to the community for credit, service, and environmental and educational programs.

NOTES

1. The canal project extends through five districts: District 1 and District 3 are in the central city, where what little land is available is very expensive; the other three districts included in this chapter are details of projects in District 3 and in Bin Thanh.

2. This study in Xom Dam (Ward 10, District 8) found that thirty-one of 157 households that were resettled in 1993 had sold and moved out by 1996.

4

Women's Access to Housing in Hanoi

Hoang Thi Lich

Many researchers in Vietnam have studied problems of urban centers and urbanization processes, including related aspects such as inhabitant structure, social background, living standards, ways of life, social issues, environment, urban architecture, and housing. They have not, however, paid attention to gender issues in urban housing reform. This chapter is a first attempt to address the differences in women's and men's use of and rights to housing in Hanoi, with an emphasis on the needs of poor women.

Vietnam is an agricultural country, with nearly 80 percent of the population living in rural areas. In many ways, urban centers in Vietnam have not developed as much as those in other countries. Decades of war have destroyed cities and towns, many of which still need to be rebuilt. Many inhabitants in these areas were displaced during and after the war. In addition, since the policy of economic renovation, or *doi moi,* began in 1986, people have increasingly been migrating from the countryside to urban centers in search of work.

These rural urban migrants need housing that is in short supply in Hanoi. They add to the demand for housing coming from urban residents and foreign businesses and competing uses of land. These factors contribute to rising prices that are minimally offset by construction of new approved housing and illegal squatter units. At the same time that prices are rising, income inequality is also increasing and subsidies for basic needs are being reduced. Thus, modernization, urbanization, and industrialization are creating many housing problems in Hanoi. Housing for the poor is an urgent need. Although 60 percent of the poor are women, the differences in women's and men's needs have been ignored by most studies. Housing is a means of earning an income as well as shelter and could offer more opportunities for poor women. This chapter focuses on these gendered aspects of housing.

To study urban housing issues that exist throughout northern Vietnam is too great a task. Therefore, I have focused on Hanoi, the capital of Vietnam, for two reasons: First, Hanoi is a large city, with a population of more than 1 million. Second, Hanoi is my birthplace, a city where I have witnessed first-hand many changes over the years. This research has drawn primarily on sources such as published and unpublished materials, as well as newspapers and government statistics. There are inevitably shortcomings that I hope to address and supplement later.

The chapter begins with a background section on the socioeconomic characteristics of housing in Hanoi before and during the process of *doi moi*. The second section focuses on women's rights to housing, a topic that is greatly neglected in current urban research. Women's use rights are discussed in terms of the changing family type, use of the home as a base for productive work, and the design of the housing unit. Next, property rights are discussed. This is followed by an examination of the particular needs of poor women. Some suggestions for future research are presented in the concluding section.

SOCIOECONOMIC CHARACTERISTICS OF HOUSING IN HANOI

Hanoi, the capital of Vietnam, is thousands of years old. In 1010, at the beginning of the Ly Dynasty, the capital of the country was moved from Hoa Lu (Ninh Binh Province) to the Dai La Citadel and given the new name Thang Long (Ascending Dragon) by King Ly Thai To. This city has remained the capital ever since, although its name was changed during several dynasties. It was renamed Hanoi in 1831. After the French colonized the North in 1882, they began to transform Hanoi by building new roads and constructing modern buildings in the European style. By 1904, the city comprised 940 hectares with 130 adjacent quarters and villages (Bui Thiet, 1995: 160). Since the August Revolution in 1945, Hanoi has been the capital as well as the center of politics, culture, and economy of the independent country of Vietnam.

Historic Overview

Before discussing housing issues in Hanoi, I would like to address urban formation in Vietnam in general and in Hanoi in particular. In Vietnam, an agricultural country, the process of urbanization has been very slow. During the traditional, feudal period that preceded the French colonization during the late 1800s, according to urban sociologist Trinh Duy Luan, "The formation and development of Vietnam's feudal urban centers did not originate from the division of labor but from the redistribution of social goods to satisfy the demands of consumers from the ruling class and to meet the need of trade exchange." Rather, the cities were "administration and trade centers set up on the base of feudal kings' and lords' citadels and buildings in areas with geographically favorable conditions for trade exchange" (Trinh, 1996: 26). The result was an agriculturally based, small, self-sufficient, closed economy in which the urban centers did not play a very important role. The social relations were similar to those existing in villages and hamlets. At the time, Hanoi consisted of thirty-six ancient guilds and streets of workmen and businessmen. Houses in the city were as small and narrow as those in the countryside.

After establishing their dominating rule over Vietnamese peoples, French colonizers began to intensify their exploitation of Vietnam's natural resources for the benefit of their homeland. During this period, many cities and towns in Vietnam were expanded, especially those with ports such as Saigon, Danang, and Haiphong.

Hanoi alternated with Saigon as the headquarters of Indochina's administration under French rule. The city was widened, and important transportation roads were built to link it with other big cities and ports. European-style houses were constructed alongside traditional ones. Canadian urban planning professor Brahm Wiesman remarked that even in 1991 "Hanoi specifically bears the stamp of a former French colonial city." The population of Hanoi grew from 119,700 in 1943 to 279,000 in 1953. Rural-urban migration was relatively slow during this period.

After the war of liberation against the French, cities and towns began to flourish. In the first ten years (1955–1965), Hanoi grew rapidly. The central bodies of the administration and Communist Party were moved from the war zones to Hanoi. Industrialization was also rapid. After the French defeat at Dien Bien Phu in 1954, the French community (colonial authorities, military officers, and traders) left Vietnam. All of their offices, buildings, and houses were taken over by the Vietnamese government, which continues to manage them. The buildings formerly used as officers' quarters are now used by many ministries, departments, and embassies. The rest of the houses have been allocated to government departments to rent to their employees. In addition, since 1955, the Hanoi Authority has been managing many of the houses left by Vietnamese who went to South Vietnam or abroad after 1954. These houses, termed "absent-owner houses," are leased to residents of Hanoi. Although the owner is supposed to be able to get the house back upon returning to Vietnam, that rarely happened until *doi moi;* it is an expensive process, because the returnee has to compensate the current residents and find them new housing. Land policy since 1955 has prohibited private ownership of land because all land is owned by the state.

The next ten years (1965–1975) witnessed the American War in Vietnam. In the North, industrial zones and cities were bombarded with U.S. airpower. To minimize the damage caused during wartime, the government ordered an evacuation of all central offices, factories, and schools from Hanoi, a situation that remained until 1973, when the Paris Agreement to halt bombing in the

North was signed. Hanoi's recovery from the war was rather quick compared to other cities and has consisted of two stages, 1975–1986 and 1986 to the present.

From 1976 to 1986, the city experienced a sluggish socioeconomic life under a centrally planned, bureaucratic regime. The citizens were unable to do business and arrange their own lives themselves, either because they were too poor to buy construction materials or because the materials were too scarce and strictly planned to sell to consumers. The infrastructure and architectural style in Hanoi changed very little. The national housing policy at this time was mainly to build and allocate housing for state employees. These houses included four- to five-story living quarters with self-contained flats and one-story tiled buildings divided into many separate flats for individual households, with shared kitchens and toilets.

Construction of these houses has taken place in two ways: First, the Department of Public Management of Hanoi has used state funds to build housing. Houses are then allocated to the ministries according to the annual plan by the state Planning Committee. The employer selects the workers who will receive the limited state housing; the Department of Public Management of Hanoi then leases housing to cadres and state employees. Second, the national government supplies funds and land to ministries and departments for construction of living quarters. When the houses are built, they are allocated by these ministries and departments.

Housing was greatly subsidized, so that rent was usually less than 10 percent of an employee's salary; sometimes it was as low as 1 percent. The criteria used to determine who would receive housing are based on several factors, such as whether the recipient has ever been allocated housing from the state; whether their current housing is smaller than the size that the state has set as appropriate for that level of work; the employee's position, with higher levels receiving housing sooner and getting larger units; seniority; the size of the family, with larger families receiving preference until the two-child policy went into effect in 1982; and outstanding performance of the employee at work. Some preference was given to women who otherwise had the same criteria as men at their level but who had children and whose husband's work unit either did not provide housing or whose husband lived separately due to job assignment. With so many criteria to consider, the selection process for housing always took a long time.

Official policy during this period was to provide only state employees with housing without taking into account the needs of people from other classes in the city. Nonstate employees were expected to arrange their own housing. When they could not afford to lease their own apartment or were not married, they usually lived with parents. Their parents' housing unit might be private (owned or rented) or state-owned. A woman had survivor rights to remain in her husband's state-allocated unit when he died, and children, both women and men, typically inherited the use rights for the parents' housing. Private housing could also be inherited during the subsidy period from grand-parents or parents. Nieces and nephews were not permitted to inherit housing; units would go to the state.

With limited capital, the state was not able to meet the housing demands for all state employees. There was little incentive to lease private housing when state-subsidized units were so inexpensive. State housing, however, was insufficient; by the end of the 1980s, only 30 percent of state employers were provided with houses. The others had to accommodate themselves in ex-tremely cramped quarters. State housing was also inadequate:

> Due to the lack of experience in planning and managing urban centers, the State paid more attention to the short-term needs of constructing residential dwellings rather than developing a master plan for the city's long-term space and infrastructure needs such as an adequate water supply and drainage sys-tem, roads and environmental sanitation. . . . The buildings lacked conve-niences and were of bad quality and monotonous architecture (Trinh and Leaf, 1996: 13).

Housing in Hanoi Since the Renovation in 1986

The implementation of renovation policies in 1986 has had great influence on housing all over the country, especially in big cities such as Hanoi. The devel-opments both of a socialist-oriented, multisectoral market economy and of rights for people to run private businesses have greatly increased the ability for people to build housing. Reduction of the subsidy system now encourages people to be self-sufficient in meeting their basic needs for food, clothing, and housing. As a result of market liberalization, those who have money can im-prove their houses.

Social differences are also on the rise. Those with money can buy rights to use land and build houses. Wealthy people may build several houses and rent them to others. Some built houses illegally along the Red River Dikes be-cause of the profit opportunities and because the authorities were slow in pro-cessing the many applications received. People unable to buy houses can now rent rooms at places closer to work. A "drifting stream" of people who are jobless in rural areas due to the lack of farmland and capital has come to the city in search of work. These people have to find their own accommodations and often set up squatter or makeshift housing on marginal land throughout Hanoi.

Adoption of the open-door policy for foreign investment has created fa-vorable conditions for investors and international organizations to open their representative offices in Hanoi (*An Ninh Thu Do Magazine,* September 17, 1996). As a result, demand for housing from foreign business representatives has grown rapidly.

Key policy changes occurred with the national Ordinance on Housing, issued in 1991, and with Decree No. 61/CP on buying and selling state-owned units to renters, issued in 1994. These policies include the sale of low-quality houses and concrete buildings as well as villas. In addition, renters of state-owned houses are entitled to transfer leases or sell their rental houses. Licensing for building new houses and repairing old ones has become quicker and easier than before. Consequently, housing in Vietnamese urban centers has changed greatly both in number and form. In 1992, the capital invested in housing construction by businesses and individuals was twice that of the government, excluding the numerous unlicensed buildings, and by 1995 one-third of the houses in cities and towns were built with private money (Trinh and Leaf, 1996: 16). The explosion in housing construction can be seen everywhere. The construction rate in Hanoi is somewhat slower than that in Ho Chi Minh City, where much of it is privately financed. According to the statistics released by the Hanoi Land and Housing Department, of the 700,000 square meters of new houses built in the city from 1991 to 1994, 70 percent were built by the people themselves (more than twice the national rate). In 1994 alone, 84 percent of the dwellings were self-financed (Trinh and Leaf, 1996: 16).

CONTEMPORARY HOUSING IN URBAN HANOI

According to the Hanoi Statistics Department, up to December 31, 1993, the total area of Hanoi was 922.8 square kilometers. The city has four urban districts (Hoan Kiem, Ba Dinh, Hai Ba Trung, Dong Da), each divided into four administrative subdistricts; there are five suburban districts (Dong Anh, Gia Lam, Tu Liem, Thanh Tri, and Soc Son); administrative subdistricts there consist of communes. In 1995, the Tay Ho area became the fifth urban district, created by combining several urban communes in Tu Liem and Ba Dinh Districts. The area of Hanoi, therefore, remains the same. This discussion will therefore focus on housing issues in the four original urban districts and the Tay Ho area, recently classified as the fifth urban district.

Hanoi's houses present a panorama of different degrees of color and light. Hoan Kiem District, which is in the center of the city, still remains Hanoi's old quarter, with streets named for thirty-six guilds that used to be the working-place and marketplace for craftsmen, artisans, and other citizens. From this quarter comes the inspiration for the well-known artist Bui Xuan Phai, who had spent his zeal and most of his life on hundreds of paintings in which he tried to express "the ancient city of Hanoi." Along the broad streets of Ba Dinh District, several beautiful buildings with French architecture and green gardens are still in good condition. Hai Ba Trung and Dong Da Districts are areas whose inhabitants are mainly state employees, businessmen, and people of the working class. Many of the multistory housing blocks built some twenty or thirty years ago during the subsidy period are located more than five kilometers away from the city center in Thanh Xuan, an area designated in 1997 as a new suburban district of Hanoi. In the central city, big hotels and high-rises have been constructed recently by joint ventures to meet the demands of foreign tourists and businessmen. Throughout the city, hundreds of small hotels with no more than ten rooms have been built.

Migrants seeking work can sometimes find space in dormitories. Others crowd in with relatives or move into homes inherited from their grandparents. The government still allocates some housing. But people increasingly trespass on land next to rivers and ponds, trespass on rubbish dumps and former graveyards, and build their own shelter. The problem of housing for the poor will be addressed more extensively elsewhere in this chapter.

The lack of housing in Hanoi is a pressing issue. According to the statistics of the Urban Planning Institute, although the total housing available in Hanoi is increasing, the per capita living area is not. In 1954, the city's average per capita area was 6 square meters. By 1993, it had been reduced to 4 square meters (Trinh and Leaf, 1996). Thus, Hanoi is the most crowded of the big cities in Vietnam; its population density increases nearest the center of the city (Nguyen, 1996). In the early 1990s, 30 percent of Hanoi's population had an average per capita housing area of only 3 square meters. Hoan Kiem is the most crowded district, with about 27,000 households living in units of 2–3 square meters and 3,000 households in units of only 1.5 square meters per person (Thanh Mai, February 7, 1996).

The quality of housing in Hanoi is also controversial. Except for recently built houses and ancient buildings, most of the houses for working people are of poor quality, come with few conveniences, and have a monotonous design. Many houses built a long time ago, whether still private or taken over by the state, have not been maintained and thus are seriously degraded. "Of the total dwelling areas of 54.4 million m² in Vietnam's urban centers at present, up to 32 million m² need repairing and 1.7 million m² rebuilding" (Trinh and Colleagues, 1996). In Hanoi, according to the Hanoi Land and Housing Department, 40 percent of the houses are one- or two-story buildings made of brick and wood, while 15 percent are poor-quality houses. Of the currently used area, up to 60,000 square meters need rebuilding, 5,000 square meters are in seriously bad condition, and 2.5 million square meters need repair. Of the buildings constructed during the subsidy period, 40 percent have foundations that have sunk. Block B-7 in the Thanh Cong living quarter, for example, has sunk 70 centimeters (Thanh Mai, February 7, 1996).

Yet the citizens' legitimate wish to buy state-owned houses to improve their housing condition, a possibility since Decree No. 61/CP on July 5, 1994, has hardly been met. According to Bui Dinh Nguyen, this is because of "cumbersome formalities of consideration and the lack of a sensible mechanism in the procedure of selling houses" (Bui, 1996).

In general, Hanoi has changed continuously in many respects over the past few years. The citizens' living standard has been stabilized and improved. The city has become more crowded and bustling with new buildings and a wide variety of goods. The new market system, however, has also created a difference in people's living standards; this can be seen very clearly in housing. Some active and wealthy people have grasped the chance to improve their lives, constructing many buildings themselves. Some take advantage of loopholes in the market regulations for housing and land to speculate in the land market. "In only a few years (1991–1994), land and housing price increased from twice to fivefold, depending on their localities, creating a widespread 'price-boom' from Ho Chi Minh City to Hanoi and other big urban centers all over the country" (Minh Thuy, 1996: 6). Specialists on market price say this is because:

- An increase in price has encouraged people to invest and speculate in land and housing.
- The renovation in the state's land and housing management policy has eradicated people's thoughts of living dependent on state-owned houses.
- Thanks to higher income and improved living standards, the people have been able to accommodate themselves.
- Legal land and housing owners have achieved the rights to use their land and houses to obtain a mortgage, guarantee a loan, and provide inheritance; they may also transfer or lease their land use rights.

In Hanoi and Ho Chi Minh City between 1992 and 1994, 60–70 percent of purchases and sales of land was speculative. Speculative land and house buying occurred with both private and state-owned land and housing. The state properties could have been legally sold with official approval at the district level but were often sold illegally, with only a subdistrict official's certification. In these circumstances, the poor hardly have a chance to accommodate themselves without state special aid programs.

The explosion of housing construction in the past few years shows an ineffective management of housing construction and use in Hanoi. In many cases houses were built illegally, without licenses and not in accordance with planning projects; these dwellings threaten the city's security and its aesthetic quality. Some of the illegal building occurs because lower-level authorities exceed their limits. The transition process produces many areas of confusion. A few years ago, for example, heads of universities had the right to allocate housing to employees, but now that right has been canceled. Some people apply for permission to build and proceed before it is granted. Others build on areas near their house, such as the construction on the Red River Dikes. "The housing management in the city has been publicly compared to a slatternly old man without necessary inner force to meet the demand of urban development" (Thanh Mai, February 7, 1996).

The state has taken some action against illegal building. Authorities have destroyed some illegal buildings on campuses; others were allowed to remain but were heavily fined. In 1995, authorities destroyed hundreds of houses built illegally within 10 meters of the Red River Dikes; jagged bricks from the structures that were removed are visible on the remaining units near the dikes.

Consequently, the housing development master plan, a strategy ratified by the government in March 1992, needs to be carried out immediately. It is necessary to remember that the main tasks in the plan are implemented by the City Chief Architect System, which only exists in Hanoi and Ho Chi Minh City. Its duty is to:

- Study and design the city plans;
- Introduce construction sites and come to an agreement on space, plan, and architecture options;
- Supervise the execution of the construction in accordance with the plan; and
- Develop related legal documents.

Yet in the master plan attention has been paid only to capital expansion and centers for culture, tourism, sports, and industrial zones—but not to housing programs for the poor in urban centers. "The question of housing policy for the poor has been raised many times in resolutions of the Party Committee and the City People's Council. This needs to be tackled both morally and constitutionally. However, there are many difficulties at present," says Mr. Ngo Xuan Hong, vice director of the Hanoi Land and Housing Department, during an interview with a correspondent from *Vietnam Economic Times* (Minh Thuy, 1996: 6).

WOMEN AND HOUSING IN HANOI

A house is a home for a family, considered to be a cell of the society. A woman's life is closely bound to her home and family. During childhood, Vietnamese girls usually live with their parents. After getting married, they move to the husband's house, where often they remain for life. It is said that one of the guarantees for a young woman's marriage is the house. Whether this is so or not depends on the husband's housing condition. However, she has a home. From this point of view, the issue of women and housing can be seen in two aspects: (1) women's housing use rights, and (2) property ownership rights.

Rights to Use the House

Carolyn Moser (1987) identifies several factors that are key to understanding differences in women's and men's use of housing. The factors are family type, home as base for productive work, and design of housing. According to a common conception, there are always two or three generations living together in a family household in developing countries. If there is a man present, the husband is the head as well as the breadwinner of the family. The man takes part in outside productive activities while the woman often takes on the housework, which consists of caring for the whole family, bearing and bringing up the children, and arranging family life. This is a "natural" gender family labor division.

However, this assumption is not completely accurate when compared to real life, especially women's roles and functions in family as well as the way that women use houses to carry out all the tasks mentioned above. The family is a changing unit. Unlike the former conception in Vietnam that a happy family should consist of several generations living together, there is an increasing tendency in Vietnam toward nuclear families. The latest study by the Center for Family and Women's Studies of two hundred households in the two subdistricts of Ngo Thi Nham and Yen Phu in Hanoi shows that nuclear and extended families account for 65–66 percent and 29–33 percent, respectively (CFWS, 1994).

We all know that women have a double role. The woman's tasks in an extended family are even more difficult. She is less influential in the family's decisionmaking but more responsible in caring for old people and children. Hanoi's average per capita housing area is only 4 square meters. In some families, three generations live together in a unit. This is very disadvantageous and troublesome for family life, especially in houses with only one room. The relations between brothers- and sisters-in-law when sharing a house are very complex and sometimes are reasons for committing crimes (something that is also noted in China; see Chapter 12). The wish to live separately can only be realized when grown children have enough money to buy or rent a house or when they are provided new dwellings by their employers.

In addition to her reproductive obligations at home, women's productive work frequently centers around the house: They raise food crops, fruit, and fodder trees; they breed pigs and poultry even in urban settings. Women engage in a wide variety of home-based work both for direct sale and through contracting. Many women are microentrepreneurs who sell goods or street foods from carts or in markets; they store the materials for sale at home and often produce them there as well (Moser and Peake, 1987; Peattie, 1982; Tinker, 1995).

Women's critical role in supporting their families is evident in a survey of 669 poor households in Hanoi that found that 24.5 percent (or 164 of the respondent households) are poor families suffering from the lack of husbands. Of the total number of 379 families with both husband and wife present, 33.6 percent of the households had women as the primary breadwinners, while 24.5 percent of the respondent households had both husband and wife as breadwinners. Only 29 percent of people questioned said that the husband was the family's breadwinner. This shows that in poor living conditions the wife's role is often more difficult and active compared to that of the husband and other men in the family. Furthermore, the health of women as breadwinner is often worse than that of a man: Women of poor health account for 50 percent as compared with 42.8 percent of men (Trinh and Colleagues, 1994).

Anyone who has visited Hanoi must have the impression of an active city rife with small production and services on every street. Many shops sell services, and consumer goods such as hairdressers, tailors, and shoemakers can be seen everywhere. On the one hand, this explosion of services results from the government's multisectoral economic policy. On the other hand, it is caused by the implementation of Resolution Nos. 176 and 127 to eliminate redundancy within the state sector. Over the past few years, tens of thousands of people have been forced to retire and become self-employed—60 percent of whom are women (a figure remarkably consistent between Vietnam and China; see Chapter 11).

This fact is reflected in the survey of poor households mentioned above, which showed that 73.6 percent of households had between one and six members working in the informal sector either as self-employed (74.2 percent) or employed (50.8 percent), with some workers in both categories. Some formal sector workers may also work part-time selling street foods, like the women selling sticky rice during the two hours before the formal job begins. The goods are produced, processed, and sold in numerous locations, including: houses (30.1 percent); marketplaces (14.0 percent); pavement (35.2 percent); and mobile or part-time vendors (34.6 percent). Comparing occupational groups, the survey authors concluded that poor women's work in the informal sector seems to be more important to family life than that of men. Women's need to use housing for both productive and reproductive activities is evident.

Housing Issues for Women

Because most housing construction is designed and built by men, women's needs have seldom been considered. Recent literature records women's complaints about the placement of toilets and bathing facilities or, in cultures where women's mobility is limited, about the small size of secluded courtyards (Peake and Moser, 1987; Dandekar, 1993). The University of Lund has sent researchers from its Center for Habitat Studies to Hanoi to work with local scholars in order to improve kitchen design (Nystrom, 1994). Equally important is the placement of cooking, bathing, and toilet facilities that must be

Table 4.1   Type of Housing in Hanoi, 1993–1994 (in percent)

	Yen Phu	Ngo Thi Nham
No amenities	28.9	42.2
Makeshift houses	9.3	14.4
Self-built houses	16.5	27.8
Shared amenities	19.5	27.8
One-story living quarters	8.2	11.3
Multistory living quarters	11.3	16.5
Full amenities	54.6	29.9
Villas	3.1	1.0
Self-contained one-story buildings	37.1	3.1
Self-contained multistory buildings	14.4	25.8

Source: CFWS, 1994.

shared, either in multifamily housing or in squatter settlements. (Efforts to consult with women in Ho Chi Minh City on such designs are discussed in Chapter 3.)

The lack of amenities characterizes much of the housing in Hanoi, where many people live in substandard or cramped quarters. A 1994 study in two subdistricts of Hanoi, Yen Phu and Ngo Thi Nham, found different patterns of housing types between them as to those with no amenities, shared amenities, and self-contained units (see Table 4.1).

More recent data collected in poor areas of Hanoi describe the wide variety of housing utilized by the poor (see Table 4.2) and clearly portray the difficult living conditions experienced by a majority of people in the city. Among the 669 houses of the poor surveyed, the average area of amenities was only 1.5 square meters per house (Trinh and Colleagues, 1996).

Due to commonly poor circumstances in Vietnam, the vast majority of people are living in below-standard conditions. In addition, the concept that "much is needed to eat but little is needed to live in" seems to create a toler-

Table 4.2   Types of Housing in Poor Areas of Hanoi, 1995 (in percent)

Types of Houses	
Self-contained flats in 4- to 5-story buildings	4.9
Self-contained flats in 1- to 2-story buildings	1.3
Flats in low-grade living quarters	18.1
Divided rooms	13.0
Self-created dwellings on balconies or corridors of buildings	2.7
Makeshift houses (made of thatch and bamboo)	20.3
Other types, including self-built houses	39.6

Source: Trinh and Colleagues, 1996: 47.

ance for makeshift and inconvenient housing conditions that lack clean water, all-weather roads, drainage systems, and the like.

The amenities in a house are very important to women, for such amenities represent a cultural way of living. Nevertheless, these issues have hardly received any attention, especially in housing for the poor. Research shows that amenities are in terribly bad condition in houses for the poor in Hanoi. Only 56.6 percent of urban households have separate kitchens. The rest must cook in living rooms or share public kitchens with two or more neighboring units (Trinh and Colleagues, 1996). Sharing kitchens is difficult; sharing toilets is even more inconvenient and unhygienic. In some areas, more than half the families must share toilets, sometimes with more than ten other families.

Houses for the poor in Hanoi are primarily found in two areas of subhamlets, with 37.4 percent living in squatter housing and 49.4 percent living in slums in older working-class districts. The isolation of housing space for the poor has helped increase their social seclusion from other groups of people. Within their areas, they can easily appropriate or illegally buy and sell public land because of loose state control. Of households surveyed, 37.4 percent do not have the required legal documents (Trinh and Colleagues, 1996). Improvements in amenities and sanitation are difficult to achieve because of the widespread poverty and adverse health and environmental effects. Women are greatly affected by the poor living conditions because they do most of the cooking and washing and must care for sick children.

Property Rights

Under Vietnamese law, land is the property of the state and so of all the people. Individuals, therefore, have land use rights but not ownership rights. However, they effectively control the property on which their houses are built, that is, dwelling land; when people sell their houses, they transfer the use of the land under their houses to the new owners.

As discussed above, although women make primary use of houses for productive and reproductive work, men typically hold housing contracts in their own names, not women. When the property clearly belongs to the woman, the title may be issued in her name. Since the mid-1990s, both spouses' signatures are required for mortgaging a house or land. House ownership is quite varied in cities and towns, especially in Hanoi, due to the fact that the housing policy carried out during the subsidy period is still effective. According to statistics for Hanoi, private houses and state-owned houses account for 47 percent and 48 percent of the total number of houses, respectively (Trinh and Leaf, 1996: 25). The figures are somewhat different in the two subdistricts of Yen Phu and Ngo Thi Nham (see Table 4.3).

Yen Phu is a working-class area with many state-built rental buildings; more than half of the inhabitants continue to rent. Data indicate another 10

Table 4.3   Acquiring Housing in Two Subdistricts of Hanoi, 1993–1994 (in percent)

	Yen Phu	Ngo Thi Nham
Inheritance	19.6	23.7
Buying from the state	5.2	8.2
Buying from private individuals	3.1	7.2
Renting	51.5	30.9
Self-erected (squatter houses)	5.2	24.7
Putting up at other people's houses	10.3	2.1
Other types	5.2	1.0

Source: CFWS, 1994.

percent of the people are crowded into rental and inherited houses. Few people are buying their homes, and only 5 percent are squatters. Ngo Thi Nham, in contrast, has fewer rental units (31 percent), but squatters make up a quarter of all inhabitants, suggesting larger areas of marginal land in this area. Inherited homes make up nearly one-third, a figure that may reflect older, more rural houses, as the number of people living with others is very small.

The allocation of state-owned houses is often based on the registration of employees in the offices that previously rented them. Under the subsidy system, women with young children were given preferences in housing allocation to help them stabilize their lives. At that time, the only value of the house was for use as a home. Due to the increase in housing prices, mortgageability, transferability, and capitalization of land use rights under Decree No. 60/CP, state-allocated houses have now obtained an inherent value in the market economy.

Vietnamese laws ensure women's equality to men. The constitution, written in 1959, says that women are equal to men in terms of politics, economy, society, culture, and family. In Articles No. 14 and 16 in the 1986 Marriage and Family Law, equal rights of husband and wife to private and common property are clearly stated. The house is the most important and valuable asset of a married couple. Both have equal legal rights in owning, using, and making decisions about common assets. Within the family, issues related to housing are not considered to be of great importance in Vietnam, except for some cases in which the couple has decided to divorce.

Under Article 42 of the Marriage and Family Law, wife and husband have equal rights as well as obligations to use common assets to ensure the family's common needs. When they divorce, there should be unanimous decision about division of assets. If not, a civilian tribunal makes the decision. The couple's assets will be divided into two parts with a recognition of the real condition of the family and each person's contribution—namely, the house will be divided into two if it is situated in a city or town. The area of each part depends on specific cases, with the larger portion usually belonging to the person who will care for the children and/or parents. Only in cases where the house is too small, or one of the couple has another place to live, will the house be allotted to one person. The other person can be given other assets or be compensated with money.

In fact, housing problems following divorce are very complicated and difficult to resolve. Women are often the ones who suffer losses. The case of Thu and Duc's divorce settlement provides an example. The case was tried by Dong Da Tribunal on April 5, 1990. The tribunal confirmed that the house was on the property of the husband's parents and that the couple only contributed to the house construction. Duc gave his wife only 1 million Vietnamese dong (about US$100) for her to move to another place. This is only one of many cases in which the wife receives a compensation that is much lower than the house's value at the time of divorce.

Control of housing is a type of savings for women, as its value often increases over time. Moreover, when a woman obtains permits for housing, she may use them as collateral to borrow money to expand her business, thereby earning more for her children and family. However, a recent sociological study of credit funds shows that very few women use their housing as collateral to borrow money even when women themselves have loan contracts in their names, perhaps because microcredit loans do not require collateral. The study also shows that women are mainly responsible for the family's budget and that women usually pay back their loans on time (Trinh and Colleagues, 1996).

However, women seldom have housing property papers in their own names. Women also suffer losses in the division of land, houses, and inheritance after their parents' death. Because women often move to live with their husbands' families, they hardly receive any part of their parents' houses unless the parents decide to sell the property. Although the law on marriage and family and the civil code stress equality between men and women in inheritance, women's shares are often less than those given to their brothers.

HOUSING NEEDS FOR POOR WOMEN

According to a 1993 United Nations report, the average monthly per capita income in poor families in Vietnamese urban centers ranged from 70,000 to 100,000 Vietnamese dong (US$650 to US$900 at the time). In Hanoi, 10 percent of the population has monthly per capita incomes of 70,000; 18 percent receive 100,000 dong (UNDP, 1995).

In Trinh Duy Luan's investigation (1996), she identifies four levels of monthly per capita income of the poor:

1. More than 120,000 dong (more than US$1,100; 13.9 percent);
2. From 91,000 to 120,000 dong (36.3 percent);
3. From 61,000 to 90,000 dong (36.3 percent); and
4. Less than 60,000 dong (less than US$550; 24.7 percent).

In contrast, the average monthly per capita income for the whole population was 220,000 dong in 1993 (General Statistics Office, 1994). With such low income levels, it is extremely difficult for the poor, especially poor women, to accumulate savings to buy themselves a house. Housing is really the most urgent problem for the poor in big cities such as Hanoi and Ho Chi Minh City. As mentioned already, the differentiation between the poor and the rich is also greater in a transitional economy. The issue of social equality, therefore, is once again posed.

Currently, no priority is given to the poor in terms of housing conditions. Most poor must arrange accommodations for themselves. The lack of concern—together with a loose control of urban space, especially in riverside subhamlets, under bridges, and remote areas—has unintentionally helped create a movement toward trespassing on or illegally buying and selling public land. Such activity destroys the environment and causes the formation of areas rife with social evils inside Hanoi. The health condition of the poor depends largely on their economic situation, housing condition, and the environment in which they live.

In order to resolve the problem of housing the poor, two different approaches need to be taken. First, houses and flats whose occupants have land use rights or valid leases need to be improved and upgraded. Second, it is imperative that as the city plans for the construction of new living quarters a certain percentage of houses be allocated to the poor and rented or sold to them at subsidized prices. In both approaches women need to be drawn into housing programs and projects, for they are responsible for childcare and are the primary users of the house, its surrounding area, and its infrastructure to generate income. Only with women's involvement can all the housing programs and projects be successful and more effective.

CONCLUSION

Housing for citizens in Vietnamese urban centers has always been an important social issue. The state and all ranks of authorities have shown concern on this issue for more than forty years. Today the socioeconomic transition is encouraging urban migration that strains the available housing in all urban centers. Housing problems are particularly acute in Hanoi, as its status as the nation's capital brings foreign residents with their requirements for office space and housing. Of the various groups that need housing demands met, women, especially poor women, require more attention.

A preliminary view of housing issues and the poor in Hanoi has been presented here. However, this overview needs to be supplemented by further research, which could include the following:

- Providing more information about the way women use their houses to earn a living in Hanoi, especially in the informal sector and small production.
- Paying more attention to housing issues for women-headed households in Hanoi.
- Proposing housing solutions for the poor in urban centers, giving them more opportunities to obtain access to land, houses, and loans in order to raise these people out of poverty and secluded lives.

Only with the involvement of women in Hanoi's urban housing programs can their practical and strategic gender needs be satisfactorily met.

5

Women and Rural Land in Vietnam

Tran Thi Van Anh

Land is an important resource for any nation. For Vietnam, a country with more than 80 percent of the population working in agriculture, land and land use are of special significance. For quite a long time, the Vietnamese people have shown sentiment and respect toward their land. For peasants, land is considered as mother, who always feeds her children. Nonfarm job opportunities are available, but in 1994, land remained the principal means of living for more than 10 million rural households, especially for female members of rural families. Women occupy 53 percent of the agricultural labor force. Female peasants do 65 percent of the agricultural work (Chu Huu Quy, 1995). As men in rural areas migrate to cities to search for jobs in recent years, women are becoming increasingly more important in agriculture.

The shift from the centrally planned economy to the socialist, market-oriented economy in Vietnam has resulted in a new form of land use in agriculture. In allocating communally held land to individual farmer households, policies for renovation created conditions for farmers to become more deeply attached to their own cultivated land and benefit directly from using the land effectively. Farmer households became the basic production units in agriculture, replacing the previous agricultural cooperatives. The changing process created an important driving force, promoting agricultural production.

Thanks to capital investment and intensive farming, the output of agricultural production has increased significantly compared to the previous period. The total output in terms of paddy increased from 13.3 million tons in the 1976–1980 period to 17.6 million tons in the 1981–1988 period and to 22.2 million tons in the 1989–1992 period. The average food availability per capita increased from 254 kilograms in the late 1970s to 294 kilograms in the 1980s and to 330 kilograms in the early 1990s. As a result, Vietnam is able to afford sufficient food for domestic consumption, preservation, and export. Vietnam's rice for export increased from 1.4 million tons in 1989 to 1.9 million tons in 1994 (General Statistics Office, 1995).

During the process of renovation, land has become a deep concern among managers and researchers as well as the general public. Under the old mechanism, land relations clearly reflected inefficiency and the "ownerless" situation. Instruction No. 100 on the quota system in agricultural production (1981) of the Secretariat of the Vietnam Communist Party initiated the adjust-ment of land relations, gradually granting landownership to farmers. Since then, legal documents on land relations have been amended, supplemented, and revised to make them suitable to the shift to the multisectoral economy under state management. Land use rights were diversified in accordance with economic development in Vietnam. Newly arising issues, however, such as farmer households with little or no land, have not yet been analyzed from the point of gender.

To date, women have quickly grasped new job opportunities in other sec-tors, including service, trading, industry, and so on. Agriculture, however, is still the main occupation of women; agriculture production attracts more than 72 percent of the total labor in the country. Women's access to and use of land therefore have great impact on the efficiency of the rural economy, especially on the work and quality of life of many Vietnamese women and their families.

This chapter first reviews the background of land use in Vietnam. The second section addresses women's access to and use of land in the periods be-fore and after *doi moi,* focusing on recent years. The final section puts forth some explanations of gender differences regarding rural land in the reform period.

HISTORICAL BACKGROUND

Land was traditionally cultivated by the community, which allocated land to each family. Land was controlled both by the community and the state until the sixteenth century. Subsequently, under the feudal system, communal own-ership was reduced and state control tightened. Land was granted as private property to aristocrats. Land reclamation also increased the amount of land under private ownership.

So by the seventeenth and eighteenth centuries, three different types of landownership existed such as private land, state land, and communal land (the land of the village or land of pagoda). Until the first half of the nineteenth century, more than 80 percent of the land was privately held (Ngo Kim Chung, 1978). In the early twentieth century, when the French invaded Viet-nam, they established plantations, increasing the acreage of land under their control. By 1930, the French controlled about 22 percent of all land then cul-tivated.

Table 5.1   Landownership in Vietnam in 1930

	Under 5 ha	5–50 ha	Over 50 ha	Public Land	Total
North Vietnam					
percent landowners	94.8	4.9	0.3	–	100
percent land	28.5	28.1	31.5	11.9	100
South Vietnam					
percent landowners	71.7	25.8	2.5	–	100
percent land	15.0	37.0	45.0	3.0	100

Source: Tran Phuong, 1969: 12–13.

Land belonging to local people was categorized into large-scale owner-ship (over 3.6 hectares), medium-scale (1.8 to 3.6 hectares), and small-scale (less than 1.8 hectares). In the North, 91.5 percent of rural households had small-scale landownership; 60 percent of the peasants had very small-scale ownership, at less than 0.36 hectare (Henry, 1932). In the South, because of the small population and large acreage of reclaimed land, large-scale owner-ship was popular (see Table 5.1).

During this period in Vietnam, few peasants were the owners of any land. In the North, 36,000 out of 74,000 people (48.6 percent) who had to pay taxes in that region were not the landowners (Gourou, 1936). In the South, 265,000 out of 1 million households were landowners. The remaining 74.5 percent of peasants were landless; they either worked for wages or cultivated the land of the landlords.

Female Peasants' Access to Land During This Period

Documents on land at the end of the eighteenth and early nineteenth centuries from twelve villages of the Quynh Coi District, Thai Binh Province, in the eastern part of the northern plain of the Red River Delta, give us a general view of the issue. Like many other areas in the North at that time, in Quynh Coi private land occupied 65.1 percent of the total cultivated land of different types. At that time, the majority of land under private ownership belonged to the landlords and the well-off. Of 471 households who owned more than 4,486 *mu* (1,614 hectares; a *mu* is one-fifteenth of a hectare) in the above-mentioned twelve villages, twenty-seven people owned more than 30 *mu*, oc-cupying 26.5 percent of land, while 101 people owned less than 3 *mu*, occu-pying 4 percent of the land (Nguyen Duc Nghiem and Bui Thi Minh Hien, 1992).

Other studies in Thai Binh Province also showed that the number of fe-male owners was lower than the number of male owners. Of 471 landowners, 114 were women, accounting for 24.2 percent. This proportion was higher

Table 5.2   Ownership According to Acreage and Gender at the End of the Eighteenth
and Early Nineteenth Centuries in Twelve Villages of Thai Binh Province,
North Vietnam

	Under 1.08 ha	1.08– 3.6 ha	3.6– 7.2 ha	7.2– 18 ha	Over 18 ha	Total
Women						
number	38	64	11	1	–	114
percent	33.3	56.1	9.6	0.8	–	100
Men						
number	63	169	76	43	6	357
percent	17.6	47.3	21.3	12.0	1.7	100
Ratio of women to the total	37.6	27.4	12.6	2.3	–	

Source: Nguyen Duc Nghiem and Bui Thi Minh Hien, 1992.

than that of three other Thai Binh regions (Kien Xuong, Thai Ninh, and Thuy Anh) and almost the same as that of Tu Liem District in Hanoi (24.6 percent).

Female landownership was small, both absolutely and relatively to male landownership. Women acquired land mainly from inheritance of family lands. Also there were cases of women buying land from the state. The majority of female landowners had less than 5 *mu*. Of 194 households who owned less than 3 mu, sixty-six households were female, accounting for 37.6 percent. In contrast, out of eighty-seven persons who owned from 10 to 20 *mu* (0.3 hectare), only eleven were women, or 12.6 percent. In the large-scale landownership group, the proportion of women was lower. There was only one woman out of forty-four persons who owned from 20 to 30 *mu,* comprising 2.3 percent. Only 10.5 percent of female landlords owned more than 10 *mu;* the figure was 33 percent for male landlords (see Table 5.2).

It is a pity that there were no documents about landless women during this period. However, since 50–70 percent of all the peasants had no land in other areas of Vietnam, many of these landless must have been women. Tenants' wives, single women, widows, and other poor women in rural areas became landless persons when their land was sold, pawned, or given as payment for their debts—or simply because they did not inherit land.

Women and Land Under the Collective Period

The main features of land use before *doi moi* were the allocation of land to poor peasants and the formation of collective land use through agricultural cooperatives. The distribution of land to the poor people was implemented in 1946–1947. The collective access and use of land took place in the North from 1960 and in the South from 1978 to the mid-1980s (see following chronology).

Land allocation to poor peasants
1945   Land rent reduction; confiscation of French land
1953   Land reform (in the South, 1955–1956)

Collective use of land
1960   Agricultural cooperatives (in the North)
1970   Land reform (in the South)
1978   Agricultural cooperatives (in the South)
1981   Contract system to group of farmers and households

Household use of land
1988   Leasing cooperative land to farmers
1993   Land allocation to farmers for twenty to fifty years

The main agricultural production unit during the period before *doi moi* was the agricultural cooperative. Peasants, both female and male, were divided into work brigades that performed all tasks related to production. Cooperative members were paid in work points according to the work done. For one workday, workers could receive ten points. In practice, work points varied by type of work, with male labor typically being remunerated more highly than was female labor. After each harvest, and after a portion was set aside for taxes, production costs, and social security expenses, individuals received shares of the crop, mostly in-kind, according to the number of work points each had accumulated.

In the years before 1960 in the North and before 1970 in the South, as well as in the years after 1981, agricultural production was based on the household economy. Farmers cultivated the land that had been allocated to them—temporarily in the past and permanently at present—using the labor and production tools of each household. After fulfilling their obligations to the state (quotas, taxes), farmers were allowed to use the products at their will.

In the agricultural cooperative, in principle, all the farming work from cultivation in the rice fields to husbandry was divided equally among all the households and types of labor, without differentiating between women and men. In practice, however, cooperative heads assigned work according to their perceptions of workers' abilities. Thus, women were more likely to be assigned traditional women's work, such as transplanting, weeding, manuring, harvesting, and animal-breeding. In general, women's work received fewer work points. One workday for transplanting earned ten points, and one workday for fertilizing received eight. Men's work earned them more points: One workday for plowing received twelve points and one workday for a carpenter earned fourteen. The point system was heavily influenced by the conception that the work was either hard or easy, either technical or simple (Tran Duc,

1991: 13). Almost all the work done by women was considered light or simple because it was done by hand, such as transplanting, or by using simple tools such as a hoe, a sickle, a pair of baskets, and the shoulder pole (Le Tho, 1990: 24). Therefore, although women might have the same number of workdays as men, their points would be lower, and thus the share of the crop they received was smaller.

Overall, women did 65 percent of the farming work (Chu Huu Quy, 1995: 159). Between 1965 and 1969, when most men went to battle, women became the main labor force in all sectors, including agriculture. The magazine *Party Construction* in 1967 remarked, "The main labor force in rural areas was women . . . to be more exact, persons who worked in the field every day were women" (Le Thi Nham Tuyet, 1975: 692). Women not only replaced men in farming work but also took part in managing activities in agricultural production. In the period between 1967 and 1969, 3,733 women worked as heads and deputy heads of cooperatives; 45,000 others were heads and deputy heads of production groups of more than 200,000 agricultural cooperatives in the North (Le Thi Nham Tuyet, 1975: 296).

Land management and use in the collective form proved to be inefficient. Farmers' interests were not paid attention. At times, workdays were not fairly recorded, resulting in serious undervaluation of each workday (Tran Duc, 1991: 17). This fact especially had a negative effect on women, because they already received fewer work points than men. Women and men cooperative members were dissatisfied and lost interest in their work. These problems were the preconditions for the renovation of agricultural policy and other issues relating to land in the 1980s.

Women and Land Under Doi Moi

The shift from the collective use of land to the household economy was based on land use rights of individuals and families and has been the core issue of the renovation process in Vietnam. Land policy renovation started in 1981 with the introduction of the contract system. Under this system, responsibility for decisions about cultivation was returned first to groups of farmers and then to individual households. The incentives of the contract system had remarkable production results in the short run. From 1981 to 1985, rice productivity increased 24 percent and food output increased 27 percent, or 5–6 percent per year on average. However, the growth rate was not maintained because farmers' interests were not secured. When production output increased, the required contributions to the cooperative by the farmers also increased.[1] So, if women worked more under the contract system, they had to contribute more. In some places, the required contributions increased 50–80 percent of output; as a result, the income of both female and male farmers clearly fell.

In 1988, a new policy was adopted that provided for leasing the cooperative fields to farmers' households for a period of ten to fifteen years. This policy was designed to encourage farmers to invest in their fields. However, in many localities, parts of the land were leased for much shorter periods (for example, for the cropping season or for only three years) (Chu Van Vu, 1991: 155). Changes in land rights made farmers reluctant to undertake long-term investments and led to the adoption of a new regulation to ensure the rights to land use by individuals and households for the long term.

The Land Law of 1993 was the most important policy in securing the land use rights of individuals. The Land Law stipulates: "Any households or individuals shall have the right to exchange, transfer, rent, inherit, or mortgage the right to use land allocated by the State" (Government Land Law, 1993: 3.2). Under this law, though farmers do not own the land, they have the right to use the land on a stable and long-term basis: Land allocation should be twenty years for planting annual crops and fifty years for perennial crops such as trees and coffee.

Together, the laws of 1988 and 1993 created favorable conditions and new opportunities for farmers to be the masters of their land and to increase agricultural production. In this process, women farmers have acquired the right to determine their own work and their family's work. Women have more rights to determine the use of their products. Women have become free to express their opinions and to innovate in their production and business in order to enrich themselves and their families (Center for Women and Family Studies, 1993). Nonetheless, although women's land access and land use have fundamentally improved under the new laws, women and men still have differential access to resources, particularly to land. Furthermore, assistance that women used to receive during the socialist period for their reproductive activities, such as subsidized daycare centers, has been greatly reduced in recent years.

LAND ALLOCATION

Many issues have been raised in the discussion of women and land in the context of economic liberalization and land reform. Among them are questions of whether women are entitled to receive land and, if so, how much and how the land will be divided; and whether women are legally entitled to transfer and inherit land in their own names. Overall, what will be the impact of the new land politics on marriage and family in rural areas? Such fundamental issues will influence how the land is used and what the quality of life for rural women will be.

Since the 1993 Land Law stipulated only general principles on land allocation, twenty-five legal documents have been issued to establish implemen-

Table 5.3   Average Areas Under Agriculture and Forest per Worker in Different Regions

Regions	Areas (m^2)
Northern mountainous areas	3,157
Northern Midlands	1,365
Red River Delta	1,787
Former 4th region	1,634
Central coastal areas	4,576
Central Highlands	3,859
Mekong River Delta	4,341
Average	2,703

Source: General Statistical Office, *Vietnam Living Standard Survey* (Hanoi: GSO, 1993): 152.

tation procedures.[2] This decree identifies that the target groups of land alloca-tion are agricultural inhabitants registered in the locality (MAFI, 1995: 6). It means that all agricultural residents registered in the locality are the target groups, with no discrimination based on gender and age. The term "land user" as used in the document is neutral, without gender discrimination. Words used in the legal document to mean persons who receive allocated land, including "households," "individual," "target," user," and "land recipient," are all also neutral. Other sections relate to the duration of land use and the certification of the right to use land, and others imply no discrimination between men and women. In other words, under the law, women farmers have the same oppor-tunities to access land as do men.

Actual Process of Land Division and Allocation

Land division and allocation depend on the physical characteristics of the land base of the locality and the specific way each locality allocates land. There are major differences in land bases across the landscape. The difference between the lowest average area per capita in the Red River Delta and the highest average area per capita in the Central Highlands is three times (see Table 5.3). Therefore, though the principles are the same, average areas per capita to be allocated is the least in the Red River Delta, the highest in the Central Highlands. As we can see, the issue of land availability is closely linked with how much land people receive in different regions and localities.

In many localities, land is allocated based on the age of the residents. For example, working-age people will receive one ration of land; people beyond working age will receive half the ration; children from thirteen to fifteen re-ceive half the ration; and children under thirteen receive one-third the ration. If the ration of land is 1,000 square meters (common in the Red River Delta),

Table 5.4   Agricultural Land in Vietnam According to the Areas and Gender of the Head of Household

Allocated Land (m^2)	Women-Headed Households (%)	Male-Headed Households (%)
0–1,000	14.0	6.5
1,001–2,000	20.6	10.7
2,001–3,000	20.6	15.6
3,001–4,000	15.2	13.4
4,001–6,000	12.1	17.4
6,001–9,000	8.2	12.2
9,001–18,000	6.7	16.5
>18,000	2.8	8.4
Total number of households	1,226	2,533

Source: Desai, 1995: 118.

people of working age will receive 1,000 square meters; people beyond the working age will receive 500 square meters; and children under thirteen will receive 330 square meters.

Working age, stipulated by the government, is from sixteen to sixty for men and from sixteen to fifty-five for women. Due to the difference in working age between men and women, women are classified as beyond the working age five years earlier. Land allocation based on working age results in women from fifty-six to sixty only receiving half of the ration of land in comparison with men of the same age. Many propose changing women's retirement age to sixty; but because the land has already been allocated, farmers will not be affected until their land lease expires in twenty years.

Land allocation on the basis of age illustrates that the acreage of each household depends not only on the number of persons in the family but also on the proportion between persons of working age and the number of elderly and children in the family. Women-headed households tended to receive less land than male-headed households because female-headed households have a higher dependent ratio, that is, they have fewer adult laborers, and women aged fifty-six to sixty are not classified as laborers. Thus, although the principle is the same and without any discrimination, the average land allocated to women was 2,223 square meters, which is lower than the average land area for men of 2,799 square meters (see Table 5.4). Further, because prior to 1993 some men held land for contract production, men were more likely to retain some of their land for contract, while women-headed households usually hold only cultivated farmland. Cultivated land and a house plot are distinct types of land and are allocated in different ways. Some people have no farmland but do have a house plot with space for a kitchen garden.

The Quality of Allocated Land

Land *quality* has many factors, including easy access to water and irrigation systems, proximity to roads and villages, and composition of soil. Since each village and commune encompasses land of different quality, households receive parcels of both better and inferior land scattered throughout the village. Although this method is meant to ensure equity, poor single women seem in fact to have received a greater proportion of the less desirable land. Madam Dam, fifty-two and a widow in Cam Ngoc, Thanh Hoa Province, said: "Everybody was allocated a piece of land in the front field except me. My land is in the field that is very far from the village." Asked, "Why didn't you speak at the meeting of the commune on land allocation?" she answered, "I did, but they told me that I was in debts with the cooperative and it was lucky for me to have even that piece of land."

It is important to note that the whole process of measuring, classifying, and numbering pieces of land in preparation for farmers to draw plots in lottery style is quite new and complicated for everyone. This process is undertaken by the land department of the commune, which consists of local leaders and some farmers, mostly men. Because of the complicated nature of the allocation and the lack of experience in setting up standards for evaluation and comparison, individual interests can intervene. In Cam Ngoc, for example, local people complained that members of the land department had more good land than did others.

Furthermore, no women were directly involved in the process (CFWS, 1993). Women, particularly poor women, are often timid and inexperienced; they lack knowledge on issues related to land policy and so do not know how to protect themselves. Once the land has been allocated to each household, it is no longer subject to communal decisions; after that, it is very difficult to adjust the size and quality of the land allocated. Even if the allocation was not fair, many people, particularly women, prefer to accept the distribution.

Yet a survey conducted in 1996 showed that many farmers were satisfied with their land allocation in places where land policies were widely disseminated and where the process and procedures were openly conducted (CFWS, 1996). Problems were settled before the official allocation was completed. Some localities worked out regulations on the management and use of land, taking into account the characteristics of the land and society (*Nhan dan,* March 27, 1996: 3). With these regulations, land allocation, management, and use have been implemented effectively and equally.

Landless and Land-Poor Farmers

Currently, the problem of farmers with no or little land is a serious issue that had attracted much attention. Lacking sufficient land to cultivate, they work as agricultural laborers. Some people may even lack a house plot and are forced to rent land for their house. This happened even though in principle all farmer households are entitled to land, because in some provinces in the South, and in the mountainous provinces in the North and in central areas, no actual land allocation took place. In the Mekong Delta, land distribution was inadequate. Many landless peasants who did not have, or did not own enough, farm equipment had either refused to accept land granted to them or had received it only in order to resell it immediately afterward. Local authorities granted land use certificates based on actual land use at the time of certification.

In the North, there are farmers who, for one reason or another, sell the allocated land and thereby become newly landless. The situation is "new" because after long periods of practicing agricultural cultivation on the collective land the concept of "landlessness" didn't exist. In other words, the fact that farmers have no land is closely linked to the transition to the market under the current state. The number of households dependent on agricultural production but, having little or no land, accounted for 5–7 percent of households in 1995. The highest figure then reported was 19 percent in Dong Thap Province, 15 percent in Minh Hai, 13 percent in Kien Giang, 9.5 percent in Tay Ninh, 9.4 percent in Tra Vinh, and 7.4 percent in Soc Trang (*Nhan dan,* March 7, 1995: 1–3).

In 1996, a survey conducted in the northern province of Hai Hung and the southern province of An Giang showed that of the 600 households surveyed, 141, or 23.5 percent, were landless (CFWS, 1996). The survey also found that in An Giang, a province in the Mekong River Delta, the rate of households without land was 45.6 percent of total households surveyed.

There are many reasons for such landlessness. A majority of these households became landless when former owners successfully reclaimed their land. Especially after the mid-1980s, failures of cooperative farms in the South were common. The former owner might then ask for the land back, and if the former owner paid compensation (usually too little), then he/she would get the land again. In other instances, households sold parts of their land, mortgaged their land, or sold all their land to others. This situation happened very often among the Khmer ethnic groups in southern Vietnam. For example, in Soc Trang and Tra Vinh, about 8,000 Khmer households sold their land; more than 4,000 households mortgaged their land. Land sales also happened among ethnic groups in DakLak, Gia Lai (Central Highlands) (Ministry of Agriculture and Food Industry, 1995). In Chu Prong District of Gia Lai, due to pressure from the unofficial land market in addition to the lack of information about laws, an entire village of the T'Rai ethnic people sold their cultivated land, then moved to the wild forest to search for new sources of land to cultivate (*Vietnam Agriculture,* April 10, 1996).

Another reason rural households became landless is due to policies utilized by local authorities. In order to pressure households to pay outstanding debts or to practice family planning, many households were given only a third or half of allocated land. The duration of this strategy was decided locally and was mainly used in the North. The rate of land deducted from the allocated land to households in Nam Ha was 44 percent, in Hoa Binh 40 percent, in Ha Bac 35 percent, and in Thanh Hoa 27 percent (Nguyen Van Tiem, 1993).

In Cam Ngoc, Thanh Hoa Province, land withheld affected 15 percent of households; in Ngoc Son, Hai Hung Province, it was 12 percent (CFWS, 1993). Among the list of households that were given only parts of their allocated land, there are many women-headed households. These families are disadvantaged, with many children, and their health conditions are not good. Because their land could not support their whole families by agricultural cultivation, some families sold their land and started to work for wages.

Farmers working for wages in the Mekong Delta account for 70–80 percent of these land-deficit households. There are many forms of working for wages, mainly according to crop and season. Some households work for wages on the spot or in their homeland. Others go to work in other provinces. In some households, the father works far from home and the wife and children work in their village. There are also some cases in which the whole family leaves the homeland and works in other places, traveling from place to place looking for work, especially Khmer families in the South. The dream to have cultivated land and a stable life is the aspiration of many farmers, especially women farmers. Mrs. Trang, thirty-six, with five children living in Soc Trang, said, "I wish to have a piece of land so that my children and I won't have to travel here and there, but my husband doesn't support me. He sold all the land and the whole family has to follow him to work for wages" (CFWS, 1993).

Additional factors are causing increased sales of farmland through formal and informal land markets. Agricultural land is developed for other purposes (*Rural Areas Today,* March 13, 1996); risks inherent in agricultural production, including natural calamities, cause many homeowners to mortgage their land. Limited support services for farmers, such as credit and education in intensive farming to help them increase production, mean that many households fail to become masters of their land; because of low production, they are forced, step by step, to sell off their land.

So far, the informal land market in rural areas has formed mainly in the areas specialized for industrial crops, near main roads, small towns, and resorts. In the informal land market, all the transactions are done by personal agreement and without official approval. Attracted by high benefits from selling land, men usually initiate the buy-sell process, often without taking into account the long-term preferences of other family members.

In trading and transferring land, women are particularly disadvantaged. First of all, information always plays an important role in trading, but women have less opportunity to access information, especially with the many changes in regulations. Women are pressured by husbands and children because of the skyrocketing prices of land and benefits achieved through trading. TV reports and dramas started to address this issue, and a 1996 film on the state broadcasting channel covered a family in which the wife and her daughter tried to keep the land to grow flowers, the traditional occupation of the family, while the husband wanted only to build a hotel on the land.

Agricultural land, especially land for rice cultivation, has been reduced. Recently, the prime minister issued an instruction to control the transfer of land from rice cultivation to other purposes. The instruction calls on the chairman of the Provincial People's Committee and ministers to take necessary measures to maintain and protect the existing areas allocated to food crops, especially rice (*Nhan dan,* May 2, 1995). The reduction of land for rice crops first of all impacts women. About 90 percent of the total farmer households in Vietnam grow rice, mainly woman's work. Meanwhile, the rate of women householders involved in growing industrial crops and forest trees is lower than that of men householders (Desai, 1995: 124). It is easy to predict negative impacts to women due to the reduction of land for rice cultivation, such as decreases in incomes, threats of unemployment and underemployment, difficult lives, and so on.

To date, intensive modern farming techniques are more accessible to men than they are to women. Training courses on agricultural technology in many localities were targeted at men. Integrated pest management technical training courses were held in almost all the provinces in 1992–1994, but only 13 percent of participants were women. Of course, the rate of women participation in the course was different in each region. The number of women participants was higher in the North (36 percent) than it was in the central areas (7 percent) and the South (8 percent) (CFWS, 1995). The data of the household survey were almost the same. Except in the Red River Delta, women have less opportunity to access intensive farming services than do men (Desai, 1995: 121). This is due to the traditional perceptions of local people concerning the role of women in agriculture. At the village level, men do not think that women are appropriate targets for training because they have no time, lack sufficient literacy, and have many obligations at home. Often, the authorities discourage women's participation. And the training itself does not provide good facilities for women in terms of time, location, gender-sensitive curriculum, and so on. So far, the government, the Women's Union, and the nongovernmental organizations have not focused their training on gender, land, and housing issues.

Land Use Certificates

Land use certificates are the sole legal document that recognized the right of farmers to use the land. Article 2 of the 1993 Land Law stipulates that stable

Table 5.5   Number of Households and Area Granted with Land Use Certificates by
Region in Vietnam, 1995 (in percent)

	Households Receiving Land Use Certificates	Areas Granted Land Use Certificates
Northern mountains	32.8	14.34
Northern Midlands	58.1	41.20
Red River Delta	18.25	13.57
Former 4th region	32.24	21.98
Central coast	12.44	7.26
Central Highlands	39.45	24.40
Eastern Nam Bo	27.97	26.33
Mekong River Delta	53.49	56.19
Average	33.88	33.48

Source: Ministry of Agriculture and Food Industry, 1995: 4.

land users are to be granted certificates of land use by the competent authorities. Although in principle the certificates are granted when the land is allocated, in practice farmers may have cultivated a piece of land for some time before receiving the certificates, as the process is very slow.

By early 1995, only one-third of farmer households had been granted land use certificates. This ratio varies from region to region, the slowest being the central coastal region, where only 12.4 percent of households had been granted certificates. Next comes the Red River Delta (18.2 percent). The northern Midlands and Mekong Delta regions are the quickest in issuing land use certificates (58.4 percent and 53.5 percent, respectively) (see Table 5.5).

Among the many reasons that have slowed the issuance process is management agencies' delay in promulgating guidelines. Only twenty of the thirty regulations needed to implement the law have been issued. Besides, due to rapid changes in the real situation, some regulations are already outdated: The land use tax was set too high to be realistic. In Ho Chi Minh City, in the first three months of 1995, only 56 of 1,524 households, or about 3 percent, came to the offices to pay the tax and receive their certificates (*Nhan dan,* August 11, 1995).

Lack of adequate records on landholdings is a major obstacle (*Nhan dan,* January 16, 1996). Funds to carry out surveying and mapping are insufficient. For example, to build a pilot land administration program applying computer technology for thirty-seven communes in Nam Ninh District, Nam Ha Province, it cost 2 billion dong, of which 250 million was contributed by the district and the remainder by the General Department of Land Administration. Meanwhile, according to the deputy general director of the General Department of Land Administration, the state has not yet had a clear-cut mechanism to solve financial problems for this work (*Hanoi Moi,* January 5, 1995).

Furthermore, after years of using and farming on collective land, many people are not fully aware of the importance of official documents that grant land use to households and individuals. Due attention has not yet been paid to the communication and dissemination of the Land Law and other legal documents among the people, particularly in remote rural and ethnic minority areas. According to the deputy general director of land administration, local authorities of many areas are themselves not fully aware of the importance and complexity of the grant of land use certificates (*Hanoi Moi,* January 5, 1995). Also, information on the effect of the Land Law on people has not yet been collected.

The slow granting of land use certificates is one of the reasons leading to unofficial selling and buying of land. Unofficial land transactions are very popular in urban and industrial areas as well as in rural areas. For example, after years of high prices for tea and coffee, an unofficial land market has developed in the Central Highlands. The director of land administration in Gia Lai Province said about 120,000 hectares of agricultural land will be granted certificates, but by February 1996 less than 20,000 hectares had been granted (*Vietnam Agriculture,* April 10, 1996). Unofficial land purchases often lead to deception, illegal occupation, and forcible sales in which local farmers, especially women, often become the victims. As the unofficial land market develops, the price of land increases, pressuring farmers to sell out. Many farmers thus become totally or partially landless, particularly in the industrial crop regions and tourist areas.

Another problem is that only the name of the head of household appears on the land use certificate, even though Article 12 of Decree 64/CP indicates that households and individuals who receive land allotments shall be granted certificates of land use. In rural Vietnam, 80 percent of the households are headed by men, who are also the holder of the household registration book. Only women who head households, including those whose husbands are absent as well as unmarried or widowed women, tend to receive the land use certificates. In some cases in Ha Bac Province, the household selects a family representative to hold the land use certificate. However, in these households, most of the holders are men.

On this issue, land administration officers do not deny the suitability of having both names of husband and wife written on the land use certificate. However, they also say that the actual name on the land use certificate is not important and that a wife, even though she is not the certificate holder, is entitled to use land like her husband. In case the husband wants to sell land, he needs the signature from the wife. Others are of the opinion that Vietnamese families respect the spirit of harmony between husband and wife and that there is no discrimination in terms of land use, regardless of who holds the certificate.

This concept stems from the realities of the process of applying individual land use rights in Vietnam, which is very new. Experience and examples show that land use rights of women may be trampled when their names do not appear on the certificates of land use. Moreover, during the process of land allocation, land disputes between members of families have not been seen; social attention has therefore not been drawn to this issue.

SOME EFFECTS OF LAND POLICY
CHANGES ON WOMEN

In Vietnam, the process of dividing extended families into nuclear families has been normal practice. Following the marriage of children, new families are set up. Parents usually stay with the elder son's family or with the youngest son's family. However, the division of households in recent years has increased. One of the reasons is the land policy (Le Tho, 1995: 63). If a young couple continues to live with parents, they are not entitled to receive either farmland or a house plot. This land policy, issued in the 1980s, encourages nuclear families. According to the national population census, in 1989 Vietnam had 12,958,000 households, an increase of 3,292,000 since 1979. On average, this represents an increase of 3.1 percent per year. The family size reduced quickly, from 5.2 persons in 1979 to 4.8 in 1989.

Independent young couples are given favorable treatment as to land and business. However, this may affect caretaking of the elderly and children. When living separately, young couples and their parents will have little chance to help and support one another. Meanwhile, the system of crèches and kindergartens in many rural areas is failing, and support and benefits provided to the elderly by cooperatives in the past no longer exist. This is a major constraint for women who have small children, for the elderly, and for those whose husbands are absent (Le Tho, 1995).

The Land Law also encouraged early marriages because land allocation was made only once; no subsequent adjustments are allowed until the lease expires (twenty to fifty years). Villagers complain that there will be no land allocation for newborns and no decrease in land when family members die. To benefit from land distribution, many couples will marry before they reach legal age (eighteen for women, twenty for men). Family pressure for early marriages even comes from extended families: A daughter-in-law increases the total land allotted to a family for cultivation even if the new couple receives a house plot (Beresford, 1994).

Outside Village Marriage

The policy of land allocation is based on fixed delineation of each administrative unit of village and commune. This means that if the number of people increases quickly the per capita allotted land area will be reduced. Therefore, before land is allotted to households, and if a woman from outside the village gets married to a man in the village, then the average land allotted all villagers will be reduced. This leads to initiatives in some villages to limit migrants to the village through marriage. In other words, marriage to outsiders, though not banned, is limited. For example, if a man in the village gets married to a woman outside the village and brings her to the village, a fine (50,000 dong in Thai Binh Province) will be imposed. So far, there is no data on the number of couples affected by such local regulations. Though the fine is small and should not prevent young couples from marrying, it violates the right to free marriage and to free residence of citizens. Moreover, this regulation shows that nonvillage women—as daughters-in-law—are a burden to the places where their husbands' families are residing. The women's right to land use in this case is at risk (Beresford, 1994).

Women who marry within the home village can continue to work on their allotted farmland. However, if they marry outside the village and go to live with the husband's family, they cannot bring their own land or continue to farm their land. Their parents' families may give them some money in compensation, but in general the young woman does not have land to till and thus will be dependent on the husband's family (Beresford, 1994). In principle the young woman can sell her land use rights or rent her land to bring some money into the husband's family, but in reality this rarely happens, as the land is allotted to the entire family and the division of land use rights becomes a family affair rather than a legal issue.

This issue is sufficiently contentious that it was covered in the magazine *State and Law* (1995/4: 61); it emphasized that daughters-in-law who move into a village after the land allocation are not entitled to receive land. If the young woman is not skillful in nonagricultural activities such as trade, she will have to rely on farming for the husband's family. This obviously places the new daughter-in-law in an unfavorable position within her husband's family because she comes without property and is viewed as a burden by her new family (Beresford, 1994).

Land Rights After Divorce

Land rights following the divorce of a couple is a newly emerging problem that has not yet been addressed, either by the Land Law or the Family and Marriage Law. The policy direction can be gleaned from the following, again from *State and Law:* "After divorce, if the wife continues to live and farm in the same village, she will be entitled to the land use rights of that land. If a wife moves away or if she does not actually work on the farm, she is not entitled to land use rights allocated to her husband's family but will instead receive compensation equal to the values of the land allotted to her" (*State and Law,* 1995/4: 61).

Upon divorce the wife usually leaves the old residence if she comes from outside the village and therefore is deprived of her land use rights. Compensation for the value of the land does not provide any assurance of future access to land. Moreover, assessing fair value is very complicated and often leads to underestimation. For example, the paper *Phu Nu Thu Do* (Capital Women) reported on a divorce case in Gia Lam District in Hanoi. The house was valued as 11 million dong, and the court decided that Mrs. Hao, the wife, was entitled to half and that she had to leave the house. In fact, the house was worth 60 million dong (*Phu Nu Thu Do,* October 18, 1995).

According to law, the land is allotted to members of the household; the wife, as a member of the household, is entitled to use her land. This right cannot be abrogated after divorce. The residence after divorce is a personal decision and should not be a decisive factor when courts allocate land to the wife. Whether she directly or indirectly farms the land is her decision. It is unreasonable to deny the allocation of land based on the fact that the wife "moves to another place or does not directly engage in farming" (*State and Law,* 1995/4: 61).

Many gaps exist in the legislation pertaining to land division in marriage and after divorce. These newly arising land disputes between family members are not covered by either law. The marriage law only deals with the house, because at the time of passage in 1986 the Land Law did not exist. The latter deals with land but does not pay due attention to disputes over land within the family. As a result, some of the temporary land regulations are too technical and do not really protect women's interests. Clearly, both the Land Law and the Marriage and Family Law need to be reviewed, especially in terms of land and house disputes between women and men.

CONCLUSION

Those who are interested in the topic of women and land in Vietnam often ask why women's access to land is often lower than men's access. How can this happen when the law defines that there is no discrimination in land use between men and women? This is even more difficult to imagine in a country with a constitution that guarantees women equal rights in political, economic, social, cultural, and family spheres (1959 Constitution: 24).

We have tried to answer these questions by reviewing the discrepancies between women's rights to land in theory and the diverse realities in the Vietnamese countryside.

The process of shifting from farming on collective land to farming on land controlled by the household or an individual has been accompanied by many theoretical and ideological discussions. By considering these discussions, we can see what issues draw attention in society and why other issues remain below the surface. As mentioned above, the 1993 Land Law is a major landmark on the road toward allocating land use to farmer households in the long term. Compared to the 1988 Land Law, the new law is more progressive, particularly in expanding the rights of farmers to land use. Although land continues to be owned by the state, the 1993 Land Law gives farmers wider rights to transfer, mortgage, and sell land use rights (Kerkvliet, 1995: 83).

Most newspapers and magazines have focused on the question of landownership and land use between the household and the state (cf. *State and Law,* "On the Right to Ownership of Land" [1992/2], with *Communist Review,* "Why Land Is Under the Ownership of the Entire Population" [1993/6]). The relationship between individual members in a household in terms of land use has not often been raised. This issue did not emerge during the process of land allocation; as a result, decisionmakers and researchers are not very aware of the potential threat of land disputes within families.

A second issue that emerged during the process of land allocation is the changing role of the farming household. In the past, when farming was done on collective land, households only existed in terms of registration and administrative management. The household did not have economic roles. The head of the household only formally represented other members in terms of demographic registration. Today, as a result of land allocation, farmer households have become a basic production unit in rural areas. Households have more resources (land) than in the past; the head of the household has a dominant role in land use decisionmaking. He or she is granted this power by law as holder of the land use certificate. In other words, the head of the household has more economic and legal power than other family members, and much more so than in the past. Disputes as to rights and obligations between household heads and other family members have increased. Obviously, along with the change of the role of household, the Land Law has created a foundation for strengthening the authority of the household head as well.

Worthy of note is the fact that even though the legal and economic position of the household head has completely changed, the underlying concept of the household remains the same. The belief that the family is a harmonious unit leads to the assumption that whoever heads the household makes no difference. In fact, granting legal recognition to the household head gives the head significant power over other family members.

Women themselves are not yet aware of these implications. Their traditional behavior of "being behind" their husbands and acting shy inhibits women from claiming rights to land use certificates. Even talking about their husband's property is considered disrespectful, a feeling that has obstructed the division of property and assets in a divorce. The lack of specific regulations on household assets and property in the Family and Marriage Law shows that these assumptions prevail among lawmakers (Ho Chi Minh City Women, January 21, 1995).

To protect the fine customs and traditions of cooperation within the family despite the challenges of the market economy, the exercise of equal rights to land use between the husband and wife will be more practical than just talking about how to maintain them. Until existing regulations and laws are revised, women will continue to be more disadvantaged than men in their access to house and land.

NOTES

1. Contributions to the cooperative included taxes, payments to the cooperative social welfare fund, and local infrastructure construction and maintenance. This was considered, in part, a way of paying back the cooperative for its contribution to contract production, especially for mechanized land preparation (plowing and harrowing) and for irrigation water.

2. Five of these documents were ratified by the National Assembly, and the other twenty were government decrees (*Nhan dan,* April 2, 1995: 1–2). The most comprehensive document concerning agricultural land is Decree No. 64/CP, dated September 27, 1993 (Ministry of Agriculture and Food Processing Industry, 1995: 167).

6

Cultivating the Forest:
Gendered Land Use Among the Tay
in Northern Vietnam

Carol Ireson-Doolittle and W. Randall Ireson

Women and men villagers in the upland regions of Vietnam continue their utilization of the surrounding hills and forests despite uncertainty about landownership and land use rights. In the past three decades, the government first mandated collectivization of all farmland; then switched to a contract system; and more recently initiated the distribution of paddy land that had been held within cooperatives. The state now assesses taxes on paddy, home garden, and residential land and has begun allocating areas for use as common village forests and as private fields. For the present, however, slowly changing customary land practices and the gender division of labor continue to influence women's access to land, forest, and house.

This chapter presents current information about subsistence foresters among the Tay ethnic group and documents how increasing market integration, rapid population growth, and in-migration from the lowlands are affecting both their field and forest utilization and gender roles. In particular, this chapter focuses on differences in women's and men's understandings of their local environment and gender differences in the collection and use of local natural resources, especially "wild" resources during a time of rapid economic and environmental changes in the highlands of northern Vietnam.[1]

The first section provides background on the Tay, their agroecosystem, and the changing political and economic contexts of contemporary northern Vietnam. The second section documents the variations by gender and class of the collection and use of natural forest products. It closes by discussing the complexity of agroecosystem changes among the Tay and highlighting the value of including gender and socioeconomic level in studies of these changes.[2]

CHANGING FOREST USE

The general pattern of villagers' exploitation of natural resources in times of rapid economic transition has been reported in numerous similar situations throughout the tropics (see, for example, ESCAP, 1986; Kunstadter, Chapman, and Sabhasri, 1978; Poffenberger, 1990). Most reports have focused on the overall human-farming/ecosystem interactions and have not differentiated human activities below the household level. However, women and men in the same household use and understand the natural environment differently. Furthermore, "development" in many Third World contexts has had negative effects on women by increasing their workloads, undercutting their traditional income-earning crafts, reducing their traditional access to important resources like land, and marginalizing and undervaluing their traditional contributions to family survival (see Sen and Grown, 1987; Blumberg et al., 1995; Charlton, 1984; Momsen and Kinnaird, 1993; Tinker, 1990).

Women more frequently than men collect forest products for family use (Fortmann, 1986; Fortmann and Richeleau, 1985; Hoskins, 1980; C. Ireson, 1991). Poor farmers particularly count on forest products to enrich their hearths, their health, and their household income, especially during bad crop years. In one area of northeastern Brazil, for example, forest-product extraction is roughly equivalent to wage labor and to agriculture in its contribution to family income and is most important for poor households and for women (Hecht, Anderson, and May, 1988). Many farming families in developing countries continue to be dependent for part of their livelihood on the forests near their farming plots (Belsky and Siebert, 1983; Condominas, 1977; Kunstadter, Chapman, and Sabhasri, 1978; Tayanin, 1994).

Women, as the main collectors of wild products, are sometimes in the forefront of efforts to conserve the natural environment and this aspect of their household livelihood. The Chipko movement in India, for example, began with groups, mainly women, who successfully protested against commercial harvesting of "their" gathering forest by hugging the trees slated for cutting. Movement organizations have since begun village-level reforestation projects in areas of degraded forest and cropland (Rodda, 1994).

Women and men have different areas of knowledge about the natural environment and different interests in preserving and using aspects of the environment. In many societies, women are often the major collectors of firewood and forest fruits, while men are more likely to grow and sell wood for poles and timber. Thus, women and men are likely to prefer different kinds of trees for reforesting degraded areas. For example, women may favor trees producing food and high-quality firewood, while men may prefer commercial timber or pulp species (see Fortmann and Bruce, 1988). These different interests might even lead directly to conflict between the interests of women and men.

Gender differences in the use of the forest and wild products in Vietnam have not yet been widely studied. Previous research of a mountain minority village in central Vietnam, studied before the village was destroyed by war, found that villagers were very dependent on forest resources. Villagers regularly gathered food, items for use, and medicinal plants from the forest and margins of their swiddens. The researcher, however, did not report gender differences in the collection and use of wild products (Condominas, 1977). More recently, others have studied various aspects of the interaction between people and the natural environment in Tat hamlet. Although researchers have found that the natural environment is an integral part of the agricultural and economic systems of the hamlet, they have not yet studied the variations by gender in the interface between people and environment.

THE HIGHLAND TAY

In large areas of the Vietnamese uplands, particularly in the northwestern area, shifting cultivation (also known as slash-and-burn or swidden agriculture) has been identified by the government as a serious threat to the natural environment. As practiced in its traditional form among the Tay ethnic group, however, this system was relatively sustainable under conditions of low population density. Rapid natural population increase, together with substantial migration of ethnic Vietnamese (Kinh) from the lowlands and intensive commercial exploitation of timber and other resources, have now created a situation in which this farming system is no longer sustainable. Tay farmers in the study area of Da Bac District of Hoa Binh Province have practiced a mix of paddy and swidden farming for generations. Paddy areas were very limited; thus, the rice supply was supplemented through swidden agriculture. Traditionally the Tay felled primary forest or secondary forest growth on previously cultivated land. After several years of cultivation, the swidden was allowed to return to brush and forest while the farmers cleared and cultivated new plots. Under traditional conditions, farmers would reuse old swidden plots after only fifteen to twenty years of fallow when there was substantial forest regrowth. Now the fallow period may be as little as three to four years in many areas, with fields being cultivated for two or three years, depending on fertility and weeds.

Today the Tay ethnic group is the largest minority group in Vietnam (Levinson, 1993: 265). They are a member of the larger Tai ethnic family, closely related to the Lao and northern Thai. Their language has many words in common with Lao, and other linguistic connections with the northern Lao dialect can be identified. Like the Lao and Thai, they build their houses off the ground on wooden piles, but other architectural details, such as the complex mortise-and-tenon joints between beams and posts and the decorative carving on the beams, are distinctive. Tay women are traditionally able to engage in trade, though male authority over females is evident in patrilocal residence after marriage and in male community leadership.

The study hamlets, Tat and Dieu Luong, are located within three kilometers of each other in Tan Minh Village of Da Bac District in the Da River watershed.[3] Tat's elevation is roughly 360 meters, while Dieu Luong's is about 600 meters. Surrounding peaks reach an elevation of 800 to 1,000 meters. Hillside slopes are steep (40–60 degrees or more) and extend down to the valley floor. Numerous small creeks flow into the main stream in the narrow valley where Tat hamlet is located. Fewer streams cut into the slopes surrounding Dieu Luong since it is located on a hillside rather than in a valley. The creeks power numerous 100-watt electrical generators and are also diverted with simple structures to irrigate the limited areas for paddy fields in both hamlets. The tropical monsoon climate has a rainy season extending from May to October. Eighty-five percent of the annual rainfall occurs during this period. Total annual rainfall averages 1,962 millimeters per year. The soil is primarily red-yellow feralitic.

THE AGROECOSYSTEM OF THE TAY

The collection, use, and sale of natural products are an integral part of the land-based subsistence and income-generating activities that make up the agroecosystem of the Tay. Changes in the local natural and socioeconomic environments are affecting these practices. The Tay of Tat and Dieu Luong practice mixed subsistence farming based on a blend of paddy cultivation in small mountain valleys and swidden cultivation, tree "gardening," forest gathering, and hunting on the surrounding hillsides. Within memory, the area was heavily forested, and wild animals including bears, deer, and wild pigs were not uncommon. Human populations were small; elders from Tat report that only seven households made their home in Tat in 1958, for example. Tat now contains nearly eighty households and a population of more than four hundred; Dieu Luong has 294 people in fifty-three households. In Tat, houses are scattered along a three-kilometer stretch of the all-weather road (built about 1976), all within about sixty meters of the road. Settlement in Dieu Luong consists of several clusters of houses built on higher ground near the rice paddies. A dirt road connects the village to the all-weather stone road in the valley at the east end of Tat. The differences in physical setting between Tat and Dieu Luong have stimulated somewhat different adaptations and a different balance among the components of the farming system, but the same components are present in both villages, as described below.

The Tay are originally settled cultivators. For a long time, the Tay have known how to convert valleys and low hills into paddy fields. In addition to wet rice agriculture, swidden agriculture claims a very important position in the economic life and in the spirit of the Tay community. Gathering and hunting natural products also are economically and culturally important to the Tay. Tay people categorize their land into several main types: forest, swidden, tree garden, home garden, animal grazing, and paddy.

Area farmers have grown rice in paddies for as long as anyone can remember, and the total area of paddy land (seven and eight hectares today, respectively, in Tat and Dieu Luong) has increased only slightly during the last thirty years. Two rice crops can be grown on most fields, because the surrounding creeks and streams are diverted by simple weirs into canals and pipes to irrigate the fields during the dry season. Men commonly are responsible for working the soil, while women are commonly responsible for transplanting and weeding. Within the last few years, paddy land was distributed to individual households for private production on the basis of household size and composition. Although farmers use new varieties and chemical fertilizers, rice yields are still low, reaching only about 1.8–2.2 tons/ha./crop. Even with double-cropping, the paddy allocations do not supply adequate rice for household needs. These small areas of paddy provide households with enough rice for two to six months every year. All households also farm significant amounts of upland rice, as well as cassava, a second variety of tuber, called *dot* locally, and minor amounts of maize and vegetables in swidden fields.

Swidden farming has also been an integral part of the Tay farming system in Da Bac. It is not a recent adaptation to population growth, as it is for many other ethnic groups, and paddy rice production is not indicative of a recent orientation away from swidden farming. Both elements combine for a "composite" paddy-swidden farming system. Men commonly select the land for swiddens and do the initial clearing and burning. Both men and women clear and fence the burned swidden area, collect the larger unburned branches for firewood, and work together to plant the swidden. Women are responsible for swidden weeding and often stay in the swidden to protect the crop as it grows. Family members work together to harvest and carry rice to the village, though women select the seed for the following year.

While both paddy and swidden farming have long been practiced by the Tay, the relative proportion of household food produced in paddy and swidden has probably changed during the past several decades. Farmers in Dieu Luong, for example, report that twenty years ago they farmed only small amounts of swidden rice and cassava to supplement paddy production. Now swidden production appears approximately equal to paddy production. In recent years, because of population pressure, the fallow period has become shorter. In both Tat and Dieu Luong, people often plant rice for only two years and leave the field fallow for two to three years before clearing the swidden again. Predictably, yields are declining.

Other crops grown in swiddens are somewhat different in Tat and Dieu Luong and are managed somewhat differently. In Tat, only a few families plant cotton in small strips near the swidden hut. In contrast, in Dieu Luong, most families have cotton swiddens. Mothers and young women process and weave cotton to make blankets, skirts, and other items for household use and for the dowries of daughters. People in Dieu Luong plant more *dot* than those in Tat, and they consider *dot* to be a crop for their children's economic use. Children older than fifteen have a portion of the family *dot* swidden. They carry up the seedlings, plant them, care for the plants, and have the right to sell the products. Children keep this money to buy clothing and things to use, or they can contribute it to daily household expenses. In Tat, on the other hand, children sell *dot* for their parents, who then use this money to purchase textbooks and clothing for the children. Ways of managing swidden land also differ, but in both hamlets the cooperative determines which hillside areas are allowed to be farmed during any given year.

In addition to paddy and swidden farming, most households maintain forest gardens and small home gardens adjacent to their dwellings. Women plant fruit trees, herbs, vegetables, and sometimes cassava and corn in their home gardens. During the middle of the rainy season, vegetables interplanted in the swidden are carried home daily, but at other times of the year the home garden plays a larger role. Availability of water (carried by small bamboo aqueducts from the surrounding streams to water-collection points near almost every small cluster of homes) facilitates maintenance of these gardens during the dry season. Forest gardens are primarily planted with various kinds of bamboo and commercial crops such as tea and palms used for roofing. Women are primarily responsible for the home garden, while both women and men report harvesting and selling crops from their forest gardens.

Domestic animals are the fourth element of the farming system. Chickens, ducks, and pigs are raised in the village. Poultry is fed some rice and corn and is allowed to scavenge during the day; hybrid pigs (only raised in Tat) are more typically penned and fed on cassava, *dot* tuber, and chopped banana trunks, while local pigs are allowed to range freely through the village, though they are fed also. Households sometimes eat chicken on special occasions. Pigs are almost never slaughtered locally but are sold for cash to purchase household necessities or rice. Many families have constructed small fishponds in recent years, taking advantage of the plentiful water supply in the area. Water buffalo provide the main source of traction for plowing and harrowing the rice paddies and are also raised as an investment. Small numbers of cattle are kept by some families, to be sold for cash as needed. Women normally care for smaller animals and sometimes for larger animals, though men sell the high-value animals like water buffalo and cattle. On average, Dieu Lu-ong households have fewer large animals than do Tat households.

Finally, wild products from the surrounding forest and uncultivated lands are harvested by villagers for their needs. Since most farming households in both hamlets experience some rice shortages nearly every year, farmers rely on wild foods to meet their food deficits. The forest can immediately and frequently supply them with food, firewood, construction materials, and other necessities for daily living: bamboo shoots, ear fungus, mushrooms, tubers, animals, medicinal plants, and the like. When necessary, villagers will chop down trees for income to purchase food, even in forests that are being restored or protected. Forest resource management in Dieu Luong is better organized than in Tat. Dieu Luong hamlet has created a group of five forest guards. Because of the guards, the forest adjacent to the hamlet still contains valuable hardwood trees. Dieu Luong also has an area of bamboo forest that is reserved for hungry periods when each family has permission to cut a determined number of bamboo lengths to sell in order to buy rice for survival.

Tat and Dieu Luong have a somewhat different balance between these five agroecosystem elements. Tat, for example, raises more large animals and some hybrid pigs, while Dieu Luong has been able to protect more of its old forest. The elements of swidden, forest, and fallow fields are not fixed but in fact all derive from the same category of land, that is, fields too steep to develop into rice paddies. In long-fallow swidden farming, a section of forest is cleared and burned and farmed in rice or cassava for several years, at which time it is abandoned. Brush and eventually small trees regrow, and if the parcel is left long enough, a young (and, later, old) forest ecosystem develops. Thus, sections of sloping land cycle among the forest, swidden, and fallow categories. The management of this cycle is a critical activity in the farming system, as the balance over time among the three categories of land use intimately affects food production, groundwater supplies, soil erosion, availability of wild plant products, and the diversity and population of wild animals. Men and women are involved in somewhat different aspects of this cycle.

Because of substantial expansion of swidden farming over the last decades, and recent government regulations prohibiting the clearing of older forests, the "sloping land" elements of the agroecosystem are now mostly constrained to a two-phase rotation between young fallow and swidden fields. Under these policies, the upland areas will likely become a mix of old timber (very small areas), plantations (palm, bamboo, acacia, etc.), and fields that rotate between bush fallow and swidden on a relatively short cycle (four to eight years). These policy- and population-driven changes have distinct implications for women's and men's collection of natural products. Men's hunting and trapping activities will continue to decline as wild animals also decline. Some species of plants gathered by women will continue to be available, however, and women's swidden work will continue to be central for family subsistence.

These government policies are just the latest in a series of laws that have altered the national policy framework for forestry and agriculture. Economic reforms initiated in 1986 and culminating in the new Land Law in July 1993 restored the family farm as the primary producing unit in rural areas and enabled market forces to direct the flow of agricultural goods and natural products. Beginning in 1988, forest-designated lands (much of which is not forested) belonging to state enterprises and cooperatives are being slowly allocated to households, with provisions to encourage the regeneration of forests on barren lands. In addition, a national project for economic and cultural development of the uplands is being reviewed for approval. If the project is approved, there will be significant improvements in roads, electricity, schools, and village clinics in the research hamlets.

Local Perception of Changes

Villagers in both hamlets report specific, mostly negative, changes in their natural environment: the serious reduction in forest; limited availability of new swidden fields; accelerating scarcity of wild products which they formerly collected; and reduced areas available for animal grazing. They also mentioned negative changes in the natural water supply and in soil fertility.

Of great concern was the reduction of the wild animal population. The animals that were previously easy to hunt are now very rare and perhaps no longer remain. Previously, about 60 percent of families in Tat hamlet had hunting rifles. Forest animals included bears, deer, pigs, foxes, and chickens. Today, only 20 percent of the families have hunting rifles. Wild pigs, bears, and deer are now uncommon. The role of hunting in family income is insignificant. Nowadays villagers trap rats, snakes, birds, foxes, and other animals mainly for family consumption and to prevent animals from destroying crops. Wild tubers, bamboo shoots, mushrooms, and ear fungus have become rarer and must be collected from far away. According to people who practice traditional medicine, medicinal plants have become harder to find, and practitioners must travel farther afield in order to collect necessary plants. Bamboo, rattan, and big logs for house construction are also becoming increasingly rare because the forest is disappearing and state forest conservation policies have become stricter.

Local people also observed positive changes in the use of natural resources. Some forest products have more value because they are easily sold (such as broom grass, bamboo, gecko, medicinal fern, and snakes). Water is not only used for drinking, daily use, and irrigation but also for small, household-level hydroelectric generation.

In contrast, most villagers reported that socioeconomic changes are positive. Roads and transportation conditions have significantly improved: Previously people took three days to walk to and from the provincial center; now they can get there and back within one day by hired motorbike and automobile. Trade has become easier: They can purchase necessities in Tat hamlet or purchase equipment and expensive articles at Cao Son market, about twelve kilometers away. Merchants regularly come to both villages to sell common household goods and consumables and to buy certain forest products and surplus cassava; some villagers act as middle merchants—buying and storing local products for sale to traveling merchants and buying outside products for sale in the hamlet. Many households have already purchased beds, radios, and television sets. A few men in both villages sometimes do wage labor (sawing lumber, loading log trucks), usually for outsiders who are harvesting timber (both legally and illegally). Dieu Luong seems to have more local "specialists," including four furniture makers, one herbalist, and several weavers.

Diseases are less common because of better hygiene and the presence of a local clinic. About one-quarter of hamlet children finish their primary education in a local elementary school. Some children continue their education in a middle school, twelve kilometers away, and in high school at the district center twenty-five kilometers away. Family planning has been implemented with noticeable results. Each family previously had six to ten children. Today, young couples have only two or three children and are using family-planning methods to maintain smaller families. Finally, wet rice is intensively cultivated by some farmers, leading to higher yield. A number of cultivation technologies, including new varieties of rice, beans, peanut, corn, and pigs, have been encouraged and applied, thereby increasing agricultural production.

Interestingly enough, some older women report no change at all. They still grow the same things in their swiddens and are still tied to their swidden work for part of the year. Women have few new opportunities, with the exception of petty trade. Women report no wage labor available for women and perceive of no cottage-industry possibilities for women.

GENDER AND CLASS DIFFERENCES IN THE COLLECTION OF NATURAL PRODUCTS

The collection of natural products varies by gender and age and is affected by the season, household needs, and the market. Women and men use different natural products to generate their shares of their families' livelihood. Women are more likely to collect plant products, while men are more likely to harvest timber and hunt and trap wild animals. The people with knowledge of medicinal plants in Tat and Dieu Luong are women. Women gather a greater variety of natural products than do men and appear to spend much more time in their gathering than do men. Women are more likely to use natural products directly, while men are more likely to sell natural products and use the income.

However, women also collect products for sale; men also collect for household use. As the natural environment around Tat and Dieu Luong has changed and some desired plants are less accessible to women, men have begun to participate in the collection of these plants. Only bamboo shoots and rats appear to be regularly harvested as a supplement to the basic staple foods of rice and cassava. Several varieties of wild tubers form an important part of the diet for those families that are not self-sufficient in rice, particularly in the months preceding the June rice harvest. Interestingly, and in contrast to other groups such as the Hmong and Lao, who often gather forest products, the Tay do not report collecting a wide variety of wild vegetables and plants for food. Instead, they appear to rely on such crops as kale, squashes, and cucumbers that are seasonally planted in small quantities in the swiddens and home gardens. It is not clear whether this is a long-standing pattern or a more recent adaptation to the heavy gathering pressure on the forest environment which has made collection of wild vegetables too time-consuming.

Women's Collection

During swidden cultivation season, the energy of many women is focused on their swidden fields, so their collection is localized to the swiddens and nearby areas. Returning home daily from the swiddens, they might bring a few ears of corn, bamboo shoots, and several tubers, all collected nearby. Some women say that even if they need income they would not collect products to sell since growing their swidden rice crop is of primary importance. In fact, one woman says that if her household were to run out of rice, others might refuse to help her if they thought she had not devoted herself fully to the swidden crop.

Women also collect a variety of products for household purposes, though the mix of products collected varies by season and is constrained by women's other responsibilities for swidden cultivation and the care of very small children. Plant products are primarily gathered by women. Fuelwood, bamboo shoots, and vegetables for the daily consumption of humans and animals, and products used to build houses, huts, and fences such as bamboo and palm leaves, are all collected by women. Women also go to the swiddens and into forests to dig for tubers during times of hunger and rice shortages. Some collection activities require hard labor by the women of Dieu Luong and Tat, such as cutting and carrying bamboo and digging fern roots and tubers. Women, often with the help of their children, also collect small animals like crabs and snails from the paddies and streams near the village.

Though men sometimes collect specific medicinal plants, women are generally more knowledgeable, and a few women are particularly expert and collect a large variety of medicinal plants, both for use and for sale. Some women also cultivate wild plants in their home gardens. One woman informant says that she sometimes collects the seeds of medicinal plants and scatters them in the new areas that she is farming, like her new swidden or the forest land that is allocated to her household. Another woman, known districtwide for her healing abilities, claims that she relies on more than two hundred natural medicinal items, most of which she was able to collect in the areas surrounding her village during the years when she was an active practitioner. She has partially trained her daughter and son-in-law, and she says that they are still able to collect some of these medicinal products from the nearby areas.

Men's Collection

Men, in contrast, seem to collect natural products less regularly and for specific needs, as for income, meat, and to repair houses. Men's collection of wild plants is primarily limited to activities requiring greater physical strength, such as carrying large pieces of fuelwood, climbing tall trees and limestone mountains to get medicinal plants, and felling fruit trees for women to collect. Sometimes the women and men of a household work together collecting palm leaves. Virtually all houses in both hamlets are roofed with layers of leaves from the local palms. Roofs must be rethatched every several years, which usually involves numerous trips to the forest over a short period of time to cut and transport the leaves to the village. Demand has outstripped the natural supply, however, and many households have now planted this type of palm on allocated forest lands near the village. This ensures a permanent supply for the household, perhaps some surplus for sale.

Men and women often collect bamboo together, usually for sale. Several varieties of bamboo are used to weave house walls and flooring and for baskets, animal cages, and other household uses. When buyers from town send word that they want bamboo, both women and men will cut bamboo in the forest and bring it to the hamlet for sale. There is considerable disagreement as to whether women or men contribute more to this activity. Bamboo shoots are also regularly sold for a small income. Normally they are sold locally, but one family reported jointly collecting about thirty-five kilograms of shoots in a recent daylong trip to the forest, cleaning and cooking them all night, then hiring a motorcycle taxi to take the husband to the district market the next day, where he sold them for 50,000 dong. Even after paying 20,000 dong for the taxi, they earned about 10,000 dong ($.90) more than if they had sold the product in the village.

Natural products from animal sources are primarily captured by men. Wild animals other than rats constitute what is best described as "variety foods" in the Tay diet. Men and boys may catch snakes, eels, and turtles and trap rats and birds.[4] No women were seen or reported catching snakes, eels, wild boars, wild chickens, foxes, and dogs. No informant reported any woman who traps rats or birds. Moreover, women do not eat natural products such as eels and monkey. When we asked why, they answered that these animals are repulsive and have a pungent or fishy odor.

Forest Use by Class

Research-team members asked local officials to identify a number of households in each hamlet as follows: well-off, middle, and poorer economic levels. Their main criteria seemed to be adequacy of food supply and ownership of large animals. Results of the study show significant differences in the role played by the collection of natural products by the economic level of the household.

A minority of Tat and Dieu Luong households are identified as being well-off. These households have enough food to eat and own large animals. Animal husbandry is the main source of income for these households. Abundant labor enables these families to cultivate extensive swiddens, with the swidden providing more of the household food than do the limited areas of paddy. Agricultural products are more commonly consumed rather than sold. Wild products are a supplementary source of both food and income for well-off households. Their wealth is not derived from the forest, but they still depend on the forest for many things, such as firewood, rats, bamboo shoots, bamboo, wood, and palm. One well-off household in Tat sold several cattle to invest in a motorcycle taxi, which has become a reliable source of income. Several well-off households supplement incomes by selling lumber that the men fell and saw in the forest.

About half of the households in both hamlets are identified as having a midlevel or average standard of living by village criteria. They have enough or nearly enough food to eat and sufficient labor for large swiddens. However, they own few large animals. In comparison to their better-off neighbors, their swiddens provide more of their income, while animal husbandry provides less. Sale of swidden products and domestic animals each contributes about one-third of total household income. Although only one middle-level Tat household reported supplementary income sources, two Dieu Luong middle households interviewed reported income from basket-making, trading, and furniture-making. Members of these households rely on wild products for food, use, and sale as much as the well-off households do, but agricultural production is still a more important source of food and income than are wild products.

Poorer families often have food shortages of several months' duration and own no large animals. The poorer households can be divided into two groups: those that may be temporarily poor because they have recently separated from their "parent" household, and those that are poor because they have many children and no surplus. New householders have very young children and are often unable to field more than one worker at a time. They often have expended all of their savings to build a new house. Poorer households depend more heavily on income from wild products than do households at any other level. Several families reported that they sell broom grass during the first and second lunar months to buy rice. Members of poorer families collect medicinal fern roots year-round except when they can harvest bamboo for sale. Almost all must find wild tubers to eat. In addition, some poorer husbands hire themselves out as laborers when possible, sawing lumber for others.

In sum, poor families rely more on wild and swidden products for income, while well-off families sell domestic animals. Middle-level families sell both swidden products and animals. Well-off families are somewhat more able to provide labor for swiddens, so they derive somewhat more of their food from swiddens, while poor families are more dependent on their small paddy plots. These limited data suggest that poor women may be carrying a particularly heavy workload, since women are almost entirely responsible for swidden production, small-animal raising, and much wild-product collection. Poor women may be producing most of the family cash income (in swidden and wild products), as well as providing much of the family food (from swidden, forest, and animal-raising). However, poor men, like those of other economic levels, are the organizers of paddy-rice production and are responsible for paddy-preparation labor. Women of other economic levels may not carry a disproportionate share of household support since large animals (usually raised by men) and men's secondary occupations are more common income sources for middle-level and well-off families.

GENDER, NATURAL PRODUCTS, AND CHANGING RELATIONS IN THE AGROECOSYSTEM

This study, highlighting the role of gender in the collection of natural products, indicates the value of integrating gender into studies of the changing agroecosystem and economy of hamlets like Tat and Dieu Luong. Women and men do collect different kinds of products from the natural environment and use those products differently. But these differences in collection activities must be placed in the context of the local agroecosystem and the larger social, economic, and cultural contexts in order to see why gender *really* matters. In addition to information about collection activities, this study describes women's and men's different responsibilities in the household economy, explores the economies of households at different economic levels, and notes Tay cultural elements (e.g., patrilocal residence after marriage, male hamlet headship) that legitimate men's authority over women in both households and the community at large.

In studying gender and one aspect of the agroecosystem of the Tay in Da Bac, one is tempted to conclude that we see a classic example of population growth in the process of causing a permanent degradation of the productive base of the physical environment, a process that disproportionately affects women and poorer families. In fact, the situation is considerably more complex. Although population growth has indeed placed significant pressures on the natural environment, and certain elements of the environment (particularly soil fertility and species diversity) are deteriorating, the human population has also changed its behavior in response to changing environmental conditions. Some of the changing behavior of local people is mediated by changes in national policy, regional economy, and culture, with women and poor people more limited in their possible responses.

Resources and resource use vary in several dimensions: over time, by location, by gender, and by economic level. Variation in time shows both long and short cycles: the gradual decline in recent decades of forest cover, soil fertility, and species diversity, on the one hand, and the more rapid rotation between forest, swidden field, and regenerating fallow on the other. Differences in resource mix between Tat and Dieu Luong illustrate the variation possible by location. Women and men do different work, know about and harvest different resources, and respond differently to changes in the natural and social environment. And households of different economic levels exploit different resources over space and time, responding to their different needs and opportunities.

Agroecosystem analysis typically analyzes the household in a farming system as a "black box"—a single unit that interacts with other elements of the agroecosystem such as rice paddies, forests, gardens, and so on. One focus of this study is to disaggregate the household unit, especially by gender, and identify the ways in which different members of the farming household understand and interact with the natural resource base. Observation of and conversation with the Tay of Da Bac clearly identify the differences in male and female roles in economic production and in knowledge. Both women and men are quite aware of the activities predominantly carried out by their spouse and children, and in at least some instances they participate in those activities. But it appears that the detailed knowledge necessary for successful regular exploitation (or conservation) of a resource is frequently gender-specific.

This study suggests several aspects of economic and agroecosystem change in Tan Minh village that might be further explored for differential effects by gender. Although two older women reported that "nothing has changed," we did observe a few new economic opportunities for women producers: Petty trade and the raising of improved pigs are the most common examples. Wage labor is now available for some men, but not women. Women have developed no cottage industries in response to changing economic conditions, though some Dieu Luong women maintain a traditional cottage industry of textile weaving and blanket-making for family use. In contrast, some men have become furniture makers, laborers, cattle ranchers, and traders in large animals and are beginning to move into the transportation business. The national family-planning program, active locally since 1992, will soon begin to have a visible impact on the health of young women and children, as well as on the time young women with fewer children have available for productive labor. Yet economic opportunities for women are still underdeveloped, so how will these healthier, less child-encumbered women use their time? The reports of women informants reveal that increased household income from increased marketing opportunities is commonly funneled into better housing, consumer items (like televisions), and investment in male-controlled items or businesses (like cattle, motorcycles, and a taxi service). It appears that profits from women's economic activities, other than those contributing to food security, may provide capital for male activities.

Changes in the agroecosystem may also affect women and men differently. Declining swidden fallow time and lower yields mean more work for women, because in order to produce the same amount of food women must cultivate more land or cultivate the same land more intensively. Sometimes available land is farther away. More intensive weeding is required, because the shorter fallow period less successfully suppresses weed growth. Loss of forest requires women to spend more time foraging at greater distances or to plant gardens to produce substitutes for forest products. Loss of forests may contribute to the seasonal drying up of streams that historically contained flows year-round. Major changes in water flow will negatively affect the double-cropping capability of current paddies, requiring families to produce more of their rice in swiddens or to purchase it. Currently, convenient drinking-water supplies may no longer be available, necessitating more female labor for water-hauling. Increasing large-animal populations requires more labor for women, as women and children are often responsible for the feeding of animals, even though men are ultimately responsible for the use and sale of larger animals.

Loss of forest has already taken a toll on animal species available for men's hunting and trapping, though this loss is perhaps mitigated by the increasing role of animal husbandry in the villages. The commodification of wild products has accelerated the pressure on the environment. Both men and women have benefited from sales of forest products, so the depletion of wild plants and animals affects both women's and men's sources of income. As agricultural growth stagnates, forest resources dwindle, and population growth continues, more families may be forced to hire out their labor in order to purchase food. At present, only men are involved in this activity, which usually requires heavy physical labor for low pay. Poor women are especially likely to suffer as their labor (in swidden and forest) becomes the mainstay of their household economy, a trend that may be well under way already.

In short, the social, economic, and agroecosystem changes that have occurred since the construction of the all-weather road in 1976 appear to have benefited men more than women, better-off families more so than poorer families. Insofar as local people have been able to influence these changes, local decisionmakers (nearly always men, and nearly always economically stable men rather than poor men) have viewed their world through the lenses of their own experiences and interests when making decisions. Outside influences have reinforced the male orientation of local decisionmaking. Yet men and women experience their local world differently and have different knowledge about and interests in that world. Knowledge of these gender differences should enable policymakers and the Tay themselves to better understand and manage the highland agroecosystem of Da Bac.

NOTES

1. The authors conducted this field research June 12–21, 1995, as part of a research team that included Bui Tuyet Nhung, Dang Thi Sy, Do Mai Lan, Duong Thi Thuan, Nguyen Quang Ha, Nguyen Thi Quy, and Tran Duc Vien; five of the eight team members were women. This chapter is a revised and shortened version of Working Paper #6 in the Indochina series for the East-West Center, which is available from the Publication Sales Office, East-West Center, 1777 East-West Road, Honolulu, Hawaii 96848.

2. Tat hamlet has since 1992 been the focus of a series of investigations by researchers from the Center for Natural Resources and Environmental Studies (CREES) of the University of Hanoi and from the East-West Center in Honolulu. These data supplemented information collected in June 1995 utilizing the Rapid Rural Appraisal and Participatory Rural Appraisal techniques, including key informant and small group interviews, participatory mapping of the village area, drawing timelines and transects, walking trips to fields and forested areas, and resource-ranking exercises.

3. Basic information about Tat is drawn from the East-West Center–CRES compilation of information gathered in Tat from February 1992 and August 1993, entitled "Preliminary Report April 1994—The Human Ecology of the Tay of Ban Tat Hamlet."

4. Some varieties of snakes are worth over 300,000 dong (US$27). In contrast, a duck is valued about 30,000 dong, one kilogram of milled rice costs about 3,600 dong, and a day's labor locally would earn 15,000–20,000 dong.

7

New Land Rights and Women's Access to Medicinal Plants in Northern Vietnam

Jennifer Sowerwine

The collection of medicinal plants from the mountainous regions of northern Vietnam has provided a significant livelihood for local women and has contributed tremendously to national health care needs since time immemorial (Son, 1996; Tran Thi Lanh, 1996; Nguyen, 1990). Since 1986, changes in land rights, market opportunities, and highland development strategies promulgated by the government are creating new land use patterns and access regimes threatening the long-term supply of medicinal plants and, consequently, women's status and income derived from the trade.

Decollectivization and allocation of land to individual households, as well as titling of land to the (most often) male head of household, are processes that are shifting formal land tenure rights toward men and creating new gendered patterns of land use. Government-sponsored reforestation and cash crop projects in highland mountainous areas are now competing with existing land uses, including swidden agriculture and medicinal plant production. These developments raise important questions about the effects of economic renovation policies, particularly changes in land tenure and concurrent land use programs, on the long-term sustainability of medicinal plant supply, as well as women's sustained participation within the market.

Recent literature documenting the gendered effects of the shift from a socialist "command" economy to a more market-oriented economy, and the privatization of government and communal landholdings, suggest an erosion of women's welfare and status. In studying the effect of macroeconomic reform on women's income and employment, Melanie Beresford argues that there has been a shift of women from more secure waged and salary employment into less secure household and informal sector work. As a result, women have less social contact, an increased burden of productive and reproductive labor, and fewer opportunities for skill development (Beresford, 1994: 3). Desai argues that since economic renovation, the gender gap has reemerged in education. Son preference is prevalent, and even though female-headed households are not significantly worse off than male-headed households, adult women's nutritional and health status is poorer (Desai, 1995). Daniel Goodkind argues that gender inequality has risen since reunification, as evidenced by unequal educational attainment, occupational segregation, and reversal of women in leadership roles (Goodkind, 1995). Although no explicit study on the gendered nature of land allocation exists, a recent Swedish International Development Agency (SIDA) publication found examples of women receiving poorer quality of land through the process.

Although there is certainly mounting evidence, particularly from urban studies among the ethnic Kinh,[1] on rising gender inequalities in Vietnam, my recent observations in several locations in the northern highland suggest that rural minority women, for whom many of the urban realities related to income, occupational, and leadership disadvantages are not applicable, appear not only to be maintaining access and control but are deriving increased benefits from the marketing of medicinal plants. This is evidenced, I observed, by their flourishing presence in the marketplace, their expressed improvement in quality of living, as well as their increased acquisition of material goods. How women in the northern mountainous region (NMR) of Vietnam are able to maintain access to and control over these resources and the benefits derived from their trade during this time of transition remains a puzzle. Will these benefits be short-lived? If women are to sustain economic gains from this market, then potential threats, such as a declining resource base due to overharvesting and competing land use claims, must be addressed. Rights, whether formal or informal, to land and housing for women are necessary to ensure secured access to the necessary inputs for full participation in the trade of medicinals.

In this chapter, I analyze the effects of economic renovation policies, in particular land tenure and land use programs, on women's role and position within the medicinal plant market and on the sustainability of the medicinal market. I begin with a discussion of the historical importance of traditional herbal medicine in both the lowland Vietnamese and highland minority health care systems and economies in the lowland and highland, turning to how production and consumption patterns have changed over time. Next, I describe the market structure, from production to consumption, for medicinal plants, providing examples of both material and cultural-symbolic roles of women in the medicinal market, as well as the importance of access to and rights in land and housing to participate in the production and exchange of medicinals. Third, I discuss how specific policies and programs associated with *doi moi* (economic renovation) are restructuring the market in ways that may threaten the long-term sustainability of the medicinal plant trade. Drawing from several case studies, I also discuss how these policies are creating new opportunities and constraints for women involved in the market. Alternative scenarios for the future and further areas for research conclude the chapter.

HISTORICAL IMPORTANCE OF TRADITIONAL HERBAL MEDICINE

According to the World Health Organization, as much as 80 percent of the world population depends on traditional medicine for primary health care needs, the greater part of which involves the use of plant extracts and their active principles (Adams, 1995: 53). Since more than 85 percent of the population in Vietnam lives and works in the countryside, and has limited access to modern medicines, this age-old system of herbal medicine has provided a means of health care for generations. "Urban" peoples of the lowland also have a long history of using herbal medicines. Historically, upland minority people would trade nontimber forest products, including medicinal plants, with lowland Vietnamese in exchange for rice, salt, and agricultural implements, indicating the importance of indigenous knowledge of medicinal plants in supplying lowland Vietnamese with herbal medicines (Mai Quang, 1974). The earliest written documentation of Vietnamese traditional medicine dates from the fourteenth century, when Tue Tinh (1255–1399), a young and brilliant physician, wrote a series of books on southern medicines with miraculous effects (The Gioi, 1993). Predating Linnaeus, Tue Tinh's books describe 499 medicinal plants and their medical qualities and group 3,873 medical formulas into ten specialties (The Gioi, 1993). This work led to a proliferation of followers, including Lan Ong (1720–1791) in the eighteenth century. Lan Ong developed the work of his master by documenting more than three hundred "recipes" or prescriptions consisting solely of medicinal herbs. Today, a street in the old town of Hanoi named after him can be found.

Traditional medicine underwent assault in the nineteenth and twentieth centuries with the arrival of French colonialists and their imposition of Western medical ideologies over the Vietnamese peoples. Claimed to be nonscientific, traditional medicine doctors were barred from practice. With the decline in trained traditional doctors, poorly qualified herbalists created a bad name for herbal treatments. During the wars with France and the United States in Vietnam, access to modern medicines was severely limited, resulting in herbal medicines becoming once again the frontline treatment for most medical conditions. After the 1945 August Revolution, which put an end to eighty years of French colonial domination,[2] traditional medicine gradually became institutionalized, due largely to the appeals of Ho Chi Minh. The Constitution of 1945 explicitly declares the national commitment to traditional medicine (Article 39). There is even a government mandate that states, "Forty per cent of all patients must be treated with medicinal plants, 35 species must be cultivated which treat seven disorders; each commune has to reserve more than half a hectare for the cultivation of medicinal plants; each person must be able to identify 5–10 medicinal plants and is required to use them for his health" (The Gioi, 1993: 31). In addition, the existence of numerous research centers, state-owned, herb-based pharmaceutical companies, and the Traditional Medicine Association of Vietnam, with more than 20,000 members, suggests both the material and symbolic importance of traditional herbal medicine in the Vietnamese culture, health care system, and national identity. Recently, there has been a return shift to medicinal herbs as the basis for pharmaceutical development, as well as for homeopathic and phytomedicines, both domestically and internationally.

Medicinal plants grow predominantly in the North and in the NMR, a region inhabited largely by ethnic minorities (11.2 million people today) who have a wealth of knowledge about medicinal plant species, their location, methods for collection and processing, and recipes for healing. It is estimated that hundreds of thousands of people are dependent on the medicinal plant industry for employment (Luong Van Tien, 1991: 13) and that more than 30 percent of the population is directly dependent on forest resources in some capacity. According to C. Rake et al. (1993), 70 percent of the medicinal plants traded in the market originates from ethnic minority communities; only 30 percent is collected from forest farms. Income generated from trade of nontimber forest products, including medicinal plants, often exceeds income derived from the sale of agricultural products such as rice (de Beer, 1993). Today, the highlands of Vietnam supply more than 557 pharmaceutical products and 458 essential oils to the Vietnamese economy (Nguyen Trong Dieu, 1995.) Yet it is unclear how economic liberalization policies and programs may affect the long-term ecological and economic viability of the industry, particularly for upland peoples, women, and the environment.

THE MARKET STRUCTURE AND ROLE OF WOMEN IN THE MEDICINAL PLANT INDUSTRY

Very little documentation acknowledges the fundamental role women play in the market for medicinal herbs and the reproduction of traditional herbal medicine historically. Yet during preliminary research conducted during December 1995 and autumn 1996, I observed that collectors, processors, and traders along the entire chain were predominantly women and that the production end of the medicinal market was largely dominated by ethnic minority women. Most of the exchanges I observed in the lowland urban areas were conducted by middlewomen of the ethnic Kinh group. These observations were drawn from market survey data collected with the help of researchers from the Center for Natural Resource and Environmental Studies (CRES), the

Center for Research and Development of Ethnomedicinal Plants (CREDEP), and the Forestry Inventory Planning Institute (FIPI) in two urban and suburban markets (Hanoi and Ninh Hiep), two midland markets (Ba Vi and Hoa Binh), and two highland markets (Lao Cai and Lai Chau).

In a market survey in Hanoi, respondents stated that medicinal plants grow primarily in the northern and northwestern mountainous provinces of Hoa Binh, Hai Hung, Nge An, Thanh Hoa, Cao Banh, Lang Son, Son La, Hai Phong, Lai Chau, Moc Chau, Lao Cai (Sapa), Ha Tay (Ba Vi), and Nam Ha. People of the ethnic minority groups as well as some Kinh collect the plants, some of which grow wild; others are managed according to traditional customs from forests or communally held land. Often, the collectors (primarily women) and their families do the initial processing, such as slicing roots and stems and leaves, drying them in the sun and over fire, and storing them in paper and plastic bags in homes. Proper storage in a dry place is essential to minimize postharvest loss due to mold, insect infestation, and the like. It is therefore crucial to have access to a house to engage in this business.

Some of the herbs are kept for local treatment by traditional healers at the village level, many of whom are women. Within the Dao[3] culture, for example, there is a clear gender division of healing. The men are the shamans in the community who perform ritualistic ceremonies for rites of passage, for healing people's spirits, and the like. The women, in contrast, are the herbalists who treat a multitude of illnesses and provide preventive tonic medicines derived from complex mixtures of several medicinal plants. A common treatment for stomachache, for example, may include up to twenty different plants and plant parts. Specialized knowledge of medicinal plants and herbal remedies appears to be predominantly held by women, which may provide them a source of power for negotiation in the future. Knowledge of plant medicines used to "cleanse" the body postpartum, or to control or space births, has peaked the interest of urban pharmacologists. However, many herbalists refuse to disclose their secret recipes. One herbalist expressed concern that her birth-control treatment, if used improperly, could have profound negative effects on humankind (Tran Thi Que, 1996).

In addition to being used for treatment locally, many of the herbs are sold by women at the local market or directly to "trading houses" or shops run by ethnic Vietnamese in the town center. Sometimes, local women travel outside the district to sell plants. Women traders from Hanoi, China, and sometimes even southern provinces come to these mountainous villages to purchase bulk quantities of botanical medicines. In some cases, for instance, where herbs are grown in provinces closer to Hanoi, such as Hai Hung and Ba Vi, local women transport herbs by bus and by car to markets in Hanoi and to a special village outside Hanoi called Ninh Hiep.

Ninh Hiep, approximately twenty kilometers north of Hanoi, is a legendary center for processing and trading in medicinal plants. Ninh Hiep is an unusual town with a long history of specialized involvement in the medicinal plant trade that is attributed to a woman named Ly Thai Lao, originally from Thanh Hoa Province. Ly Thai Lao, as the legend goes, recognized the intelligence of the people of Ninh Hiep and therefore decided to settle there and teach the citizens of Ninh Hiep how to use medicinal plants. The symbolic importance of this woman is reflected in a temple that was built in her honor. The temple has become a meeting place where the traditional medicine association of Ninh Hiep holds its monthly programs. It is also a place in which her image hangs proudly on the wall, where daily incense offerings to the "goddess" reaffirm the town's identity in the medicinal plant sector. Inside, on the altar, there is a sign: "We will remember you forever" and "Traditional medicine will develop forever."

Although the cultural importance of medicinal plants in Ninh Hiep remains strong, production and exchange relations around medicinals in general have changed due to changing ecologies and market opportunities. In the past, forests surrounding Ninh Hiep supplied plants for medicine. Today, for Thuoc Bac, or northern (Chinese), medicine preparations, herbs are imported from China; for Thuoc Nam, or southern (Vietnamese), traditional medicine, plants are purchased from numerous northern provinces, such as Lao Cai, Thanh Hoa, Hai Bac, Yen Bai, and others listed above. The emergent traders who travel to the China border to purchase herbs, and those who market processed herbs from Ninh Hiep to Lan Ong Street in Hanoi, are women. It is the women, I was told, who market the plants to and from China and Hanoi while their husbands stay at home and work on the farm, take care of the children, and engage in handicrafts and leatherworks. This is because of the fear that the men would spend all their earnings from the trade before it reached home.

There are domestic as well as international consumption ends for this market, including Hanoi, Saigon, China, and numerous other foreign markets such as Taiwan, Korea, and, increasingly, Europe. Second to the town of Ninh Hiep, Lan Ong Street in Hanoi is the most well-known historical market for medicinal herbs in the North. According to the tradespeople on the street, there are more than one hundred vendors, many of whom are women and all of whom run their businesses out of the ground floors of their homes. Adequate space for secondary processing and storage is vital at this stage of the market. Security in housing is key to ensure stability in the market. If, as in the case with land titling (see Chapter 5), the businesses are titled in the name of the male head of household, then the woman's entitlements to her fair share of the company in the event of divorce, death, and other misfortune are precarious. The next section will discuss more specifically how the effects of particular policies under *doi moi* are creating new opportunities and constraints for women in the market and threaten the sustainable supply of particular medicinal plants.

THE DISSOLUTION AND RE-CREATION OF POLITICAL BOUNDARIES AND ECONOMIC CONTROL

Since 1986, the Vietnamese government initiated a series of *doi moi* (economic renovation) policies in an attempt to fuel industrialization and development of the Vietnamese economy. Three sets of policies in particular have had an immediate and significant impact, particularly along gender lines, on the opportunities and constraints for people residing in the highlands. The policies are: (1) the reduction in government subsidies for education, health care, and the like; (2) trade and market liberalization; and (3) decentralization of land and forest ownership/management, titling both agricultural and forest land to individual household heads. These policies and associated programs have resulted in an increased demand for and supply of botanical medicine, profound changes in land tenure relations along gender lines, changes in land use practices and cover, criminalization of certain land use practices, and changes in housing structures.

The reduction of government subsidies for modern health care, combined with trade liberalization, caused a pronounced increase in demand for and extraction of medicinal herbs from the NMR to meet national health care objectives as well as export targets. Due to the sheer cost of Western medicine and its treatment regime, many Vietnamese, particularly in rural areas, have shifted back to traditional botanical medicine. A bed, for example, in a Western-style hospital costs $4–7 per day, while at the Central Traditional Medical Institute it costs less than $1 (*Vietnam News,* 1998). With an estimated GNP per capita at $200, this discrepancy is significant. Domestic pharmaceutical companies are exploring new leads for drug development, including conducting studies on traditional herbal remedies. A recent article stated that "the demand for herbal materials for use in modern medicines has increased from 20–30 percent to 40–60 percent in the past 10 years" (*Economic Times,* 1997). During the period 1986–1990, export targets of medicinal herbs were to generate $6 million of revenue for the state (Shiva, 1990). At only a few dollars per kilogram at market price for medicinal herbs, this increase in demand has tremendous potential to decimate the supply through overharvesting. Although there are some species that are now being intensively cultivated under government programs to meet this high demand, many are still being collected from the wild or from areas where plants have not been intensively cultivated. Secure tenurial rights provide greater incentive to cultivate medicinals for long-term supply.

Trade liberalization has restructured the social organization of the medicinal plant market as well. With the opening of the market, about ten years ago, gathering in marketplaces was again legalized. At the Kim Boi market in Hoa Binh, for example, the women interviewed used to travel for two to three days, with a pack on their backs filled with herbs, to Lang Son, Nam Ha, Thai

Binh, Quang Linh, coastal areas, and so on to sell their plants. However, since markets were legalized, some sixty or eighty women now sit in an open marketplace once a week; buyers, primarily from Ha Tay and the coastal provinces, come to purchase plants directly from them. As a result, women of the neighboring province in essence have taken over as middlewomen for the women of Kim Boi market, freeing up time for leisure activities for the latter.

The opening of international borders has also resulted in a tremendous surge of people participating in the medicinal trade and flow of plants beyond nation-state boundaries. Traders from both Ninh Hiep and Hanoi expressed an increase in participation rates and volumes traded domestically and with China during the past ten years. Taiwanese, Chinese, and other foreign businessmen have begun placing orders for large volumes of specific medicinal plants. One seller in Sapa said that four or five years ago a Taiwanese businessman requested such a large volume of co nhung and co hoa plants that populations of those plants are now difficult to find in the region. Although the government is attempting to regulate import-export flows of goods, Rake et al. estimate that 70 percent of the total collection and sale of medicinal plants is carried out through undocumented across-the-border sales. With providers being ill-prepared for such an increase in demand, an intensification of harvesting is threatening the ecological populations of some of the rarer and most valuable medicinal plants.

Land allocation, a third element of economic liberalization, has resulted in women's traditional rights to land being undermined through the legalization of land rights with title in the male head of household's name (Grady, 1996; Schenk-Sandbergen, 1996). This is legitimized through the allocation and administration of land use certificates, thereby securing long-term legal rights in land to the male head of household in both rural and urban areas. The process of allocation in itself is inherently biased toward male, Kinh-speaking populations. Women in the highlands rarely participate in the process of land allocation, because they are not informed about the policies and process of land allocation generally and, in some cases, are excluded outright. Ethnic minority women often do not speak the Kinh language of the government authorities in charge of the allocation process. One of the land allocation officials expressed the overall bias to an Oxfam UK mission: "The head of the household is the man because he makes the decisions in the family" (OXFAM, 1996). Men, as a result, have the ultimate ownership rights and power to decide how the land is used. Depending on the nature of intrahousehold negotiations, a woman may see her choice of land use converted into some other use that is preferred by her husband.

Title in land is important not only for security purposes in the event of divorce, long-term out-migration, and death but also for access to government services and credit programs, status in community, and the like (Agarwal, 1997). As men increasingly migrate to urban centers for work, it is becoming particularly important for women to have equal formal rights of landowner-ship, as women increasingly are left with the responsibility of land manage-ment. For the purpose of access to and control over medicinal plants, power to decide how land is used may be linked to formal ownership title as evidenced by other countries. This may become critical as government programs—to en-hance the productivity of land—encourage conversion of lands away from fallow, communal, and food crops and toward cash crop and plantation forestry.

In an effort to fuel the economy, the Vietnam government is encouraging new landowners to "regreen barren lands" through cash crop production and reforestation initiatives, such as those outlined in Decree 327.[4] So-called bar-ren lands are often communal or fallow lands that are vital to meeting house-hold needs, particularly during times of crisis. Women in particular rely on these lands to meet household nutrition, health, housing, and fiber needs (Agarwal, 1994; Fortmann and Rocheleau, 1985; Hecht et al., 1988; Kun-stadter et al., 1978). Few ecological studies have been conducted to determine the exact location of medicinal herbs in Vietnam. But evidence from other Southeast Asian countries clearly shows the abundance of medicinal plants and trees grown on so-called barren land or wasteland (Agarwal, 1997; Caron, 1995; Hoskins, 1982). Converting this land to monocrop fruit and tim-ber crops may result not only in a decline of access by poor women-headed households but also may result in furthering the destruction of medicinal plant habitat, threatening not only urban supplies but local consumption of medicinal plants—often the only line of health care.

National parks, which would seem to conserve natural resources ulti-mately in the interest of the state, provide a somewhat different example of how national policies create boundaries between people and resources that traditionally have played an important role in providing supplementary foods, shelter, fuelwood, and medicines for the community's well-being. The Dao in Ba Vi, who were relocated off the mountain when it was designated a national park in 1973, were allocated insufficient land to meet their food needs. As a result, members of the communities intensified collection and sale of medici-nal herbs and firewood from the park itself to generate cash for food. In essence, the criminalization of their traditional land use practices has resulted in fines being imposed when caught gathering within the boundaries of the park, yet gathering continues. The Muong of Hoa Binh and the Kinh in Ninh Hiep cited similar reasons for increased participation in the medicinal market: insufficient agricultural land. Although formal access is denied, we see women and men engaging in everyday forms of resistance (Scott, 1985) to obtain the necessary plants and other forest products to meet subsistence needs. Both processes of land tenure change (decollectivization and establish-ment of national parks) to increase productivity and conserve biodiversity have, in essence, created barriers to the well-being of rural poor families, shifting the burden to the poorest of the poor—and to the environment itself. If officials granted local villagers access rights to harvest medicinal plants from the park, incentives to harvest more sustainably might just ensure long-term productivity. Allocating title to land in buffer zones may also provide incentives to cultivate medicinal plants and harvest sustainably (see Sowerwine et al., 1998, for more discussion).

Lastly, intensification of the market for medicinals is increasingly reflected in the built environment, modes of transport, and communication. In specific localities of medicinal plant processing and trade, one can see a proliferation of new buildings, with the construction year (mostly between 1988 and today) embedded in the front wall. Interview respondents consistently talked about how new lines of communications and transportation have made the trade of medicinal herbs more efficient and more intensified. As Ms. Nam, a Kinh woman of Ninh Hiep, said, "With improved communication technology, shipments of lotus seeds arrive quickly and easily from Cambodia to HCM city to Ninh Hiep." Ms. Lan, a Dao woman of Ba Vi, concurred: "I used to have to treat patients by carrying a bundle of plants on my back, and traveling house to house, I would be gone for up to three weeks. Now, with improved roads and a car that I was able to purchase, I am able to treat patients as far away as Hanoi, Thai Binh, and Thanh Hoa provinces. I also can bring many more plants with me on each trip."

CONCLUSION

The reduction of central state control over resource management decisions, including the shift of unit of production from the cooperative to the household, giving title to men, combined with the reduction in state subsidies in education, health, agriculture, and other areas, appears to be shifting resources and benefits to men. Since liberalization, however, new markets and increased demand for medicinal plants have provided numerous women of both highland minority and midland Kinh communities higher incomes that may even translate into new sources of power. However, as the preceding section points out, government policies designed to increase land productivity (land titling, reforestation, cash crop promotion) may undermine not only women's access to and control over the resource base but also the resource base itself, as state-supported monocropping patterns compete with local practice of medicinal plant cultivation. Overharvesting is another threat, as lowland agents representing state pharmaceutical companies and foreign interests (Taiwan and Hong Kong) broker deals with local government officials to harvest all of a certain species, leaving insufficient material for regeneration.

Trade liberalization is also changing the structure of the market, as medicinal plants are being imported in greater quantities than before. Will Chinese plants substitute for particular domestic plants and lead to greater specialization in both China and Vietnam? How will it affect rural women involved in the market? Successful efforts by women to negotiate access to medicinal plants may reveal the importance of informal networks of social and political capital (Berry, 1994, 1993, 1989; Verdery, 1996) necessary to guarantee women's continued and increasing prominence in the market. Innovation in cultivation and innovation in processing techniques present two means of adding value by which women in the northern upland and urban centers may be capturing benefits from the burgeoning market of medicinals. Rights, whether formal or informal, to land and housing are key elements necessary for women to maximize the potential benefits derived from the marketing of medicinals.

Assuming that decisionmaking authority goes hand in hand with legal title, providing women equal or independent title in land is therefore crucial to ensuring women's continued role in the medicinal plant industry, meeting both reproductive and productive goals. As Bina Agarwal demonstrates in her work (1997), the assistance of "gender-sensitive" nongovernmental organizations (NGOs) can be helpful in facilitating women's ability to gain rights in land, to access goods and services that are often denied propertyless women, and to provide a forum through which women can share ideas and become more assertive in making claims. In Vietnam, for example, NGOs, in conjunction with the Women's Union, could lobby for women's individual rights in land, regardless of marital status, provide women with small-scale loans for land improvement, and provide training in sustainable production of medicinal herbs.

Although there have been some recent efforts by a consortium of international NGOs and bilateral aid organizations[5] to discuss the effects of land allocation on the poor, representatives from Action Aid said there was no explicit emphasis on gender disaggregated analysis. Oxfam UK, however, has been conducting some investigations in the northern province of Lao Cai, looking at the gendered allocation of land use certificates. Intrahousehold decisionmaking with respect to land use, allocation of labor, and access to capital and other government services along gender lines are areas of possible future research that will shed light on the ways in which women are negotiating access to and control over medicinal plant resources and the benefits derived from their trade.

The collection of medicinal plants from the NMR has provided a significant livelihood for local women and has contributed tremendously to national health care needs since time immemorial (Son, 1996; Tran Thi Lanh, 1996; Nguyen, 1990). Since 1986, changes in land rights, market opportunities, and highland development strategies promulgated by the government are creating new land use patterns and access regimes threatening the long-term supply of medicinal plants and, consequently, women's status and income derived from the trade.

Decollectivization and allocation of land to individual households and ti-tling of land to the (most often) male head of household are processes that shift formal land tenure rights toward men and create new, gendered patterns of land use. Government-sponsored reforestation and cash crop projects in mountainous highland areas are now competing with existing land uses, in-cluding swidden agriculture and medicinal plant production. These develop-ments raise important questions about the effects of economic renovation policies, particularly about changes in land tenure and concurrent land use programs on the long-term sustainability of medicinal plant supply as well as women's sustained participation within the market.

NOTES

1. The ethnic Kinh comprise 87 percent of the population and reside mainly in the lowlands delta regions.

2. It wasn't until 1954, at the Battle of Dien Bien Phu, that the French forces were defeated and French occupation came to an end.

3. The Dao (pronounced "Zao") are the ninth largest of the fifty-three ethnic groups in Vietnam, numbering 475,000. Other names used to describe the Dao are Iu Mien, Mien, and Yao.

4. See Sikor (1994) for a good description of this policy.

5. These included Action Aid, Care, GTZ, Oxfam Belgium, Oxfam UK, and SIDA.

PART TWO

Laos

8

Gender and Changing Property Rights in Laos

Carol Ireson-Doolittle

Male-dominated political and economic systems may be subverting women's traditional and constitutional rights in the Lao People's Democratic Republic as land is formally registered in the name of the "head of household" (see Chapter 9). Land allocation and titling processes are part of a broader social and economic change to integrate Laos into regional and global capitalist economies.[1] Laos has experienced dramatic social and economic changes since 1975, when it was united under a victorious communist government allied with Vietnam and the Soviet Union. These changes have had different impacts among the people of Laos that comprise the various ethnic communities and may reinforce women's secondary status to the detriment of women, their children, and community cohesion. The lowland Lao women will be particularly affected if traditional matrilineal rights are eroded by the introduction of a single set of laws for the country. Women who are able to exercise control over economic resources are active and effective builders of family, village, and community well-being in Laos, as elsewhere. The abrogation of women's property rights may leave families and communities in disarray during a turbulent time of social and economic transformation.

HISTORICAL SKETCH

The impact of change occurring in Laos today can best be understood in the context of earlier turbulence in this small country. During the eleven-year American War that polarized this tiny country, the Pathet Lao (communist) formed a stable government in December 1975 by forming a coalition with their former rival, the Royalists. The war had devastated the country: Upwards of one-third of the population was displaced from homes; unexploded ordnance littered farm and forest lands; and about 10 percent of the population, including most educated Laotians, fled into exile during the early years of communist rule (Ireson and Ireson, 1989). Women's resourcefulness had been sorely tested during the war. Some women lived in caves to avoid the bombings, cultivating fields at night or working in government offices or hospitals during the day. Other women took the place of absent men, guiding family-owned buffalo in plowing and harrowing. Still other women, not knowing male agricultural skills, obtained meager assistance from relatives or migrated to towns to earn their living with their bodies in the flourishing wartime sex trade (Ireson, 1996). Rural landownership at this time was based on use rights and customary inheritance practices, which varied by ethnic group.

Communists initially brought a rigid, centrally controlled model of communism to the newly reestablished country. Villagers who did not choose to flee returned to the land, rebuilding and establishing once again a mixed-subsistence economy based on paddy and hillside agriculture, animal husbandry, and forest foraging, though the land was now officially owned by the new government. Zealous government cadres organized paddy farmers into collective work groups and then into villagewide cooperatives. In cooperatives that actually functioned, women received work points in their own names, though they often received less for a day's work than did men. Individual marketing was politically incorrect, so lowland Lao market women and other marketers[2] stopped buying and selling, leaving many villagers with no market for their goods. Production fell as people produced only for their own use (Ireson, 1996).

Urban dwellers, including civil servants and students, planted large gardens around their homes and public buildings to provide for their own needs. The new government, a one-party state that ruled by decree, struggled with socialist production organizations (village agriculture cooperatives and state-owned enterprises), marketing arrangements (state stores ostensibly linked to village cooperative stores), and schooling, but many of these organizations and arrangements proved inefficient, ineffective, and culturally inappropriate.

The process of implementing socialism, however, did solidify socialist rule throughout the country and did establish at least a few grades of school in many remote villages. People's hard work and government efforts did successfully reestablish normal social life for most people. Ethnic minorities were more recognized by the new government than by previous regimes and were more integrated into national life. The new government declared that men and women should enjoy equal rights and delegated the task of women's emancipation to a mass organization, the Women's Union. Governance during the early years was by national policies and decrees unevenly implemented by state and local Party and government officials according to their own interpretations. Costs for running the government and reconstruction at that time were almost entirely financed by other communist states, as systems of taxation were poorly developed, the country and most of its citizens were impoverished, and capitalist and Western governments were viewed with suspicion.

INTRODUCING A MARKET ECONOMY

With the creation of perestroika and glasnost in the Soviet Union, Laos began to experiment with its own version of "opening." The Friendship Market, established on an island in the Mekong River between Thailand and Laos in 1985, opened a period of sporadic small-scale trade with Thailand. The Fourth Party Congress in 1986 fashioned the New Economic Mechanism to stimulate the domestic economy, to increase the monetization of the market, and to broaden international trade facilitating Laos's entry into the regional economy. As Lao officialdom sought wider participation in the modern world, it began to create a Lao version of the modern state, with governance by law rather than by decree, and the establishment of a judiciary rather than depending on people's courts.

The Investment Code of 1988 was followed by numerous other laws institutionalizing elements of individual ownership. The demise of the Soviet Union gave further impetus to Laos's cautious opening to international trade, aid, and investment. Local entrepreneurship was once again legitimated during the mid-1980s, though in fits and starts. State and local governments began to document and arbitrate customary land use rights by determining the boundaries of land and forest areas available for use by villagers in each village. Throughout the country the transportation and communications infrastructures are being expanded and upgraded.

Today, external economic and political forces are sweeping over this small nation, listed by the United Nations as among the least developed (see Bourdet, 1997, for details). International aid organizations multilateral, bilateral, and nongovernmental—are growing in number and importance; increasingly, regional companies are seeking permits to do business in Laos. Laos's regional economic participation has recently been certified by admission to the Association of Southeast Asian Nations (ASEAN), the major regional forum for intergovernmental cooperation (Stuart-Fox, 1998). As Western consultants, international bank officials, Japanese aid workers, and Thai businesspeople promote rapid economic transition toward a market economy in ways that they think will benefit both Laos and their own profits, ordinary Laotians are increasingly impacted by these external forces.

Recent developments in Laos demonstrate the ease with which customary, individual, and even village rights to land can be abrogated when corporate profits and foreign exchange earnings are at stake. Both commercial logging practices and hydropower projects illustrate this disregard for customary rights. Land use customs vary somewhat throughout the country, but in general, village heads and administrative committees are responsible for planning and monitoring land and forest uses in their areas and for mediating land disputes. Since neither the village nor individual citizens have clear title to the land that they oversee and use, they have no legal means to control use (or misuse) of this land by outsiders (Rigg and Jerndal, 1996: 160). So, without any notice and compensation, a village's foraging forest may be logged, devastating both forest and watercourses in the area, as I discovered during a study of village forest use in 1989. The logging company in question harmed an important aspect of the village economy as company loggers damaged, destroyed, and extracted trees, wild foods, medicinal products, and other non-timber forest products used by villagers in their everyday lives (Ireson, 1989, summarized in Ireson, 1996: 182).

Dozens of hydropower projects have been considered for Mekong tributaries in Laos. By 1994, contracts and memoranda of understanding had been signed for twenty-two such projects (Hirsch, 1996: 214). The impact on villagers in the dam area is barely considered in the plans. One observer of Lao dam project decisionmaking enumerates the many actors in the process: the Lao government, northern-based construction and equipment companies, the World Bank, bilateral aid agencies, the Mekong River Commission, private consulting firms, nongovernmental advocacy groups, and journalists. She notes that Lao citizens most affected by these projects, however, are not included.

Sadly, the one group that has so far had little influence on the hydrodam discussion in Laos is the rural villagers whose subsistence is derived from a combination of rain-fed agriculture, hunting, fishing, and gathering from the forests. Hydropower will affect such communities directly by inundating their fields and homes, wiping out their fish stocks, blocking river transport routes, and destroying their forests—in short, undermining their primary sources of food, medicine, and income. "The political clout of these rural people is not likely to increase for many years to come" (Usher, 1996: 126).

Philip Hirsch underscores this lack of effective compensation for impacted citizens. Dam schemes in Laos are designed mainly to provide electricity to Thailand as well as foreign exchange for the Lao government as Laos becomes part of an emerging regional resource economy driven by Thai economic activity. These national and international interests quickly redefine the legitimacy, or lack of it, that local people possess with respect to legal recognition of claims over their livelihood base. Without formal, legal ownership of the land and water that forms the basis for their livelihoods, local people are unable to resist the more powerful national and international interests pressing for dam construction and are equally unable to secure compensation for the loss of their homes and livelihoods. Though some villagers may be offered a resettlement option, the schemes are unlikely to compensate local people for the loss of access to rich common-property resources (Hirsch, 1996: 219).

An exception to this disregard for consulting with local people is Swed-Forest, which has specific directives to stimulate participatory development and encourage sensitivity to gender issues. Unfortunately, many of the project directors still think of land allocation as a family issue and don't realize that it makes a difference whether women sign the contract along with their husbands (interview in Vientiane, June 1997).

IMPACT ON WOMEN'S TRADITIONAL PROPERTY RIGHTS

In a context where customary land rights are often disregarded, it is not too surprising that women's customary rights to land might also be ignored. Current land allocation and titling processes are occurring in response to pressure and funding from multilateral lending agencies and bilateral Western aid donors. The governmental departments actually allocating land and creating model land-titling pilot projects are among the most sexist of the departments in a widely male-dominated government, as recounted in this volume. For example, all-male teams from the strongly male-dominated Department of Forestry register household land, including the land inherited by the wife from her parents, in the name of the "head of the household," who is always understood to be male unless there is no adult male in the household.

Buffeted by these winds of change, women's customary and constitutional rights are at risk. Organizations and institutions that might protect and support women's customary rights and improve the position of women in patriarchal ethnic groups exist but are not powerful or are in the early stages of development. These include the Lao Women's Union and the Ministry of Justice, both of which have attempted to insert gender sensitivity into the Land Law and Forest Law, seemingly to no avail. Educational systems, which might eventually enable women to understand and challenge laws and practices that maintain their secondary status, are still primitive, with few supplies, poorly paid teachers, a curriculum still under development, and incomplete coverage in rural and especially minority areas. Even if these systems were strong and well developed, however, women of different ethnic groups would have differential access to them based on their power and autonomy in their own cultures.

ETHNIC DIFFERENCES

Among the lowland Lao, for example, the child who stays home to care for her elderly parents usually inherits the house and much of the paddy land. This child is commonly the youngest daughter. When she marries, her husband moves into her household (Ireson and Ireson, 1993). Ethnic Lao women also carry out a number of economic activities, some of them independently of their husbands. These women collect, cultivate, and craft products from forests, fields, and raw materials for both family use and for sale. Some of these women regularly engage in trade and businesses. Once family needs are met, most lowland Lao women are free to keep the money they earn. Many choose to buy additional goods for their families and to reinvest in their ongoing economic activities. The level of autonomy associated with these resources enables these women to make some of their own decisions and to participate with a strong voice in family decisions. Economically resourceful women are also able to augment their families' well-being, contribute to the local temple, and indirectly influence village matters. More recently, women with economic resources have been able to send their children to school and to choose to limit the size of their families (Ireson, 1996).

Land inheritance and landownership by women is an important component of lowland Lao women's autonomy, power, and effectiveness. Traditional inheritance and ownership patterns have also shaped the social, economic, and political networks that enable villages to function effectively. Since usually daughters inherit, lowland Lao villages commonly comprise, among others, groups of sisters or female cousins related through their aunts. A wife's relatives rather than a husband's relatives are more likely to live in the village. She, then, is central in constituting labor exchange groups, in informally negotiating solutions for village conflicts, and in contributing household resources and labor to extended family events like weddings or ordinations of sons or male relatives into the monkhood.[3]

Women of midland and upland ethnic groups have fewer customary rights and sources of autonomy than do lowland women. Midland Khmu women, for example, work very hard in all aspects of the household economy but rarely market their own produce and, therefore, do not control any income they may have generated. Most Khmu households are quite poor and own no paddy land, so most women's work directly contributes to family subsistence rather than income generation (Ireson, 1996).

The patriarchal clan structure of Hmong society, an upland minority group, allows a Hmong woman little opportunity to control her own labor or products. This situation was exacerbated by the growth of opium production encouraged by French colonists. Men work in the opium fields and sell this lucrative product, but women's continuous labor is essential for optimal opium production. One researcher believes that the economic importance of opium production distorted the already strongly male-dominated husband-wife relationship so that it became much more a relationship between a boss and a laborer (Tapp, 1989).

If the gender equality enshrined in the constitution were enforced, both Khmu and Hmong women might be able to gradually improve their subordinate position. Recently, new economic opportunities and the model provided by lowland women have inspired some Khmu and even Hmong women to market their own products. However, allocating land to male household heads, and formally giving household heads land title, only reinforce the already subservient position of midland and upland women. Potential social benefits often accruing from women's autonomy and equality with men, like additional economic resources from her economic activities, smaller family size, and increased likelihood of daughters' attending school, are thereby lost.

POOR WOMEN, THEIR FAMILIES, AND PROPERTY

Formalizing property rights has a variety of implications for Laotian society in the future. The current ways of carrying out property registration seem to have especially negative impacts on women. Registration of property with individuals or households facilitates the purchase and sale of property. Some new landowners are already selling their land and heading into the hills to build on and cultivate "unowned" land. If this response is widespread, desirable land is likely to concentrate in the hands of people who already are well-off, while the seller-migrants are likely to increase the overall level of hillside slash-and-burn fields (swidden) with negative environmental consequences.[4]

Other displaced farmers migrate into urban areas for employment. Few former farmers are likely to have the skills needed by modern businesses, so they may swell the ranks of the urban unemployed. Laos has few of the urban squatter slum settlements common in much of the urban Third World, but the commodification of land and the subsequent mechanization of agriculture may introduce some of the same "pushes" for urban migration experienced throughout the urban Third World.

Poor women of all groups may see their workloads increase without any ability to improve their situations. Some villagers with access to the reconstructed north-south Route 13 in the Paksane area have already sold their now-valuable land. When men sell the household land, they may use the resulting capital to begin a new business (trucking, for example); women who sell off their land no longer have access to farmland. If they have no capital to open a business and do not receive the benefits from their husbands' businesses, they must become agricultural laborers or move into the hills to cultivate high-labor, low-yielding swidden plots to ensure the survival of their families (Trankell, 1993). Women with customary rights to land are often the gardeners and orchardists producing for urban markets. If these women lose property rights, this high-quality agricultural land may be purchased by agribusinesses and its production converted to cash and even nonfood crops for sale regionally. Skillful gardeners who currently supply urban markets may then be supplanted by agricultural laborers cultivating cash or even nonfood crops for export, affecting the quantity and the quality of food available for domestic consumption.

In summary, the form and process of creating a "modern" type of ownership currently being undertaken in Laos may institutionalize marked gender inequality despite constitutional guarantees for equality. Furthermore, these overall changes in the structure of the agricultural system may have a variety of other negative consequences.

NOTES

1. A nation without private property is not inviting to investors or Western-dominated multilateral lending agencies. The poverty of Laos's government following the demise of its Soviet-bloc sponsors forces it to seek outside capital to support its operations.

2. A number of expatriate merchants left Laos with the change in government. These included Chinese and South Asian merchant families.

3. The ordination ceremony involves arranging for food and ritual events, providing, perhaps weaving, the yards and yards of cloth needed for the monk's robes, and other uses. Traditionally, a woman's willingness to pay the costs of ordination determined whether a young man could become a monk (Lefferts, 1993). Such sponsorship earned spiritual merit for the woman.

4. Some longtime swidden cultivators like the Khmu have developed environmentally sustainable swidden systems, but these systems require careful attention to sustainable cultivation practices and a long fallow period (see Tayanin, 1994). New swidden cultivators are unacquainted with these cultivation practices, and even the Khmu cannot sustain their traditional system when population density forces farmers to reuse fallow fields after just a few years, the common situation in most parts of the country today.

9

Reforming Property Rights in Laos

Manivone Viravong

Lowland Lao women's power and decisionmaking ability in the home contrast strongly with their lack of power outside the home. This contrast has set the stage for their loss of traditional property rights as male-dominated governmental agencies formally allocate and register land use rights. This chapter introduces Lao women's traditional rights in land and discusses how recent history and current government policies and practices may be undermining lowland Lao women's traditional property rights and most likely reducing their decisionmaking power in the home and community. It concludes with a discussion of strategies to avoid these negative effects.

LAND ALLOCATION, LAND TITLING, AND CHANGING LAND RIGHTS

Laos is landlocked, ringed by five countries: China, Vietnam, Cambodia, Thailand, and Myanmar. Primarily a mountainous country, its poor infrastructure results in limited access to rural areas, where four-fifths of the people live, and makes communications among the various ethnic groups and between local and central administrative levels extremely difficult. One of the least populated countries in the region (only 4.6 million people), population density is about 17 persons per square kilometer (CPC, 1995a). As much as 60 percent of its area is considered forest, although shifting cultivation practices and new forest industries are reducing forest cover (CPC, 1995b). Most of the arable land is found along the banks of the Mekong River and its main tributaries, where lowland Lao, who are predominantly matrilineal by tradition, settled and have lived for centuries. The types of geographic divisions also categorize the different ethnographic composition of the country: lowland Lao (Lao Lum) live mainly along the Mekong River and on the nearby plains; midland Lao (Lao Theung, including Akha, Khmu, etc.) live in the slopes of mountains and in the plateaus; highland Lao (Lao Sung, including Hmong and Mien) live high on the mountain ridges. Lowland Lao comprise more than half of the population of Laos and are the focus of this chapter.

Tradition, Land Rights, and Socialism

Prior to 1975, Western-influenced governments adopted a mixture of feudal land tenure and the French legal system of land administration. During that period, land was by and large owned by royal families (northern and southern), though villagers in many parts of the country lived on and worked their land with little royal interference. The Free Lao movement and subsequently the Pathet Lao were created by a number of people who detested royal rule, colonialism, and foreign domination. It was a popular movement that involved all classes of people; women could participate and had equal opportunities and rights. The Pathet Lao became the government of the entire Lao People's Democratic Republic in 1975. Until the recent enactment of decrees and laws, land was owned by the government in the name of the people, but cooperatives and households had unsecured rights to use the land. Traditional land tenure and inheritance patterns were still practiced among some lowland Lao. After 1975, however, official land redistribution schemes and use by cooperatives often superseded traditional land rights.

Women's customary domestic power among the lowland Lao has been exercised politically by women of the royal family in the past. In the fourteenth century, the queen and later queen mother, Keo Nhotfa (highest sky princess) and Keo Thevi (highest queen), was the most powerful, influential, and intelligent queen and monarch the Kingdom of a Million Elephants ever had. She was the daughter of the king of Angkor (a Khmer king) who was given to King Fangum, adopted son of the same king, before sending him back to the Kingdom of Lan Xang (a major kingdom in Laos during the thirteenth and sixteenth centuries). She reigned with her husband and helped to transform many laws for the assurance of position for women and to the general benefit of Lao women. This may be the origin of the current matrilineal social organization of lowland Lao society. After her husband died, she became reigning queen for some time before her son, King Samsenthai, ascended to the throne. The period of King Samsenthai's reign witnessed the most prosperous epoch of the Lan Xang kingdom. She drafted many laws and created many traditional rules and practices that gave Lao women powerful positions and legitimate rights and created honor and respect for women within the family and in society at large. Because of her intelligence and her deep comprehension of family as well as of public affairs, she was, as the first woman monarch, able to change royal inheritance, giving daughters the right to succession of the throne that formerly had been reserved for sons only.

For lowland Lao, the birth of a daughter is a relief and an assurance to the parents as she will, for sure, be the one who will stay home and look after them in their old age. Consequently, inheritance passes on to the daughters, particularly the youngest one, who will usually reside in the parental home and inherit at least the home, if not most of the parents' properties. A wedding ceremony normally takes place at the bride's home, because, traditionally, the groom will have to move to the bride's home after marriage. The couple will live there until they can build their own house, normally not far away from the wife's parents' home. However, if the wife is the only daughter of the family or the youngest, the couple will usually reside permanently with her parents. Because the husband lives in the wife's house, he has to respect his wife and her parents and family elders. If he wants to do something on the property, he has to ask permission or at least consult his wife and her parents and other family members. By tradition, he will not have any rights to the property, unless his wife agrees to give or share it with him after being granted the property from her parents. Traditionally, there is no formal registration of land and property. However, it is always understood that both husband and wife have equal rights to any common property acquired during the marriage. In the event of divorce, often the settlement will result in the wife keeping the property and the husband moving out. If the wife does not want to keep the property, she can sell it, either to her former husband or to someone else (see Ireson, 1996).

In the past, written laws have been less important to most lowland Lao families than have traditional customary rights. A middle-aged or elderly woman who has not yet passed on her inheritance is the center of domestic power and is the central pole of the family. In traditional religious ceremonies, although the old men perform the ceremonial duties, or sessions, the elderly women are the ones who sit in the middle of worshipping family members and guests and host the official ceremonial exchanges. Yet barriers still limit women's entrance into the public arena. Officials and decisionmakers are not prepared to share power with women in government institutions and in corporate establishments today—and probably for some time into the future (Ngaosyvathn, 1993).

The traditional family comprises at least three generations: grandparents, normally from the mother's side, parents, and children. Domestic affairs like food, clothing, and welfare are normally decided by the mother; farming business, house construction, and official affairs are normally discussed among adults; grandparents normally have the final say. However, the husband takes care of formal papers. This is where loopholes exist to impinge women's customary rights and may even be the starting point for abuse of power in the family that may eventually lead to further legal complications as land and property become marketable commodities.

The groundwork for this abuse of power is laid during childhood, when it is often necessary for girls to stay home and help the mother with household chores. This limits their opportunities to attend school for the long period necessary to get higher education. Girls have to care for younger brothers and sisters while the parents work. Girls have to support the welfare and well-being of the family, so they attend school for only a few years. As a consequence, girls and boys from the same family grow up with different skills and objectives in life. Education is said to be important and necessary for boys, because they have to deal with the exterior and official worlds. Women thus need not worry over the formal aspects of life; the men take care of it. However, there are different levels of divisionmaking, and the public division is always more authoritative, higher, and more influential than that of the home. Education is therefore the key to women having access to all resources, including power. The land allocation and subsequent land titling process also revolve around the accessibility to both land and to the formal land registration procedures. The ability to read, comprehend, and process a legal document is of utmost importance. If even half the women could read and write, many problems that women face in land titling today might not have happened.

The New Economic Mechanism

The New Economic Mechanism (NEM) is a cornerstone of modern Laos. Within a few years of the NEM's promulgation in 1986, the country opened up to the outside world, as the political hard line was softened and a market economy was introduced. The NEM provides the foundation for economic liberalization, foreign investment, and privatization of state-owned industries. Political and economic barriers to these activities were removed; controlled prices and production quotas were taken away. Currency was stabilized by introducing a market exchange rate, and inflation was reduced. Road construction has opened rural areas to socioeconomic change (Trankell, 1993). Reform of the public sector was also initiated to bring down government expenditures. As a result, many civil servants, especially women, left the government and entered the private sector. These women decided to forego their career opportunities for good family and financial reasons: civil servant husbands earn so little that wives and other family members must support them (Dessallien, 1991). But this shift of women out of state employment removed women from state jobs that might eventually have led to leadership positions.

The first Constitution of the Lao People's Democratic Republic was passed by parliament and officially promulgated in 1991. Since then, many urgent, crucial laws have been established to facilitate economic development and to regulate government policies and individual rights and interests. Equality between women and men has been included in the Constitution and in laws on family, inheritance, and property. However, despite these gender-related laws, women are still being treated and looked at as unequal partners, even in the areas addressed by the laws. Legal reform also started to take place soon after the introduction of the NEM, and the Ministry of Justice, along with an entire judiciary system, began to develop. A law school was created in 1989, first to train judges for the judiciary and then to offer a full law school curriculum. This institution is the first academic institution to advocate gender equality by assigning a 50 percent quota for female law students.

Decrees on Urban and Forest Land

As the country opted for a market economy, houses, land, and forests began to be valued in economic terms and were in rising demand. The boom in private house construction and skyrocketing land prices peaked during 1992–1993 and continue today. Encroachment on nonowned land increased as residents and farmers sold houses and fields for short-term profits and began to cultivate and to build on nonowned urban land and to clear forest land for cultivation (Leacock et al., 1993). Land and property disputes started to become features in civil courts, with up to 95 percent of civil court cases involving land disputes (interview with chief judge of civil court, 1996). Increasing commercialization of these resources and ensuing conflicts required governmental regulation. The initial regulating mechanisms were three decrees from the prime minister addressing, respectively, land and house ownership in urban areas (Decree 99), forest and forest land control and management (Decree 169), and land allocation throughout the country (Decree 186).

Decree 99 was proclaimed in 1992 to regulate land and house ownership in urban areas like Vientiane, Savannakhet, and Pakse. It specifies who has the right to own land and buildings (only Lao citizens) and invalidates the claims on houses and property of Lao refugees who fled more than ten years previously. The law also delineates responsibilities of property owners, such as paying taxes, and limits land use to domestic residence and farming for home consumption. This decree was issued to ease land disputes and court cases arising from the escalation of land prices.

Decree 169, promulgated in 1993, regulates use, management, and control of forest land and its products. It was the most comprehensive legal document ever to be produced for the natural resource sector of the economy. Regulating forest use is critical as the forest and forest land are developed to generate income to finance the country's development. Its objective is to ensure that the accrued benefits go back to local people and to provide for the sustainable use of forests, forest land, the environment, water sources, and wildlife. This decree provided the basis for the later Forest Law by classifying forest types; describing forest management contracts between individuals, families, communities, and the state; describing forest land tenure rights; and regulating hunting and the extraction of timber and nontimber forest products.

Decree 186 ("Regarding the Allocation of Land and Forest Land for Tree Plantation and Forest Protection") was issued in 1994. This is the most interesting and important decree because it opens ways for hope and prosperity as people gain greater access to land. The decree also relates to women both economically and socially, as discussed below. This decree has also attracted the most public attention, as land reform represents an important policy initiative, especially in view of agrarian reform under a socialist regime. Many divergent interests are involved in land allocation, from poor farmers—particularly those of ethnic minorities—to commercial companies. The decree is primarily meant to address poverty issues and to redirect the practice of shifting cultivation to more stable, sustainable modes of agricultural and forest production. Under this decree, land could be allocated to individuals, families, communities, enterprises, and government organizations. Decree 186 is regarded as the first step to legalizing land tenure and land use rights and transferring these rights to use land as collateral. Officially, Laos has land use rights rather than ownership rights, but in practice people believe that the land is their land, once they have rights to use a piece of land. For example, the decree states that "forest lands allocated to individuals and enterprises for [forest] plantations are regarded under their ownership. The State secures their right to use, transfer and to inherit such lands according to the laws" (Article 17).

All three decrees are "gender-neutral"; however, Decree 169 indirectly brings up gender when it notes that "in addition to the above mentioned rights, the state also recognizes the right to use forests, forest land and forest products in accordance with customs of villagers" (Article 4, paragraph 3). As noted above, lowland Lao women, especially youngest daughters, customarily inherit land and other property from parents. In addition, all decrees and laws normally follow the Constitution, which mandates equal rights between women and men in all aspects. As soon as the decrees were announced, the government began drafting more comprehensive legislation for presentation to parliament for a vote. During the interim of several years, many groups tried to influence the scope and details of the proposed laws.

WOMEN'S ATTEMPTS TO INFLUENCE THE PROPOSED LAND LAWS

In the wake of NEM, the ensuing economic boom, and the resulting increase in land prices, disputes over land and property have accumulated in courts at all levels. Some of the cases clearly have a gender aspect, as in intrafamily disputes between husband and wife. Systematic land registration, land valuation, a standard system of land titles, and mechanisms for the transfer of landownership are urgent needs in the transition toward a market economy. So even before the Forest Law and the Land Law were in place, "pilot" land allocation and land titling programs were initiated. One land titling project targeted four cities in mainly lowland Lao areas (Vientiane, Savannakhet,

Pakse, and Luang Prabang). Although the objectives of the project seem to be valid in the current situation concerning land tenure, socioanthropologists have expressed concern that the project might impinge on existing customary rights of women to inherit and own land when the registration and titling processes somehow deal with men only. Yet if the project succeeds in taking all sociocultural factors into consideration, customary rights might be better legally documented (Anon., 1995; World Bank 1995, 1996).

Once the three land-related decrees were promulgated, various localities and projects began implementing aspects of the decrees (Agriculture, 1995; CPC, 1995a; Connell, 1994; Forest Service, 1995; Hansen and Sodarak, 1995). As land was allocated in response to the decrees, the actual forms used to register land called for the name of the "head of the household." Nearly all field-workers (many were from the Department of Forestry, a nearly entirely male and strongly male-dominated department of the Ministry of Agriculture and Forestry) interpreted this to mean the husband. Usually only the names of widowed women were included as "heads of households." Such registration of the newly distributed land is important because proof of allocation may be presented to obtain title to the land with full property rights (Eggertz, 1996; Gaston, 1995).

During the process of preparing the Land Law, a number of gender specialists were consulted, and a draft of the law was officially presented to the Lao Women's Union for study and comment. Unlike other institutions in Laos, the Lao Women's Union has the mandate to be involved in the drafting of all laws, because women's rights and issues are on the cutting edges in all sectors (LWU, 1993). The Women's Union was critical of a land titling process proposed in the draft law, fearing that it might disenfranchise women who have inherited land in the customary lowland Lao way or who neglected to have their names included on the title when household resources were used to purchase the land.

The Ministry of Justice has also been an important player in the national debate over land titling and allocation. Ever since the implementation of these decrees, many issues keep on surfacing, including gender. Issues of women and their rights to receive, own, and transfer land were first brought up in meetings by the Lao staff of international nongovernmental organizations, in local community meetings, and in commercial circles (Chagnon, 1995; Choulamany-Khamphoui, 1994). Concerns were expressed that women might lose the opportunity to get a share in this land allocation process unless the question was raised to officials at all levels of the implementing agencies. These concerns incited the Lao Women's Union and the Ministry of Justice to organize a countrywide seminar series ("Legal Issues in Land and Property Ownership of Women") to generate awareness and attention to gender in land allocation and titling processes. These seminars required the cooperation of many government parties and organizations at both central and local levels.

A second aim of the seminars was to mobilize the awareness of women in regard to their legal rights in landownership, in addition to their customary rights that are normally undocumented. The seminars were well attended and did succeed in attracting wide government and public interest. Lively debates continued throughout the day, with new questions being generated even at the end of the day. Participants included government officials representing relevant institutions having direct and indirect administrative support for the implementation of Decree 169, Decree 186, and the Land Titling Project (Department of Land and Housing, Ministry of Finance), local administrations and representatives from provincial and district levels, representatives of the Lao Women's Union at all levels, and, most importantly, officials of the Ministry of Justice, especially those from the provinces.

The seminars were initiated at the right time and addressed the right issues. They focused on increasing awareness as to the existing legal rights of women, on discussing the need to make sure that women are included in land allocation processes, and the fact that agencies produce tenure documents with the names of both husband and wife, not just the household head, as previously. The seminars also attempted to promote men's willingness to respect women's rights and to educate women to stand up to protect their rights by providing information about obtaining legal help.

Utilizing these seminars and its own administrative structure, which extends to the village level, the Lao Women's Union has been diligent in trying to get women to speak up for their rights and to understand how customary rights are changing. The village Women's Union can play a very important role in village conflict resolution, since governing committees must include the head of the village Women's Union. A strong Women's Union advocate for women's customary land rights at the village level can assist women who formally complain to the village committee that their land rights have been violated. Uneducated women who are not informed of their rights, however, are unlikely to make such a formal complaint, so additional strategies are needed to protect women's rights to land. Decree 169 and the subsequent Forest Law requires the appointment of local people to supervise and, in some cases, implement the law. At provincial, district, and village levels, members of the Lao Women's Union normally are invited to take part to represent the interests of women, but the committees remain male-dominated. Of course, the government advocates equal rights policies, and the Constitution spells out these rights clearly, but stronger female representation on these committees would be a force to be reckoned with and help ensure that these rights are taken into consideration (KPL, 1997).

As a result of these activities, people even in remote parts of the country have heard about the changes and have attempted to get involved in the process. The land allocation program continues to receive enormous attention during this most dynamic period of transition. No previous historical period has witnessed this magnitude of socioeconomic development. Land allocation questions have excited the curiosity of even the smallest community (Savanakhone and Phonekeo, 1995). Yet for all these efforts of the Women's Union and its supporters, they were frustrated in their hope that the Land Law, in its final form, would contain more gender-sensitive language and articles. It does not.

Impacts of the Forest and Land Laws

The Forest Law was passed in 1996 and was followed by the Land Law in 1997 (Bailey, 1997). The two provide a comprehensive legal framework for land use ownership rights, though the implementing agencies must still provide more detailed regulations and procedures. As in the three decrees, both laws are "gender-neutral." Women are not explicitly excluded (or included) from land allocation or titling processes. In practice, however, the land titling project, the model land allocation project, and other land registration procedures continue to use forms registering the head of household, nearly always construed to be the husband if he is present. Since husbands are responsible for official activities outside the household, they commonly handle the registration of household land. Men sometimes register property under their own name even though it belongs to their wives. With the Land Law, a male property owner can then use this land as collateral for a loan and can lose it. A wealthier man might take a second wife, sell the first wife's property registered in his name, and use the money to establish a home or business for his new wife. In land and property disputes like this, courts must interview both husband and wife. However, women can and do own and manage land quite successfully (Viravong, 1995). For example, many Vientiane landowners are women, often women who left government jobs when the size of the civil service was cut after the NEM was implemented. In my personal experience, about 80 percent of property transactions in urban Vientiane are carried out by women.

It is here, in the implementation process itself, that concerned citizens, Women's Union members, and government officials can have the greatest effect. Without continued, concerted efforts at all levels to reorient these male-dominated processes of land allocation and land titling, lowland Lao women are likely to forfeit ownership of property inherited from their parents during this transition period, when legal documents (land allocation certificate, land title) are supplanting customary property rights. Furthermore, these male-dominated processes not only tend to disinherit lowland Lao women but also perpetuate women's powerlessness among the more patriarchal midland and upland ethnic groups.

*Policies and Strategies to Address the Disinheritance
of Lowland Lao Women*

Some strategies have already been attempted to include women's legal rights in the land allocation and titling process. Although they seem like good ideas, they have been insufficient so far. These include the education of officials responsible for the process itself (the seminars sponsored by the Ministry of Justice and the Lao Women's Union), the concerned response of the Lao Women's Union to drafts of the two laws, and the possibility of Women's Union involvement at the village and district levels as land is being allocated and registered. The challenge remains: In real, practical implementation, how far is the issue of equality between women and men in landownership being addressed? Obviously, additional monitoring and follow-up must be carried out to ensure equitable application of the policy in the field.

Continued training and monitoring of allocation and titling teams, gender awareness, and women's constitutional rights seem essential. Implementing agencies might be required to train team members and to include female staff, perhaps even on loan from the provincial or district Women's Union.

Greater efforts must be made to ensure that information about the land allocation and registration processes is made available to all affected women. Local Women's Unions should be trained to identify cases where the process has disinherited a woman and to support women who wish to make a formal complaint of inequity at the village and district levels. The Women's Union, in concert with the Ministry of Justice, has already begun this educational effort. Now this effort must move into districts and villages to build a strong and informed network of village women who can stand up for their rights to land. Village- and district-level efforts to educated and support village women in equitable land distribution and titling might be well supported by a legal advice center for women that is in the planning stages. Its usefulness will depend on how widely its services can become available to women throughout the country.

Successful legal challenges to these allocation and titling processes may be possible in the future. But the court system is still young, so it may take some time before it is possible to challenge the constitutionality of these processes and the resulting skewed land distribution. Even recently, when women have brought suit in court their voices seem less likely to be heard and carry less weight than opposing male voices.

The challenge of implementing constitutionally mandated gender equality still remains for Laotian women of all ethnic groups during Laos's economic transition. This requires more information, education, institutional change, and community development to enable women to have equal access to all opportunities and resources so they can best contribute to the sustainable development of their country.

PART THREE

China

10

Chinese Women's Housing Rights: An International Legal Perspective

Dia Warren

Since its founding in 1949, the People's Republic of China has implemented legislation and used administrative and educational means to provide women with a more equitable position in Chinese society than existed in imperial China. Chinese women were "liberated," at least in theory, and given paper rights that are generally aligned with international human rights standards.

This chapter uses the international definition of "property rights" to explore those rights as they exist for Chinese women, with particular reference to housing. The move toward equal rights is still ongoing in the area of property. Legal guarantees have been put in place but are not consistently applied. Nor do women, the beneficiaries of the laws and decrees, see them as meaningful solutions, if the women know the guarantees exist at all. Thus, the ostensible right to housing is in reality neither full nor equitable. This chapter will show how the Chinese housing allocation system, though not inequitable under the laws as they have been written, undermines the values of equitable ownership, acquisition, management, administration, enjoyment, and disposition of property that are recognized as international rights in the 1979 Convention on the Elimination of Discrimination Against Women (CEDAW, Article 16). The chapter will then explore how legal and administrative mechanisms are failing to compensate for this. In the market-oriented economy, only a combination of complete commodification of the housing market with appropriate enforcement of legal guarantees and greater attempts to combat social barriers are likely to ensure a full realization of Chinese women's property rights.

THE RIGHTS TO PROPERTY AND HOUSING AND THE RELEVANCE FOR CHINESE WOMEN

CEDAW was the first international agreement to extend property rights to women.[1] It represents a binding set of goals that all signatory countries are to

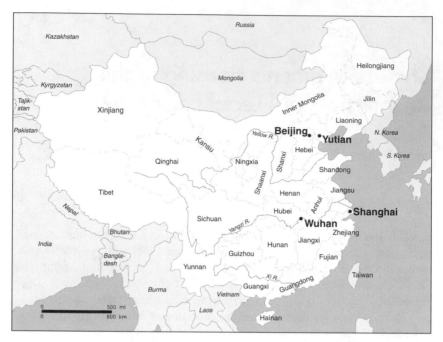

China

strive toward. The participant countries agreed, among other things, that women shall have an equitable legal capacity with men to conclude contracts and to administer property and the opportunities to exercise that capacity (CEDAW, Article 15[2]). Women shall have the freedom to choose their residence and domicile (CEDAW, Article 15[4]). Finally, Article 16(1)(h) provides the same rights for both spouses in respect of the ownership, acquisition, management, administration, enjoyment, and disposition of property, whether free of charge or for a valuable consideration.

The terms "housing rights" and "property rights," both protected by the CEDAW rubric, are often used interchangeably in international law. *Property* rights are generally recognized as a central component of sustainable development and a preserving force of human rights, including the right to self-determination, the right to sovereignty over all natural wealth and resources, and the right to the establishment of a new international economic order. Mainstream development theory recognizes the importance of property rights to ensure human dignity and personal liberty. International law recognizes the right to property but treats it as an enabling process that is applied through the market system (Sachar, 1992).

The right to *housing* is traditionally viewed as a subsidiary and defensible human right. It has been called "a fundamental requirement related to a primary need" and "an essential prerequisite for the pursuit and exercise of a variety of other human rights" (Sachar, 1992). Housing, which implies shelter but also affects security, health, family economy, individual autonomy, and personal dignity, is the most basic building-block among property rights generally.

In China, the enabling mechanism for market-driven distribution of property rights is absent, and housing rights are subsumed by a complex bureaucratic process. Property is communal; land is owned by the state or rural collectives (Chinese Constitution, 1992, Chap. 1, art. 10). This includes house sites, but individuals maintain some form of rights in housing.

The Chinese concept of property rights theoretically separates ownership rights from use rights, and neither were codified until the 1982 constitutional provisions and the 1989 Civil Code came into effect. The Chinese concept of a "right in things" is a compilation of four powers and functions: possession (*zhan you*), use (*shi yong*), disposition (*chu fen*), and benefit (*shou yi*) (Epstein, 1989: 184). Under the Civil Code, all people hold the right to "possess, use, benefit from and dispose of one's own property in accordance with the law" (Civil Code, 1987, Article 71). Although these use rights are not the equivalent of full ownership rights from a Western perspective, this constitutional language is similar to that of CEDAW.

Land in China is collectively owned, so an individual member of a collective unit, such as a rural cooperative or a state-owned work unit (*dan wei*), does not own the land itself. Individuals are guaranteed *use* rights to their property (Civil Code, 1987, Articles 74, 75). Thus, an individual's rights are limited to contractual ownership or use rights to the housing unit as provided by *dan wei*. The rights in the housing unit are jointly owned, with the individual retaining use and inheritance rights, but not the right to transfer ownership, rent to others, and give away or borrow against his or her home. A co-owner shares in the enjoyment of rights in the common property and in the undertaking of obligations in connection with the housing unit (Civil Code, 1987, Articles 78, 80). Land is mostly owned by villages in rural areas. Families in the collective are allocated cropland and housing sites, and individual family members get an undivided equal interest in that land. However, the right is limited—it is not transferable, and the land must be worked to be retained (Baker, 1995: 381).

China therefore protects public (state) and collective ownership and, simultaneously, conditional individual and private ownership. As property rights defined in the Universal Declaration of Human Rights (UDHR) and CEDAW provide for collective or individual use, Chinese rights thus nominally meet international standards. In fact, since "state property" is defined by the Civil Code as being "owned by the whole people," Chinese people are by definition each property shareholders. This is theoretically more personal property interest than is guaranteed by the United States and most other industrialized nations.

The Chinese separation of use rights and possessory rights does not facially violate international law. International legal standards generally allow the state some degree of control over personal property, allowing for certain safeguards against abuse. The UDHR codifies the right to property as follows: (1) Everyone has the right to own property alone as well as in association with others; (2) no one shall be arbitrarily deprived of his property. The right may be regarded as an inalienable one, limited only for "the purpose of securing due recognition and respect for the rights and freedoms of others and of meeting the just requirements of morality, public order and the general welfare in a democratic society." In fact, the redistributive powers of the socialist system attempted to surpass these basic international norms by theoretically erasing inequalities to provide citizens with a more uniform, if minimal, standard of living. Discrepancies in housing under the socialist system did not technically distinguish among groups of people. Any inequities in housing were to be based on occupation, seniority, and location.

These assurances of property and housing rights have been specifically extended to Chinese women. Article 13 of China's 1982 Constitution incorporates the right of *citizens* to their own income, savings, houses, and other lawful property and to inheritance. Article 48 guarantees that women "enjoy equal rights with men in all spheres of life, in political, economic, cultural, social and family life." Violation of this constitutional property right provides a basis for civil liability, and further legal protections are written into civil and family laws to protect the equal enjoyment of property rights. Attempts to assure women some form of equitable property rights were begun as early as 1950. One of the initial laws seeking to extend rights to women, the Marriage Law of 1950, gave women the right to possess and manage family property.[2] In addition, women had the right to use their own family name, inherit property, and receive alimony if divorced. Agrarian land reform assured women and children in rural areas a legally protected share in the family land. Family law in post-Mao China has rapidly expanded in recent years. The 1985 Inheritance Law explicitly states that daughters as well as sons can inherit parents' property.

More general guarantees of women's rights were born when the 1979 Organic Law of the Local People's Congresses and Governments gave provincial legislatures partial power to enact laws and regulations for the first time. Over a five-year period in the early 1980s, twenty-eight provinces passed women's rights protection regulations. The notable exceptions, Yunan and Xizang, did not follow suit most likely because of sensitive minority issues (Siao and Chao, 1994, introduction). The local regulations in turn prompted the promulgation of national legislation. This legislation, the Law of the People's Republic of China on the Protection of Rights and Interests of Women (the Women's Rights Law), was also intended to implement China's obligations as a party to CEDAW. The Women's Rights Law thus adopts similar language to that used in CEDAW: "[a] woman shall enjoy equal rights with her spouse in possessing, utilizing, profiting from and disposing of the property jointly possessed by the husband and wife according to law, which shall not be affected by the status of income of either party" (Women's Rights Law, 1992, Article 43).

The Women's Rights Law says that "[t]he State shall guarantee that women enjoy the equal right, with men, to property" (Article 28). More specifically, the Law nominally protects common property in case of a divorce and succession rights (Articles 29, 31). The Women's Rights Law introduces two new rights. First, it gives women the right to sue for monetary and nonmonetary damages. Secondly, it contains a ban on discriminatory housing allocation practice and provides for a right to redress.

China's legal guarantees to property thus stand up to international standards and provide women with assurances of legal and administrative recourse in an attempt to eliminate traditional sexist social traditions. Although the right to housing was specifically addressed in the Women's Rights Law, such laws and policies do not necessarily translate into practice.

Despite its grand pretensions, the Women's Rights Law has been criticized as consisting more of form than substance, as it lacks legal enforcement mechanisms, and whatever protection there is remains at state discretion. The language is all too often ambiguous. Article 44, for example, provides: "If the wife has no housing to live in at the time of divorce, the husband shall help her in this regard whenever he can afford to." Because this is an ambiguous legal standard, the main strength of the Women's Rights Law may be as a consciousness-raising tool rather than as an effective legal tool (Jordan, 1994: 96; Stearns, 1993: 54; J. Hecht, 1995: 4–6).

The Women's Rights Law has accorded some degree of protection against discriminatory housing allocation practices. But it does not yet seem to be consistently applied, and the question remains whether it adequately combats discrimination against women as a group or merely serves the few individuals who have access to the system. Specifically, the Women's Rights Law gives no independent jurisdiction to the courts. Furthermore, patriarchal and virilocal practices, and women's ignorance of their own rights, may impede many cases from reaching the courts at all.

China's laws, such as those protecting inheritance rights, rights to succession, and policies regarding the division of common property, seek to protect a person's lawful share in property. How property is divided in the event of divorce provides an illustration. For example, in the case of a divorce, each spouse may be awarded an equitable share of the value of their common property. Since goods are attributed value, individual shares in such joint assets can be calculated. (On a side note, proving the value of joint assets is becoming increasingly problematic as ways of generating income diversify. The filer has the burden of proving the value of the couple's assets in a divorce case, and the majority of the time this is the woman [Chen, 1996].) Unlike goods, housing cannot be attributed value and thus cannot be equitably divided in a divorce. As the house does not have a market value, and since house use rights are allocated by the *dan wei,* the couple does not hold full and divisible rights in the house. Severe housing shortages and economic constraints compound the problem, because additional housing is often simply unavailable.

Furthermore, Chinese socialism, like its counterparts in Eastern Europe and Russia, proved ambivalent about changing ingrained attitudes regarding gender roles (Jancar, 1978: 73–75). The women's movement was secondary to the state's development, and it thus failed to address adequately many deeply ingrained ideas about family structures and traditional gender-defined roles. Chinese women talk of the "double day" they worked under full socialism, a recognition of how their traditional responsibilities at home did not change even as women were incorporated into the workforce. The bureaucratic nature of the Chinese government left ample room for officials to circumvent official policies, impeding any national efforts to address policy implementation. However, sexist practices and beliefs are not limited to the male officials responsible for sidestepping equal rights legislation. Concerned China scholars recognize the need to involve women and battle women's own feudal gender stereotypes as a step in strengthening their role in today's reforming society (Li, 1994; Wen, 1990). Greater education about their legal rights will encourage women to act on their own behalf.

RURAL CHINA

In rural areas, land is collectively owned, and almost all land belongs to the villages. Family members each have an undivided equal possessory interest in the land allocated to that family, which may include both house site and cropland. As in urban areas, however, this use right is limited. The right is not transferable. If an individual sells or leases her home, she is not eligible to apply for another house site (Law of the PRC on Land Management, Article 38; China Laws on Foreign Business, 1993 Paragraph 14–715).

Rural women typically leave their family and village to join their husband's home (see Chapter 15). The woman maintains a legal resident status (*hou kou*) in her natal village, and she may regain the right to have housing there if she returns. Under Article 38 of the Law of the People's Republic of China on Land Management (1986), a person leaving the village will automatically lose her share of housing rights. The Women's Rights Law delineates the procedure for recovering housing rights in the woman's native village. Local administrative agents have the power to order relief and administer discipline. A common village practice is to reallocate land every few years, but this practice may be changing with longer contracts occurring under the household responsibility system.

In reality, these paper protections are often meaningless. The village authority, which is also responsible for allocating the rights, is responsible for itself and will not necessarily hold itself accountable to a woman seeking housing. Moreover, the presumption is that women will leave their family home only to marry into another (divorce is extremely rare, and unmarried women's migration to the city to work is considered temporary). Thus, women receive a share in their parents' or in their spouse's family property. In case of divorce, a woman may technically be allocated housing rights in her husband's village; however, this is rarely practiced, as the housing distributor is its own regulator. Furthermore, there is such a strong social stigma attached to divorce that a divorced woman may be castigated within the local community if she chooses to stay (and a large proportion of the village would be relatives of her former husband). Often, the only option is to return to the family home and village. Even then it is often difficult to acquire land rights. The same factors discussed above—cultural biases against divorced women, lack of bureaucratic checks—may stand in her way, and in addition there may not be housing available. The village periodically readjusts rights, at which point the woman may receive a land allocation (but longer land contracts will make this less likely).

Another new trend curtailing women's legal property rights is a concern. The current perceived imperatives of family farming and the need to avoid reproduction restrictions have increasingly driven couples to avoid registering their marriage. By not obtaining state sanction for their marriage, women forfeit the legal guarantees to property that they have. Laws proscribing de facto marriages simultaneously increased in the 1980s, compounding the problems facing these growing numbers of couples. Protection of property arrangements associated with unlawful cohabitation differ sharply from those related to marriage, and joint ownership will often not be recognized by the court in case of divorce, usually to the disadvantage of the woman (Palmer, 1995: 116–117; see also Jordan, 1994: 70–74).

URBAN CHINA

In urban China, women usually live with their parents until they marry and then live in a house belonging to their husband's work unit. Women who remain single usually have difficulties finding housing units of their own. Housing reform is in its early stages, and most housing units are still distributed by the *dan wei*. Under the distribution system, women often receive fewer housing vouchers and are ineligible for newly constructed homes (Croll, 1995: 158). A woman's *dan wei* could until recently legally refuse to allocate housing to a woman and otherwise impede her ability to find housing (Jordan, 1994: 72). In her work describing Chinese women's lives, Elizabeth Croll writes: "Officially, the older single woman has no existence separate from or independent of her family. For instance, she cannot have a registration separate from her parents' household and therefore has no individual right to separate housing or other benefits" (Croll, 1985: 158). However, many Chinese are sympathetic with the *dan wei* because urban centers suffer chronic housing shortages, and *dan wei* may merely avoid double allocation to each family.

Following the promulgation of the Women's Rights Law in 1992, discrimination remains pervasive. The All China Trade Union Female Workers Department surveyed 103 *dan wei* in five regions after the Women's Rights Law was passed and found excessive housing discrimination.[3] Out of 14,279 apartments built in the few years preceding the survey, women received only 8.7 percent. More than four-fifths of the housing was allocated to male workers in surveyed regions. The discrimination took several forms. Allocation would be purely based on gender, even to the extent that if the man transferred *dan wei,* and his wife remained with the original *dan wei,* she would be obligated to give up their joint housing. Alternatively, women had some severely limited rights to housing. In Hebei, one factory's rules required a woman to be employed for twenty years before she became eligible for housing, while men had to work for four years before their housing right accrued (All China Trade Union Female Workers Department, 1976).

The woman in this situation has no individual use rights to her home, and in the case of a divorce she cannot receive adequate compensation, as the house is not communal property. (Any use of the house, such as for a home-based industry, does become communal property, and wherever it can be assigned a monetary value, each individual's share in that aspect of the property is, technically, guaranteed.) Despite the protection in the Women's Rights Law and its clarifications, *Zhongguo Xinwen She* reported in 1990 that up to 90 percent of urban women have difficulty finding housing after divorce (despite very low divorce rates) (*Zhongguo Xinwen She,* April 28, 1996). In the state-run system, housing allocation in case of divorce is an administrative nuisance, as the *dan wei* cannot command the additional housing unit. Should a couple divorce, and if a woman's own unit does not assign her a house, she is forced to seek housing with family or friends. Until well into the 1980s, the necessary role of the *dan wei* in a couple's marital living situation could even influence their ability to divorce. In an exploration of Chinese divorce trends, William J. Goode found that "many or most courts and civil affairs offices required a letter of permission from the spouses' work unit before they would process the divorce request, even when the couple was in agreement" (Goode, 1993: 311).

POSSIBLE SOLUTIONS, OLD AND NEW

To combat the problems inherent in protecting individual property rights, the Supreme People's Court issued clarifications regarding property rights protection, particularly in the case of divorce. According to the court's 1988 "Opinion (for Trial Use) of the Supreme People's Court on Questions Concerning the Implementation of the General Principles of Civil Law of the People's Republic of China," joint property rights are to be respected upon dissolution of a partnership, and in case of divorce the Marriage Law is to be followed. Administrative remedies are provided to combat discriminatory housing allocation (the effectiveness of which will be discussed below), but little exists to preserve a woman's equal share in marital property. In 1993, the Supreme People's Court issued a detailed clarification of Article 44 of the Women's Rights Law, which, although noncompulsory, may guide the courts to a more thorough protection of women's property rights in the event of divorce. More recently, in February 1996, the court issued a circular on how to resolve division of public housing in a divorce case.

The Supreme People's Court directive sets forth guidelines to determine when housing and rental rights become jointly owned by a married couple. The directive urges courts to consider equity when dividing common housing, by requiring a living allowance or by requiring both people to live in the shared home for up to one year while they arrange other housing. One Beijing lawyer with the *fulian,* the state women's organization, described a 1994 divorce appeal she handled after a local court ordered the divorced woman to return to her parents' home. The husband's *dan wei* refused to give housing to women in general, and the woman could not get assigned housing from her own *dan wei* since the husband's had already provided it. The *fulian* lawyer argued that the court should apply the 1993 directive, as the lower court had not done. Ultimately, the appeals court ruled that the couple should remain in the home together for one year (Pi, 1996).

Although the court can urge equitable division of "common" housing rental rights, in reality those rights ultimately belong to the *dan wei.* And supervisory structures controlling the *dan wei* are poor. The *dan wei* can interfere with women's legal rights by avoiding transfer of the home.[4]

Reasons for discrimination in housing allocation are related to women's limited ability to enforce their evolving legal rights. They include: (1) male dominance in positions of control, (2) lack of adequate independent legal recourse against *dan wei,* (3) insufficient access to legal aid and judicial ignorance of the recent policies, (4) women's own lack of adequate legal education and knowledge of their own rights, and (5) no effective independent channel that women can use to protect their rights.

There are two highly visible mass organizations advocating on women's behalf in China. The chief institution advocating for women's interests is the *fulian* (All China Women's Federation). A primary goal of the organization is to "rectify the tendency to neglect work concerning women" (Jancar, 1978: 108). The women's sections of the Trade Union compose a second such mass organization; its focus is on women's labor issues.

The *fulian* has sought to increase its role during the post-1978 period of economic reform; however, as it is strongly affiliated with and promotes the policies of the state, the *fulian*'s ability to advocate for women's interests is most effective on an individual case basis. (For an explanation of the role of the *fulian*, see Croll, 1958: 136–142.) The *fulian* remains a party instrument and continues to tailor policy according to the dictates of the Party rather than the needs of the people it serves. In the view of its most adamant critics, the *fulian* asserts itself as "an institution of social administration when it ought to be representing women" (Barlow, 1994: 345). The organization's self-effacing posture in relation to the state means that it "lacks an independent will" and thus the very wherewithal to do anything.

Despite these criticisms, the *fulian* can be and has been instrumental in promoting women's rights. The national *fulian* was a key player in the creation of the Women's Rights Law, for example, although some measures for which it actively lobbied were never effectively incorporated. The *fulian* also offers individual guidance and sees education and employment as the most important issues. Moreover, there are three lawyers on staff at the national headquarters (for a group whose membership is almost one-half of the Chinese population, or .6 billion people), and a few at district levels. Legal services are limited for marital disputants, and if a woman knows her rights and does seek out help, the resources may nevertheless be financially out of her reach.

When approached by an individual, the *fulian* may be most helpful as a mediator. If a woman has a problem with her housing situation, for example, the *fulian* may help her negotiate a solution with the *dan wei*. Within Chinese government structures, this is an effective resource, as problems are often settled through informal means.

Given the shortcomings of legal and administrative solutions, reconciling housing rights with full property rights may be the only hope of effectively granting women full and equitable housing rights. Ann Jordan posits that as long as housing remains a work-related benefit the divorce provisions contained in the Marriage Law and the Women's Rights Law will be ineffective (Jordan, 1994: 74). The Chinese government is now actively seeking to correct the problems inherent in their supply-side housing system, problems that include an excess of overpriced apartments, built for foreigners and the newly rich, and severe shortages of available affordable housing. Theoretically, complete commodification of the housing market will help clarify women's and men's property rights and eliminate discriminatory practices in housing acquisition by attributing a financial value to a home. Housing reform would put the right to housing within the analytical framework of property rights generally. Housing rights could thus be effectively protected by the market characteristics of property administration.

All Chinese scholars and activists interviewed by this author believe that a market-controlled housing system remains a remote and unreliable solution. First, many believe complete commodification of the housing market is too distant. It not only requires new housing be built; the government must also convince or compel people who have lived in heavily subsidized homes for decades to purchase. Second, as discussed below, the method of housing reform itself has built-in inequities. Housing commodification without the addition of effective legislative protection will be an incomplete remedy for the housing problems facing Chinese women.

Housing reforms vary in different cities and regions. The Shanghai April 1996 round of reforms illustrates some of the potential problems common to each. The plan introduced a three-tier pricing system at which a family could buy their home at a price adjusted to their buying power. The home could be subsidized, sold at cost, or sold at profit (United Press International, April 11, 1996). A type of mortgage arrangement was implemented to make purchasing housing more accessible to the general population. Under this payment scheme, workers pay 5 percent of their salary into a fund that is matched by their *dan wei*, which will then provide low-interest loans to home buyers (see Chapters 2, 12, and 13). The ownership rights purchased in this kind of scheme will remain contingent upon the pricing structure adopted (O'Neill, 1996; *Hong Kong Ching Pao*, February 1, 1996). The purchaser buys the house she currently lives in. A new home owner may only acquire partial rights initially, while the *dan wei*, as previous owner of the home, retains the rights to transfer and sale. The current reforms, which are run by an external bureaucratic agency, may ensure more equitable disbursement, provided that regulations, such as those in the Women's Rights Law, are followed.

In order to implement housing reforms, the state must compel families who have relied on heavily subsidized homes to give that housing up. Furthermore, the escalating costs of housing construction and the difficulties of calculating incomes, particularly as a large fraction of family income is derived from secondary sources such as household-based industries or remittances, could continue to impede reform. Before this round of reforms, even a "comfort housing" program that supplied housing at cost was under attack. City workers' average monthly salary is 500 yuan ($60), and the price of a comfort home in Shanghai or Guangzhou is priced at 1,000 to 1,500 yuan ($602) per square meter, which would require twenty to thirty years of savings to purchase (United Press International, April 11, 1996).

Finally, the nature of land rights themselves will not change. Although a Chinese buyer may purchase full *use* rights, the land itself will technically revert to the state in seventy years. Whether housing will remain affordable otherwise is questionable in China's booming economy. One source cites that rents were raised in Shanghai by 50 percent annually, while income increased 25 percent annually since 1990 (O'Neill, 1996). However, once pure commodification of the housing market is obtained, there will be equitable ownership rights across groups of people. The problems cited above, such as Chinese *dan wei* ignoring the Women's Rights Law and mandating sexist housing allocation, and of a divorced woman being compelled to leave the family home that is the property of her husband's work unit, will no longer be practiced.

To provide an effective guarantee that women receive fair treatment under housing reforms, an independent monitoring mechanism, or a strengthened forum in which those who may have suffered discrimination can air grievances, is advisable at this early stage of the reforms. In addition, strengthened training and education programs would help inform women of their rights. Nevertheless, despite additional structural protection, the social barriers cited above (lack of legal awareness and education, lack of a sufficient channel to register complaints with the system, and weak enforcement of the laws) will continue to impede Chinese women's equal enjoyment of property rights.

CONCLUSION

Property rights in China are not absolute but are seen as a compilation of ownership and use rights and are subject to state policy. However, this treatment of rights is accepted under international legal definitions.

China's course of reform shows that there is no contradiction between treating public ownership as the main form of property rights and cherishing the individual citizen's right to own property: The two notions are mutually complementary and beneficial. This is plain not only from the above-mentioned expansion and increase of individually owned property but also from the all-round growth and prosperity of mixed economies embracing both individual economy and private ownership (Rodriquez, 1992, Paragraph 252).

Chinese officials believe that housing reform need not impact the traditional conception of property rights, that it can be conducted with "Chinese characteristics." Currently, discriminatory practices regarding the ownership, acquisition, management, administration, enjoyment, and disposition of property impede women's rights as human rights and have a negative impact on social development. Legal reforms such as the 1993 and 1996 directives may provide the impetus to change the status quo, but without awareness by the judiciary and the women themselves there is unlikely to be full realization of equality. A solution may come once housing is regulated by the market, if the transition period recognizes and accommodates women's concerns.

NOTES

1. Although China, Vietnam, and Laos are members of CEDAW, the United States is not. A right to own property is also mentioned in the following United Nations documents: Convention on the Status of Refugees (1951) (China is a member); Conventions Relating to the Status of Stateless Persons (1954); International Convention on the Elimination of All Forms of Racial Discrimination (1965) (China is a member); Declaration on the Rights of Disabled Persons (1975); International Convention on the Protection of the Rights of All Migrant Workers and Members of Their Families (1990).

The International Labor Organization provides for the control of ownership and land use rights in its basic aims and standards (Convention No. 117 on Social Policy, 1962). Several regional documents also address property rights.

2. The Marriage Law of 1950 also outlawed bigamy, concubinage, foot binding, child betrothal, and bride sale. It made men responsible for children conceived out of wedlock and granted women free choice of occupation.

3. The exact date of the report and the years of the survey are unavailable.

4. The role of the *dan wei,* however, is shrinking as market reforms progress.

11

Housing Reform in Urban China

Gale Summerfield and Nahid Aslanbeigui

For the past four decades, the state and collective work units (*dan wei*) in China have provided almost all urban residents a small apartment or room. This housing was highly subsidized: Workers spent only 1–5 percent of their incomes on rent. Although either spouse could apply for housing from her/his respective work unit, the couple would usually live in housing provided by the husband's unit, as he would be more likely to have a better job and therefore better housing. In practice, many work units would allocate housing only through the husband. Single people, especially women, were expected to live with their parents or in dormitories.[1] Because socialist policies also heavily restricted migration from rural areas (and millions of urban youth were sent to rural areas during the 1960s and 1970s), the demand for housing in the urban sector did not expand too rapidly. Increases in the urban population would lead not to much more construction but to more cramped use of available subsidized housing; sometimes several generations shared a room. Homelessness and squatter settlements in the cities did not become issues until after the market reforms that began in the late 1970s, when millions of rural residents rushed to cities.[2]

Although housing reform is integral to efficiency-driven transition policies, it is still in its infancy in the late 1990s. Most specialists agree that a successful reform would end the relationship between state work units and housing, eliminate the housing subsidies, and sell off publicly owned housing.[3] These changes would increase reliance on the market allocation of resources and reduce the size of government involvement in the economy.

This chapter examines the gender aspects of these reforms, which have largely been ignored. As usual, the household remains a black box in the existing literature and in official decisions on housing reform, that is, the individual family members are assumed to be impacted equally.[4] After providing a brief background on housing reforms in urban China, this chapter focuses on neglected gender issues surrounding a few major themes: the separation of

Table 11.1   Annual Completed Housing Space in Some Provincial Chinese
Municipalities (in million sq.m.)

	Beijing	Shanghai	Tianjin
1979	2.845	2.160	2.064
1980	3.757	3.043	2.424
1981	4.330	2.976	3.272
1982	4.450	3.946	3.714
1983	4.891	4.059	3.779
1984	4.200	4.382	3.859
1985	4.757	4.886	3.397
1986	5.010	4.909	4.000
1987	5.817	4.862	2.937
1988	5.979	4.630	2.694

Source: World Bank, 1992: 6–7.

housing provision from work units, rental price reforms, home ownership and property rights, and housing conditions, environmental regulation, and urban planning. The concluding section focuses on the impact of these reforms on women's agency (capabilities of acting in their own and others' interests) and strategies (actions taken in their own and others' interests).

BACKGROUND OF THE REFORMS

Since the post-Mao reforms, per capita GDP has grown at an average annual rate of 8 percent (1978–1995) compared to the previous 4.8 percent (1965–1980) (World Bank, 1997: 3; UNDP, 1994: 182). The looser migration rules have led to growth in the urban population at a rate of "3–5 percent per annum, depending on the legal classification of the migrants involved" (World Bank, 1992: ix). By 1992, 28 percent of the population lived in the urban areas, up from 19 percent in 1960; by the year 2000 China is projected to have 47 percent of its population living in the cities (Davis et al., 1995; UNDP, 1994: 182). Almost 100 million people relocated from the countryside between 1980 and 1997; approximately one-third of these migrants were women.[5]

The increased urban population and per capita income have created what the World Bank has called an "insatiable demand" for housing (World Bank, 1992: ix). In response to this demand, the average annual number of new units has increased from 1.67 million before the reforms to more than 10 million since 1982 (World Bank, 1992: 1); the increase for Beijing, Shanghai, and Tianjin is shown in Table 11.1, reported in square meters (sq.m.).

Table 11.2 indicates that average living space per capita more than doubled in urban areas since the reforms, growing from 3.6 sq.m. in 1978 to 7.5

Table 11.2   Living Space in China[a]

| | Through Investment by | | Living Space Per Capita (in sq.m.) | |
	State-Owned Units & Collective- Owned Units	Urban Individuals	Urban	Rural
1978	38	3.6		8.1
1980	92	3.9		9.4
1983	115	25	4.6	11.6
1984	107	40	4.9	13.6
1985	125	63	5.2	14.7
1986	121	72	6.0	15.3
1987	110	83	6.1	16.0
1988	108	94	6.3	16.6
1989	83	78	6.6	17.2
1990	107	65	6.7	17.8
1991	117	68	6.9	18.5
1992	146	86	7.1	18.9
1993	178	98	7.5	20.7

Source: State Statistical Bureau, 1994: 281.
a. Floor space of newly built residential buildings in urban areas (in million sq.m.).

in 1993 and 8.47 in 1997 (*Xinhua,* 8/24/97). The increased supply of housing, however, has not kept up with the increased demand, and a shortage persists. Four million households have an average per capita living space of less than 4 sq.m., and 34 million sq.m. of old housing requires major repairs (FBIS, 10/7/96). Young married couples may find themselves waiting longer than a year for a small apartment; until then, they live separately, often with parents or sometimes in an apartment provided through parents. Homeless migrants, termed the "floating population," have become a common sight camped outside the train station in wealthy cities like Guangzhou. Similarly, squatter villages have sprung up, like Zhejiang village in Beijing.

In the mid-1980s, housing was still highly subsidized, and urban households allocated a mere 1 percent of their incomes to housing fees, which were insufficient to cover even maintenance costs. Despite the lack of cost recovery from existing housing and reforms that emphasized cost reduction, state and collective work units continued to build new housing, increasing urban living space from 38 million sq.m. in 1978 to 178 million sq.m. in 1993 (see Table 11.2). The World Bank reports that by "one conservative calculation, the share of rental subsidies rose from 7 to 16 percent of the total average compensation package of workers, between 1979 and 1988" (World Bank, 1992: x). To be competitive with nonstate businesses, state firms have had to reduce their expenses; welfare functions are being eliminated or transferred to the state.[6]

Chinese officials recognize that housing reform is linked to other transition-oriented policies directed at labor markets, state-owned enterprises, and social security (FBIS, 5/28/96). Therefore, in the late 1980s, they began to place more emphasis on housing reform. By the end of 1988, only "7.5 percent of newly built, publicly owned housing was sold to households, along with 0.3 percent of the pre-existing stock" (World Bank, 1992: 26). In 1988, the first comprehensive reform plan, to be implemented in all cities, counties, and towns in 1990, was proposed. Experiments were conducted in two trial cities: Yantai in Shandong Province (northern China) and Bengbu in Anhui Province (central China) (World Bank, 1992: 28); other areas such as Beijing and Shanghai have applied their own versions of housing reform (see Chapters 12, 13, and 14). Because the reform was more complicated and less popular than anticipated, the proposed implementation date of 1990 was postponed. The Shanghai reforms (which drew on the Singapore model) were very influential in the State Council decision on housing reform issued in 1994 (see Chapter 2). This national regulation permitted some variation among regions in applying the main features of the reform: development of a housing market and sale of public housing units, the creation of housing accumulation funds, rent reform, and acceleration of inexpensive housing construction. The so-called Comfortable Housing Policy began in earnest in 1995 following the State Council decision. Financed by central and local governments, it made provisions for low-cost apartments for the poor and middle-class families (FBIS, 9/27/96). A more extensive national housing reform was introduced in July 1998. This package requires work units to sell new housing to residents; older units are to have higher rents or be sold. The new policy also seeks to stimulate the economy by getting more of people's savings into the housing market (*Asia Pulse,* 5/19/98; *Xinhua,* 12/24/97).

HOUSING REFORM: THEMES AND ANALYSIS

The Separation of Housing Provision from Work Units

A key goal of housing reform is to break the connection between employment and housing. Since 1949, most new apartments have been provided by work units, and urban residents are reluctant to give up the security of subsidized housing. Although they may venture out to start their own businesses or work for foreign firms, many urban dwellers have remained in these units by keeping one family member on the state payroll. State-owned enterprises, however, are increasingly pressured to become cost-effective by laying off surplus workers. Efficiency in the production process and in labor use requires that workers be able to find affordable housing that is not tied to employment. In keeping with China's gradualist approach to reforms, the current stock of public housing could be run by a number of rental management agencies, eventually to be sold off for renting or ownership. During the 1980s, officials had already begun arranging for new housing units to be built by several work units, spatially separate from the work site. In the 1990s, they are instituting management companies to collect rents and maintain properties (FBIS, 8/29/96).

The separation of housing from the work unit has gendered impacts not yet recognized in policy discussions. We analyze the various aspects of this issue in more detail below.

Location.   Both positive and negative gender impacts can be expected from changes in the location of dwellings as housing is separated from the work unit. Freedom in choosing the location of apartments would enable women and their families to select areas with lower rents so that they could acquire newer, larger apartments, equipped with more amenities, such as private bathrooms with hot and cold water and kitchens with gas ranges and refrigerators. Under the existing system, because most housing has been spatially linked to the husband's work site, women have been the main commuters (Gaubatz, 1995b: 31). Shorter commute time for the woman could benefit the family as a whole by increasing the available time for her activities within the home.

Current policies have paid too little attention to the importance of earning a living from the housing unit, an attractive alternative for women since it allows them to combine their childcare tasks with paid work opportunities (see Chant, 1996b; Tinker, 1994). At least 5 million (about one-fourth) of the licenses to run private businesses in Chinese cities were held by women at the end of the 1980s (see Croll, 1995: 123). Many of these activities are conducted from the home. The main form of dwelling since the early 1980s has been the apartment high-rise, providing relatively limited opportunities for retail trade and services from the unit. The trend for urban centers, however, is positive; such centers plan for more specialized neighborhoods with shopping and recreation areas and offer women opportunities for connecting home and work in new ways (see Gaubatz, 1995b).[7]

Central cities are prime locations and are increasingly more expensive, making it difficult for ordinary workers to find affordable housing there. The average price for purchasing an apartment was 2,205 yuan per sq.m. in 1998, an increase of 10.3 percent from 1997 (Asia Pulse, 7/98). The price in the center of large urban areas was two to three times higher. Although housing owned by the work units was being sold below market value in 1998, the cost was 200,000 yuan or more in large cities (Poole, 1998: 18; Wang Lihong, 1996: 1–2). With the new housing regulations in the mid-1990s, planners are promoting low-priced, comfortable housing, but it is unlikely that these units will be built on prime property. Long commute times and congested city streets are problems associated with the location of many of the new apartments that are being built in the suburbs. For some families, though, the reduction in well-being from longer commutes would be offset by better housing, and they could be expected to relocate voluntarily.[8]

Divorce. At present, divorce poses a serious problem for women who live in housing units provided by the husband's work unit. Divorce typically results in the woman losing her housing and moving back to live with her parents. If this is not possible, the woman may be compelled to remain living with her former husband for a year or more while she looks for a new dwelling. The situation has been problematic enough for the law to provide that "in a case where the husband and wife live in a house allocated by the unit to which the husband belongs, if the wife has no housing to live in at the time of divorce, the husband shall help her in this regard whenever he can afford to" (Croll, 1995: 190). How strongly this is enforced is subject to question, and up to 90 percent of urban women find it difficult to locate housing after divorce (see Chapter 10). Lack of housing can also be a disadvantage to the mother in custody disputes (Li Zhang, forthcoming). If housing is allocated by means other than work units, it is not necessarily the woman who would lose her place of residence.

Social Security. The provision of guaranteed, subsidized housing in urban areas has not only been a form of "brick and mortar wages" (World Bank, 1992) but also an important component of social-security benefits (Pudney and Wang, 1995). The dissolution of the link between housing and the work unit essentially removes this source of security for urban residents. Although China has achieved low levels of urban poverty by developing-country standards (World Bank, 1997), these gains could be threatened if the potential problems of the combined reforms are not anticipated. The 1997–1998 Asian currency crisis is a reminder that market systems require some type of social safety net.

Housing's role in poverty alleviation is more than provision of shelter; housing units are productive assets through which income can be generated (Moser and McIlwaine, 1997: 48; Tinker, 1994, and Chapter 1 in this volume). Low-income housing has a distinct impact on the opportunities of female heads of household, the elderly, the unemployed, and rural-urban migrants.

The removal of guaranteed jobs, moreover, has already weakened housing security; a person who is permanently laid off from her/his state-owned enterprise job or whose work unit declares bankruptcy cannot expect to continue living in the work unit's housing. Women are more likely to lose their jobs as firms cut costs.[9] During the wave of layoffs that occurred before the

Table 11.3   The Status of Women in China

	Female	Year
Female/male ratio	94	1992
Adult literacy	68% (compared to 92% for men)	1992
Share of administrative and management jobs	11%	1980–1989
Share of unemployment	65.65%	1987

Sources: UNDP, 1994: 144–146; Summerfield and Aslanbeigui, 1992: 60.

Tiananmen Incident in the late 1980s, for example, firms laid off twice as many women as men (Summerfield, 1994; Croll, 1995). Table 11.3 shows that although women make up less than half the labor force, they comprised 66.65 percent of the urban unemployed in 1987 and 64 percent of those identified as surplus labor in 1988.[10] Women are discriminated against in the labor market because firms consider them more expensive compared to men (due to maternity leaves and health care costs, such as prenatal care, that the firm had to cover) and because of traditional biases (Summerfield and Aslanbeigui, 1992: 60).

The separation of employment and housing may make access to housing harder for women who do not have the support of a husband or a father regardless of whether they are gainfully employed; the gap between women's and men's wages is increasing, and women face growing discrimination in the emerging labor market. In the housing market, women face a direct bias—managers may not want to rent to single women whom they consider immoral—as well as an indirect bias—rising prices will make the differences in wages more obvious.

Rental Price Reforms

In addition to eliminating the burden of subsidized housing from state-owned enterprises, a successful reform would have to allow rents to reflect the scarcity value of housing. The 1988 reforms suggested a onetime rent increase for some areas to cover maintenance, depreciation, management, interest charges, and property taxes (Pudney and Wang, 1995: 143). A simultaneous onetime wage adjustment would enable people to meet this cost-of-living increase. The wage compensation would be made in the form of housing coupons or contributions to the housing fund (see discussion below) and could be used only for housing. In other areas, rents would be allowed to increase slowly without comparable increases in wages (Wang and Murie, 1996: 979). The 1994 state decision promoted increases in rental fees to cover costs. All of these components are included in the 1998 reforms.

The gradual removal of subsidies and the development of a small housing market have resulted in a wide range of rental fees. In Beijing, tenants of subsidized housing typically pay about 1.3 yuan ($.16) per sq.m. per month (Wang Lihong, 1996: 1–2). "The average price of a private rental is 5,000 yuan (US$600) a month and a young couple would have to spend their entire salary just on the rent" (Agence France-Presse, 5/6/96). In Shanghai, a subsidized unit often costs around 30 yuan per month, but a similar, privately owned apartment may cost 2,000 yuan a month (Agence France-Presse, 6/1/96). During the early 1990s, the average rental fee for a state-owned housing unit increased from .3 yuan per sq.m. to .6–1.2 yuan per sq.m.; the proportion of two-earner family income spent on rent has increased from 1.04 percent in 1993 to 5 percent in 1995, and in cities like Daqing it has reached 15 percent in a single jump (FBIS, 5/28/96). Even with more emphasis on the provision of inexpensive housing during the comfortable housing campaign of the mid-1990s, one purpose of the reform is to let rental prices rise compared to the old subsidized rate; the market will no doubt lead to large jumps in rents from 30 to 50 yuan per month in central urban districts, but the empty units that cost 5,000 yuan per month indicate the planners have overestimated the demand for high-end apartments.

As rental prices increase, women's opportunities in the labor markets will influence their access to housing, particularly if they are single, divorced, or widowed. Although some women entrepreneurs are finding greater success in the context of the general market reforms, many others are having difficulties finding jobs and are more likely to be laid off than are men. Everything else being constant, gender-based employment discrimination that leaves women with either low or no wage income would be more harmful in the context of a "free" housing market.[11]

The proposed wage increase to offset the rental price increase appears to be gender-neutral. The specifics of implementation, however, have significant gender implications, and the lull over these issues is problematic. Consider, for example, a firm that hires both women and men but mainly allocates housing to male workers. If only those who receive the housing allocation are given the wage increase (not the practice in the experiments reported to date but a possible scenario in the variations of housing policy reform), then it would generally be the men who would receive the increment. This could potentially lead to different pay for the same work, mainly differentiated along gender lines, resulting in a larger wage gap between women and men. If, in contrast, wages are increased across-the-board to make up for higher rental fees, men would typically receive higher wages that they would pay back to the work unit to cover the higher rental fees. If women also receive the higher wages even though they were not receiving the housing subsidy directly, they do not pay the wage back as rent to their employer and, thus, they become a relatively more expensive factor of production (the hidden, nonpecuniary wage discrimination that existed through the housing subsidy is removed); this moderately higher wage for women could lead some employers to discriminate more in decisions about whether to hire women or men. In practice, however, the wage increment is usually paid to all workers at the firm and can only be used for rent. This practice obfuscates the gender differences, provides a right to a share in the housing fund for women, who may not have directly received housing allocations previously, and makes negative effects on women less likely as the work unit begins the process of unburdening itself from housing provision.

Home Ownership and Property Rights

An estimated 20 percent of China's urban housing is privately owned (World Bank, 1992: 8). During the 1980s, it became more common for several work units to buy apartment buildings together and for these dwellings to be separate from the work site. Although the direction of these changes was desirable to reformers, most people still pay such low rents that they have little incentive to take on the expense of buying and maintaining a private dwelling unless pressured to do so.[12] In 1997, approximately 58 percent of the housing sold was bought by individuals, a gain of 27 percent from 1996 (*Xinhua*, 1/24/98). Thus, individual investment in housing is increasing (also see Table 11.2), but private residential construction is well below that of state- and collectively run units. Since work units can no longer supply highly subsidized units after July 1998, the percentage of individual purchases is expected to rise significantly (and officials hope this will stimulate the economy).[13] Tenants have had "rights in perpetuity to live in a housing unit" in addition to receiving substantial subsidies (*Xinhua*, 1/24/98: 46). Increased incomes, the desire to accumulate wealth, higher rental fees, and the elimination of other social-security aspects of housing are expected to boost the demand for home ownership. It is reasonable to assume, however, that a free housing market in China will be characterized by the coexistence of privately owned and rental units.

The appropriateness of housing construction is another problem. Until the early 1990s, much of the construction of private dwellings centered on expensive units expected to return a high profit. Although people in the high-income category are considered more likely to purchase housing as opposed to renting (World Bank, 1993a: 48), neither they nor foreign investors have bought as much as speculators anticipated. More than 50 million sq.m. of new housing, targeted to wealthy domestic and foreign investors, have not been sold because the price is too high for average and low-income families (*Asia Pulse*, 7/98; Wang Lihong, 1996: 1–2).

The average price per sq.m. of commodity houses was 1,710 yuan ($206) in 1995. But most apartment prices in major cities are much higher. In Beijing, the price per sq.m. of a downtown commodity house is 5,000 yuan ($602) to 7,000 yuan ($843). Even houses in remote suburbs could be as high as 2,000 yuan ($241) per sq.m. The price is about 10,000 yuan ($1,200) in the city center of Shenzhen, Guangdong Province. In general, a two-room residence downtown costs about 300,000 yuan ($36,000), the equivalent of a middle-income worker's salary for thirty years (Wang Lihong, 1996: 1–2).

To increase the supply of affordable housing, Chinese authorities have guaranteed a 15 percent rate of return to foreign investors. They are also promoting and partially subsidizing the comfortable housing project for low- and middle-income groups; middle-income families will be asked to pay explicit costs of building the unit, and low-income families will receive additional subsidies. The construction area of the project reached 11.7 million sq.m. by the end of October 1995—a 7 percent increase over the same period in 1994 (FBIS, 9/27/96; 12/4/95). Mortgage lending restrictions have exacerbated the problems in getting people to buy housing units. Mortgage interest rates are also high, required downpayments are frequently 40 percent or more, and the duration is relatively short (ten to fifteen years) at present. Monthly interest rates for fifteen-year loans run about 1.0 percent, requiring thousands of yuan in interest payments each month (Reuters, 9/28/96). To attract people to home ownership, banks have indicated that they will relax some of the terms on mortgages. In addition, the state has mandated housing accumulation funds as part of its reform programs in the 1990s; these are similar to the funds in Singapore, but a lower contribution is required (see Chapter 2).[14] Workers at state firms and offices must pay 5–15 percent of their earnings into these funds, which can only be used for housing maintenance, remodeling, and purchase. Policymakers plan to use the money paid by new buyers as part of a reinvestment fund for additional construction; work units, however, have often sold units to their employees at subsidized rates, giving liberal seniority discounts, and the 1994 state decision on housing includes measures that stipulate what should be charged (Wang and Murie, 1996).

Ownership issues for women are often part of a family decision because purchasing an apartment or larger unit is so expensive. Because the family is the institutional focus of individuals, the name of the person who signs the title is rarely questioned (although it would be unusual for the wife to sign by herself). The law guarantees rights to women in theory. In practice, however, women's rights are far from guaranteed. This volume is focused on emphasizing the importance of women's explicit rights to use and own property even when they remain in a marriage for life. These rights affect how women are treated inside and outside the home in a variety of ways; they become critical for staying out of poverty in case of divorce or of the husband's death. If the family lives in an apartment owned by the husband's parents, the wife (and often her children) are in an extremely weak position for maintaining rights in a dispute even if they have contributed financially to purchasing the house.

Having one's name on the title is not a guarantee of legal protection but is a step closer to it.

Women, who typically have lower wages, are automatically at a disadvantage in purchasing property, especially those in the single, divorced, or widowed category. The young female workers who have migrated from rural areas are particularly affected since, as Laurel Bossen argues, when they leave their villages behind, they also leave the right to the "household estate" to their fathers and brothers (Bossen, 1994: 6).

Availability of credit is one of the main limitations for women in acquiring property; this is especially significant for single women. With credit reform and housing accumulation funds, women may have a better opportunity to own property. The traditional rules and women's inferior position in the labor markets, however, will create an environment where they may not have equal access to credit and mortgages. As recommended in the Habitat II guidelines (from the UN meeting in Turkey in June 1996), women need flexibility in downpayment, collateral, and scheduling payments (URL: http://pan.cedar.univie.ac.at/habitat/gender/gen1.html, 9/96).

Housing Conditions, Environmental Regulation, and Urban Planning

Post-Mao China has witnessed a significant expansion in the number of apartment complexes and high-rises. The broad boulevards of urban centers give China's cities a modern look. They hide the haphazard planning of the cities and the inferior quality of the housing occupied by the majority of the urban population. Industrial and residential areas, for example, frequently intermingle (World Bank, 1993a: xxiv). People, especially young children and pregnant women, are exposed to dangerous levels of industrial pollutants. At least five of China's cities are among the world's ten worst in terms of air pollution.

The new high-rises are not of very high quality, and lack of maintenance and damage from air pollution have cut their longevity in half (World Bank, 1992: xii). The apartments are still small; not all have access to piped water, and when they do they may not have hot water. Private kitchen areas, however, usually contain a stove, fueled by cans of compressed gas, and a refrigerator; they are marked improvements in terms of convenience and reduced indoor pollution from cooking. Private bathrooms are now enjoyed by approximately half of urban residents (see Table 11.4).

With the housing reform in progress, the government is also facing issues of urban planning but has not addressed gender issues directly. As new units are constructed and older units are renovated, zoning laws have to change and industries must be relocated, often to the perimeter of the city. New residential housing is also most often located in the suburban rims of the cities, where more land is available. These must be kept separate to reduce health

Table 11.4   Housing Conditions of Households in Chinese Towns and Cities, 1992

	Towns	Cities
Living space per capita (sq.m.)	8.52	6.84
Percent with access to piped waters for exclusive use of the household	58.77	44.50
Percent with no access to sanitary facilities	47.56	71.93
Percent with exclusive use kitchen	66.21	71.17

Source: World Bank, 1992: 22–23.

problems. The differential impacts of urban planning on women and men include issues such as commute distance, provision of daycare near the home, green spaces used for gardening to supplement the family's diet at low cost, facilities such as elevators, access to piped water, and private (or easily accessible) kitchens and bathrooms.

As planners transform the cities from walled compounds centered at the work units to neighborhoods spatially distinct from the workplace, they have considered some aspects of environment and amenities that are important to women and their families. In Nanjing, for example, two large comfortable housing projects, started in 1996, include "primary schools, kindergartens, cultural and recreational centers, commercial service networks and property management offices, to provide good social management services. Twelve other cities throughout China are building such exemplary houses also" (FBIS, 9/25/96).

Planners are paying some attention to broader environmental issues as well. They have abandoned several proposed construction sites on the outskirts of Beijing because of inadequate infrastructure for water supply and the low level of the water table (FBIS, 8/28/96). They have expressed concern about planting trees and protecting the environment to improve living conditions (*Xinhua,* 8/29/97). Still, there is no effort to foster a participatory process in these projects that would involve women at all stages of development. Chinese officials, for example, should not lose sight of the fact that many women use their homes for home-based activities such as preparing foods and goods for sale, or other microenterprises (see Chapter 1; Chant, 1996b; World Bank, 1992).

The traditional *hutong* design presents one format that could be incorporated into some of the modern housing designs. These closed courtyard compounds have some advantages over high-rises because they have space to grow fruit trees and vegetables, and many families run microenterprises out of them. They lack plumbing, however, and the old shared toilet houses are inconvenient and dirty and sometimes explode from lack of maintenance; many of the courtyards have been filled in by squatter families setting up housing units. Designing units that are environmentally sound and still permit access to customers could benefit women and their families significantly.

CONCLUSION: AGENCY AND STRATEGIES

After the Communist Revolution, China's housing policy provided a cramped security to urban residents; housing units consisted of one or two rooms where toilet facilities were down the hall or outside of the living quarters. Kitchen facilities were elementary, with few refrigerators; charcoal stoves contributed to indoor pollution.[15] The provision of housing as security (or a basic "human right") with minimal attention to comfort accorded well with the official socialist ideology of hard work and dedication to the state.

Women shared this security. Occasionally, they received the family's apartment in their own name; more often, however, they received their state subsidies indirectly through housing allocated to their husbands, fathers-in-law, or, when younger, through their own fathers. Thus, women's limited property rights did not stand on equal footing with those of men. In return for housing and other basic guarantees, women's agency and strategies were defined by the state. Although their agency expanded with the provision of essentially universal primary and secondary education in the cities, they faced severe constraints on strategies. Housing was shelter and a place to take care of children but could not be used for personal income-earning activities.

Market reforms have unleashed a torrent of pent-up consumerism and entrepreneurship. New apartment high-rises transform the skylines of Chinese cities. Women who move to these new apartments receive some reduction in their double burden: new units have private bathrooms and kitchens with gas stoves; it is easier to take care of children's needs and other family members in this type of housing; and the reduction in time necessary for homemaking allows women to consider other strategies for improving their quality of life (see Chant, 1996).

Reforms, however, have been a mixed blessing for women. The new forms of housing have not altered property rights significantly.[16] Despite the existence of laws that guarantee women property rights, including the law on women's rights in 1992, little has changed in this area; housing is still mainly provided by the husband's work unit or through his parents, giving him the larger share in official rights.

Ignoring gender issues in housing reform plays into an implicit acceptance and strengthening of traditional gender biases. Men are assumed to have the responsibility to provide housing for their family, and women may base their decisions about whom to date or marry on such financial arrangements (Agence France-Presse, 6/1/96). Although men are pressured in this traditional arrangement to supply for the family, they are still empowered by having more rights in acquiring and retaining property and in getting jobs that pay higher wages.

The specification of property rights is an important area for women's security and opportunity to participate fully in development. For both rental units and purchased homes, it matters whether women have their names on the leases as full partners or owners and whether they have the right to pass the housing on to their children, resell the property, sublet it, and rent rooms out. Renting rooms even in tiny dwellings has been a way for poor women to supplement incomes in many developing countries and could be useful to urban Chinese women also (see Tinker, 1997b). Operating microenterprises from their homes allows poor women to combine childcare with income-earning opportunities. "Gender sensitive housing investment may be one of the few means by which individuals and households can cushion themselves against further deterioration in living standards or construct an escape route out of poverty" (Chant, 1996b: 47).

Success of the housing reform depends on numerous interrelated changes not only in the housing market itself but also in the labor and financial markets, environmental legislation, and the legal structure. Although the goal of reform is to establish a private market in housing and improve allocation of resources, this should not be a market for men only. As the reports from the UN's Habitat II Conference in Turkey in June 1996 summarize, a gendered policy for urban reform needs to include women in the decisionmaking at all levels.

NOTES

1. There were many exceptions, of course. For example, in the 1950s single women could be asked to adopt one of the many orphans whose parents had been killed in the war. They were provided housing and possibly housekeepers as well (based on personal interviews). Widows, however, typically remained in the housing unit provided by the husband or were allocated housing from their own work units.

2. Before the reforms, migration was effectively controlled by requiring people to register for jobs, housing, and ration coupons for grain and cloth; the state kept track of migrants and prevented most illegal migration. Since jobs were guaranteed for most people (those "waiting for employment" were relatively few), and housing was usually provided, homelessness was not a problem. With the market reforms, however, the state cannot easily control the flow of migrants who no longer need the state jobs and ration coupons; furthermore, officials have not made strong efforts to stem the flow. Registration (*hu kou*) is still needed for sending a child to a public school.

3. See World Bank (1992) and Pudney and Wang (1995) for detailed descriptions and criticisms of housing reform in China.

4. "Household" refers to people living together in a housing unit whether they are related or not; "family" refers to related individuals whether they live together or not. In general, these terms are used interchangeably in the literature unless the differences alter the analysis. We will follow this practice of using both terms freely.

5. Chinese statistics distinguish between migrants who settle in one city and transients who move frequently among cities or between the urban and rural areas; these transients are called the "floating population." The percentage of women who are among permanent migrants (40–45 percent) is much higher than that in the floating population (20–33 percent) (Wei Jinsheng, 1995).

6. As key suppliers of urban welfare benefits, state-owned enterprises have had to hire more employees than they need, to provide childcare, health care, and maternity benefits, as well as subsidize housing of their workers.

7. The division into specialized neighborhoods is both a return to traditional urban arrangements (which had neighborhoods and streets devoted to production and sale of specific goods) and an example of newer urban developments with neighborhood shopping centers observed in cities throughout the world. The neighborhood is more specialized than before the reforms but less specialized than in traditional Chinese cities.

8. Officials often force residents to relocate to less convenient sites when housing is torn down to make room for expensive apartments and new buildings. The destruction of the older *hutong* dwellings in Beijing is currently such an issue (Bezlova, 1996; Gaubatz, 1995a; for a discussion of the hutongs, see Wei and Bu, this volume). China is not known for permitting demonstrations against official policies; housing, however, is one of the few areas that has generated so much concern among some affected groups that some have taken to the streets (Bezlova, 1996). Usually these are older residents who have lived most of their lives in an area that is scheduled for new businesses or upscale housing and are being involuntarily relocated to other apartments, sometimes requiring four hours of commute time daily.

9. The labor force participation rate of urban Chinese women is over 70 percent—one of the highest in the world. In 1978, at the beginning of the reforms, women comprised about 28 percent of the workers in state-owned enterprises and about half the workers in urban collectives that provided fewer benefits and were less likely to have access to housing (Research Institute, 1990: 239). Thus, women had less housing security as individuals because they were less likely to have a job that supplied housing and they were less likely to be assigned a unit even when they did work for such a firm. The reduction in housing benefits, however, affects them as family members and individuals.

10. This ratio remains remarkably consistent for unemployment, layoffs, and those identified as "surplus" in both China and Vietnam (see Summerfield, 1997; see also Chapter 4).

11. At the same time that market reforms in China have led to discriminatory labor practices, they have also opened some doors to women: Many new job opportunities exist for younger women in the hotel industry, export-processing plants, and private businesses, although working conditions and low pay levels remain a problem.

12. At times, apartment buildings have been privatized involuntarily. The tenants who were not normally part of the decisionmaking process have often been forced to vacate because of the high prices of the units (personal interview with a resident of Fujian Province). This is becoming more common nationally since the 1998 reforms (Poole, 1998: 18).

13. Work units, however, pushed the limits of legality by buying many units at below-market prices just before the July reforms in 1998. These will be distributed to favorite employees who may then purchase them at subsidized prices (Poole, 1998: 18).

14. The funds were initiated as part of the Shanghai model in 1991, drawing on Singapore's practice (see Fei, Pyle, this volume).

15. The elite—government officials, cadre, and workers at state-owned enter-prises—typically received the best housing; intellectuals and others with "bad class" backgrounds were allocated smaller units.

16. Property rights can be divided into ownership rights and use rights. Land is still owned solely by the state in both urban and rural areas. Housing has been owned by individuals in rural areas throughout the communist period and now can be owned by urban residents. Use rights to both land and housing have changed since the market reforms.

12

The Impacts of Shanghai Housing Reform

Fei Juanhong

Food, clothing, housing, and transportation are basic necessities of human life. Only by assuring its citizens decent living and working conditions can a society achieve stability and unity. Therefore, one of the important goals of our country, China, as income grows in the transition period is to overcome housing difficulties and thus improve living conditions. This chapter examines housing reforms in Shanghai, discussing aspects that particularly affect women. The first section provides the context of the current housing situation and problems in Shanghai. This is followed by a discussion of the reforms in the 1980s and 1990s. The remainder of the chapter addresses how the changes affect women in terms of employment and family life, such as residence patterns and divorce. Key issues are summarized in the conclusion.

CURRENT SITUATION AND PROBLEMS OF HOUSING IN SHANGHAI

Before 1949, the housing shortage in Shanghai was extremely serious, with a great disparity in quality between the rich and the poor. In 1949, there were altogether 23.6 million square meters (sq.m.) of housing in Shanghai (Office, 1991: 214–215), 33.7 percent of which were occupied by the rich, who made up 10 percent of the total population. The remaining 66.3 percent of the houses (among which one-fifth were unsafe), were jammed with the laboring people accounting for 90 percent of the total population (Sun, 1983: 151–155).

Since 1949, the government has shown great concern over the housing problem. Housing has been constructed in a planned way (see Table 12.1). During the twenty-eight years from 1950 to 1978, 17.93 million sq.m. of housing was completed in Shanghai. Especially since the end of the Cultural Revolution

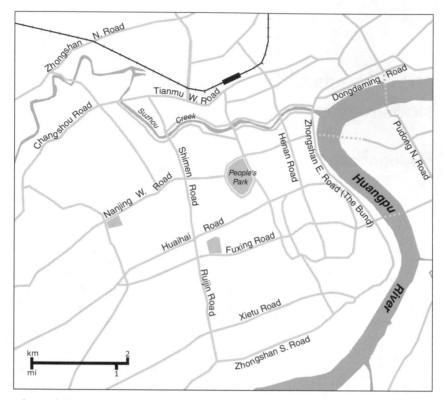

Shanghai

that marked the beginning of the reform period, housing construction has been rapid, with 43.68 million sq.m. of new residential construction in the ten years from 1979 to 1989 (Office, 1991: 214–215). From 1991 to 1995, another 35 million sq.m. were added (Zhang and Gao, 1997). Meanwhile, the housing standards and living conditions have been raised to a certain degree after years of effort. The average living space per capita in Shanghai proper grew from 3.9 sq.m. in 1949 (Office, 1991: 214–215) to 4.5 sq.m. in 1979 (Sun, 1983: 151–155). Since the economic reforms, the average living space per capita has greatly increased, reaching 6.4 sq.m. in 1989 (Office, 1991: 214–215), 8.0 sq.m. in 1995, and 8.5 sq.m. in 1996 (Shanghai Statistics Bureau, 1997: 10).

Per capita living space in Shanghai, however, is still inadequate, and the construction of housing since the reforms is not exceptional compared to other Chinese cities; in 1994, for example, the average living space per capita had come up to 8.73 sq.m. in Beijing, 8.38 sq.m. in Guangzhou, and 8.10 sq.m. in Hangzhou, all exceeding Shanghai's figure of 8.0 sq.m. in 1995 (Planning and Finance, 1995). In 1989, only half of the apartments in the city

Table 12.1   Newly Built Housing and Average Living Space per Capita in Shanghai, 1949–1996

	Newly Built Housing (million sq.m.)	Average Living Space per capita (sq.m.)
1949	23.59[a]	3.9
1950–1978	17.93	
1979		4.5
1979–1989	43.68	
1989		6.4
1991–1995	35.00	
1995		8.0
1996	12.30	8.5

Sources: Shanghai Statistics Bureau, 1997: 10; Office of Shanghai Housing System Reform, 1991: 214–215; Zhang and Gao, 1997; Sun, 1983: 155.
    a. The statistic for 1949 is the number of total houses.

had their own kitchen and toilet. The quality of housing was still low in 1995, with 1.65 million sq.m. of existing houses in Shanghai in need of extensive repair (Zhang and Gao, 1997; Office, 1991: 214–215). A more critical issue was that 61,500 families in Shanghai had an average living space per capita under 4 sq.m. in 1995. In addition, there are lots of newly married couples who are in urgent need of houses every year. Millions of rural-urban migrants add to the demand for housing. The contradictions of the housing shortage in Shanghai have been very serious for a long time, partly because of the deficiency before 1949, and partly due to the two following reasons.

One factor contributing to the housing shortage is rapid population growth. Shanghai is a metropolis with a very large population. In the early 1950s, it had a population of 5 million residents. Childbearing peaked in the 1950s, but millions of people moved to Shanghai during the 1980s. In the mid-1990s, there are more than 13 million residents (plus several million temporary migrants), and the density of population in the city proper is around 11,000 people per square kilometer. Apparently, the sharp increase in population pressure has greatly sharpened the original contradictions in the housing shortage in Shanghai.

Another factor in the housing shortage in Shanghai is the system of constructing and allocating housing. In China, land is owned by the state. Between 1949 and the late 1970s, residents in cities and towns were not allowed to build or buy houses individually. Thus, most of the houses were public ones. Even in 1990, after the reform of allowing personal purchases, private residences accounted for only 21.4 percent of existing houses in Shanghai (Yang and Wang, 1992: 222–223). Since 1949, the housing system in Chinese cities and towns has been a method of administrative allotment, characterized by low rents. Under this system, staff and workers were provided, at little cost, with houses by the units they worked in as a kind of welfare. In the years just following 1949, rent accounted for 6–10 percent of family expenses in cities and towns, but this figure dropped to 0.73 percent in 1989 (Yang and Wang, 1992: 222–223).

With the rise of living standards following economic reform, it has been quite evident that the traditional housing system could not satisfy people's growing demand for housing anymore. First, the government as well as the enterprises are not in a position to raise the huge funds required to speed up the construction of houses. Second, the traditional housing system also runs counter to the economic incentives in a socialist market economy and hinders the further development of economic reform. Therefore, the reform of our country's housing system in cities and towns is imperative. In fact, it has been placed on the agenda as a key component of economic reform in the 1980s.

HOUSING SYSTEM REFORM IN SHANGHAI

Since Deng Xiaoping initiated the overall design for housing system reform in 1980, Shanghai has experienced two stages in its process of housing reform, 1980–1990 and 1991 to the present. During the first stage (1980–1990), two main measures were taken. One was to end the practice of state and local governments undertaking the whole investment for housing construction. It was made clear that enterprises would settle the housing problems of their staff and workers by themselves. The other was to introduce commercial housing to the public.

The second stage began on February 8, 1991, when the municipal government in Shanghai put forward a systematic document named "Executive Plan of Housing System Reform in Shanghai." It defined the guidelines of gradually bringing the construction, exchange, distribution, and consumption of housing into the orbit of a planned commodity economy. It also formulated certain principles in the reform, such as "realizing the commercialization of housing and letting people earn their own houses step by step" and "establishing a mechanism of raising housing construction funds through joint efforts by the state, collective and individual."

The major components of the reform are:

1. Using a public accumulation fund. This is a long-term fund specially reserved for housing in the social-security sense; it is jointly paid by staff and workers in cities and towns and their work units; it is owned by staff and workers.
2. Raising rents and giving subsidies. The rent of public housing will be increased progressively. At the same time, staff and workers are granted relevant subsidies.

3. Rationalizing houses with bonds. Staff and workers must now buy a certain amount of housing construction bonds when they rent public houses.

4. Selling preferential houses. While allotting houses, every unit must put into effect the principle of selling before renting to encourage staff and workers to purchase houses at preferential prices.

These four points are the main aspects of housing reform in Shanghai; the first and fourth points (the public accumulation fund and rationalizing houses with bonds) were first implemented in Shanghai (drawing on the Singapore model discussed in Chapter 2). Other areas in China are trying different systems; the second point (raising rents and wages), for example, is associated with the Yantai model. Based on the various models of housing reform in the country, the "Decision of the State Council on Furthering the Housing System Reform in Cities and Towns" was officially promulgated on July 18, 1994, as the guide to national reform. It advanced a pluralistic approach for housing reform, including use of housing accumulation funds, rent reform, sale of public houses, development of a real estate trading market and socialized housing maintenance and management markets, and acceleration of construction of appropriate housing that is "cheap but good."

THE IMPACT OF HOUSING REFORM ON WOMEN IN SHANGHAI

Housing reform is linked to many other necessary economic reforms in the transition to a market-oriented economy, such as reforms of the financial and monetary systems, the wage system, the social-security system, and construction and management systems. So it is a gradual process that is implemented step by step. Although not yet having achieved substantial progress, the Chinese housing reform has advanced toward commercialization of housing with more than ten years' practice.

Every major social change will have different influences on various social and gender groups. What is the influence of the current housing reform on women as a special gender group in the society? The following analysis examines this question from the angles of employment and marriage.

Employment and Housing Reform

The specific plan of the Shanghai housing reform shows that neither establishing an accumulation fund nor increasing rental fees for housing cuts the umbilical cord that links housing and the work unit. These changes do, however, establish a new type of relation between housing and employment as well as income.

First, the prerequisite for the enjoyment of housing benefits is to be employed. The accumulation fund is designed to increase the ability of laboring families to solve their housing problems; it is paid by the laborers and their work units together and belongs to laborers. A housing subsidy is given by work units to their workers and staff, who rent public houses, to offset the increments in rental fees. It is clear that these two kinds of housing welfare are given by work units to their own workers and staff members. In other words, only the people in formal employment can enjoy them.

Second, how much one can enjoy the housing welfare is based on his/her wage (high or low) and his/her work unit's economic benefits (good or bad). The housing subsidy in Shanghai accounts for 2 percent of one's wage or retirement pay. The accumulation fund also is paid according to a set percentage of one's wage; in 1991, it was 5 percent in Shanghai. Obviously, the higher one's wage, the more one's work unit pays for his/her accumulation fund. In 1997, another measure has been adopted in Shanghai: "to establish the system of supplementary accumulation fund," that is, the units with good economic benefits can raise the percentage contributed to the housing accumulation fund, in order to push the switch from the allotment of housing in kind to allocation via money and the market (*Wen Hui Bao,* 1997).

How does this new relation between housing and employment as well as income affect women? During the period of "full employment and low income," although dwelling houses were allocated by work units, the link between employment and housing was not as critical since almost everyone worked and unemployment[1] was very low at that time. With the development of economic reform in depth, the rate of unemployment in Shanghai has grown. In 1982, it was only 0.2 percent, then it rose to 2.4 percent in 1993; in absolute numbers, 12,000 unemployed people in 1982 grew to 129,700 in 1993 (*Almanac of Shanghai Statistics 1992:* 100; *Sociology,* 1994, No. 3: 10). Most of the unemployed are women. In recent years, the proportion of women among the unemployed population is 55–58 percent, which is far above the proportion of women in the employed population (42 percent) (Shanghai Women's Federation, 1997: 54). There is no doubt that housing reform will put these women at a disadvantage. On the one hand, they cannot enjoy housing benefits such as the accumulation fund and housing subsidy. On the other hand, they have to pay the rising rent with their low income after being laid off. Even if they find another job, they will probably be at a disadvantage, because women have been in an unfavorable position in the labor market since economic reform was initiated; they tend to be informally employed either as temporary workers, who cannot enjoy the benefits of formal workers, or as part-time workers, who either do not receive benefits or only receive partial benefits.

Moreover, in the past, the general level of housing in Shanghai was low, and housing standards were strictly controlled by the government, so the differences among groups and individuals were not great. At that time, houses were allocated according to one's title, family size, length of service, and so on. There was no direct relation between housing distribution and income distribution. Commercialization of housing, however, requires organization of construction, distribution, exchange, and consumption of houses in light of economic market rules. Under the effect of the economic lever, the situation of one's housing is largely determined by one's income. In this way, the enlargement of differences in income distribution will necessarily bring about the enlargement of differences in housing distribution.

First, gender differences in housing distribution will increase. At present, more women than men are concentrated in jobs with lower pay. An investigation made by the National Labor Department in 1988 shows that the female-to-male ratio in employment income in Shanghai among workers and staff members in July 1988 is 88:100 (*The Investigation of Shanghai Women's Social Status,* 1994: 112). At present, the amount of housing accumulation fund is very small, and purchase of new private houses is not common yet; only 700,000 sq.m. was sold to individuals out of 2.34 million sq.m. of commercial houses sold in 1980–1990 in Shanghai (Office, 1991: 214–215). Over time, however, these market reforms will become more influential, and women's lower income will not only provide them fewer work-related housing benefits than men but also will lower their ability to rent and purchase houses relative to men.

Second, housing distribution tends toward polarization. At the time of "eating from the common pot," everyone's income was low, and there were no great differences in housing. People neither had money nor were they allowed to buy dwelling houses. Since economic reform, some people became rich quickly, and income distribution now tends to be polarized. When housing is put into the market, those with strong economic strength naturally will take the lead in renting and purchasing high-standard dwellings. By comparison, those people who have difficulties in housing already and now have difficulties in the market economy will not have the possibility to be allotted a house and have little or no money to buy one or pay rising rents. Although the housing reform is based on several models, the policy of commercialization of housing will put these people in a disadvantageous position.

The phenomenon of polarization in housing distribution appears among women, too. In recent years, a number of successful women are emerging as entrepreneurs, merchants, business owners, staff members in foreign-funded enterprises, and so on. These women with high incomes are most capable of improving their housing first. In addition, some wealthy single women are beginning to rent and purchase high-grade dwelling houses. By comparison, women working in enterprises in a bad economic situation, who have low incomes and heavy family burdens, and who have been laid off or compelled to take early retirement cannot easily improve their housing; although they may be married, their total family income will be affected by the woman's loss of income.

Housing reform also offers women new opportunities to make a life and advance their careers by using their houses as the means of production. Housing reform is a part of economic reform. Since the beginning of reform, one can find in Shanghai that many houses along the streets are used as shops such as hair salons, restaurants, dressmaking shops, and groceries. Usually these shops are not large, and many of their owners and employers are women. They may be laid off from their original work units, or they may be trying to improve their financial condition by engaging in a new job. Some of them use their dwellings directly for shops. Others exert great efforts to exchange their original houses for ones along the streets, then transform them into shops.

Marriage and Housing Reform

Though women participate in social labor as do men, women retain the main role in families. They manage house affairs and bring up children. All these activities are engaged in mainly at home. Therefore, housing is a more important factor for women than for men. For a long time, the shortage of housing in Shanghai has greatly limited marriage and family life. This has expressed itself first in the postmarital residence of women.

Postmarital Residence.   According to surveys in 1982 and 1993, the virilocal residence (living with the husband's family) and the unilocal residence (nuclear family not tied to residence area of either set of parents) are the main residential forms for postmarital women in Shanghai (*Study of the Urban Family in Contemporary China,* 1995: 125; *The Chinese Urban Family,* 1985: 322–324). During the past forty years, however, dramatic changes have happened. Virilocal residence is the traditional residential form for postmarital women and is a product of patriarchy. As shown in Table 12.2, after the establishment of new China during the 1950s and 1960s (with transformation of the family system and promotion of the perception of equality of sexes and consciousness of independence of youth), the percentage of women/couples who chose virilocal residence dropped by one-half in comparison with the preliberation period, and the percentage of women/couples who selected unilocal residence increased rather quickly (12–20 percent). From the late 1970s to the early 1980s, in contrast, the proportion of virilocal residence rose radically, even exceeding the rates before 1949, while unilocal residence decreased swiftly, lower than the period before 1949. This was not caused by any new change of family system or perceptions. Lack of housing in Shang-

Table 12.2   Shanghai Urban Women's Postmarital Residence by Marriage Year (in percent)

	pre–1949	1950–1957	1958–1965	1966–1976	1977–1983	1984–1993	
Virilocal	58	28	28	42	63	61.3	
	(45)	(25)	(20)	(36)	(56)		
Unilocal	34	58	46	32	22	30.6	
	(47)	(67)	(62)	(44)	(24)		
Uxorilocal	6	9	21	17	13	7.5	
	(7)	(6)	(16)	(19)	(17)		
Other	2	5	5	9	2	0.6	
	(1)	(2)	(2)	(1)	(3)		
N (persons)	130	109	81	114	190	173	797[a]
	(813)	(418)	(252)	(441)	(379)		(2,303[a])

Sources: Study of the Urban Family in Contemporary China (Shanghai: China Social Sciences Publishing House, 1995): 125: a survey of 33 neighborhoods in 10 districts of Shanghai in 1993.

Note: Virilocal refers to couples living with/near the husband's family; uxorilocal refers to living with/near the wife's family; unilocal is independent of either parent group, the typical nuclear family.

For comparison, the results of a sample of three subdistricts of Shanghai carried out in 1982 are given in parentheses under the 1993 survey results; these are taken from *The Chinese Urban Family* (Shanghai: Shandong Publishing House, 1985), 322–324.

a. Total number of observations in the study.

hai has seriously limited the selection freedom of women as to postmarital residential forms.

Judged by specific time, the Chinese birthrate peak in the 1950s brought the attendant increase of the marriage rate in the 1980s. In Shanghai, the marriage rate in 1978 was .78 percent and rose to 2.45 percent in 1981.[2] Because of the Cultural Revolution, which lasted for ten years (1966–1976), few housing units were built between 1970 and 1980; new housing construction in that decade provided only 21.1 percent of the total housing built from 1949 to 1980. Therefore, in 1989 there were more than 400,000 female youths of marital age without houses for their marriage (Sun, 1983: 151–155). Some young women made having a house a prerequisite in selecting their boyfriends. At the same time, the housing shortage also made women return to the traditional virilocal residence. The more limited the supply of housing, the more often virilocal residence was used.

Since housing reform in the 1980s, with its increase of newly built houses, the percentage of unilocal residence has risen again; the virilocal residence has tended to decrease (see Table 12.2). Therefore, it can be predicted that additional development of housing reform will give women more freedom in selecting postmarital residential forms, and unilocal residence will become more common as the supply of housing increases.

Family Life

The housing shortage has been one of the most serious social problems in Shanghai. It has hindered the upgrade of quality of life for Shanghai residents. Some have not been able to obtain the basic housing conditions that ensure human dignity. For example, at the end of 1982 there were 44,000 families in Shanghai for which the living area for each person was less than 2 sq.m. There were 602,000 families in which three generations lived in one room (Sun, 1983: 151–155). A study in 1982 of 635 married women at the Changchun Subdistrict, Hongkou District, Shanghai, showed that in 51 percent of the families the wife and husband had no room of their own. If analyzed by family types, 61.4 percent of nuclear families, 35.4 percent of stem families, and 39.2 percent of united families lived in one room (*The Chinese Urban Family,* 1985: 155).

Because of poor living conditions, there has not been enough space among family members. The women who lived in a room with growing children or in-laws were in a very awkward situation for their family life. Moreover, this living environment could easily cause tense relationships among family members, especially between daughters-in-law and mothers-in-law. In a room, whatever was done by the daughter-in-law could be seen by the mother-in-law, and whatever was said by the mother-in-law could be heard by the daughter-in-law. It often happened that contradictions between mother/daughter-in-law set off conflicts between husband and wife and dissolution of the marriage in the end.

Since housing reform was initiated, investment in housing construction has become multilateral, and this has speeded up construction. From 1979 to 1989 and from 1991 to 1995, about 1.43 million families (4.7 million people) moved into new houses (*Shanghai Housing System Reform,* 1991: 215; Zhang and Gao, 1997). This means that about one-third of Shanghai residents obtained new rooms or apartments. In 1996, the average living space per capita grew to 8.5 sq.m. (Shanghai Statistic Bureau, 1997: 10). At the same time, the living quality has improved as well. In the past, living conditions in Shanghai were characterized by small, dark, low rooms with coal stoves and no private bathrooms. Now, the percentage of apartments with gas ranges and private toilets has increased greatly. Moreover, the neighborhood environment has been given more attention than before. Trees and grasses have been planted, and facilities such as shops, schools, and hospitals are being arranged. As economic reform has brought about a general improvement in living standards for common people, housing reform has brought about comprehensive promotion of residential conditions. This helps women acquire the dignity they should have in family life. As family members get some individual space at home, family contradictions have decreased a great deal. At the same time, decent living conditions and comfortable homes can play a positive role in promoting the physical and mental health of women, helping them to achieve more success in their work.

Divorce

Since the reforms and opening-up, the divorce rate in Shanghai is starting to rise, from .004 percent in 1978 to .05 percent in 1983.[3] In terms of divorced people, there were 60,642 who divorced in 1982 and 101,875 in 1990 (*Statistical Data of Shanghai Women*, 1994: 132–133). Over time, people are taking a more tolerant attitude toward divorce than before, and the law has been modified accordingly. The housing shortage, however, has often been a blockade to women who want to rid themselves of unfortunate marriages. In order to protect the interests of women and to weaken the negative impacts of divorce on them, the law states that houses owned or rented by a couple will be shared by them while they divorce. Since the dwelling house is not big enough for most families in Shanghai, in practice it is often very difficult to split or exchange a house for two. Thus, housing often becomes a main issue in hindering the divorce of a couple.

Yet as seen from Table 12.2, about one-half of married women in Shanghai are in virilocal residence. This often makes women victims in the event of divorce. After divorce they have no place to live. Although we have not yet collected data to support this view for all of Shanghai, an investigation was made in the Dongchen District in 1997 and can be used as a reference. In ten subdistricts, 61.1 percent of divorced women have no housing.

So what will be the impact of housing reform on divorced women? The main reason for divorced women to fall into a passive position in housing is that they frequently live in their in-laws' house or live with their husband in a one-bedroom apartment that was assigned by his work unit. Therefore, once these women get divorced, they must leave. It should be pointed out that their selection of virilocal residence is not based on traditional perceptions but is a constraint imposed on them by objective material conditions. Housing reform makes it possible for women to change the dependence on their husbands in housing. On the one hand, with commercialization of housing, more dwelling houses can be established, and there are more ways to get them. On the other hand, working women can get the same rate in the accumulation fund for housing and enjoy the same rights in applying for loans from this fund. It can be expected that housing rights will take a form of joint ownership by a couple, and the unfavorable situation for divorced women on housing will be gradually changed.

CONCLUSION

In sum, for a long time, women in Shanghai have not had rights to housing in their own names: before marriage, they live in their parents' house; after marriage, they live in their in-laws' house. The housing shortage has strengthened the tradition of virilocal residence. Housing reform contributes to more freedom for women to select the type of residence and break from the old, patriarchal pattern. Along with the general improvement of living standards of common people since the economic reforms, housing reform can help women to get ownership rights for housing. Not only can unmarried women own their own houses; married women will also be able to own houses jointly with their husbands. Certainly, the continuing improvement of living conditions brought about by housing reform will further raise the physical and mental health and quality of life of women.

Nevertheless, with the gradual deepening of the reform and development of the market mechanism in China, gender-based differences and polarization of personal income have become more and more apparent and will be reflected in housing reform. The gains from the housing reform for women and men are different. Even among women, the housing gap will be broad and deep. Therefore, in developing housing reform, a major social issue is how to decrease the negative influences for women living in disadvantageous economic situations.

NOTES

1. Before 1994, unemployment was referred to as the rate of waiting for jobs.
2. Marriage rate: Divide the number of people who get married by the average number of population that year (*Almanac of China Population 1985:* 268).
3. Divorce rate: Divide the number of people who get divorced by the average number of population that year (*Almanac of China Population 1985:* 268).

13

State and Market Provision of Housing in Shanghai

Barbara Hopkins

> You must seize the last few years of the 20th century. This is Shanghai's last opportunity.
>
> —Deng Xiaoping, the late Chinese premier, during his last visit
> to Shanghai in 1994, addressing senior municipal leaders
> (Shanghai Star, *August 15, 1997*)

Thirty years of postrevolutionary neglect left Shanghai's housing stock in need of improvement and expansion. In the 1980s, enterprise reforms brought increased investment, and housing policies began the evolution toward market provision. Today, Shanghai officials, caught in a race to become a world-class city, are taking policy cues from the government-supported markets in Singapore and Hong Kong. Meanwhile, Shanghai's progress is being watched closely by national policymakers in Beijing and mayors of other Chinese cities who are following in the race to modernize. Therefore, the impact of Shanghai's housing reform on women needs to be explored.

The welfare of women is not the primary concern of policymakers facing the intercity competition for international recognition. Shanghai officials expect to be "the biggest financial centre in China by the end of the century, the biggest in the region by 2005 and a global financial centre by 2010" (Muzinet, 1997). They have set out to capture the world's attention by presenting an imposing skyline to rival Hong Kong's[1] and by catching up to the standard of living in so-called advanced countries. Shanghai is adding 220 skyscrapers, including the Shanghai World Financial Center. At 460 meters, it will be the world's tallest building once it is complete early next century (*Star News,* 1997). In theory, the imposing building will show the world that Shanghai is a financial center. The tall buildings of the financial district, the fancy department stores, the lights of Nanjing Lu, and the elevated roads and bridges across the Huangpu River all show the world that Shanghai is a cosmopolitan city in a class with other major cities of the world such as Hong Kong, Singapore, and New York.

Although these changes in city planning and housing policies are transforming Shanghai's landscape, the development of consumer culture is transforming women's relationships to their homes and occupations. City leaders interpret the growth of consumerism as a sign of Shanghai's sophistication and wealth. Statistics on the rising consumption by Shanghainese "show that local citizens now more prefer modern lifestyles" (*Shanghai Daily,* 1997). Consumption of personal computers, air conditioners, and microwave ovens shows the world that Shanghai citizens are "advanced." However, "modern" lifestyles may not always improve the lives of all women.

Housing reform is changing the quantity, quality, and distribution of housing in Shanghai. This reform is taking place within the context of the changes in attitudes about city planning and the changes in women's relationships to their homes and workplaces. These changes involve both costs and benefits that are not equally distributed across Shanghai society. It is the interaction of all of these forces that will determine the impact of housing reforms on women's lives as Shanghai moves to a market economy.

PROVISION OF HOUSING

Housing was not a priority before market reforms. Shanghai had insufficient funds for investment in housing. Investment in housing came to a complete halt at the beginning of the Cultural Revolution. Well into the 1980s, one-half the city's population lived in housing built between 1890 and 1920 (Hyslop, 1990). The housing shortage was exacerbated by a rapid increase in population after the Cultural Revolution. Many young people sent to the countryside began to return. At its peak, in 1978–1980, net inward migration reached more than 400,000 people, raising Shanghai's population to 11.5 million— over twice its size in 1950 (White, 1996).

Reforms have increased the stock of housing. Average living space per person, excluding kitchens and toilets, was 8.6 square meters in 1997—up from 8.0 in 1995 and 4.5 in 1979.[2] According to government officials, living space will soon reach 10 square meters per person (Zhang, 1997).

The government is interested not only in increasing the stock of housing but also in providing a minimum standard. The government upgraded the definition of hardship cases in 1985 to all those living in less than 4.0 square meters of living space per person. They plan to relocate all hardship families to new flats. By 1997, 30,221 of the 73,794 households living in cramped housing had been moved to larger flats. The government plans to improve the housing of the remaining 43,573 households by the year 2000.[3] Reforms have increased the range in housing quality. Women are likely to be disadvantaged in the provision of higher-quality housing either by enterprises or the market.

ENTERPRISE PROVISION

Before reform, work units and the municipal government allocated housing. Housing frequently represented part of the benefits package provided by one's work unit (*dan wei*). The distribution of housing was determined by the type of work unit and its place within the centrally planned economy (Lee, 1995). Local governments provided housing for those who did not work for work units or whose work units could not provide housing (Gaubatz, 1995b). Within work units, housing was allocated based on a set of criteria developed by central authorities, including the rank of the worker as well as marital status. Many authors in this volume have suggested that women were disadvantaged by this process because of assumptions that they would live with their parents before marriage and in housing provided by their husbands' work unit following marriage.

Reforms in 1980 created an opportunity for enterprises to invest in housing projects for their employees. Investment in housing increased by 59 percent in 1980 (Chu, 1996). Most of the financial resources for the new construction came from enterprises. Newly created development companies initially sold much of the new housing to enterprises. Individual buyers who bought before 1988 frequently purchased their housing at discounted prices through their employers (Chu, 1996). Most of the increase in the housing stock between 1980 and 1993 was in staff quarters. Staff quarters increased from 14,013,000 square meters to 63,580,000 square meters (34 percent of total housing stock to 60 percent of total housing stock) (Chu, 1996: 347). This represents 77 percent of the increase in housing stock between 1980 and 1993. Despite the growth of the private market since 1993,[4] staff quarters continued to increase as a share of total housing stock. In 1996, staff quarters increased to 94,200,200 square meters of housing space (more than 70 percent of total housing stock) (Shanghai Municipal Statistics Bureau, 1997).

Thus, enterprises dominated the allocation of housing as the housing stock increased. The quality of an individual's housing depended on the financial resources of his or her work unit. "Better work units provide better housing, and this housing tends to be located in districts in which better schools are located" (Gaubatz, 1995b: 39). Despite the rhetoric of labor market equality, men were more likely to have better jobs that provided better housing. Thus, families will rationally choose to receive housing through the husband's work unit. In much of China, it is quite rare to find family housing allocated by the wife's work unit. However, anecdotal reports point to cases without housing discrimination where many women received the housing benefit and then shared it with their husbands. A friend of mine working at a risky joint-venture job lived in staff housing provided to his wife by her work unit. Another colleague told me that the majority of women in her work unit receive housing directly rather than through their husbands. I have found no comprehensive data on housing allocation by sex. In a survey of women's status in Shanghai, housing is noticeably absent from the data on employee benefits (China Women's Federation, 1994).

The survey did ask about decisions on housing in marriages, however. Although most people, 56 percent, indicated that the decisionmaker was not clear, 10 percent indicated that husbands were dominant, while only 3 percent indicated that wives were dominant. Thirty percent indicated that decisions were jointly made. This may simply indicate that rational women agree with their husbands that, if the husband's work unit provides higher-quality housing, they should accept it. Although there is no direct evidence on which partner's work unit provides housing, commuting times indicate that more men live near their place of work than women. The percentage of men with a one-to fifteen-minute commute to work is almost twice that of women, but still only 11.15 percent (see the discussion related to Table 13.3). This clearly represents only a small fraction of staff housing, yet there is no reason to assume that housing located far from work is any less likely to be allocated to women employees in favor of men than housing near work. Thus, although disparities do exist, they do not seem as severe in Shanghai as elsewhere.

Yet disparities may increase as the labor market continues to develop. Competition in the labor market is likely to shift the allocation priorities of enterprises. Subsidies to purchase housing or higher-quality housing allocations are already being used to attract desirable employees. In an environment where employers have artificially raised entry requirements for women recruits and 75 percent prefer to hire males (Croll, 1995), housing will not be used to entice women to work for a particular enterprise. Women attempting to find work in "male" jobs are not likely to receive housing benefits—if they can find work at all.[5] If the current scarcity of affordable housing in the private market continues and enterprises use housing predominantly to attract "desirable" employees, some women may be forced into female-dominated professions solely to obtain housing.

MARKET PROVISION

Housing reforms are designed not just to increase the housing stock but also to commodify it. For the Shanghai municipal government, commodification has meant that housing would be set at prices that reflected the quality of the units. Discounted prices were offered early on to help workers afford housing. Even with discounts, however, the average family had no incentive to invest in housing when rents were so low, and few had resources to finance a house in any case. Therefore, in 1991, following the Singapore model (see Chapter 2), the government imposed forced savings to a housing fund. However, at 5 percent of monthly income for 1993, savings requirements in Shanghai are much lower than they are in Singapore. Rents were raised, yet they remain low. Average per capita expenditures on rent were only 50 RMB (yuan, the Chinese currency) for all of 1996. Recently, incentive packages have been directed toward nonresidents to attract buyers and revitalize the sluggish real estate market. The Shanghai construction industry has tapped into the wealthy migrant population through its "blue card" strategy, which offered residence permits to Chinese buying property in Pudong. Enterprises in Pudong have also taken advantage of the program for their employees (Xin, 1997).

Private ownership is still an insignificant part of the market. Between 1983 and 1990, 753,000 square meters of new housing were sold to local individuals at discounted prices. Between 1988 and 1993, 738,000 square meters of new housing were sold to individuals at market prices (Chu, 1996). Together these private sales of new housing represented less than 12 percent of total housing space in 1993.[6] Ownership statistics for 1996 were unavailable. However, single houses and new apartments, which are likely to be private, represent only 2.3 percent of the total urban housing stock. If all of the sales in the secondary market represent new sales of old housing, private purchases of old housing between 1986 and 1994 still represent less than 1 percent of the 1996 housing stock.[7]

As with enterprise provision, market forces can generate disparities in the allocation of housing to women and men. Markets tend to have a broader range of housing quality. Assigning market values to housing stock leads to an allocation according to income. Those with higher incomes will be able to afford higher-quality housing. Thus, inequalities in labor markets will generate inequalities in the new distribution of housing. Since women are disadvantaged in labor markets, women will be disadvantaged in housing markets (see Chapter 12). In Shanghai in 1990, 70 percent of women earned less than 200 RMB per month compared to 44 percent of men. Only 5 percent of women earned more than 300 RMB compared to 12.5 percent of men (China Women's Federation, 1994; see Table 13.1).

Private housing opportunities for all but the very well-off have been limited. In 1994, housing prices in the secondary market approached market values of 2,114 RMB per square meter (Chu, 1996 #36). In 1995, the value of residential houses sold in Shanghai averaged 2,477 RMB per square meter. An apartment providing the minimum goal of 10 square meters per person for a young couple with a child would be a bit larger than a spacious master bedroom and would have cost almost 75,000 RMB.[8] The average wage in Shang-

Table 13.1   Share of Employees Earning Various Monthly Incomes in Shanghai by Sex, 1990

Monthly Income (RMB)	Population (%)	Men (%)	Women (%)
1–50	0.22	0.46	0
51–100	6.5	2.63	10.13
100–150	19.43	25.9	12.52
151–200	31.61	34.3	4.83
201–300	32.29	23.73	3.06
301–400	6.88	3.62	0.64
More than 400	1.64	2.16	1.16

Source: China Women's Federation, 1994.

hai was higher than in most of China, but at 9,279 RMB per year, 75,000 looks pretty steep—even when both parents work.

However, even if an average family could afford it, would it be able to find a 30–square meter apartment for sale? As Table 13.2 implies, most of the new commodity housing has been intended for overseas Chinese and nouveau riche entrepreneurs. Those who were displaced by housing projects downtown on rare occasions receive housing in the new housing projects. Most are relocated to new housing in remote suburbs such as Pudong, separated from central Shanghai by the Huangpu River.

The take-a-risk-and-get-rich-quick atmosphere that market reforms have created in Shanghai has done more to promote luxury housing than affordable housing. Private developers motivated by profit prefer building luxury housing, because they want to sell to the highest bidder. Furthermore, in 1992, overseas land developers entered the market concentrating on the overseas market. Developers have been competing vigorously for the upscale market. Buildings for overseas residents rose from 220,000 square meters in 1992 to more than 11 million square meters in 1996 (Wei, 1997). By late 1997, 95 percent of funds spent in Shanghai on new housing went to developers who attract only 5 percent of buyers (Chen, 1997a). In the first quarter of 1997, housing units sold in the new markets had an average floor space of 147 square meters per unit. Compared with old walkups in China (at approximately 55 square meters of usable floor space per unit), or luxury high-rises in Malaysia (at 120 square meters per unit), or even my own spacious American two-bedroom apartment (90 square meters), 147 square meters seems lavish (World Bank, 1992). Developers have produced more than can be sold. Unused housing was 11 percent of the total in 1994, 18 percent in 1995, and 19 percent in 1996, with further increases expected for 1997 (Chen, 1997c).

Recent declines in the housing market have prompted calls to develop home mortgages available to individuals. However, the credit market may be biased against women. Although the market for bank mortgages is undevel-

Table 13.2   Housing Projects in Shanghai

	Total sq.m.	Units	Average Size	Prices	Costs (per meter)
Projects before 1993					
Commodity housing					
Tian He Project	7,600	92	83		
Hui Yi Garden	8,250	33	250	8,215/sq.m.	
Hu Lang Garden	50,000			37,278	3,896
Jian Guo					3,173
Relocated residents					
Ordinary citizen			45–50		
Hui Yi Garden					1,300
Hu Lang Garden			50		
Jian Guo			60		950
Ying Xiang			71		
1997 projects					
JuYuan residential quarter Pudong	450,000	5,694	79		4,444
Pudong's Blue Card Residents		506		282,609/	
Jiangwan new city			30/ capita	flat	
LongHua			69		3,000
Jing'an renovation of old housing	100,000		no change, but 6 sq.m. for kitchen and toilet added	30,000– 40,000	
Jin'an new city	200,000	>3,000	<67		
Average new construction Jan.– Mar. 1997 totals	1,069,000	7,259	147		
Increase	574,000				
Past based on increase	475,000				

Source: World Bank, 1993; Internet news articles for projects in 1997 (see notes).

Note: Information is based on available information and should not be considered a random sample.

oped, it is not unthinkable, given the attitudes about women expressed by employers, that future loan officers will reject a woman's efforts to secure a home loan without a husband.

THE ROLE OF THE STATE AND THE NEED FOR AFFORDABLE HOUSING

Although new mortgage policies may help, the Shanghai municipal government will not be able to achieve the goal of improving housing quality for those in less than 4 square meters of space solely through commodification. Although market incentives encourage the production of more housing, they do not eliminate poverty housing conditions. The existence of slum housing is not unique to centrally planned economies. Cities with real estate markets also have low-quality housing and shortages of low-income housing. A wealthy country like the United States has a homeless population, despite the freedom to purchase housing. Hong Kong, the epitome of a free-market economy in its manufacturing and trade sectors, houses 45 percent of its residents in public housing (Smart, 1995). Without public housing programs, those who cannot afford quality housing will not be able to get quality housing.

Vice Mayor Xia Keqing has publicly admitted that too much luxury housing is being built. In June 1997, he instituted a new policy stating, "Nobody is allowed to use new land for real estate projects this year."[9] Addressing the problem again in September, Wu Zhengtong, deputy secretary-general of the Shanghai Housing Reform Office, emphasized that "housing should be commercialized instead of free distribution." However, he explains that allocating housing depending on income means that "high-income families should buy from the market, while medium-income families should purchase housing provided by the government and lower-income families should rent state-owned houses." Thus, the government is still responsible for increasing the availability of affordable housing.

Unfortunately, the drive to build a world-class city distracts Shanghai officials from developing low-income housing that could best meet women's needs. In fact, much of the development of a "modern city" represents conspicuous waste.[10] Shanghai's urban planners recommended building tunnels under the Huangpu River rather than building bridges. Planners argued that tunnels would be less costly because they could be built only 15 meters down, while a bridge would have to be 55 meters above the river to allow ships to pass. Despite this advice, Zhu Rongji, then mayor of Shanghai, chose the Nanpu Bridge "simply because a bridge is a highly visible monument while a tunnel is not" (Sung, 1996: 179). Winter sleet closed the bridge in early 1993, indicating another advantage of tunnels. The additional resources needed to build the bridge, including the land needed to construct the ramps that would go up 55 meters and the additional fuel required for trucks to climb the bridge, could have been better used.

THE LOCATION OF HOUSING

Housing reform redistributes the population. The increase in the stock of housing allows many people to move to new locations. Housing markets may be able to rationalize the distance from home to work by allowing families to move closer to the woman's work (see Chapter 11). However, housing reform also coincides with adoption of a new spatial design for Shanghai that concentrates residential and commercial areas. These changes in the city plan separate residential from commercial areas and, thus, home from work.

Table 13.3   Urban Shanghai Residents' Commuting Times, 1992–1993 (in percent)

	Population	Men	Women
0 minutes	18.86	11.15	26.09
1–15	8.61	11.15	6.23
16–30	21.93	23.68	20.29
31–60	24.25	26.63	22.03
60–90	7.86	7.43	8.26
>90	18.49	19.96	17.1

Source: China Women's Federation, 1994.

The prereform plan for Shanghai was intended to minimize transportation time, but it failed. The old plan called for balancing the population density and creating self-contained neighborhoods and towns. Satellite towns were developed to relieve overcrowding in the city. They were designed for specific industries that would provide workers with all the amenities in coordinated communities. Workers' apartments were to be located near factories, commercial areas, schools, medical clinics, markets, and other public amenities (Fung, 1996). For women, the idea of self-contained neighborhoods could mean that women needed less time to get to work and childcare. Daily shopping and errands could be done quickly without venturing too far from home.

Unfortunately, this project was not successful. The lower priority of nonproductive construction meant that satellite towns developed near industry without the amenities. Therefore, most of the workers did not relocate to satellite towns but instead commuted from the center of Shanghai. Central Shanghai, with housing inherited from before the revolution, was not able to achieve the goal, either. Only a small share of the population lived near one spouse's work. Even if housing could be provided close to work, husbands and wives might work far apart. Thus, housing provided by the husband's *dan wei* may be far from the wife's work. With the underdeveloped transportation system, residents faced time-consuming commutes to and from work. For women who are currently receiving housing from their husband's work unit close to his job, markets could allow them to move closer to the wife's workplace.

I am not optimistic that housing reform will lead to significant improvements in commuting time in Shanghai. Commuting times for men and women longer than fifteen minutes are not notably different (see Table 13.3). Thus, most women are not commuting significantly longer than men. For more than 26 percent of Shanghai residents, the commute is more than one hour (China Women's Federation, 1994: 267). The allocation by work units may still be arbitrarily far from the place of work, because enterprises located in a congested part of town could provide additional housing for workers only by locating it far away. Furthermore, in the climate of partial reforms where housing has been commodified, but purchased primarily by work units, work units may have chosen less expensive locations to build or purchase housing.

The presence of a market does not guarantee that affordable housing will be located near women's jobs. First, the balanced and self-contained neighborhood is no longer the goal of urban planners. Shanghai is to be a modern industrialized city patterned after Hong Kong, Singapore, even New York. This requires creating a fashionable downtown. Before reform, planners were moving housing outside the city center to reduce the population density in the center (Chan, 1996). Now planners are making room for commercial interests. The Bund has been designated as one of the central business districts. The stock of housing has declined in the central districts of Huangpu and Nanshi since 1985. Other areas within the inner ring road have been designated as commercial districts intended for development of retail sales. The region between the inner beltway and the planned outer beltway will be used for housing, city industries, and service facilities. The separation between work and family that the market brings is developing into a spatial separation between office and home.

Second, the new work opportunities available to women tend to be in the financial and commercial districts. The financial and commercial districts, as well as many of the new cultural facilities and hotels, are inside the inner ring road. Much of the growth in jobs for women comes from commerce and clerical work (Croll, 1995). These jobs are more likely to be downtown, away from the new housing construction. Dropping one's child off at daycare may require additional side trips that further lengthen the commute. This problem is exacerbated by the decline in the number of kindergartens that has coincided with market reforms.

The new model for urban development limits women's opportunities to choose a desirable location. The current city plan forces families to choose between amenities and the size of one's apartment. Housing in the city center is the most cramped. In 1996, housing in the central districts of Huangpu, Nanshi, and Luwan had residential building space ranging from 8.7 to 10.35 square meters per person (see Table 13.4). The southern and western districts of Xuhui and Changning provided the most space, at 17.6 and 16.5 square meters per person respectively. However, Xuhui and Changning, along with Jing'an, include most of the new luxury-housing developments. These three districts have 72 percent of the independent fenced housing in Shanghai but only 22 percent of total residential building space. Thus, the averages overstate the size of an apartment available to an ordinary Shanghai citizen moving to those districts. The central districts offered the most retail services, cinemas, and doctors. Other districts offered more space in one's apartment as well as more green space. Xuhui, in the south, currently has the only subway access to downtown. Pudong is behind all other areas in the provision of

Table 13.4 Amenities by District in Shanghai

	Personnel in Retail Sales / 1,000 Capita	Hospital Beds / 1,000 Capita	Doctors / 1,000 Capita	Secondary Schools	Student Teacher Ratio	Public Green Areas per Capita (m²)	Per Capita Dwelling Space (m²)
Central districts							
Huangpu	290.10	5.89	7.12	17.00	14.87	0.88	8.74
Nanshi	85.72	6.38	5.14	29.00	15.69	0.24	10.35
Luwan	96.30	7.55	7.98	26.00	13.54	0.54	11.77
Jing'an	99.47	8.93	7.86	19.00	14.70	0.20	12.77
Southern and western districts							
Xuhui	59.26	10.67	6.72	51.00	14.98	2.29	17.55
Changning	57.48	4.91	4.56	34.00	15.63	2.58	16.50
Northern districts							
Putuo	47.59	4.00	3.33	52.00	13.53	1.63	13.01
Zhabei	69.54	5.14	3.97	42.00	5.23	1.05	13.96
Hongkou	66.44	6.20	4.82	46.00	15.15	1.02	14.02
Yangpu	45.63	4.53	3.79	60.00	16.76	1.96	14.88
Outlying districts							
Minhang	49.96	5.32	3.76	42.00	14.46	4.08	10.15
Pudong	43.51	3.29	2.89	84.00	16.84	3.45	14.89

Source: Shanghai Statistical Yearbook, 1997.

amenities. Because of this, many Shanghai residents have resisted moving to Pudong. Transportation to work is likely to remain a problem despite construction of a subway system that will link Pudong and Puxi (Shanghai's center west of the Huangpu River). City planners have identified four commercial districts for continued development to provide retail services to residential areas: Xujiahui, in the southwest in Xuhui; Wujiaochang, in the northeast in Yangpu near the border of Hangkou; Zhenru, in the northwest; and Huamu, in Pudong (Chen, 1997b).

Although the distribution of amenities by district is improving, the concentration of retail services and the construction of high-rise apartments create a modern-style separation between commercial districts and family housing. The new focus away from balanced and self-contained neighborhoods in favor of separate shopping and residential districts may pose additional costs to women. It increases transportation costs by increasing time required for daily shopping and other errands. Shopping time is likely to increase. The urban planners are unlikely to notice, because it does not show up in any of the statistics used to measure the health of the economy.

This division between commercial districts and family housing facilitates the conceptual break between public and private life and separates commercial activities from activities in the household. This separation disadvantages women trying to combine work and family responsibilities by making income-generating activities in the household more difficult. High-rises reduce community spaces for selling goods. Advertising tailoring services, for example, is much more difficult from the tenth floor than from the ground level. Even if space were available, the increased separation between residential and commercial areas places household entrepreneurs far from the market.

QUALITY OF HOUSING

As housing stock increased, so did the quality of housing. The older lane houses were built before 1930 and had no toilet and kitchen facilities. In 1995, only 5,480,000 Shanghai residents, less than 60 percent, had access to coal or gas (State Statistical Bureau, 1995). The new staff quarters are equipped with independent toilets, kitchen facilities, and balconies. For those who can move into the new apartments, modern conveniences offer the promise of saving time and improving quality of life. Providing individual kitchens for each unit makes food preparation easier. Installing more gas cooking units to replace coal is likely to reduce the incidence of lung cancer among Chinese women. Tap water within the apartment also allows residents to take advantage of washing machines. Consumption of washing machines has now reached 82.2 percent of households (*Shanghai Daily,* 1997). Purchasing a washing machine could further lighten women's workload. With 46 percent of women in Shanghai spending more than half an hour a day doing laundry, there is much to be gained.[11]

However, these gains are dependent on specific gender roles. Socialism was expected to liberate women by giving them independent status as workers and releasing them from the drudgery of housework by socializing childcare and cooking duties. Canteens would reduce the need for kitchens by providing most meals. Shanghai never fully achieved this socialist dream. Nevertheless, the political rhetoric in socialist China supported women who chose nontraditional roles by presenting the role of women as no different from that of men. Women who exemplified the state's view of appropriate behavior were women who succeeded at traditionally male occupations (Croll, 1995). Those could be interpreted as occupations contributing to the development, especially industrial development, of a strong socialist China compared to the "feminine" occupations that mirror services women provide within families, such as education of children, sewing, and cleaning. This emphasis on national goals rather than the family meant that women were judged by their work lives and not by their abilities as homemaker. In a study of the intergenerational changes in women's relationship to their kitchens, Xu Min describes the views of Mrs. Zhang, a 63-year-old retired doctor:

> Most women of Mrs. Zhang's generation are proud of being professional women. To them, "housewife" is a title for those who are incompetent, and

therefore have no social position. Furthermore, such a small field as the kitchen was thought to be absolutely the wrong place for them to attain personal value. In their times, a woman who devoted herself too much to housework was likely to be regarded as a "backward element" by society. . . . For this reason, Mrs. Zhang has spent very little time on cooking and housework in her life, not even as much as her husband has done (Xu Min, 1995: 61).

However, Mrs. Zhang should not be seen as representative. As with socialist goals for urban planning, socialist goals for women's liberation were not achieved. Survey research shows that even in Mrs. Zhang's generation Shanghai women are doing more than half the housework (Sun, 1990). Furthermore, propaganda cannot be taken as representative of the average Chinese person's attitude. The propaganda itself fails to recognize the need for a change in male behavior. Even with government-provided childcare and canteens, houses need to be cleaned and clothes need to be washed. The propaganda's focus on changing female consciousness ignores the need for housework to be done. Nevertheless, compared to Japanese and British men, more urban Chinese husbands do at least some housework (Stockman, Bonney, and Xuewen, 1995).

The socialist emphasis on public commitments, like work, rather than private commitments, like family, has been eroded by a new consumerist domesticity. Housing reform coincides with this increase in domesticity. Many leisure activities have shifted from public spaces to private homes. Consumption of home entertainment goods has grown tremendously. VCRs are now in the homes of one in five families in big cities like Shanghai (Wang, 1995: 160). With a greater focus on home and family life, homemaking skills are in greater demand. The value of one's home and the nature of its decoration are a reflection of status. Thus, Elizabeth Croll describes "male definitions of a preferred or desirable marriage partner . . . [as] one 'who is beautiful, tall, healthy, soft, kind, well-mannered, loyal, virtuous and one who is skilled in domestic crafts (e.g., sewing, cooking and so forth) and can take care of the children'" (Croll, 1995: 157). This new domesticity is in conflict with women's desire for an independent self (Croll, 1995). However, if Mrs. Zhang's daughter, Mrs. Wang, a thirty-five-year-old university lecturer, is an example, there is a greater emphasis on the importance of housework and, in particular, the value of work in the kitchen than for the revolutionary generation (Xu Min, 1995).

If the standards for the appropriate level of housework are increasing as women acquire labor-saving devices, then the burden of housework may actually increase. As variation in housing quality increases, the wealthiest families most likely will set the standards for provision of household services.[12] Not only can these families afford more labor-saving devices; they are also hiring live-in maids from rural areas of Shanghai, Zhejiang, and Jiangsu. Many of the new consumer goods represent higher-status alternatives to household production performed by women. Thus, women in households too poor to afford the consumer goods are under an additional burden to meet new standards for "keeping up with the Chens." This higher standard will be increasingly more difficult for relatively poor women to maintain, requiring more work and creating symbols of class divisions. Without washing machines, for example, it is much harder to wash clothes every time they are worn, but if those with washing machines set a new standard (as they did in the United States), then anyone not adhering could be perceived as dirty, where they were not before.[13]

If there were no social pressure, women would still have to negotiate a division of labor at home. Based on a time-budget survey conducted in 1987, women did almost twice as much housework each day as did men, spending 236.99 minutes each day compared to 116 minutes for men (Sun, 1990: 194). A woman's bargaining power in the negotiations is based on her ability to survive independently. Women with greater independence can threaten to leave if the existing distribution is not acceptable. Independence is dependent on the ability to generate income and the ability to obtain separate housing. Thus, a fair distribution of housing is crucial for women's ability to define their own roles.

CONCLUSIONS: WOMEN'S LIVES AND HOUSING REFORM

It is too early to correctly predict the impact of housing reform upon women. Shanghai appears to have had relatively good access to housing for women compared to other parts of China. Disadvantages in the labor market, however, will spill into the distribution of housing, both through enterprise allocations by employers, which are more interested in recruiting male employees, and market allocations based on income. Potential biases in the credit market may or may not arise. Because 88 percent of women in Shanghai are married, lower access as a work benefit may be felt mostly as lower bargaining power at home. Married women purchasing housing in the marketplace will likely be unaware of any biases, since most housing decisions are made jointly between husbands and wives.

For the 10 percent of women who are widowed or divorced, access to housing could be a serious problem.[14] Nevertheless, relative disadvantages in the market take place in the context of a rapidly increasing stock of housing that increases everyone's access to housing. It is possible that even if disparities increase, women's access to housing could still increase. If divorced or widowed women do have difficulty in gaining access to housing, it is unlikely that any policies short of specific government programs to target single women will solve the problem. For example, the market will not force banks to make loans if loan officers consider single women a higher risk. Only special government programs will be able to offer single women loans in this climate.

The opportunities for women to change the location of their housing are also contradictory. Once the market is fully developed, women and their families will be able to choose the location of their homes rather than receiving a specific assignment. The potential benefits of this change, however, may be overshadowed by changes in city plans that separate residential and commercial districts. Modern spatial structure and housing styles where high-rise apartments are built in suburban neighborhoods may not be the best choice for satisfying women's needs. Long distances between concentrated apartment complexes and most jobs imply long commutes. High-rise apartments that emulate wealthier cities are not likely to facilitate women's productive activities in the household. Finally, replacing widely dispersed open markets with modern grocery stores increases the time needed to get to the store to pick up a few things, offsetting the benefits of refrigerators.

Finally, although self-contained units with private toilet and kitchen facilities represent an improvement in living conditions, changes in the gender roles that result from renewed emphasis on domesticity may increase the burden of women's household labor. Women's ability to bargain for a more favorable division of labor may depend on their own access to housing as well as disparities in income. It is too early to tell what the final outcome will be. Ultimately, the ability for women to control the burden of housework, as well as their access to housing as the market develops, will depend on a commitment by the government to guarantee opportunities in the developing job market.

NOTES

1. "Shanghai wants to be like Hong Kong. But Shanghai officials don't realize the pretty buildings in Hong Kong didn't come first," John Crossman, Shanghai representative of Jardine Fleming Securities (Muzinet, 1997). Emulation of more "developed" cities by "underdeveloped" cities is an extension of Thorstein Veblen's theory of the leisure class developed by Paulette Olson (Olson, 1998). The status hierarchy of developed, developing, and underdeveloped nations generates the desire for those on the lower ends of the hierarchy to display success by emulating those above them in the hierarchy. Thus, rather than choosing construction projects based on their efficiency and effectiveness, projects are chosen for their ability to display to the world that Shanghai has arrived.

2. The 1995 data come from Shanghai Data Online. The 1997 data are the figures reported to Jiang Zemin by members of the Shanghai Municipal Government at the 1997 Party Congress as reported by Chinese news sources. Data for 1979 come from Chapter 12.

3. Figures provided by Li Siming, director of the Shanghai Housing Relief Office (Lao, 1997). Based on these figures, the number of households living in less than 4

square meters at the end of 1995 would have been 60,665. Given the discrepancy between this number and the number provided in Chapter 12 (61,500), one should be somewhat cautious about the accuracy of these numbers.

4. Effective demand for the ordinary housing market accessible to local Shanghai residents peaked at 872,000 square meters in 1990 and then fell again to 558,000 square meters in 1992. In 1993 and 1994, it increased to 1,449,000 and 1,334,000 square meters respectively (Chu, 1996).

5. Interestingly, a frequently used excuse for discrimination against women in the labor market is that women receive more benefits in terms of maternity leave and women's days off. However, few have discussed the advantages of hiring a woman who does not receive the housing benefit.

6. These figures do not represent housing produced by government, work units, and cooperatives and sold to workers.

7. Calculated from Table 14.15 in Chu, 1996, and the *Shanghai Statistical Yearbook,* 1996.

8. This household would be smaller than the average of 3.91 persons. The cost is calculated based on 2,477 RMB per square foot. In 1995 5.386 million square meters were sold for 13,282.7 million RMB (*China Statistical Yearbook,* 1996).

9. "Land Supply Frozen, Authorities Bid to Revive Slumping Property Sector," Chen Qide, June 20, 1997, URL: http://china-window.com/shanghai/sstr/97/6m/6m20d3.html.

10. The concept of emulation and conspicuous waste is explained in Paulette Olson (1998). Conspicuous consumption must be highly visible and wasteful in order to provide evidence to the world that you have "made it" and can afford to waste resources.

11. Data calculated from Tables 4 and 5 (China Women's Federation, 1994: 268).

12. This is the process of emulation described by Thorstein Veblen, where people from all socioeconomic classes attempt to follow the lifestyle of the wealthy as a status symbol (Veblen, 1931 [1899]).

13. Improvements in household technology in the United States did not lighten women's workload. "Time saved by the greater efficiency of household technology tended to be replaced by time spent transporting goods and people or by meeting the greater need to demonstrate the value of homemaking" (Coontz, 1988: 350).

14. These data come from China Women's Federation, *Shanghai funu shehui di wei diao cha* (A study of the status of Shanghai women) (1994).

14

The Housing Situation for Women in Beijing

Wei Zhangling and Bu Xin

The United Nations includes housing as part of its focus on development that is human-centered and can be sustained for generations in balance with the natural environment. In 1996, the United Nations held the Second Human Residence Congress (Habitat II) in Istanbul, Turkey. Habitat II explored human and environmental protection in the course of worldwide urbanization. It maintained that resolution of urban housing problems should not ignore rural housing problems. If rural living conditions and housing circumstances are adverse, there will be more rural residents pouring into cities; urban problems, including housing, will become more serious.

The United Nations proclaimed 1996 as the "International Year for the Eradication of Poverty." Housing problems are closely linked with poverty. As in other developing countries, many poor people in China are living in the vast rural areas, urban slums, and illegal squatter settlements. Transients, without regular shelter, have to cope with the double crises of housing and poverty.

This chapter gives some background on traditional housing in Beijing, contrasting it with Shanghai; this is followed by a discussion of the main factors that contribute to the shortage of urban housing: inadequate investment in housing construction, rapid urbanization, and deterioration of existing units. The chapter then addresses issues that particularly affect urban women.

BACKGROUND

Housing in Beijing is a mixture of modern high-rises with the traditional *hutong* (alley) and *siheyuan* (courtyard) housing patterns that create a unique scenery for the city. As early as the Yuan Dynasty (1206–1368), people referred to *hutongs* as the narrow passages between houses and other buildings; the Chinese character for *hutong* means "to walk slowly, and now walk, now stop," which is typical of a person going through the maze of narrow alleys. Afterwards, *hutong* has been a general term for northern Chinese alleys.

The *siheyuan* is the traditional Chinese dwelling compound with rooms around a courtyard. A simpler version of the courtyard design is called *sanheyuan,* because the rooms have only three sides (*san* means three, and *si* means four) and a wall in front of them. Both are quadrangles. The rooms and windows of these compounds all face toward the inside courtyard rather than the outside world. The traditional architectural design reflects the needs of the closed family. A quadrangle is a closed society. In traditional Chinese society, men were considered superior and women inferior. The woman had to abide by the "three obediences" (to father before marriage, to husband after marriage, and to son after the death of husband) and the "four virtues" (morality, proper speech, modest manner, and diligent work)—spiritual fetters imposed upon women in feudal society. Women were admonished against showing their faces in public, and the traditional dwellings provided corresponding rooms for them, especially boudoirs, much like the Muslim tradition of keeping women secluded in harems. The closed dwelling houses, especially the *siheyuan,* kept women from the outside world.

Since the Opium War in 1840, when the big Western powers invaded China, the Chinese indigenous culture has been challenged by the West. During the following years, more than half the colonial buildings were centered in the eastern trading port of Shanghai. As a blend of traditional Chinese and Occidental architecture, the *lilong* (lane) dwellings emerged in Shanghai; the *lilongs* resemble the *hutongs* of Beijing but reflect the Western influence as well. Before 1949, the *lilong* dwellings were mostly inhabited by the middle and petty bourgeoisie. The *lilong* dwelling in Shanghai was more open than the *siheyuan* in Beijing, and women in Shanghai could more easily go outdoors. In this pre-1949 period, more women in Shanghai entered the workforce and more women in Beijing had bound feet and were confined to their courtyards.

Since the founding of the People's Republic of China in 1949, an earth-shaking change has been taking place in social stratification. People of the "good" class status and family background have replaced those of the "bad" class status as residents of the *siheyuan* in Beijing and *lilong* in Shanghai. There was a continual shortage of housing. Large numbers of illegal, simply built houses emerged in Beijing's *siheyuan hutongs* and Shanghai's *lilongs;* the courtyards of many of Beijing's *siheyuans* were filled in with makeshift housing units, and the average living space of the *lilong* dwelling was only 4 square meters per person (*Ireland Times,* August 3, 1995). As a result, the *siheyuan* has been transformed into *dazayuan* (a compound occupied by many different households); and the *lilong* has grown into what is called *gezilong* (pigeon house). Correspondingly, the *hutongs* and *lilongs* have become more narrow and crowded, and the traditional dwellings have been seriously degraded.

HOUSING ISSUES IN BEIJING IN THE 1990S

In China, the gap between the rich and poor has increasingly widened. The standard of living is lower in the countryside compared to the cities in terms of average income, diet, health care, and general consumption levels. The housing situation, however, is not as serious in the countryside as it is in the cities. The density of population in the cities is too great. In 1995, the population in the cities and towns reached 347.5 million. With rapid urbanization, as China develops, the urban share of the growing population has increased from 10.6 percent in 1949 to 28.9 percent in 1995 (State Statistical Bureau, 1995). As the gap between the cities and countryside becomes wider, as the contradiction between more people and less land in rural areas becomes more intense, and as increments in farmers' incomes slow, surplus labor moves from the countryside to Beijing and other Chinese cities. The contradiction between the rural and urban population is becoming more acute. Millions of rural migrants are making a living in the cities; they not only compete with the local residents for work but also make urban housing problems more serious. A common phenomenon in the history of industrialization in Western countries—"the rich get richer, the poor get poorer"—has now become a more serious problem in the period of economic transformation in China, as people living in dangerous or makeshift housing become the poor class.

According to studies in urban sociology, there are three basic problems of urban housing throughout the world: shortage, poor conditions, and high rents and costs. In China, the shortage of housing is the main problem in urban areas. In 1995, 5 million households were living in units where the average living space per person was less than four square meters. A survey of 1,055 people in Chinese cities in 1996 found that 42.7 percent considered housing a major problem, especially for young people whose income was between 500 and 1,500 yuan per month (CCTV, 1997a, b).

Three factors contribute to the shortage of housing in Chinese cities: investment in housing construction, urbanization, and deterioration of existing units.

Investment in Housing Construction

Housing construction cannot keep pace with the increasing requirements of housing. From 1949 to the period of the First Five-Year Plan (1953–1957), investment in construction of dwelling housing constituted 9.1 percent of total investment in capital construction. During the first three years of the First Five-Year Plan, there were a total of 67 million square meters of dwellings completed, as well as cultural and welfare facilities (Wang, 1988: 74). Because of long-term political movements, however, people were educated to put the interests of the state foremost and think of their own lives and interests less. Under this doctrine, investment in construction of housing was squeezed out by investment in capital construction for production. In 1958, the proportion of investment in housing decreased abruptly to 3 percent. During the Cultural Revolution (1966–1976), housing construction was replaced by phrase-mongering. In 1970, the proportion of investment of capital construction in housing was at a low of 2.6 percent. As the cult of the individual ran rampant, millions of "worship tablets to Chairman Mao" were built; these were demolished later, and overall they were an enormous waste of building materials. As a result of the lack of investment in housing, the total living space in urban areas was approximately 277 million square meters in 1978; more than 6.8 million households were living in areas with less than 4 square meters per person, and 1.9 million families were homeless. These urban residents, living in poor conditions, comprised more than one-fourth of the total urban population. The average living space per person had fallen from 4.5 square meters before 1949 to 3.6 square meters in 1978 (Yang, 1991: 162).

The economic reforms since 1976 have pushed forward social and economic development and have given impetus to housing construction. In both city and countryside, the level of housing has been greatly enhanced. The housing industry has been developing at an unprecedented rate, and millions of people have benefited from the economic reforms. Nevertheless, housing construction still lags behind the increasing requirements of the people. In 1994, China had 267 million families, and every year about 10 million newly married couples join their ranks (Information Office, 1994: 28).

Authorities have decided to build more two-room apartments and fewer one-room, three-room, and four-room apartments to meet the urgent requirements of the large number of nuclear families. Construction of two-room apartments currently constitutes more than 60 percent of housing construction. The approach is beneficial to one-child families, as well as to young and middle-aged mothers.

After Deng Xiaoping's inspection tour to southern China in 1992, the development of real estate made a "great leap forward." Between 1991 and 1992, completed investment in real estate projects increased 117 percent. Between January and May 1993, completed investment increased 115 percent from the corresponding period of 1992 (Z. Dai, 1993). Overstocking of high-grade commodity houses, however, has resulted in buildings worth billions of yuan lying idle; by 1995, there were 17 million square meters of expensive, high-grade flats and garden villas overstocked throughout the country. Use of funds for these costly properties hampers other construction, especially dwelling house construction (Shao, 1995). Since 1989, the proportion of dwelling houses in commodity housing development has decreased by 2 percent each year; it comprised 81.8 percent in 1992 and was only half of construction in some of the open coastal cities (Z. Dai, 1993). Construction of office buildings, halls, hotels, and hostels has been increasing rapidly. The overheated real estate industry has contributed to inflation.

Urbanization and Housing

In the process of urbanization, villagers who find jobs in the cities aggravate the crisis in housing. In recent years, some 60–80 million rural workers are going to the cities to work for at least part of the year. About 20–30 million cross into different provinces or regions; this movement is growing and was 20 percent greater in 1995 than during the previous year (Fu, 1996). At present, more than 100 million people shuttle between the city and countryside to make a living. At the end of June 1996, the nonnative population in Beijing was 3.3 million; of these, 63.7 percent are male and 36.3 percent are female.

The rural-urban migrants cannot easily find good, cheap housing in the cities. The men usually engage in construction, remodeling, and waste recovery—the hard and dirty work. Women often work as waitresses and housekeepers. The new migrants are in an unfavorable situation when they compete with the locals for rental housing. Local people frequently complain about the rising rent, inflation, unemployment, pollution, lack of safety, and immorality that they attribute at least in part to the migrant workers. Women, especially those who are single, widows, divorced, or poor, are frequently the targets of criminals.

Environment and development are important issues of worldwide concern. Natural disasters and environmental pollution have brought death, deformity, and miscarriage to people in general and have had a particularly harsh impact on women and children, who constitute 60–70 percent of the victims of natural and manmade disasters. More than 30 million women suffer from homelessness and hardship related to environmental problems (Report of the PRC, 1994).

In the mid-1980s, the Chinese government began the work of helping the poor on a large scale. According to authorities, the number of people living below the poverty line decreased from 125 million in 1985 to 87 million by the end of 1992. Women and children comprised 60 percent of the poor. The government has set up the "Program for Helping the Poor to Overcome Extreme Difficulties," with the goal of lifting these 87 million people out of poverty by the year 2000 (Report of the PRC, 1994).

Deterioration of Existing Units

Many houses that were built before 1949 and during the Great Leap Forward (1958–1961) and the Cultural Revolution are worn down. These decaying buildings obstruct the normal daily life of their residents and make already tense housing problems, such as several people living in a small room, even more critical. According to surveys of dwellings' quality, the proportion that is acceptable ranges between 40 and 50 percent.

In the cities, especially the big cities, renovation of old buildings has been carried out on a large scale. During the 1990s, millions of urban households have been relocated to newly built housing. On August 2, 1996, the Department of Construction promised to undertake standardized service in thirty-six cities. In the course of housing reform, even though many people's salaries are increased to compensate for the rising prices, others—especially the elderly, those with low wages, and those who have lost their jobs—still have difficulties with the higher prices. To address these problems, the government is constructing a "safety net" for the urban poor (J. Chen, 1997). As of March 1997, 156 cities were establishing a safety-net system for the absolute poor.

An investigation into urban housing problems reveals the phenomenon of the serious shortage of houses for residents coexisting with the vacancy of numerous newly built, beautiful commodity houses. These houses are too expensive for ordinary urban residents. Some experts suggest that the high cost of land use and taxes are the main reasons for the high prices (Cong, 1996). It is common for land use and taxation to constitute 39 percent of the cost, architectural installation 51 percent, and miscellaneous expenses the remaining 10 percent.

HOUSING REFORMS AND THE TRADITIONAL *HUTONG* DWELLINGS

The authorities have had to make a choice between economic growth and the preservation of cultural relics. In the face of a large number of traditional dwellings inside Beijing, city planners are evaluating two courses: (1) build high-rises to meet growing demands for housing while repairing and rebuilding the *siheyuan* dwellings; and (2) build high-rises but also tear down *siheyuan* dwellings in order to build multistory office buildings, bazaars, and high-grade flats. In China today, the two plans have been adopted simultaneously. A large quantity of traditional dwellings—old and dangerous houses—have to be torn down. Beijing has been in first place among Chinese cities in the volume of rebuilding old and dangerous houses. In 1994, there were sixty-six districts under construction for rebuilding old and dangerous houses, eight districts for new buildings, and 3.824 million square meters for starting or continuing work. In 1995, such rebuilding increased nearly 60 percent. Since 1992, the authorities in Beijing have promoted joint investment with foreign businesses in rebuilding old and dangerous houses. At the beginning of 1996, however, foreign tradesmen participated for the first time in such construction without government partners (Hu Wenzong, January 12, 1996).

Only four old architectural blocks in Beijing are currently classified as objects of preservation of cultural relics. Similarly, in Shanghai many of the traditional *lilong* dwellings have been torn down in the transformation from low-rise brick-and-wood construction into high-rises and large mansions. In 1995, the *lilong* dwellings constituted 40 percent of local housing. In the mid-1990s, 160,000 new flats have been built every year in Shanghai. These already take up 8 million square meters of land.

CONCLUSIONS: HOUSING RIGHTS FOR WOMEN IN BEIJING

A traditional Chinese adage states, "When the husband gets rich and honored, his wife also gets high status." Today, that has changed: "A woman who works hard and achieves success can hardly equal one who gets married to a good, successful man." A woman's housing condition is still mainly determined by her husband's or father's social and professional status. Most housing for urban Chinese residents has been assigned through the work unit to the husband. This is how most housing is still assigned. In such a situation, women have less say, and single women, widows, and divorced women are apt to lack equal opportunities.

When people are relocated from the old housing, they are often given units much farther from work sites. The longer commute times to the new apartments are a burden to families, especially for the women responsible for household chores. Buying one's own house is expensive, and credit is a focus of reform in 1997. Individual housing loans currently constitute less than 10 percent of national real estate credit funds (Wang, 1997: 25). The 1997 Regulation on Personal Housing Mortgage Loans extends the period for repayment of loans from the current five to ten years to twenty years; staff and workers who have paid into accumulation funds in their work units can get limited low-interest loans. Although the regulation is an improvement for urban residents, it does not address the particular needs of women. Employment competition usually favors men, and many women workers have been forced to retire early or have been laid off since the reforms began. These conditions make it more difficult for women to buy houses. In buying housing from the state-owned enterprises, the years of work at that unit help determine the price: The longer a person has worked at the firm, the lower the price. If both wife and husband are employed by the unit, their combined years of work are used to determine the price. Therefore, workers with only their own years of work are at a disadvantage; in the current work environment, this proves to be an even greater disadvantage for single women, widows, and divorced women because they have lower pay on average and fewer options.

Housing conditions, together with wealth and power, are an important index of the social status of a modern Chinese. In sum, it is a long march to reach the goal of equal rights between women and men.

NOTES

Editors' note: The Chinese estimates of poverty focus on a narrow definition of those who are the most poor; in 1995 the World Bank increased its estimates of the number of poor based on international definitions of poverty.

15

Changes in Housing Patterns for Rural Chinese Women

Li Weisha

The current rural housing pattern in China is linked to a cultural heritage of several thousand years. This pattern has reflected the continuity of tradition, but it is now changing as it is deluged by waves of modernization. This chapter examines changes in rural housing and residence patterns since economic reforms began in the late 1970s. The paper begins with a discussion of the traditional virilocal clan pattern in marriage and housing and the role that it plays in the subordination of women. The current residence pattern and perceptions of it are then discussed. This is followed by an examination of how economic reforms are affecting traditional housing and residence patterns, focusing on rural Hubei Province in central China; property rights of widows are addressed in that section. Finally, the chapter presents some conclusions about the emerging trends.

TRADITIONAL HOUSING AND RESIDENCE PATTERNS

The traditional housing pattern in most of rural China has two characteristics. One is clan residence, namely, with father and male siblings; the other is virilocal (or patrilocal) residence, where the woman lives at her husband's family's house. This is the prerequisite for maintaining patrilineal clan residence.

In clan residence, a man can grow up and inherit his father's business, living in the same area from birth to death. A woman, however, moves to live with and assist her husband when she marries. She is separated from the place of her own birth for the rest of her life. This residence pattern provides the man with the right of inheritance of property (house and land use). The cultural concept associated with this residence pattern is that the woman is an outsider: She does not belong to her original clan because she will leave when

231

she marries, and she never becomes a full member of her husband's clan, even though she bears children who become members and lives with the clan for the rest of her life. Most villages comprise just one or two clans and a few people from various clans, so that many residents share the same last name. In this context, the tradition of the woman maintaining her father's surname is part of the mechanism that keeps her separate from the husband's clan.[1] The woman clearly has subordinate status in marriage and family.

Furthermore, in traditional marriage, a man could have several wives and concubines and also had the right to discard a wife (the practice of taking multiple wives or concubines was forbidden by the Marriage Law of 1950, and both parties were granted the right to appeal for divorce). With this traditional marital and family status, the woman lives precariously, because she faces possible competition from other women and threats of being discarded by her husband. In feudal society, it is a great shame for the woman to be discarded by her husband and driven back home. Usually, such shame is shared by her parents' family, and they will treat her badly for humiliating them. Divorce is not an option frequently chosen by rural women.

Over time, of course, the clan residence pattern, influenced by natural disasters, pestilence, and wars, has been gradually eroded. The impact of urbanization and immigration has forced extended families and clans to be divided, and marital status has experienced a qualitative change. Still today, however, virilocal clan residence is found throughout most of rural China.

CHANGING RURAL HOUSING AND RESIDENCE PATTERNS

Although the traditional customs have been handed down both consciously and unconsciously, the rapidly growing Chinese economy has greatly changed the patterns of production and lifestyle in rural areas during the past two decades; simultaneously, these changes have altered the perceptions of people in villages.

A survey of residence patterns of rural communities in five provinces of China in the early 1990s is summarized in Table 15.1. The data demonstrate that clan residence is still the main form of residence in the rural areas, with 65.4 percent of rural residents living in the same house with the husband's parents. The contrast with the cities is striking; only 31.7 percent of families in urban China retain the traditional housing pattern. And though 27.9 percent of couples in rural areas now have a separate house and live independently of the extended family, they usually live in the village of the husband's clan. Thus, they still retain the virilocal tradition. Yet the increase in nuclear families in rural areas is a notable change in terms of housing and property rights.

The current perceptions of 1,208 (mostly male) respondents in rural areas are reported in Table 15.2 (Institute of Sociology, 1994).[2] When asked which

Table 15.1   Chinese Women's Housing and Residence Patterns upon Marriage, 1992 (in percent)

	Total	Separate Housing	Shared Housing with Husband's Parents	Shared Housing with Woman's Parents	Other
Rural areas	100.0 (24,186,900)	27.9	65.4	5.9	0.8
Urban	100.0 (5,991,900)	58.4	31.7	8.4	1.5

Source: Institute of Demography, Chinese Academy of Social Sciences, 1993.

residence pattern they preferred, 30.1 percent stated a village based on a single clan/surname. Another 18.8 percent would like to live in villages where a few clans are centered. This is slightly less than half of the total (48.9 percent). Almost 10 percent prefer the urban pattern of scattered residence, not related to where the parents live, and the rest have no preference. With respect to all answers, the difference between women's and men's responses was very small.

The benefits of cooperation and mutual aid in production are key reasons for the traditional pattern of clan residence. In the survey summarized in Table 15.2, almost two-thirds of the respondents said that they would first turn to members of the same (husband's) clan for help in difficulties (Institute of Sociology, 1994). In contrast with the traditional reliance almost exclusively on family for help (before the People's Republic of China), approximately 44 percent would ask help from neighbors (with different family names) and friends. The responses from women and men were similar, with slightly more women saying they would seek help from the clan first (62.1 percent for women, 59.3 percent for men). This consistency between women and men can be attributed to similarity in cultural traditions. The development

Table 15.2   Perceptions of Residence Patterns in Hubei, 1993 (in percent)

	Total	Same Clan Surnames	A Few Clans/ Surnames (Still Concentrated)	Scattered	Indifferent
Total	100.0	30.1	18.8	9.8	41.3
Women	100.0 (382)	30.1	16.3	10.7	42.9
Men	100.0 (826)	30.2	19.9	9.8	40.6

Source: Institute of Sociology, Hubei Academy of Social Sciences, 1994.

of the rural market economy has led families to appreciate the value of cooperation with neighbors; the tendency toward nuclear families has weakened the connections between the extended family, and the clan tends to be more scattered as people move to seek new economic opportunities. These factors weaken the traditional reliance on the clan.

The traditional pattern of clan residence in rural areas is not only a mutual-aid union but also one of the main modes of basic district management. In traditional society, the clan elder manages his clan in a patriarchal mode with absolute authority. The current Chinese rural communities are administered by an autonomous organization, the village committee. The village committee has to be approved by local rural governments after democratic elections. In this system, several natural villages form an executive village for administration. This executive village brings together the various clans from smaller villages, where single clans dominate. All sorts of daily affairs will be divided and managed under supervision of local governments according to a legal system. In China, the establishment and modification of a modern legal system is a social revolution in this century. The change of management of basic rural districts has reduced the patriarchal authority of the feudal clan and changed the scope of clan activities. Rather than making all key decisions for clan members, clan activities now center on marriage and funeral arrangements and mutual aid during harvests. Since the executive management system has replaced the clan management system, the traditional clan elder system has almost disappeared. This is one reason why many respondents reported that they do not care whether residence is in a clan-centered village or not (see Table 15.2).

RURAL HOUSING CHANGES IN HUBEI PROVINCE

Since economic reforms began in 1978, the rapid development of the Chinese economy has greatly improved farmers' standard of living, and the improvement of housing conditions in rural areas provides evidence of these gains. Because housing in rural areas has been and remains private, the type of housing reform observed in the city (where state subsidies are being removed) has not occurred. Land use rights have been returned to family control, but there are limits on how much land can be allocated to housing. Thus, the main housing changes in the countryside have come through the higher incomes that farmers are earning since the reforms and their ability to expand their existing unit or build new ones. A survey of families in rural areas of Hubei Province (central China) in 1996 demonstrates that the average number of family members has been falling and the average housing area (referring to living areas excluding the bathroom and toilet, kitchen, corridor, and temporary houses) has been increasing (see Table 15.3).

Table 15.3   Housing of Rural Families in Hubei Province, 1981–1996

	Average Number of Permanent Family Members	Average Room Space per Family Member, End of the Year (sq.m.)	Residence Increase per Family Member (percent)
1981	5.76	13.80	NA
1986	4.98	19.92	4.35
1991	4.57	23.23	16.62
1996	4.26	26.56	14.42

Source: Hubei Provincial Statistical Bureau, 1997.

The housing area in 1996 almost doubled that of fifteen years earlier, with the most rapid gains occurring during the mid-1980s. These improvements benefit all family members. In the first five years of the reform period, the improvement in the farmers' standard of living centered on food supply. As income increased, the farmers started to build new houses in the mid-1980s. In the early 1990s, construction of new houses slowed, mainly because housing is a fixed asset that can be used for many years. In the mid-1990s, however, many farmers are no longer satisfied with their simple 1980s houses and have started to invest in internal facilities, decoration, and remodeling. Since China has a large population and lacks land resources, all local governments try to control the area allocated to building residence structures, and farmers are increasingly building multistory units to increase living space without taking up more land. A national survey of children reveals that 19 percent of them live in multistory buildings, and the average housing area per person is 17.9 square meters (more than twice that of urban areas) (China National Bureau of Statistics, 1993). Most children (75 percent) live with their families in single-story houses, where the average housing area per person is 12.4 square meters. The remaining 5.4 percent live in housing with an average area of 11.5 square meters per person (China National Bureau of Statistics, 1993).

Building a house is a major family decision. Who is the main decision-maker among family members? Respondents to a national survey overwhelmingly reported that the husband and wife would make the decision jointly (76.25 percent) (Institute of Demography, Chinese Academy of Social Sciences, 1993). And while 17.14 percent responded that the decision would be made by the husband alone, only 2.28 percent said that the wife would make the decision alone. The wife would only make the decision alone if the husband were absent for some reason.

The development of the rural economy has sped up the tendency for nuclear families. Between 1981 and 1996 in Hubei Province, for example, the

Table 15.4   Attitudes Toward Widows and Property

	National			Rural Areas			Urban Areas		
	Total	Women	Men	Total	Women	Men	Total	Women	Men
Strongly agree	5.5	5.2	5.9	7.9	8.7	7.1	3.1	1.9	4.6
Agree	38.1	40.9	34.8	44.2	45.8	42.5	31.7	36.3	25.9
Don't care	10.6	9.5	11.9	9.0	7.9	10.3	12.2	11.1	13.7
Uncertain	19.9	18.5	21.6	17.7	16.9	18.6	22.2	20.0	24.9
Disagree	25.1	25.2	25.0	20.5	20.0	21.2	29.8	30.2	29.3
No response	0.8	0.7	0.9	0.6	0.8	0.4	1.0	0.6	1.5

Source: Liu, Shiying, chief ed., 1994.

average number of family members has fallen by 1.5 persons, and nuclear families are growing in rural areas. Although the residence pattern is still virilocal, the growth of nuclear families and choice in marriage partner have led to more emphasis on the relationship between wife and husband and laid the foundation for greater equity in the relationship. It is increasingly common for rural couples to have discussions when making major decisions—such as whether to build a house. This promotes the woman's status within the family.

PROPERTY RIGHTS OF WIDOWS

To understand the changing ideas about women's roles and status, a survey of 1,900 people was carried out in Hubei Province (Liu, 1994). The attitudes toward a widow's remarrying and related property issues were addressed. As shown in Table 15.4, more than half of the respondents (52.1 percent) agreed that "a widow should dedicate the properties of her former marriage to her former husband's children and family"; this is 17.3 percent more than for urban respondents.

Because land is collectively owned in rural areas and individuals only have use rights for it, the house is an important part of the family property. According to the traditional clan and virilocal residence customs, women have no right of inheritance. A married woman, who lives with her husband's family, has no right to remarry and inherit the property if her husband dies. Even though the laws of the People's Republic of China state that women are equal to men and have the right to inherit property, such provisions are seldom enforced in rural areas. It is common for attitudes to change more slowly in rural areas than they do in the city. Despite the relatively traditional residence pattern that provides no great incentive for change, attitudes are slowly changing. More than one-third (38.2 percent) of rural residents were either

Table 15.5   Attitudes Toward Widows and Property Related to Educational Background, 1993

	Total	Illiterate	Junior Primary School	Senior Middle School	Middle School	College and Over
Strongly agree	5.5	4.4	8.2	6.5	2.1	1.4
Agree	38.1	50.0	48.1	32.1	31.6	15.7
Don't care	10.6	12.3	8.2	11.5	9.8	21.4
Uncertain	20.0	11.4	14.8	21.6	2.1	22.9
Disagree	25.1	21.1	20.4	27.8	26.9	38.6

Source: Liu, Shiying, chief ed., 1994.

uncertain (17.7 percent) or disagreed with (20.5 percent) the idea that widows should turn all their property over to the husband's family.

It is notable that women, especially women in rural areas, maintained traditional views more so than men. Different views are related to educational background of the respondents (see Table 15.5). The higher the level of education attained, the more likely the respondent is to reject the traditional view on widows and property. The percentage of illiterates who "strongly agree" or "agree" that widows should turn over all property is more than three times greater than those who are college-educated; the percentage of college-educated, in contrast, who "are uncertain" and "don't agree" is approximately double those who are illiterate. People who receive higher educations are more likely to be influenced by laws and concepts of equality between women and men; those with less education are more likely to hold traditional views. Those with traditional views are more likely to live in rural areas, and many of them are elderly; women comprise two-thirds of the rural elderly.

CONCLUSIONS

As the Chinese economy continues to develop, profound changes can be expected in housing and residence patterns for both women and men. Already, millions of people from rural areas have migrated either permanently or temporarily to cities. Because property rights are limited (land cannot yet be owned and sold) and because east-central regions of China are densely populated with little average arable land per capita, movement within most rural areas can be expected to be limited. In these areas, the traditional dominance of a single clan within a village will probably continue for some time, though some mingling of families can be anticipated. Increased migration to less populated western China can also be expected, but it is not clear at this time that traditional virilocal residence patterns are changing there. Mainly in coastal regions and near a few inland cities, it is likely that the scattered urban pattern will emerge where people with many different surnames live in an area.

As rural incomes continue to increase, it is likely that the cycle of construction and remodeling of houses will be shortened. Because of population pressures on limited land, housing will no doubt change from single-story to multistory dwellings, and the quality will be improved through better amenities and decor.

The tendencies toward nuclear families and freer choice in marriage together make the choice of residence after marriage less connected to areas of clan dominance. Men marrying into the bride's family face less discrimination than before. As the marriage residence areas become more flexible, a major source of traditional discrimination against rural women is reduced. As economic reform continues, rural areas are more exposed to television, cellular phones, computers, and transportation. These changes bring in new ideas to people living in remote areas; they may make them more open-minded and lead to additional changes in lifestyle. In addition, the developing legal system is replacing the traditional patriarchal system and reducing the range of clan activities. Most importantly, the continued and expanded availability of education for rural girls means they are prepared to adapt to the commodity economy in use of land and housing for income-generating activities as well as more comfortable lifestyles.

The trends in rural housing and residence patterns as observed in Hubei Province are mainly positive for women: larger homes with more amenities; reduction in power of the clan and greater decisionmaking power of wife and husband in the smaller, nuclear family about a range of issues, including housing and land use; more acceptance of matrilocal residence; and movements toward clarifying legal property rights, an especially important area for widows. Housing was already private in rural areas before the reforms, so the changes have been more indirect since the reforms through gains in income that permit better housing and through restructuring of economic activities. In sum, there are many reasons to be optimistic about continued improvements for rural women's access to housing.

NOTES

1. In contrast to the view of independence that is associated with a woman maintaining her own name upon marriage in many other countries, it was traditionally a custom associated with a woman's not belonging to the husband's clan in China. After the founding of the PRC in 1949, the practice of the wife and husband keeping their own names was frequently mentioned as a positive indicator of similar status and independence in the Chinese media also.

2. Although the interviewers are aware of the importance of getting women to answer questions, they often encounter difficulties in this area. Rural women usually avoid responding to household surveys and let their husbands and other family members answer questions. This is a reflection of the traditional concept that men are responsible for external affairs and women for internal affairs.

16

Changing Land and Housing Use by Rural Women in Northern China

Li Zongmin

China has a long tradition of male control over resources and decisionmaking. That tradition has been pervasive in the vast rural areas of China. Since 1949, one of the major stated objectives of China's social and economic policies has been to achieve equal rights for both sexes in all spheres of life. Economic independence of women was viewed as a prerequisite to independence in other spheres of life. Government policy has advocated increased work outside the household by rural women. The government has paid particular attention to ensuring that laws and regulations relating to sexual equality are enforced.

At the end of the 1970s, the People's Republic of China (PRC) began the reform process that brought its system of agricultural communes to an end. The large units of production were broken up, and management of and income from land were distributed to the farm households in a smallholder production system (Bruce and Harrell, 1989). This was called the "household responsibility system."

My research has focused on how changes in land and housing have affected women and their work, including intrahousehold resource allocation between the sexes, particularly the allocation of family labor. This chapter first discusses the case-study area, Dongyao Village, and the land reform process in the early 1980s. Impacts of the land reallocation on the lives and work of women are then addressed. This is followed by a section focusing on housing. The chapter then considers the impact of rural industrialization on women's use of land and housing. In some households, women have become an increasingly important factor in the family's economic life as men become involved in nonagricultural activities. Women are replacing men in the fields as the main source of labor in agriculture. Finally, some remaining problems are examined.

Many foreign scholars have studied related problems from different perspectives. There have been investigations of the issue of women's work in agriculture, their domestic sideline activities, and the sexual division of labor since the establishment of the household responsibility system (Croll, 1983, 1985; Summerfield, 1994); the impact of China's rural reform on women's status (Qian and Mei, 1987); women's participation in productive labor outside the household (Judd, 1990); the comparative study of the process by which women's roles change (Kelkar, 1987); and the impact on women's status of the change of kinship relationships since the rural reform (Bao, 1989).

In 1987 the All China Women's Federation began a study of rural women's education, training in production skills, health care, and family planning. In 1988 the Institute for Rural Development of the Chinese Academy of Social Science studied rural women's occupations. In 1989 the Institute of Sociology of the Chinese Academy of Social Science began a study of changes in marriage and relationships in rural families. These studies had not been published at the time of my fieldwork. Also, some official and nongovernmental women's organizations and institutes have been established since the Chinese reform.

What researchers have not yet done is to explore gender aspects of the organic link between farmers and the change in the land tenure system. This link is fundamental to the design and implementation of an appropriate land tenure system, which, in turn, is vital to the development of agriculture and to the maintenance of women's efficiency in farming. Due to the tremendous internal differences in population, geography, economy, society, language, and culture in the vast countryside of China, a sound analysis of these issues must begin with careful local studies. Therefore, this research was framed as a case study of families in a single village, though it is hoped that in the future it may be possible to expand such inquiry to other, differently situated villages in other parts of China.

DONGYAO VILLAGE

I chose Dongyao Village in Yutian County, Hebei Province, as the locale for the case study. Yutian is not strictly representative, because it has been a focus of experimental programs in rural reform since 1987, and farmers there have better access to services and credit. Yet the experience of women in Yutian can highlight issues that will be faced elsewhere in China in the future. I had carried out earlier research there in 1987, and there were practical advantages to continuing my work in that location in 1992, given the brevity of the time available for the case study.

Dongyao Village is located about 4 kilometers from northwestern Yutian Town (the area just outside the town gate). Yutian is near Beijing in eastern Hebei Province, lying at the southern end of the Yian Mountains and the most western edge of the city of Tangshan. Dongyao's location is in the middle of a triangular region about 60 kilometers from Tangshan, 120 kilometers from Beijing, and 130 kilometers from the city of Tianjin (see China country map).

Population and Land Use in Dongyao Village

Dongyao Village had a total population of 1,014 in 1992, at the time of the research, with 245 households. The labor force was 510 persons (half male and half female, including those in industry and construction as well as in agriculture). In the village, 23 families were selected as study units (12.5 percent of the total number of households). Within the 23 families, 127 persons were interviewed. Sixty-four of these were women, of whom 37 worked outside the home. Women make up 70 percent of the agricultural labor force in the case study families.

The average number of members per family is 5.52 persons (the average for Yutian County is 4.14 persons per family). The figure of 5.52 may be related to a large, extended family comprising several generations. There were two kinds of households: the extended family (at least three generations living together) and the nuclear family. The extended family today is different from that of traditional Chinese rural society. The traditional extended family comprised several parallel families of several generations living together; the modern extended family consists of a son and his spouse living with his parents and their unmarried children. Usually, sons will establish a separate household when they marry or several years thereafter.

The layout of the village is simple. There is a central residential area, with small gardens in some yards. Near this section are larger garden plots and, beyond these, irrigated and nonirrigated farmland.

The total land area is 2,512.4 *mu* (a *mu* is one-fifteenth of a hectare). The cultivated area is 1,875 *mu:* 175.3 *mu* in irrigated rice, 1,483.6 *mu* in irrigated wheat and corn, 201.3 *mu* in irrigated garden crops, and 14.8 *mu* in nonirrigated tracts. The residential and industrial area is 443.1 *mu:* 333.6 *mu* for residential, 19.0 *mu* for threshing ground, 85.7 *mu* for industrial, and 4 *mu* for the cemetery. Roads account for 96.5 *mu;* the area under water, 56.3 *mu* (33.9 *mu* in hollows and 22.4 *mu* in ditches); and the unutilized area, 41.5 *mu*. The area of unutilized land has declined greatly since 1949, as has cultivated land per capita, from 3.5 *mu* in 1949 to 2.5 *mu* in 1958 and to 1.8 *mu* in 1991. In 1949, the average farm size for an average household of 4.14 persons was 14.49 *mu*.

Since 1982, Dongyao has become a site of surplus labor as population grew and land reserved for farming declined. During the period 1982–1991, population increased by 8.8 percent, while total cultivated area (2,023 *mu*) declined by 148 *mu* (20 *mu* went to village industries, 18 *mu* to township industries, and 110 *mu* to county industries).

Grain cultivation predominated in Dongyao before 1982, but there has been a recent shift toward producing cash crops such as vegetables, potatoes, and watermelon. Figures for share of output value, available for Yutian as a whole, show this to be a more general trend. In the years immediately before 1975, wheat and corn accounted for more than 90 percent of the value of total agricultural output. By 1982, however, grains had declined to 55 percent of total value, and more profitable market crops made up 30 percent. In order to increase the output of farmland, cultivation has been increased from two crops per year (wheat and corn) to three (cabbage, wax gourd, and Chinese cabbage, or cabbage, corn, and cauliflower). By the late 1980s, some households had ceased grain cultivation altogether.

Changes in Income

Annual per capita income in Dongyao rose from 45 yuan[1] before 1980 to 1,100 yuan in 1991, well above the average figure for Yutian County (789 yuan). Much of this increase can be attributed to the switch from grains to more profitable crops in agriculture and the growth of nonstate rural industry. The production brigade (now the village committee) started to build the first village industry, a brick production unit, in 1980. Per capita income rose to 300 yuan that same year. Among the 23 families that I interviewed, the highest annual household income was 1,827 yuan, and the lowest was 391 yuan. Some of the earnings of the wealthier family came from nonagricultural sources as well as agricultural and sideline[2] earnings, but the lower-income family depended solely on farming. The average annual income for a full-time agricultural family is 1,016 yuan; this is about two-thirds of the average for a part-time agricultural family (1,514 yuan).

LAND REFORM IN 1982:
THE CHANGE FROM THE COMMUNE SYSTEM
TO THE HOUSEHOLD RESPONSIBILITY SYSTEM

Under the communist system, land is owned by the state in urban areas and by the collective in rural areas. Before the reforms, land was controlled by the brigade; now, after the breakup of the commune system, the administrative village is in charge. Although the community retains ownership of the land under the household responsibility system, use rights are contracted to the families. The changes in the organization of agricultural production from the commune system to the household responsibility system began in Dongyao Village in 1979. In June 1979 a new system for agricultural production was adopted, based on the reform experience of the rural areas in Anhui and Sichuan Provinces, which allowed 12 percent of communal working brigades to practice *lian chan ji chou,* whereby income was no longer distributed by the work-point system but was based on output per member.

At the end of 1980, the brigade in neighboring Xiaochenfu Village divided the land and other collective property among member households. The people in Dongyao were very much shocked by this. At that time, peasants said, it seemed as if there were an "earthquake" in the vast countryside of China because radical changes would take place almost every day in rural areas.

At the beginning of 1982, Dongyao (on directive from the Yutian administration) also allocated communal land to individual households. Each production team had its own area of land that was distributed to member families on a per capita basis.[3] The land was first divided into categories by quality, and each household received a share of each type of land. Plots were distributed by lottery. Each family originally received about 10.09 small parcels of land, the smallest of which was less than 0.1 *mu*. In the second half of 1982, the collective properties and draft animals of the production brigade were divided among the production teams, then among constituent production groups by the teams themselves. For example, seven households would get a cow, or four households would get a handcart.

The community has two types of land: irrigated and nonirrigated. The irrigated land was divided into food plots and responsibility plots. The food plots are intended to provide basic consumption needs based on an average of 400 *jin*[4] of grain per person annually; the household receives 0.5 *mu* per person as a food plot, and this is excluded from grain quotas. In addition, they receive 1.0 *mu* per capita of irrigated land as a responsibility plot and must sell a quota of grain from this plot to the state at prices set by government purchasing agents; the typical quota is 190 *jin* per *mu* each year. The nonirrigated land was divided equally among the households as responsibility plots (amounting to about 0.12 *mu* per person).

If a household's home parcel was larger than what its size warranted, the excess was subtracted from its food plot. When the number of people in each family increases, and if it is not time for the redistribution of land whereby the household is given more land, the grain quota for the family will be proportionately reduced, allowing more to be consumed or sold at market price.

The changes in the organization of agricultural production stimulated farmers' enthusiasm for production and resulted in the growth of output, but the farmers were soon faced with new problems. First, there were increased disputes over resources, especially over access to systems and equipment that could not be divided among households, such as canals, some agricultural machinery, and well pumps. This led to fighting even between relatives during the busy planting and harvesting seasons. Families allocated most of their labor to farming and very little to public works. Second, much existing farm machinery could not be used effectively because of the small scale of the parcels, and farmers returned to manual and draft cultivation. Many households had to purchase their own equipment, while previously the implements had served the needs of several households. The cost of pump and draft ani-

Table 16.1   Changes in Cultivated Land Plots and Area in Dongyao Village

	1982			1991		
	Total	Irrigated	Unirrigated	Total	Irrigated	Unirrigated
Land area	9.08	6.69	2.38	7.65	6.05	1.50
Parcels/ household	10.09	6.50	4.40	5.06	1.50	3.56
Average area (*mu*/parcel)	0.83	1.02	0.54	1.49	4.43	0.42

Source: Fieldwork, 1992.

mals, for example, was 98 yuan for each family in 1983. Third, the collective property and agricultural installations were either sold or not properly maintained. Three levels of the canal system (the main canals of the county's project, the branch canals of the commune's project, and the small canals of the village's project) deteriorated because nobody maintained them. Soon, farmers complained that the fields were inundated near the pumping station while the fields farther away were dry.

By the period of the study, Dongyao had redistributed land three times since the household responsibility system was introduced in 1982. At the initial distribution in 1982, land per capita varied from 1.6 to 2.2 *mu* among the four production teams. In 1986, the first adjustment of the land distribution occurred; land per capita fell slightly, to 1.5–2.1 *mu*. In 1989 the second adjustment of the land distribution resulted in per capita allocations of 1.5–2.0 *mu*. The redistributions were set off in each case by the need for land for nonagricultural uses; thus, the ever-smaller land allocations do not reflect much growth in the number of households but a smaller agricultural land base. Although national policy now calls for long-term contracts, farmers in Dongyao today farm without written contracts and remain vulnerable to redistributions.

In addition to transferring land to industrial use, the readjustments consolidated land that was too fragmented to be easily cultivated. The principle of adjustment in Dongyao was to consolidate small pieces of land into relatively large parcels, using land of middle quality as the standard (0.9 *mu* of high-quality land or 1.1–1.2 *mu* of poor-quality land was considered equivalent to 1.0 *mu* of standard land). After the 1989 reallocation, the number of pieces of land was limited to six per family (each household in Dongyao has an average of 5.06 pieces, as shown in Table 16.1). Land access for the household became easier than previously.

Since the reforms, the household replaced the collective as the basic unit of production, management, and decisionmaking. Farming has become a business. Households now make decisions about how to use land, what to produce, how much to sell, what inputs to use, and so on. The head of household has become the "team leader." Generally, the land distributed to a family is registered under the name of the male head of household.[5] If the male head dies or migrates to an urban area, the household's land may be registered under the wife's name or, if there is an adult son, under the son's name.

Due to the change in the household's role, the individuals' roles and the division of labor inside the family have changed, too. In the past, all persons were commune members who obeyed the collective's prescribed division of labor. The heads of household were to make decisions only on their own family's consumption of the grain distributed by the collective. Under the household responsibility system, the male as head of household has become a manager, completely in charge of input and output. As team leader, he may make decisions on household production and management. The women have participated in all parts of agricultural production, not merely obeying assigned tasks and performing designated labor. As villagers, they have a right to a portion of land and other resources. As family members, they have taken part in almost all activities of production and management.

THE IMPACT OF LAND REFORM ON WOMEN'S WORK AND LIVES

The government in Mao's time (1949–1976) had advocated that women should take part in social activities and economic production outside the home. The government focused more on equality than on profit, urging that women work together with men and have equal economic rights. In the Deng Xiaoping era, after 1976, the government seemed to stress the productive role of women even more. In fact, one can see from the Dongyao case that Chinese rural women now have more options for accessing production resources than ever before. They participate in labor-allocation decisions in a more diverse local economy, with opportunities for agriculture, sidelines, and nonagricultural enterprises.

The law stipulates that men and women have equal rights of access to land. As long as one is a resident of a village, she or he has the right to use a share of the land that has been evenly allotted among the village's residents. Officials assume that it does not matter whether a male or female comes forward to represent the family in contracting its share of land from the authority for the household responsibility system, and usually the husband signs the contract for land use rights. In the land reform that took place when the PRC was founded in 1949, households could own land, and whoever stepped forward to contract the family's share of land became the legal landowner.[6] But the current transformation does not delegate the ownership of land to households; rather, it gives families the right to use the land. In other words, even though the family member who became the legal owner of the family's share of land could decide whether to let others have access in the earlier land reform, all family members are by law guaranteed access to their own share of land under the more recent transformation.

In reality, due to the influence of the prevailing model of marriage in the Chinese countryside, women are hardly equal to men in their actual access to land. Even though both men and women have increased access to resources under the new system, women still have less than men. As elsewhere in rural China, Dongyao Village observes the so-called *cong fu ju* marriage custom, which means that a woman moves in with her husband's family upon marriage (see Chapter 15). In the rural areas, since women are supposed to leave their parents' family for good upon marriage, the household treats unmarried women as temporary members. Few families provide a dowry for their daughters, and wedding expenses are usually covered by the bridegroom's family. In case a woman becomes a widow, she can continue to live with her late husband's family; but if she divorces, she is likely to return to her parents' household. This marriage model has an impact on women's access to land and other productive assets under the household responsibility system.

First, as a member of their parents' family, unmarried women are entitled to a share of land in the village where the parents live. Yet upon marriage and moving away from the village, these women go through a period during which they are, in effect, landless. This happens because at the current stage of the household responsibility system landownership rests at the village level, and one is entitled to access to a share of land in the village when one is a resident. But once she or he moves away from the village, she or he loses that access. Theoretically, a female newlywed is entitled to a share of land in her husband's village, but because a village redistributes its land only periodically the woman has to wait until the next land redistribution to obtain her share. With long-term leases, redistribution should be infrequent.

Second, if a married woman lives with her husband's family, her father-in-law is, more often than not, the head of the extended family. In this case, her legally guaranteed access to a share of land has only nominal meaning, because all decisions over how to make use of that land are made by the household head. Although in the era of the commune system a woman took orders from the production team leader, now she becomes a passive laborer ordered around by her father-in-law.

Third, when a woman lives with her husband in a nuclear family, the family will receive a share of land for her. These are young families with better education and without the restrictions from their parents or parents-in-law such as those prevailing in extended families. After 1982, when the land was redistributed to the households, 80 percent of all existing families in Dongyao divided into smaller units. This might have been an effective way of reducing

---

Box 16.1   Interview of a Young Couple

Cong Niaqian and his wife are 28 and 29 years old, with a five-year-old child. They separated from their extended family two years ago and have become fully aware of the benefits of their autonomy as a nuclear family. The wife told me that when she was with her in-laws, it was like living before the household responsibility system of 1982. Her husband's income from his industrial job had to be handed over to her mother-in-law. She never received any money, even though she worked all year long. She had to request money from her mother-in-law if she wanted to visit her parents. Within this larger family unit, she and her husband were not required to break their backs working. It was her father-in-law's role to work that hard. But today, she has her own family, and they have their own land. Everything they do—all their work—is just for themselves, and she is able to join her husband in making decisions about production and the family. So she always works very hard in the fields and doing the family chores. She knows how much she gets for the work that she does.

The young wife is hopeful for the future and saves money because she wants to build a new house for a daughter-in-law when the time comes. Other rural women think along the same lines when they have unmarried sons.

---

disputes over property, clarifying property rights, and allocating labor and resources within the family. In these young households, women will take part in the decisionmaking concerning both production operations and family affairs (see Box 16.1).

Finally, if a married woman divorces and moves away from her former husband's village, she again goes through a period during which she is, in effect, landless until a redistribution of land takes place in her parents' village. This is true with regard to housing as well, as discussed in the following section. She will live with her parents and will have a house again only if she remarries.

Allocation of Labor within the Rural Household
Since Land Reallocation

Women in the surveyed families have different patterns of life than men; they work considerably longer daily hours and have slightly less education. Women who are classified as farmers or housewives/farmers tend to work longer each day than other women, especially if they are married. Their aver-

---

Box 16.2   Conversation with Wang Jinyu and His Wife

Wang Jinyu made the straightforward statement that both of them do the farmwork together. But he does the skilled work and his wife does the manual and unskilled work. The house chores are her duty. He thought that women had no ability to manage farmwork. His wife told me that she does the same work as her husband. But her husband does only farmwork and nothing else. He might play mahjong with friends, but it is her duty in the evening to do all the chores. She never has any leisure time.

---

age age is 38 years, their average schooling is 4.46 years, and their average daily labor is 14.3 hours. Women in the age group of 35 to 50 years work the most hours daily. A woman in this age range is typically married. She must care for not only her children but also her in-laws. She is responsible not only for the household chores but also for the family farm. The husband is still the head of household by custom, though not by law. The traditional division of labor continues in many ways: Men do technical work and women do manual or unskilled work. Husbands still make the decisions regarding agricultural production and tend to do that farmwork that is customarily considered unfeminine, such as guiding the plow, sowing seeds, and making beds for planting. The tradition that men are in charge of business outside of home and women are solely responsible for domestic affairs endures. (For one family's allocation of labor, see Box 16.2.)

Based on the occupations of family members, families can be divided into two categories: full-time agricultural (75 percent of households in Dongyao) and part-time agricultural (25 percent of households). In the part-time agricultural family, usually the husband has already left agriculture and works in a village industry or, for example, as a carpenter or village doctor. These men work outside of agriculture most of the year except for periods of peak labor demand during planting and harvesting. Their wives are in charge of the management and yields of responsibility land and food plots as well as sideline production. So the rural middle-aged woman, as the one in the house, becomes the main agricultural laborer of the family. These women bear two burdens: household chores and farm production. It is impossible for them to leave the house and the land and look for a job. Women are also limited by their own perceptions. These middle-aged women generally have little education and, being traditional in their views, are not able to face the challenge of the new social division of labor.

Even though there are difficulties in women's access to land of their own, it is clear that their roles in agriculture have been growing under the house-

---

Box 16.3   A Production Model

Cheng Guirong is in her forties. Her husband works outside the village. She is famous in the village for her farm production and is able to do almost any kind of farmwork. She even does some work that women traditionally did not do. She manages about 9.59 *mu* of family land, drives a walking tractor, and carries over 300 *jin* of products by bike to sell in the street. The earliest change she made in the village was to switch from growing grain to producing vegetables. The vegetables on her land had matured when the vegetables on other lands were just germinating. She knows much about the farmwork and market prices for her produce. Many men praise her for achieving prosperity through industry. Even though she can make decisions about production and chores in the family due to her ingenuity and ability, she still considers her husband to be the head of household and, therefore, the decisionmaker.

---

hold responsibility system. In the part-time agricultural households in Dongyao, almost all agricultural income is produced by women's labor. In the full-time agricultural households, the husbands acknowledge that their wives should be given half the credit for the household's agricultural production. In other words, more than 50 percent of agricultural income should be credited to women. Household sideline income is attributable mainly to women.

Decisionmaking Within the Household

The expanded role of women in agricultural production has been accompanied by a greater role in agricultural decisionmaking. Although this conclusion might not be readily drawn from the collected data, it became apparent from the interviews. Due to the influence of traditions and customs, when asked who in the household makes decisions, both the husband and the wife may say it is the husband. Yet one detects that the wife also participates in the decisionmaking process concerning agricultural production matters. The husband says that although he has the final say he makes decisions only after consulting his wife in eight out of ten cases. The fact that the wife is often very familiar with production procedures, labor inputs, and market prices implies her involvement in decisionmaking in these areas (see Box 16.3).

The days when the husband made all decisions are gone forever. The image of the husband wielding all the power in the household is becoming more and more simply symbolic. In reality, for a widening range of decisions, it is more likely that the wife is the one who calls the shots. Nowadays, women have their own views on family development, child education, and spending.

More important, they doubt neither their ability nor their right to assert those views. For instance, when the Zhous talked about this issue, the husband said that decisions were made after consultation with each other, while the wife said, firmly, that she could make her own decisions.

FAMILY HOUSING

After the Communist Party took control of China in 1949, it confiscated the land of landlords and distributed it to the poor. Often it took the landlords' houses as well, but other rural residences remained privately owned. As the process of collectivization began in the late 1950s and continued into the 1960s, houses of rural people were not appropriated. They remained privately owned. The communist system permits private property in things, including houses, but not in land. So the land on which the house stood was owned by the collective, but the house itself was privately owned. This meant that it could be used and inherited by the children of the owner (usually the sons), but it could not be sold.

The ownership of a house is registered in the name of the head of household, typically the husband. The house has generally been built by the parents of the husband for his marriage, and so the title is in his name. The wife is generally from another village and moves to join her husband in this house. She has no legal interest in the house.

In case of divorce, the wife must leave the house, and she will usually return to her natal village. In the event the husband dies, ownership passes to the widow, who can remain in the marital house. If she remarries, she may move to her new husband's home or may remain in her house, depending in part on whether the new husband has a house and on whether the children are adults who need a house. Legally, the new inheritance law enacted by the Communist Party gives the wife and every child, male and female, a right in the deceased's property. After the death of both parents, the arrangements will be influenced by who among the children already has a house. By Chinese custom, the oldest son would usually get the family house, but today the situation is more complex. A designation by the parents will often decide the question.

Although the house belongs to the head of household, his ownership is surrounded and encumbered by duties to other family members. These go with his status as head of household, and the family sees the house not as "his" house but as "their" house. This is true of the wife as well, though she understands what would happen in the case of dissolution of the marriage.

The large increase in income that the household responsibility system has brought in Dongyao has led to a building boom in private housing. From 1958 to 1982, virtually no new private homes had been constructed; no one had any savings to build houses. Between 1982 and 1992, 80 percent of the households in Dongyao built new houses. The old houses were made of mud brick with sheet-metal roofing. The new houses are more diverse. They are built of combinations of brick and concrete, with wood trim and wood or metal window and door frames. The roofs are made of clay tiles.

The housing boom took place in part because of pent-up demand for housing but also, to an important extent, because the house is the major capital item that is privately owned. Investment in houses is a secure, safe way of saving. Houses became a symbol of the living standard of a household. Housing was a solid investment that could be passed to sons. The daughters of the family, as noted earlier, would move away from the village when they married.

This trend has created competition for land between agriculture and housing. The Village Economic Cooperative must give permission for the building of any new house, and for the commitment of land to this purpose, if new land is needed. This land must sometimes come from agricultural land. If a family builds more than one house, for instance, a house for each of three sons, the farmland of the family will be reduced accordingly. The new house will often be occupied by the son and his family, with the parents staying on in the older house. Or sometimes the parents become effectively houseless, shifting from the house of one son to another.

RURAL INDUSTRIALIZATION AND WOMEN'S CONTRIBUTION

At about the same time that agriculture was reorganized from the commune to the household responsibility system, village-owned industries started to develop. Although this change in production organization freed large numbers of surplus laborers from land-based activities, the formation of industries provided a new outlet for workers. The movement of labor from agriculture has accordingly provided rural industry with its necessary labor resource, and it is transforming both the structure of employment in rural areas and the lives of farm families. Between 1981 and 1991, Dongyao started five village-owned enterprises (a tin factory, a knitting mill, a plastics factory, a cardboard-box factory, and an artificial diamond factory) that have profoundly influenced the economic development of the village, the progress of the resident families, and the division of labor within the individual households.

By the end of 1991, the earnings of village-owned enterprises had reached 196,955 yuan, amounting to 54.58 percent of Dongyao's total income of 360,856 yuan. Agricultural income made up 45.42 percent of the total. As of 1991, 513 laborers resided in Dongyao, of whom 373 were involved in agriculture and 164 worked in village-owned enterprises. Among the village's part-time agricultural households (about 25 percent of resident families), nonagricultural income accounted for 40–50 percent of total family income.

With the development of village-owned enterprises, Dongyao has been able to invest its industrial earnings in agriculture. Since 1981, Dongyao has spent more than 200,000 yuan to purchase farming implements and has added 26 new machine-operated wells, thereby greatly improving the conditions for farming.

Since 1982, Dongyao Village has also used its industrial earnings to renovate the village's central elementary school, provide funding for an all-farmers'-children wind band, and pay educational taxes for the households (this last expenditure amounts to 30,000 yuan annually). In addition, the village has repaired old roads and built new ones, improving the living environment of the village.

THE IMPACT OF NONSTATE RURAL INDUSTRY ON WOMEN'S WORK AND LIVES

Industrialization is a critical step for the development of a market economy in the rural areas and is changing the role that women play in society. The biggest change that the industrialization process brings to a farming community is to loosen the traditional bond between the farmer and the land. But the extent to which the bond is eased is not the same for both men and women. In the case of married women, who shoulder the burden of household chores in addition to farmwork, attachment to the land remains the same. Most young unmarried women (average age of twenty to twenty-two years) work in village industries. For these young women, the slackening of the bond to agriculture does occur—but it is only a temporary change and contingent upon their single status. Although it was a giant step forward for women in rural northern China to change their status from housewife to farmer, it is an even bigger step for a farmer to become a factory worker. The latter is especially true for women. Among Dongyao's 164 factory laborers in 1991, 101, or 61.6 percent of the total, were women.

The women employed by nonagricultural industries tend to be better educated than their farmer counterparts and parents, with a mean of 8.3 years in school. On average, women workers in Dongyao's five factories had received a junior high school diploma, while only 38.3 percent of those remaining in farming had that much schooling. However, this may be a function of the younger ages of women who are factory workers. For all types of work, generally speaking, garment cutting, cardboard making, supervising, and operating machine tools are regarded as skilled occupations, and women comprised only 15 percent of those doing skilled work. Most women were assigned to unskilled tasks, and they earned salaries that were about 75 percent of those received by male coworkers for the same work.

Generally, 95 percent of female workers quit their jobs upon marriage, for an overriding purpose for their factory employment is to earn themselves a dowry. Once married, they retire from the factory jobs to take care of their families and assume farming responsibilities.

The characteristics of female industrial workers accompany the temporary nature of the change in the social role and status of women. Almost all the women employed in Dongyao's five factories were short-term employees. The temporary nature of their employment may partly account for the lower proportion of women doing skilled work. The fact that they worked to earn themselves a dowry while they were unmarried did not meaningfully change their societal role.

RURAL WOMEN'S CHANGING ROLES

The combined effect of the household responsibility system and rural industrialization is that women have gradually come to form the main labor force in agricultural production. In the era of the commune system, more than 60 percent of rural women took part in agricultural production on collective farms, but the share of men in farm work was also high. The kind of work done by women tended to be labor-intensive and to require little skill or training. At the time, there was a saying that jobs demanding skill were made for men, and women were supposed to do unskilled work. Under the household responsibility system, agricultural activities are organized and carried out with the family as the basic operating unit.

Agricultural production is a highly seasonal activity, and both planting and harvesting require intensive labor input. In the commune system era, mutual help was a method of labor division arranged by the collective. Since the commune system was dissolved, mutual help has evolved into a voluntary and good-willed relationship among neighbors and relatives. In forming a network of mutual help, the social connections on the maternal side tend to play a more prominent role. Usually, a mutual-support network operates among relatives residing in the same village, though networks with out-of-village participants linked through in-laws are not uncommon. Moreover, mutual help is basically an equality-based labor exchange, and it helps effectively to solve the problem of labor shortage in busy seasons.

Since the mid-1980s, rural women have begun doing work with which they were never previously associated. The development of nonagricultural industries in the rural areas has brought the recruitment of men and unmarried women for the labor force, leaving married women behind to take care of family-based agricultural production. In these families, married women not only plan and execute almost all agricultural production; in the cases where no help is available from grandparents, they also raise poultry and do household chores.

Under the auspices of village-run enterprises, the Dongyao Economic Cooperative has over the years purchased some farming implements. At the time of this fieldwork, Dongyao had three tractors, one 75-horsepower planter, and three rotating plows. The Cooperative coordinated plowing, planting, and harvesting, all done with machines, at the village level. Meanwhile, other production conditions have also seen significant improvement. For example, when Dongyao redistributed its land in 1982, the village had only 28 machine-operated wells, with more than 100 *mu* of land relying on one well for irrigation. At that time, quarrels among relatives were not uncommon because households competed with one another for limited water resources. Now the village has 54 machine-operated wells. The improvement of production conditions has helped make women the main labor force in agriculture.

Table 16.2 describes the changes in work patterns and transfers of tasks between male and female laborers before and after 1982, when the rural reform started in Dongyao.

The Changes in Division of Labor Between Male and Female Since 1982

As shown in Table 16.2, there are three basic categories of labor, namely, housework, agriculture, and nonagriculture. The traditional principle for dividing work is the same across all labor categories—that is, skilled tasks for men and unskilled tasks for women—and remains largely unchanged. What has been revised is the definition of "skill." Furthermore, new tasks have been added to the labor domain.

Changes in the living conditions of the household have resulted in adjustments in housework. For example, before 1982, farmers had to fetch water from public wells at long walking distances from their homes. Now that burden has vanished, as every family has a pump well in its yard. Furthermore, more than 80 percent of the households have TV sets (20 percent are color sets, which were considered luxury items only a few years ago). About 25 percent of the families have washing machines and 5 percent have VCRs. Therefore, operating and maintaining these valuable household electrical appliances have become a new task, reserved mainly for men.

The clearest changes in household chores affect tasks once done only by males but now done also by females, for example, storing grains and vegetables in a cellar, food processing, trading produce in farmers' and state markets, building houses and walls (with bricks), and transporting produce by

Table 16.2   Division of Labor Between Males and Females in China, Before and After 1982

Labor	Before 1982			After 1982		
	F	M	All	F	M	All
Housework						
Cooking	*			*		
Washing	*			*		
Shopping for consumables			*			*
Cleaning	*			*		
Taking care of old parents	*			*		
Baby-sitting	*			*		
Child education				*		
Storing grain and vegetables in a cellar		*				*
Carrying water		*				
Food processing		*				*
Feeding livestock	*			*		
Trading produce in farmer and state markets		*				*
Building houses (building with walls, using bricks)		*				*
Building houses (setting a roof beam)		*			*	
Digging wells		*			*	
Transporting produce by bike or tractor		*				*
Using household electrical appliances					*	
Agriculture						
Seed selection	*			*		
Plowing		*				*
Guiding the plow		*			*	
Sowing seeds		*			*	
Raising seedlings			*			*
Making beds for planting		*			*	
Weeding			*			*
Spreading fertilizer			*			*
Spraying insecticide			*			*
Irrigating fields	*			*		
Managing pumps & farm machinery		*				*
Driving a cart or a tractor		*				*
Digging irrigation ditches		*			*	
Constructing reservoirs		*				
Building railways & roads		*				
Molding adobe blocks—mixing mud		*				*
Molding adobe blocks—carrying shovel	*					*
Molding adobe blocks—trawling blocks		*				*
Harvesting grain			*			*
Shelling, threshing, and drying grain	*					*
Winnowing, sifting, and grinding grain	*					*
Putting grain in storage		*				*
Delivering tax grain to the state		*				*
Feeding draft animals		*				*
Nonagriculture						
Village industry					*	
Managing industrial operations				*		
Transportation				*		
State employees		*				*
Service/trade (running restaurants and shops)						*
Construction		*			*	

Source: Fieldwork, 1992.

bike and tractor. But the house tasks customarily done by women are still women's work, for example, cooking, cleaning, washing, taking care of elderly parents, baby-sitting, children's education, and feeding livestock. On the one hand, women's participation in the work of the family is obviously broader than before; on the other hand, women's burdens are clearly heavier.

In agriculture, the concept of "skill" has altered. Some jobs formerly thought of as skilled have been transferred from men to women and are now characterized as unskilled, for example, managing pumps and farm machinery, driving a cart and tractor, molding adobe blocks and mixing the mud, putting grain in storage, and feeding draft animals. These jobs used to be regarded as so heavy, and requiring so much skill, that women were not allowed to try them.

Industrialization brought new tasks for both men and women. Before 1981 there was no industry in Dongyao. Occasionally, male members of the commune had been assigned to a construction team by the production brigade for work in nearby towns or on construction sites. Legally, both men and women had equal opportunities to be employees in the state's or the county's industries. In reality, however, the opportunity for a woman was nil unless she were admitted to a university; then, after graduation, she could be assigned by the government to be a city resident and a state employee. Now, with the rapid development of village-township industries, women have had more economic opportunities. They have been able to work in the local enterprises and to be saleswomen. Yet few women reach the managerial level in the factories of Dongyao.

Reasons for Changes in the Division of Work Between Men and Women

The changes in the division of labor between men and women are directly related to changes in the economy of Dongyao. Because agricultural production is based on the household economy, housework and agricultural activities must be coordinated within a family. Men, especially heads of households, are customarily responsible for the important matters in the family's economic operations. Due to the improvement in both economic and living conditions, the nature of these family economic activities has been dramatically changed, as has the division of housework.

Women now assume some of what were once considered to be male responsibilities, that is, tasks that were important or even vital to the family. For example, the storing of grain used to be a man's job simply because grain, partitioned and distributed mainly according to accumulated work points by the production brigade, was vital for the subsistence of the whole family. Storing grain is less important nowadays, since almost no family lacks grain for food. Men have been "upgraded" to what they consider to be more important jobs, such as operating and maintaining household electrical appliances, while once-important tasks such as storing grain have been "downgraded" to women.

Since the land was distributed to families, the principle for dividing agricultural production has also been changed: enough for the state's quota, sufficient for the collective's share, all the remaining for the family. The volume of the remaining portion is related to the total volume of the family's production. This market economy–oriented production and distribution system has provided strong incentives for rural women to participate in agricultural production.

In addition, flourishing industrialization in rural areas has attracted and absorbed large numbers of male and young female workers to industry, leaving the burdens of agricultural production to married women.

Public Labor Duties of the Commune System

During the study period, it was observed that some of the public-labor duties, such as constructing reservoirs and building railways and roads, had vanished from the family's work list. Under the commune system, members had been awarded work points for labor, even for public labor. For the farmers, therefore, it did not matter which work was done, only how many work points could be earned. After the reforms, the specific task performed made a difference, and the state or the collective could not ask the farmers to work on public projects without fair compensation. Hence, public-labor duties, which used to be part of the family's normal work schedule, are becoming nonagricultural businesses.

Restrictions on Women of Traditional Ideas and Customs of Division of Labor

Although significant improvements and changes have been taking place in the rural women's lives, there clearly remain many restrictions imposed by traditional ideas and customs on women's roles in housework, agriculture, and nonagricultural work. Women are still not allowed to participate in some production and household activities even though the labor is not beyond their physical abilities. For example, women are not allowed to set roof beams when building a house, and they are not permitted to dig wells. In fact, they cannot even watch the processes due to the belief that if women were allowed to watch the house would collapse and the well would dry up. Guiding the plow and sowing seeds are also still not women's work, since many people believe that a woman's performance of these tasks would result in poor crops. These jobs were skilled work and earned top work points during the commune period. Today, they are still considered as skilled and, hence, not women's work.

THE ROLE OF EDUCATION

To assess the impact of education, individuals were categorized in roles and occupations by their relative levels of formal schooling. Women tend to have spent one year less in school, on average, than men. The differences in level of education are indeed significant as far as family roles are concerned. Generally speaking, the generation of grandparents (typically above age 60) is illiterate. On average, the household heads (male), with a mean age of 47.6 years, have had 6.2 years in school, while their wives, with a mean age of 46.5 years, have had only 3.6 years of schooling. The younger generation (sons, daughters, sons-in-law, daughters-in-law) has had an average of 6.16 years in school. Females in this category have a mean educational level of 6.9 years, two times more than their mothers and mothers-in-law. The younger males have the same average amount of education as their fathers, which reflects the traditional priority given to males in the Chinese rural education system.

Occupation is another important factor reflecting the different levels of education for females, while on average the levels of education for males are similar across vocational categories. The female agricultural workforce has a mean level of education of 4.46 years, while the nonagricultural female labor force, a group of young women with an average age of 20.7 years, has 8.3 years of schooling, which is equivalent to the completion of middle school. The data show that young, unmarried, and educated women have better economic opportunities than do middle-aged, married, and less educated women.

Households with higher incomes are placing more emphasis on the education of their children. Child education was regarded as very important by all twenty-three families interviewed. Achievements in education were considered to be an honor to the family. Some families even thought that to have a child going to college was more important than to have a family income exceeding 10,000 yuan (a figure signifying wealth). More significantly, the education of female children is receiving more and more attention. At the time of writing, Dongyao had two youngsters attending college, and both were female. In the eyes of many farmers, to leave the countryside and find a job in the city is the best opportunity that a child of farmer parents can have, and that, in part, explains why they consider the education of their children to be important.

There is another reason for farming households to emphasize their daughters' education. Farming households believe that the best way out of rural poverty for their daughters is to marry a good husband; and to marry a good husband, one has to have a good education. Unlike male siblings, who are expected to inherit the family property and carry on the family name, a daughter will leave the family sooner or later and therefore needs a good husband to maintain her own well-being.

In addition, farmers have learned that education plays an important role in agricultural production.

PROBLEMS FACING WOMEN

Since the household responsibility system was initiated in the early 1980s, women have been presented with more opportunities than they ever knew existed before. Now women are not only participating in all sorts of agricultural activities but also organizing household sideline production in response to market demand. In so doing, they are contributing to family income in a very tangible way. Moreover, a majority of unmarried women now can enter non-agricultural industries as they wish. It is true that at the current stage of development of village-owned industries most women are still limited to finding employment within the boundaries of the village. But this is temporary. One cannot overestimate the significance of these women's beginning to see opportunities beyond agriculture and even beyond village boundaries. Seeing these new openings, rural women are awakening from their passive past and, for the first time, recognizing their true independence.

The above having been said, women living in today's rural China also face new problems.

The Need for Better Community Services

Women shoulder the dual responsibility of taking part in production and doing household chores and caring for children. Society tends to see that dual responsibility as women's natural duty. During Mao's era, production was assigned the top priority for political reasons; in rural China today, production is being assigned the top priority because it is directly related to the market economy. Although Dongyao's women are being presented with more opportunities, they also face the problem of being overburdened. The women's overload problem is due to the following two factors:

1. They work too much in the field. This is especially true of those households in which both husband and grown children work in the factories. In these households, the women do all the fieldwork, and only in busy seasons—like planting and harvesting—do they get some help from their husbands, children, and relatives. Introducing technologies to minimize manual labor would also help women's health, as the level of exertion required in agricultural production, sideline production, and household chores is frequently detrimental.
2. They lack help from social services. All public services that existed in the commune system era—like kindergartens, public mess halls,

and barefoot doctors—have disappeared with the dissolution of the old system.

Until the market begins providing more services, a reasonable way to solve the work-overload problem is for the local village government and non-governmental organizations to develop community services, which could include food processing, baby-sitting, clothing manufacture, health care, and geriatric nursing. One pitfall that should be avoided is the so-called communist-style, charge-free services prevalent under the commune system, which provided assistance that was ill-conceived in the first place and did not last even through the initial stages. The services should be fully compensated. As for technical issues such as how much to charge and how to pay, many options can be explored. At Dongyao's current level of economic development, the farmers can neither afford nor sanction elaborate and high-priced services.

Baby-sitting provides a good example. Farmers need childcare during the busy seasons only; yearlong baby-sitting is neither necessary nor affordable. Being aware of that, the village could establish seasonal daycare services during the summer and fall busy seasons by organizing high school students, who are out of class during school recess, as well as elderly people, who can no longer work in the field but are still able to look after children. By providing such services, the village relieves the women of two responsibilities: taking care of the children and cooking lunch for them.

Another area in which the village could start providing a service is food processing. In Dongyao, there are already a few privately owned food-processing mills that are engaged in rice and flour preparation, saving women the considerable labor that was necessary when more primitive processing methods were used. But cooking is still done in a very traditional fashion in Dongyao. Since all households share the same cooking style and methods and every household cooks more or less the same dishes every day, a community food-processing service to provide semifinished products is readily conceivable. The service could be either based on barter or paid for in cash, thereby improving its sustainability and popularity among the farmers. By making use of unused labor scattered among many households, the service would save on fuel and agricultural equipment as well as labor and cost.

Women's Educational Needs

The limited education women have received is more and more an obstacle in their struggle to grasp the new opportunities coming their way. Of the generation of females currently of parenting age, women have on average received 3.6 years of schooling, while the men on average have received 6.2 years. Judging either by age or by the role this generation is playing in the household economy, these women are the backbone of their households. But because they suffer from a poor education, their development opportunities are limited.

When asked about educating the next generation, more than 50 percent of the parents indicated that they were willing to pay however much it took to support their children's going to college, if the children would study hard enough to make their way to that level. Farmer Zhou Lianfu, for instance, had a daughter going to college, and supporting her for a semester accounted for one-third of the family's total yearly expenditures; yet the family could not be prouder of her.

The fact that the girls of the next generation are receiving a better education than their mothers did indicates that education has begun to be valued in the rural areas. Government support is needed to encourage this trend. History has, time and again, proved that education is the key to improving women's social status and, finally, to liberation.

If young women in rural areas are not well educated, they will not be able to play a significant role in local development in the future. In fact, education is not yet considered as important and valuable as it should be. Two young women who taught at the village's elementary school were among those interviewed. They reported that their monthly salary was 70–75 yuan, less than the average amount received by a factory worker (about 100 yuan per month). Such low salaries paid to teachers are no help in sustaining educational quality and in encouraging people to pursue further schooling.

Creating Better Work Opportunities and Conditions for Women

In the part-time agricultural households of Dongyao (25 percent of the total), women shoulder the responsibilities of agricultural production, sideline production, and household chores. In rural China today, much of this women's work is still done in the traditional, manual fashion, which is detrimental to women's health. In a conversation with a practicing physician in Dongyao Village, we learned that the percentage of women contracting nephritis, appendicitis, and metroptosis was still high. When we address issues like developing community services and improving education, we should also seek ways to improve women's working and living conditions in very practical, health-ensuring terms. Until better conditions are created, the day of real liberation from women's overload will never come.

CONCLUSIONS: WOMEN'S ACCESS TO LAND AND HOUSING

Although the access of women to land and housing as members of families has improved dramatically in recent times, their legal position remains very vulnerable. While the marriage continues, the situation may be satisfactory; when the marriage ends in divorce, the woman loses the land and house—and the benefit of all her efforts over the years.

In the case of land, the lease could be made jointly to the husband and wife, with both their names appearing on the document. In the case of houses, the law on inheritance is reasonably adequate. The problem area is divorce, which cuts off all a wife's right to the house. Accordingly, there is a need for legal reforms that recognize a woman's contribution to the building and main-tenance of the house and provide her with compensation for that contribution.

NOTES

1. In 1997, US$1 was equivalent to 8.11 yuan.

2. "Sideline production" refers to activities such as raising pigs and chickens and making handicrafts.

3. The production team was the basic unit of agricultural production during the commune system. Usually, a commune was composed of several production brigades that were administrative villages; one brigade, or village, was composed of several production teams. Dongyao had four production teams in that period.

4. A *jin* = 0.5 kilogram = 1.1 pounds.

5. Although legally the Chinese system does not designate a head of household, claiming that all individuals are equal under law, in practice the husband usually func-tions as the head of household, at times being permitted to sign legal contracts in his name only.

6. The initial land reform gave ownership rights to individuals. Soon, however, land was collectivized in stages. The smallest unit of agricultural production in 1954 was the mutual aid group, consisting of 608 households (later it was called the brigade). The elemental agricultural producer's cooperative (in which distribution of production was based on the amount of work that each member did and the amount of land s/he contributed) was composed of 20–50 households in 1955. A more advanced cooperative was established in 1956 to include 10 or more villages. In 1958, this method of organization changed to the people's commune, in which the basic account-ing unit was the production team, consisting of a small village or a part of a larger vil-lage (25–50 households). A rural people's commune was composed of 1,500–5,000 households and managed every aspect of rural life. The commune replaced the town-ship as the primary-level unit of local government. During this period, there were changes in the names, tasks, and responsibilities of accounting and production at all levels. At the base, however, a unit was composed of 608 households, then came a di-vision of 20–50 households. Although the tasks and names of the production units changed, the farmers still worked with their relatives and neighbors in the same labor sections.

Conclusion: What We Know—and What We Need to Know

Irene Tinker and Gale Summerfield

The authors in this volume present what we know about the various ways housing and land policies were implemented in China, Laos, and Vietnam under their communist regimes and how the current governments are adapting these rules and regulations to promote a market system. The persistence of traditional custom in regulating women's access to house and land, despite years of Communist Party rule, is an implacable theme running through the chapters. Yet the recent societal transformations accompanying the transition to a market economy are challenging these customary practices more profoundly than they were challenged under the nominal equality of the command economies. This apparent contradiction is at least partially explained by the changing roles of women in the present economic transition, a change that contrasts with the patriarchal control typical of communist regimes.

The previous adherence to rhetorical equality meant that allocation of housing in urban areas was theoretically available to both women and men; rural land was collectivized, and all able-bodied people were obliged to work. What is clear from the chapters is that the prevailing construction of gender in various social groups continues to affect both the interpretation of the law by local officials and the expectations of women about their rights within the family.

What is changing as a result of rapid economic transformation is the social construction of gender. Women's roles are changing, and so are men's roles. When men migrate from the farm, women become farmers. When factories prefer women workers for assembly jobs and export processing, families release them from customary farmwork. When factories lay off proportionately more women than men, women find that their bargaining power at home also falls. When forest resources become commercialized, women's knowledge may give them equal access to participation in the trade. When education provides access to increased income, girls—who gained greater access to education in the communist period—may also benefit.

Under communist regimes in these countries and in Eastern Europe, the party was patriarchal, and women's roles at home were only slightly altered. Despite the provision of childcare facilities for urban women workers at state-owned enterprises in China, Vietnam, and Eastern Europe (Laos lacked such enterprises), and occasional official exhortations for men to help with housework and childcare, the requirement to work outside the home resulted in excessive "double day" burdens on women. The collapse of centrally planned economic systems under Communist Party control has resulted in women being laid off first because the managers of firms and government offices, still influenced by cultural attitudes toward women, consider them more expensive than men—mainly due to maternity leave—and less efficient workers because they have to perform domestic roles in addition to work.

The change to the market economy, then, has forced some women back into traditional familial roles within the household or within family enterprise as firms eliminate "surplus workers." At the same time, the reforms have opened new possibilities for women. The weakening of China's strong clan and family control permits greater mobility and decisionmaking by rural women. In Vietnam and Laos, where women's roles have never been as subject to the patriarch, women are reasserting their traditional trading activities while continuing to benefit from the governments' provision of education to girls as well as boys.

The weakening of customary controls, especially in rural China and Vietnam, may free women from many family pressures, but it may also mean that women are no longer provided with a house or access to land through their husbands. Divorce exacerbates this erosion of traditional rights at the same time that it allows women themselves more independence. While divorce appears to be primarily an urban phenomenon, women's rights to land and house are issues in rural as well as in urban areas not only in these three countries studied but throughout the world. Increased migration, not only to cities but abroad, plays a critical role in these changes; but legal migration has only recently been allowed in China and Vietnam, a fact that further complicates women's rights to house and land.

Authors in this volume examine these significant trends as they play out distinctively in the three countries and among various groups within each country. The immensity of China, with its regional variations, long experience under communist rule, and recent successes with economic transformation, presents very different patterns of women's changing rights to house and land than those found in the newly emerging, primarily rural Laos, with its dominant ethnic group influenced by a matrilineal past. In Vietnam, the North retains elements of Confucian custom overlaid by a longer exposure to a command economy while the South, which experienced a shorter exposure to communist control, reflects more of its Southeast Asian heritage. Such variety lends texture and detail to the issues discussed in this volume and makes any generalizations difficult. The trends undermining the more traditional constructions of gender, and the impact they are having on women's lives, thus gain added importance as a way of interpreting the diverse information presented. The following material presents some conclusions based on the path-breaking set of chapters in this volume, but much more research is needed to explore these trends throughout the region and to test and document them more thoroughly.

HOUSING RIGHTS UNDER COMMUNISM

Housing security is one of the basic human rights that officials in the socialist planning phase of these Asian countries have frequently contrasted with the Western concept of human rights as individual freedoms. However, the authors show that the full state provision of housing was limited to a minority of mainly urban residents, with the greatest numbers of those living in state housing in China. This is logical considering the population of the country and the fact that the communist regime in China has lasted over forty years. For the same reason, more residents of Hanoi were provided with housing than was the case in Ho Chi Minh City, where communist control began much later. In predominantly rural Laos, the war discouraged urban migration. The public housing in Vientiane, financed by the Eastern bloc countries, was begun late in the regime and remained largely unfinished with the collapse of those regimes.

Housing that was provided by the state through work units was usually small but varied by employer, with party officials often living in larger units and at times occupying spacious confiscated villas. Until recently, throughout the region several generations of one family lived together in most government housing. Because shelter was scarce, unrelated singles or even several families were at first required to share rooms in Hanoi. Married women shared in the housing provided by the state, but they were not fully equal partners, despite state rhetoric of equality. Although the rules permitted allocating housing to either husband or wife, work units typically gave rights to the male in the family. Single people from the same city lived with their parents, and young couples had long waits for units.

Most rural residents had to provide their own housing, but they benefited to some extent from guarantees on use rights to the land and low-cost building materials. In rural areas of China and Vietnam, patrilocal patterns were prevalent, though Laos illustrates the interesting contrast of matrilineal rights to land and house. Various types of private markets flourished in these countries except in the most intense period of the Cultural Revolution in China

(1966–1976). Women often used their homes to earn income as well as for shelter. This income-earning aspect has increased considerably during the economic transition that began in 1976 in China and in the mid-1980s in Vietnam and Laos. Women prepare foods, handicrafts, and equipment to sell, operate small hair-styling shops, and engage in a myriad of market-supported activities in and in front of their housing units, making the lower-level units in multistory housing extremely desirable. Thus, women's agency is increasing as they decide how to use their housing to generate income even as their housing security becomes less certain.

Women who have high incomes or whose husband works for a successful company or influential bureaucracy have vastly improved their housing since the reforms. In Vietnam, universities and ministries allocate land for their workers and may subsidize the cost of building; as a result, Hanoi is ringed with developments of three- and four-story, single-family residences rising up from lots that average fifty square meters. Old public housing is also for sale to those residing in the units, but there is little incentive to buy these tiny, unimproved rooms with their shared utilities, especially as the rents are minuscule. Since rents and subsidized housing are tied to low wages, the Vietnamese government is unlikely to follow the Chinese government decree to end subsidized housing in the near future.

Apartment complexes with modern amenities are more typical in China than are single-family residences. Since the reforms, state-owned enterprises have used investment funds to satisfy the pent-up demand of their workers for better apartments and found loopholes for subsidizing units even when privatized. As the Chinese government vows to withdraw from supplying housing, it has looked toward Singapore as a possible model for providing housing in a market-based economy. The Singapore government stresses housing rights as human rights and argues for a strong role for the state in providing it. The government's use of a compelled housing accumulation fund forced employees to accumulate monies for buying housing units; this concept is already in use in many parts of China. Once again, however, the patriarchal nature of Singapore's socialist government rests on a secondary role for women (as it repeatedly stresses the role of male as head of household and receiver of state subsidies) and authoritarian political processes. Although the Singapore model is important to understand because of Singapore's influence in housing and other areas in China and Vietnam, this model offers limited insights into incorporating women's rights into housing policy.

Rapid migration to urban areas in China and Vietnam began illegally when residential restrictions were in place. These migrants were ineligible for government employment, which in turn provided access to housing and schools. Squatter settlements and increased crowding in existing housing stock have intensified as the restrictions on internal mobility have decreased. The chapters on China in this volume have briefly referred to women in this "floating population"; they note the tensions between urban residents and migrants as millions move from the countryside to the city, thus adding to the already great demand for low-cost housing in the cities. The studies of squatter settlements and urban crowding in Hanoi and Ho Chi Minh City are more expansive. Poor women in these squatter areas have been active in establishing or improving infrastructure and environmental conditions (such as sanitation services), but their efforts are frequently undermined by lack of clear rights to housing and developers' goals of earning profits from the rapidly rising prices for inner-city land.

In all the countries, housing policies to promote a private housing market have moved slowly in contrast to many other reforms, reflecting the population's fears about the removal of housing guarantees. These reforms, however, are considered integral to the market-oriented reforms, especially in terms of cutting subsidies to unprofitable state enterprises, promoting labor markets, and establishing new social-security systems.

Policymakers both locally and in international organizations have treated housing reforms as a family issue thought to be gender-neutral since most women are married. The authors in this volume have pointed out the numerous ways that the assumption of gender-neutrality is wrong. The discussion of housing reform stresses the gendered aspects of rising income inequality, patrilocal traditions, employment discrimination, housing shortages, prices, separation from work units, and changing institutions. To date, most policymakers, especially in studies of Vietnam and Laos, seem more concerned about land reallocation in rural areas than about urban housing issues, a bias that reflects assumptions about poverty as primarily a rural phenomenon. In fact, the disparity of income between rich and poor is an urban as well as rural phenomenon; this particularly affects women heads of households and is leading to an increasing feminization of poverty.

LAND RIGHTS AND ACCESS UNDER COMMUNISM

The change from communal farming back to household control over land has been a dramatic one in all three countries; land, however, continues to be owned by the state in all of these countries. Because the laws designated the farm household as the unit for the reallocation and registration of land, the laws encouraged the creation of independent households as opposed to extended family living arrangements. Although the laws in Vietnam and Laos provide that women as well as men have equal rights to registering the land, customary attitudes have once again prevailed: Women and men acquiesce to the land being registered under the husband's name alone as head of household. This is true even in Laos, with its matrilineal roots. Laos law allows wealthy women to buy land; the limits on number of hectares prevent con-

solidation by one wealthy family. But in the countryside, the process of transferring titles to private families has in actuality resulted in a transfer of lands
from the women's side in the matrilineal tradition to the control of the husband, mainly through the simple omission of having the wife be at least
cosigner on the new titles. In both countries, representatives of government
agencies and nongovernmental organizations have organized workshops
where women are encouraged to exercise their legal rights to land and house.

Land reform in China began in 1979, when the household responsibility
system replaced communal working brigades. Since then land has been real-
located several times in order to adjust for land taken out of agricultural production for rural industry and to respond to natural population increases and
new residents, such as young women who marry men living in the village.
The allocation of land to a family, however, ignores unmarried women's
rights and reiterates women's role in marriage. As a result, women lose their
rights to land or house if they divorce. New wives, moving to their husband's
village, are also at risk under the land reallocation system because the long-
term family land contracts will stop the redistributions that typically occurred
periodically to give them a share in village land. Because land reallocation is
more recent in Vietnam and Laos, this problem is only beginning to emerge in
these countries.

Rapid economic changes have also encouraged a redistribution of tasks
on the farm; married middle-aged women are increasingly doing the farming
as men and young women look for jobs in rural industry or migrate to the
cities, at least temporarily. A more hidden gendered aspect occurs in the allocation of land for contracts to grow commodities specifically for market
(rather than the allocations based on provision for the family); these areas in
Vietnam have more frequently been allocated to men, and anecdotal evidence
indicates that the pattern is similar in China.

FINAL AND FORWARD THOUGHTS

Taken together, the chapters in this volume underscore the critical nature of
legal reforms for establishing women's rights to house and land while emphasizing the persistence of cultural traditions of patriarchy. The destabilizing effects of recent rapid economic transitions seem to have been a greater factor
in undermining custom that restricts women's agency than the many years of
communist control and its emblematic equality. The authors illustrate how
women as individuals and as family members take advantage of new economic opportunities, such as opening small businesses, expanding markets in
medicinal herbs and vegetables, and exporting goods. Although some com-
mentators will equate this added economic activity with a greater burden on
women, most feminists believe that women's agency and, hence, their house-

hold bargaining power are increased as women make their own economic decisions and control their own income.

At the professional level, women are also able to expand the scope of jobs in mass organizations as the role and importance of the Women's Unions in Vietnam and Laos and the Women's Federation in China increase. Even the minimal opening of a civil society has also provided women with new professional opportunities. Many authors stress the crucial importance of education for women in taking advantage of these new economic possibilities.

At the same time that economic change undermines restrictions on women, the same forces of change may jeopardize customary protections of women, including their access to house and land. Divorce may force a woman out of her house in urban and rural areas, since men tend to maintain rights to property. Examples are given of men selling their farmland even when their wives were producing crops on the land because the women had failed to register their claims to access.

This blatant inequality has aroused activist women in all the countries studied. Working with government ministries and nongovernmental organizations, women in Vietnam and Laos have organized workshops to educate women on the importance of ensuring that their names appear on the title to urban housing or on the rental contract as well as on land titles in rural areas. Such joint control is central to equal rights for women: It affects their status both in society at large and within the family; it becomes critical in times of stress such as divorce, abandonment, or death of one's husband.

Overall, this collection of studies establishes the critical importance of women maintaining their rights to house and land in the face of economic transformations that alter customary rights and responsibilities. Emphasized also is the crucial need for women to preserve whatever gains they achieved during the communist period, such as access to education and employment. In this volume, women's changing property rights during the transition periods have been documented in the three communist countries in East and Southeast Asia. Given the tremendous variety of cultures and regions presented, only general trends can be ascertained, but the intertwining of laws, custom, and economic change provides powerful insights that call for further research not only in these countries but throughout the world. Such research is urgently required to design policies that will truly address the problems of women's rights to house and land in this changing world.

Bibliography

ACHR (Asian Centre for Housing Reform). 1998. E-News No. 13, Monday 19 January: maurice@ksc9.th.com.

Adams, M. 1995. *Technical Report: Forest Products, Harvesting, and Utilization Component.* Paper presented to a Project Formulation Workshop for the FAO of the UN in the series Sustainable Conservation, Management, and Utilization of Tropical Rainforests of Asia.

Afonja, Simi. 1990. "Changing Patterns of Gender Stratification in West Africa." In *Persistent Inequalities: Women and World Development,* I. Tinker, ed. New York: Oxford.

Agarwal, Bina. 1997a. "'Bargaining' and Gender Relations: Within and Beyond Households." *Feminist Economics* 3(1): 1–51.

———. 1997b. "Editorial: Re-Sounding the Alert—Gender, Resources and Community Action." *World Development* 25(9): 1373—1380.

———. 1994. *A Field of One's Own: Gender and Land Rights in South Asia.* Cambridge: Cambridge University Press.

Agence France-Presse. 1996. "Shanghai's Youths Grapple with Housing Woes." June 1.

———. 1996. "Serious Fraud from Illegal Renting of Government Flats." May 6.

Aggarwal, Narendra. 1998. "S'pore Is Still Tops." *Straits Times Weekly Edition* (April 25): 2.

Agriculture and Forestry Service of Sayaboury Province. 1995. "Land and Forest Allocation, Sayaboury Province."

All China Trade Union Female Workers Department. 1976. "Guanyu zhufang fenpei nan nu bu pingdeng wenti de diaocha baogao" (Investigation of housing inequality among men and women). Howard Yao, trans.

Almanac of China's Population 1985. 1986. Beijing: China Social Sciences Publishing House, 268.

Almanac of Shanghai Statistics 1992. 1992. Beijing: China Statistics Publishing House, 100.

An Ninh Thu Do Magazine, 9/17/96.

Anon. 1995. "Discussion Paper on Proposed World Bank/Ausaid Land Titling Project for Laos." Vientiane. Internal AUSAID document.

Antoine, Philippe, and Jeanne Nanitelamio. "Can Polygyny Be Avoided in Dakar?" In *Courtyards, Markets, City Streets: Urban Women in Africa,* Kathleen Sheldon, ed. Boulder, CO: Westview, 129–152.

Asia Pulse. 1998. "Profile—China's Real Estate Industry." July 30.

———. 1998. "Alert—China to Implement Housing Reform Plan in July." May 19.

Bailey, Stephen. 1997. "Revision of Forestry Law Translation." Vientiane: Swedforest. Unpublished report.

Bakari, Jana Patterson. 1995. "Women, Work, and Housing in Tanzania." Field report based on a Fulbright grant.

Baker, Mark. 1995. "Forgotten Legal China." *Houston Journal of International Law*: 383.

Bao, Singui (translation). 1990. "The Unknowns in Rural Women and China's Development." *Intellectual Women* (in Chinese), vol. 1, at 245–265. Zhengzhou: Henan People's Publisher.

Bapat, Meera. 1987. "Women and Housing: A Training Manual." Bombay: SPARC (Society for Promotion of Area Resource Centres, mimeo).

Barlow, Tani E. 1994. "Politics and Protocols of Funu: (Un)Making National Woman." In *Engendering China: Women, Culture, and the State*, Christina K. Gilmartin, Gail Hershatter, Lisa Rofel, and Tyrene White, eds. Cambridge: Harvard University Press.

Belsky, Jill, and Steve Siebert. 1983. "Household Responses to Drought in Two Subsistence Leyte Villages." *Philippine Quarterly of Culture and Society* 11: 237–256.

Beresford, Melanie. 1994a. "Impact of Macroeconomics Reform on Women in Vietnam." A report prepared for UNIFEM. Hanoi. Unpublished.

———. 1994b. *Impact of Macroeconomic Reform on Women in Vietnam.* UNIFEM, VIE/93/w02, Hanoi.

Berry, Sara. 1994. "Resource Access and Management as Historical Processes—Conceptual and Methodological Issues in Access, Control, and Management of Natural Resources." Occasional Paper No. 13/1994.

———. 1993. *No Condition Is Permanent.* Madison: University of Wisconsin Press.

———. 1989. "Social Institutions and Access to Resources." *Africa* 59(1).

Bezlova, Antoaneta. 1996. "China: Beijing to Tear Down Historical Residential Area." Inter Press Service, November 27.

Blanc, Cristina Szanton, with contributors. 1994. *Urban Children in Distress: Global Predicaments and Innovative Strategies.* Switzerland: Gordon and Breach; UNICEF.

Blumberg, Rae Lesser. 1991. "Income Under Female Versus Male Control: Hypotheses from a Theory of Gender Stratification and Data from the Third World." In *Gender, Family, and Economy: The Triple Overlap*, Rae L. Blumberg, ed.

Blumberg, Rae Lesser, Cathy Rakowski, Irene Tinker, and Michael Monteón, eds. 1995. *EnGENDERing Wealth and Well-Being.* Boulder: Westview.

Boris, Eileen, and Elizabeth Prugl, eds. 1996. *Invisible No More: Homeworkers in Global Perspective.* New York: Routledge.

Boserup, Ester. 1970. *Woman's Role in Economic Development.* London: George Allen and Unwin.

Bossen, Laurel. 1994. "All Words and No Deeds: Rural Women's Property Rights in Reform China." Paper presented at the World Bank Conference Gender and Property Rights, Montreal, Canada.

Bourdet, Yves. 1997. "Laos: The Sixth Party Congress, and After?" *Southeast Asian Affairs 1997*: 143–160.

Bruce, John W., and Paula Harrell. 1989. "Land Reform in the People's Republic of China, 1978–1988." LTC Research Paper, no. 100. Madison: Land Tenure Center, University of Wisconsin.

Brush, Stephen B., and Doreen Stabinsky, eds. 1996. *Valuing Local Knowledge: Indigenous People and Intellectual Property Rights.* Washington, D.C.: Island Press.

Bui Thiet. 1995. *Hanoi Dictionary of the Names of Localities.* Hanoi: Culture and Information Publishing House.

Bui Xuan Nguyen. 1996. "Hanoi Is Selling Housing to Subscribers According to the New Procedures," *Hanoi Moi* (Sunday newspaper), September 7.

Buvinic, Marya, and Geeta Rao Gupta. 1997. "Female-Headed Households and Female-Maintained Families: Are They Worth Targeting to Reduce Poverty in Developing Countries?" *Economic Development and Culture Exchange (EDCC)* 45(2): 259–280.

Buvinic, Mayra, Nadia Youseff, with Barbara von Elm. 1978. "Women-Headed Households: The Ignored Factor in Development Planning." Washington, D.C.: International Center for Research on Women.

Caron, C. 1995. "Magic, Wind-Borne Fear, and Nature's Nerf Ball: Ethnobiology in Siruvattukkadu Kombai." Newsletter, Institute of Current World Affairs, May 5.

CCTV. 1997a. "Can Housing Dreams Come True Through Personal Housing Mortgages?" *China TV Guide*, Life Column, Department of Economics, no. 14.

———. 1997b. "Medical Treatment and Housing Are Main Urban Problems Considered by Staff and Workers at Present." *China TV Guide*, Life Column, Department of Economics, no. 14.

Centre for Family and Women Studies. 1996. "Survey Data. Land Allocation Issues." Hanoi. Unpublished.

———. 1995. "Women and IBM." Hanoi. Unpublished.

———. 1993. "Women and the Household Economy." Hanoi. Unpublished.

CFWS (Center for Family and Women's Studies). Various years. "Family and Education in the Family." Institute for Social Sciences and Humanities: Hanoi, unpublished.

Chagnon, Jacquelyn. 1995. "Comments and Suggested Insertions on *Proposed Lao Pdr Land Titling Project—Inception Report*." Vientiane. March 4.

Chan, Roger C. K. 1996. "Urban Development and Redevelopment." In *Shanghai: Transformation and Modernization Under China's Open Policy*, Y. M. Yeung and Y. Sung, eds. Hong Kong: Chinese University Press.

Chant, Sylvia. 1996a. *Women-Headed Households: Diversities and Dynamics in the Developing World.* New York: Macmillan.

———. 1996b. *Gender, Urban Development, and Housing.* New York: UNDP Publication Series for Habitat II, vol. 2.

Charlton, Sue Ellen M. 1984. *Women in Third World Development.* Boulder: Westview.

Chen, Jian. 1997. "Constructing a 'Safety Net' for the Urban Poor." *Wenhui Daily* (April 29).

Chen, Peter S. J. 1979. "Policies Affecting the Family and Fertility Behavior." In *Public Policy and Population Change in Singapore*, Peter S. J. Chen and James T. Fawcett, eds. New York: The Population Council, 187–202.

Chen, Qide. 1997a. "Leader Wants Changes: 'Housing Should Be Built for Common Residents.'" URL: http://china-window.com/shanghai/sstr/97/9m/9m05d2.html, *China Window*, September 5.

———. 1997b. "Modern Metropolis Looms: New Urban Blueprint Will Guide Development." URL: http://china-window.com/shanghai/sstr/97/10m/10m14d3.html, *Shanghai Star*, October 14.

———. 1997c. "Too Many Empty Houses: Experts Call for Measures to Help Revive the Market." URL: http://china-window.com/shanghai/sstr/97/8m/8m26d2.html, *China Window*, August 26.

————. 1997d. "Housing Relief on Way for Crowded Families." URL: http://china-window.com/shanghai/sstr/97/6m/6m17d2.html, *Shanghai Star.*

————. 1997e. "Land Supply Frozen, Authorities Bid to Revive Slumping Property Sector." URL: http://china-window.com/shanghai/sstr/97/6m/6m20d3.html.

"China Links Housing with Income." 1996. *United Press International* (April 11).

China National Bureau of Statistics. 1993. "China Nationwide Sample Survey of Children's Status in 1992."

China Women's Federation 1994. *Shanghai funu shehui di wei diao cha* (A study of the status of Shanghai women). Shanghai Juan: Shanghai.

The Chinese Urban Family. 1985. Shandong Publishing House.

Chiu, Stephen W. K., K. C. Ho, and Tai-lok Lui. 1997. *City-States in the Global Economy: Industrial Restructuring in Hong Kong and Singapore.* Boulder: Westview Press.

Choulamany-Khamphoui, Outhaki. 1994. "Information on Land Registration and Titling Issue." Data extracted from "Report on Gender Studies: Strengthening and Restructuring Irrigation Development Project." Vientiane: Irrigation Department, Ministry of Agriculture and Forestry. November. Unpublished.

Chu Huu Quy. 1995. "The Relationship Between Rural Development Strategies Toward the Year 2000 and the Human Resources Development in Vietnam Countryside from Gender Perspective." Hanoi: Committee for Social Affair and CIDA, 149–160.

Chu, Rebecca L. H. 1996. "Housing." In *Shanghai: Transformation and Modernization Under China's Open Policy,* Y. M. Yeung and Y. Sung, eds. Hong Kong: Chinese University Press.

Chu Van Vu. 1991. "The Land Relation in the Countryside—the Situation and Measurement." Pham Xuan Nam, ed. Hanoi, 149–163.

Chua, Beng-Huat. 1997. *Political Legitimacy and Housing: Stakeholding in Singapore.* London: Routledge.

Chua, Mui Hoong. 1996. "Local Election Versus By-Election." *Straits Times Weekly Edition* (December 21): 14.

————. 1995. "Executive Condo Scheme a Milestone in HDB Policy." *Straits Times Weekly Edition* (September 9): 15.

The Civil Law Teaching and Research Section of the Central School for Politico-legal Cadres. 1958. "Fundamental Problems of Civil Law of the People's Republic of China." Beijing: Law Press.

Condominas, Georges. 1977. *We Have Eaten the Forest.* New York: Hill and Wang.

Cong, Yaping. 1996. "House Selling." *Guanming Daily* (January 19).

Cong san (Journal of The Central Committee of The Communist Party of Vietnam).

Connell, John. 1994. Field level study on the work in the selected field areas (Phin and Lao Ngam districts). Vientiane: Swedish International Development Authority (SIDA)–Laos. Unpublished report.

Constitution of the Democratic Republic of Vietnam. 1945.

Construction Ministry. 1995a. "Second National Conference on Urban Issues."

————. 1995b. "Seminar on Community Based Housing Finance." Unpublished proceedings.

"Convention of the People's Republic of China of 1992." Chap. 1, art. 10.

"Convention on the Elimination of Discrimination Against Women." 1979.

Coontz, Stephanie. 1988. *The Social Origins of Private Life.* London: Verso.

CPC (Committee for Planning and Cooperation). 1995a. "Sayaboury Province Land and Forest Allocation." Vientiane: Committee for Planning and Cooperation. January 30–February 1. Unpublished results of conference.

————. National Statistical Centre. 1995b. *Lao Census 1995, Preliminary Report 2*. Vientiane: Committee for Planning and Cooperation.

Croll, Elizabeth. 1995. *Changing Identities of Chinese Women: Rhetoric, Experience, and Self-Perception in Twentieth Century China*. London: Zed Books.

————. 1985. *Women and Rural Development in China: Production and Reproduction*. Geneva: International Labour Office.

————. 1983. *Chinese Women Since Mao*. London: Zed Books.

Dai, Kejin. 1991. "The Life Experience and Status of Chinese Rural Women from Observation of Three Age Groups." *International Sociology* 6: 35.

Dai, Zigeng. 1993. "Real Estate Industry: How to Lower the Temperature." *Guangming Daily* (July 26).

Dandekar, Hemalata, ed. 1993. *Shelter, Women and Development: First and Third World Perspectives*. Ann Arbor, Mich.: George Water.

Dao Ngoc Tan. 1996. "The Need for Land Use Regulations in Kienxuong." *Nhan dom*, Mar. 28.

Dao The Tuan. 1995. "The Peasant Household Economy and Social Change." In *Vietnam's Rural Transformation*, Benedict Kerkvliet, J. Tria, and Doug J. Potter, eds. Boulder: Westview Press.

Davis, D., et al., eds. 1995. *Urban Spaces in Contemporary China: The Potential for Autonomy and Community in Post-Mao China*. Cambridge: Cambridge University Press.

de Beer, Jenne. 1993. "Nonwood Forest Products in Indochina—Focus: Vietnam." Working paper submitted to the Food and Agriculture Organization of the United Nations, Rome.

Department of Statistics. 1992. *Yearbook of Statistics, Singapore*. Various years.

————. 1991. *Census of Population 1990 Advance Data Release*. Singapore: SNP Publishes.

————. 1983. *Economic and Social Statistics Singapore 1960–1982*. Singapore.

————. *Census of Population*. Singapore, various years.

Desai, Jaikishan. 1995. *Vietnam Through the Lens of Gender: An Empirical Analysis Using Household Data*. Hanoi: United Nations Development Programme (September), 118.

Dessallien, Christian. 1991. *Social Implications of the New Economic Mechanisms in Laos*. Vientiane: United Nations Development Programme.

Deyo, Frederic C. 1991. "Singapore: Developmental Paternalism." In *Minidragons: Fragile Economic Miracles in the Pacific*, Steven M. Goldstein, ed. Boulder: Westview Press, 48–87.

Dowall, David, and Giles Clark. 1991. "A Framework for Reforming Urban Land Policies in Developing Countries." Washington, D.C.: Urban Management Program Policy Paper, World Bank.

Drakakis-Smith, D. W., and Yue-man Yeung. 1977. "Public Housing in the City-States of Hong Kong and Singapore." Occasional Paper No. 8. Canberra, Australia: Development Studies Centre, Australian National University.

Du Yongjian and Zhang Zhilan. 1996. "Thoughts About the Deepening of Housing Reform." *Construction of Town and Country* (June): 29–31.

Duy Khanh. 1996. "Land in Giarai—Enduring (Long-Lasting) Pain." *Nong nghiep Vietnam* (April 10): 8.

Dwyer, Daisy, and Judith Bruce, eds. 1989. *A Home Divided: Women and Income in the Third World*. Palo Alto, Calif.: Stanford University Press.

East-West Center–CRES. 1994. "Preliminary Report—The Human Ecology of the Tay of Ban Tat Hamlet." Unpublished.

Economic Times (Thoi Bao Kinh Te), quoted in *Vietnam News*. 1997. December 3.

Eggertz, Daniel. 1996. "Interim Report on Legal Aspects of Land Allocation: Minor Field Study." Vientiane: Lao-Swedish Forestry Program. January. Unpublished draft report.

Egziabher, Axemite, et al. 1994. *Cities Feeding People: An Examination of Urban Agriculture in East Africa*. Foreword by Irene Tinker. Ottawa: IDRC.

ENCO (Environment Committee of Ho Chi Minh City and École Polytechnique Fédérale de Lausanne). 1996. "Metropolisation, Sustainable Development, and Pollution of Natural Resources—the Case of Ho Chi Minh City." Report published by École Polytechnique Fédérale de Lausanne, Switzerland.

ENDA (Environment et Développment du Tiers-Monde-Vietnam). 1996. "Survey of Women's Perception of Housing in Three Districts of Ho Chi Minh City." Unpublished report.

Epstein, Edward J. 1989. "The Theoretical System of Property Rights in China's General Principles of Civil Law: Theoretical Controversy in the Drafting Process and Beyond." *Law and Contemporary Problems* 52: 177.

ESCAP 1986. *Environmental and Socio-economic Aspects of Tropical Deforestation in Asia and the Pacific*. Bangkok: UNESCAP.

Fagerstrom, Minh Ha. 1995. "Evaluation of the Impact of Land Allocation in the Area of the Sweden-Vietnam Forestry Cooperation Programme Vietnam." For the Sweden-Vietnam Forestry Cooperation Program, Hanoi.

Farvacque, Catherine, and Patrick McAuslan. 1991. *Reforming Urban Land Policies and Institutions in Developing Countries*. Washington, D.C.: Urban Management Program Policy Paper, World Bank.

Fawcett, James T. 1979. "Singapore's Population Policies in Perspective." In *Public Policy and Population Change in Singapore*, Peter S. J. Chen and James T. Fawcett, eds. New York: The Population Council, 3–17.

FBIS. 1996. "Beijing Apartment Buildings to Occupy 40-Sq-Km Area." August 28.

———. 1996. "Chinese Minister Gets Un Human Settlement Prize." October 7.

———. 1996. "Expansion of Property Management in Beijing Urged." August 29.

———. 1996. "Minister of Construction on China's Housing Construction." September 27.

———. 1996. "PRC: Commentary on Urban Housing Reform." May 28.

———. 1996. "PRC: Construction of 'Comfortable Housing' Projects Stepped Up." September 25.

———. 1995. "Status of 'Comfortable Housing' Project Viewed." December 4.

Fernandez, Warren. 1997. "Big Swing to Pap." *Straits Times Weekly Edition* (January 4): 1.

———. 1996a. "Parents Hold Key to Passing on Values: Prime Minister." *Straits Times Weekly Edition* (February 24): 1.

———. 1996b. "Prime Minister Goh Urges Young to Rally Behind Him." *Straits Times Weekly Edition* (August 24): 1.

———. 1994. "Confucian Values Helped Singapore Prosper: Senior Minister Lee." *Straits Times Weekly Edition* (October 8): 24.

Folbre, Nancy. 1986. "Cleaning House: New Perspectives on Households and Economic Development." *Journal of Development Economics* 22: 5–40.

Forest Service of Luang Prabang Province. 1995. "Basic Guiding Manual on Initial Land and Forest Allocation in Luang Prabang Province for Leading Committee and Technical Staff." Luang Prabang: Forest Service. January. Unpublished.

Fortmann, Louise. 1986. "Women in Subsistence Forestry: Cultural Myths Form a Stumbling Block." *Journal of Forestry* 84(7): 39–42.

Fortmann, Louise, and John W. Bruce. 1988. *Whose Trees? Proprietary Dimensions of Forestry.* Boulder: Westview.

Fortmann, Louise, and Dianne Rocheleau. 1985. "Women and Agroforestry: Four Myths and Three Case Studies." *Agroforestry Systems* 2: 253–272.

Fu, Weishai. 1996. "Five Outstanding Characteristics of Stable Social Development." *Guangming Daily* (January 24).

Fung, K. I. 1996. "Satellite Towns: Develoment and Contributions." In *Shanghai: Transformation and Modernization under China's Open Policy*, Y. M. Yeung and Y. Sung, eds. Hong Kong: Chinese University Press.

FYI Financial Statistics. 1996. *The Vietnam Business Journal* 4(4).

Gallin, Rita. 1995. "Engendered Production in Rural Taiwan: Ideological Bonding of the Public and Private." In *Engendering Wealth and Well-being: Empowerment for Global Change,* Rae Blumberg, Cathy Rakowski, Irene Tinker, and Michael Monteon, eds. Boulder, CO: Westview, 261–283.

Garrett, Patricia, Jorge Uquillas, and Carolyn Campbell. 1987. "Interview Guide for the Regional Analysis of Farming Systems." Ithaca, N.Y.: Program in International Agriculture, Cornell University.

Gaston, Graham. 1995. "Land Tenure, Use Rights and Titling of Agricultural and Forestry Land. Report 2—Specific Suggestions." Vientiane: Nam Ngum Watershed Management and Conservation Project, Ministry of Agriculture and Forestry. Unpublished report. October.

Gaubatz, Piper Rae. 1995a. "Changing Beijing." *Geographical Review* 85(18): 79.

———. 1995b. "Urban Transformation in Post-Mao China: Impacts of the Reform Era on China's Urban Form." In *Urban Spaces in Contemporary China: The Potential for Autonomy and Community in Post-Mao China*, D. S. Davis, R. Kraus, B. Naughton, and E. Perry, eds. New York: Cambridge University Press, 28–60.

General Department of Statistics of Vietnam. 1995. *Statistics on Vietnamese Women (1984–1995).* Hanoi: Statistical Publishing House.

"General Rules of the Civil Code of the People's Republic of China." 1987. *China Law Reports* IV, James V. Feinerman and Lee M. Zeichner, trans., 91–110.

General Statistics Office. 1995. *Statistical Year Book* (English ed.). Hanoi.

———. 1994. *Vietnam Living Standard Survey 1993.* Hanoi.

———. 1993. *Vietnam Living Standard Survey 1992.* Hanoi, 152.

Gilmartin, Christina K., Gail Hershatter, Lisa Rofel, and Tyrene White, eds. 1994. *Engendering China.* Cambridge: Harvard University Press.

The Gioi Publishers. 1993. *Vietnamese Traditional Medicine.* Hanoi.

Goh, Sunny. 1994. "Family Unit Reason for East's Success: Senior Minister." *Straits Times Weekly Edition* (March 5): 5.

Goode, William J. 1993. *World Changes in Divorce Patterns.* New Haven: Yale University Press.

Goodkind, Daniel, 1995. "Rising Gender Inequality in Vietnam Since Reunification." *Pacific Affairs* (May).

Gourou, Pierre. 1936. *Les Paysans du Delta Tonkinois.* Paris.

Government of Vietnam. 1995. Civil Code of Vietnam. Hanoi: National Political Publishing.

———. 1994. Annual Statistics of 1993 of Hanoi. Hanoi: Statistical Publishing House.

———. 1993. *Land Law 1993.* Hanoi: Gov't of Vietnam.

———. 1992a. Constitution of SRVN. Hanoi: Law Publishing House.

———. 1992b. Written Materials on Marriage and Family Law. Hanoi: Law Publishing House.

Grady, Heather. 1996. Executive Director of OXFAM UK/I. Hanoi. Personal communication.

Grant, Miriam. 1996. "Moving and Coping: Women Tenants in Gweru, Zimbabwe." In *Courtyards, Markets, City Streets: Urban Women in Africa,* K. Sheldon, ed. Boulder: Westview.

Greaves, Tom, ed. 1994. *Intellectual Property Rights for Indigenous Peoples: A Source Book.* Oklahoma City, Okla.: Society for Applied Anthropology.

Han, Fook Kwang. 1995. "Pitfalls of Growing Too Quickly." *Straits Times Weekly Edition* (September 9): 15.

Hanoi Moi. 1996. "Hanoi After Three Years Has the First Main Architect." September 27 (article signed by K.O.).

Hansen, Karen Tranberg. 1996. "Washing Dirty Linen in Public: Local Courts, Custom, and Gender Relations in Postcolonial Lusaka." In *Courtyards, Markets, City Streets: Urban Women in Africa,* K. Sheldon, ed. Boulder: Westview.

———. 1989. "The Black Market and Women Traders in Lusaka, Zambia." In *Women and the State in Africa,* Jane L. Parpart and Kathleen A. Staudt, eds. Boulder, CO: Lynne Rienner, 143–160.

Hansen, Peter, and Houmchitsavath Sodarak. 1995. "Environment, Socio-Economic Conditions and Land-Use in Thong Khang Sub-District, Northern Laos." Luang Prabang: Shifting Cultivation Stabilization Project. Lao Swedish Forestry Programme. January. Unpublished report.

Harvard Institute for International Development. 1994. *Vietnam Economic Reform Towards Flying Dragon.* Hanoi: NXB Chinh tri quoc gia.

Hashemi, Syed M., Sidney Ruth Schuler, and Ann P. Riley. 1996. "Rural Credit Programs and Women's Empowerment in Bangladesh." *World Development* 24(4): 635–653.

Hecht, Jonathan. 1995. "The Legal Protection of Women's Rights in China: Discretionary Enforcement of Human Rights Norms." *China Rights Forum* (Fall): 4–6.

Hecht, Susanna, A. B. Anderson, and P. May. 1988. "The Subsidy from Nature: Shifting Cultivation, Successional Palm Forests, and Rural Development." *Human Organization* 47(1): 25–35.

Henry, Yves. 1932. *Economic agricole de Indo-china.* Hanoi.

Hirsch, Philip. 1996. "Dams and Compensation in Indo-China." In *Resources, Nations, and Indigenous Peoples: Case Studies from Australasia, Melanesia, and Southeast Asia,* Richard Howitt, ed., with John Connell and Philip Hirsch. Melbourne: Oxford University Press, 212–222.

Ho Chi Minh City reports, Land and Housing Department. 1995. "Urban Houses in Ho Chi Minh City." Ho Chi Minh City.

———. People's Committee of Ho Chi Minh City. 1996. "Development Plan of Ho Chi Minh City Up to the Year 2010 and Socioeconomic Orientations for the Period 1996–2000." Unpublished report.

———. Statistical Office. Various years. *Statistical Yearbook of Ho Chi Minh City.*

Hoang Trung Hieu. 1995. *Questions and Answers on the Marriage and Family Law.* Hanoi: Youth Publishing House.

Hoodfar, Homa. 1996. "Survival Strategies and the Political Economy of Low-Income Households in Cairo." In *Development, Change, and Gender in Cairo: A View from the Household,* Diane Singerman and Homa Hoodfar, eds. Bloomington: Indiana University Press.

Hooper, Emma, and Kanta Singh. 1991. "Women and Shelter in Nepal." Report to the Ministry of Housing and Physical Planning, Government of Nepal. Kathmandu: Culpin.

Hoskins, Marilyn. 1982. "Social Forestry in West Africa: Myths and Realities." Paper presented at the annual meeting of the American Association for the Advancement of Science.

———. 1980. "Community Forestry Depends on Women." *Unasylva* 32(130): 27–32.

Hu Wenzhong. 1996. "Foreign Tradesmen Participate for the First Time in Rebuilding Old and Dangerous Houses in Beijing with Their Investment Only." *Guangming Daily* (January 12).

Huang Xiyi and Li Ling. 1989. "Rural Women's Roles and Status in the Development of the Mountainous Areas." In *Proceedings, Conference on Global Empowerment of Women,* November 1989, Washington, D.C., 38–42.

Hubei Provincial Statistical Bureau. 1997. *Hubei Statistical Annual.*

Huff, W. G. 1995. "What Is the Singapore Model of Economic Development?" *Cambridge Journal of Economics* 19: 735–759.

Hyslop, J. S. 1990. "The Spatial Structure of Shanghai City Proper." In *China's Spatial Economy: Recent Developments and Reforms*, G. J. R. Linge and D. K. Forbes, eds. Hong Kong: Oxford University Press.

Ibrahim, Zuraidah. 1994. "Prime Minister: New Steps to Strengthen Family." *Straits Times Weekly Edition* (August 27): 1.

———. 1995. "Prime Minister Spells Out Art of Government, Singapore Style." *Straits Times Weekly Edition* (September 23): 1.

Information Office of the State Council of the PRC. 1994. *The Situation of Chinese Women.* Beijing.

Institute of Demography, Chinese Academy of Social Sciences. 1993. "Sample Survey of Current Chinese Women's Status." Wanguo Science Publishing House.

Institute of Rural and Urban Planning. 1995. Strategy for urban development. Unpublished report. Hanoi.

———. 1995. "Policy for Housing and Environment Improvement for Poor People." Unpublished report. Hanoi.

Institute of Sociology, Hubei Academy of Social Sciences. 1994. "Research on the Evolution of the Relation Between Chinese Rural Clan Collectives and Functional Collectives."

Interviews (by Dia Warren), Wen Zhi Hong, Vice Secretary-General of the Guangzhou Women's Federation. Guangzhou, December 1990.

———. Chen Ming Xia, Senior Research Fellow of Law Institute, Chinese Academy of Social Sciences, Deputy General Director of Chinese Marriage Law, Institute of China Law Society, Member of the Board of Directors of Chinese Marriage and Family Research Institute. Beijing, July 16, 1996.

———. Pi Xiaoming, Attorney, All China Women's Federation. Beijing, July 22, 1996.

The Investigation of Shanghai Women's Social Status. 1994. Beijing: Chinese Women's Publishing House, 112.

Ireland Times. 1995. (August 3).

Ireson, Carol. 1996. *Field, Forest, and Family: Women's Work and Power in Rural Laos.* Boulder: Westview.

———. 1991. "Women's Forest Work in Laos." *Sociology and Natural Resources* 4: 23–36.

———. 1989. "The Role of Women in Forestry in the Lao Pdr." Vientiane: SilviNova Forestry Consultants with the National Institute for Social Sciences, the Swedish International Development Authority, and the Department of Forestry of the Ministry of Agriculture. Unpublished.

Ireson, Randall, and Carol Ireson. 1993. "The Lao of Laos." In *Encyclopedia of World Cultures*, Volume 5: *East and Southeast Asia*, Paul Hockings, ed. Boston: G. K. Hall.

———. 1989. "Laos: Marxism in a Subsistence Rural Economy." *Bulletin of Concerned Asian Scholars* 21(2–4): 59–75.

Islam, Nazrul, Amirul Islam Chowdhury, and Khadem Ali. 1989. *Evaluation of the Grameen Bank's Rural Housing Programme*. Dhaka: Centre for Urban Studies, University of Dhaka.

Jancar, Barbara Wolf. 1978. *Women Under Communism*. Baltimore: Johns Hopkins University Press.

Jordan, Ann D. 1994. "Women's Rights in the People's Republic of China: Patriarchal Wine Poured from a Socialist Bottle." *Journal of Chinese Law* 8: 47–104.

Judd, Ellen. 1990. "Alternative Development Strategies for Women in Rural China." *Development and Change* 21(1): 23–42.

Kandiyoti, Deniz. 1988. "Bargaining with Patriarchy." *Gender and Society* 2(3): 274–290.

Kelkar, Govind. 1987. "Women and Rural Development Programs and Organizations in Contemporary China and India." In *Women Farmers and Rural Change in Asia*. Kuala Lumpur: Asian and Pacific Development Center, 41–103.

Kerkvliet, Benedict J. Tria. 1995. "Rural Society and State Relations." In *Vietnam's Rural Transformation*, Benedickt J. Tria Kerkvliet and Dong J. Porter, eds. Boulder: Westview Press.

KPL News Agency. 1997. "Turning Up the Volume on the Voices of Lao Women." *KPL News Bulletin*. April 26, 1997. Vientiane.

Kunstadter, Peter, E. C. Chapman, and S. Sabhasri. 1978. *Farmers in the Forest: Economic Development and Marginal Agriculture in Northern Thailand*. Honolulu: University of Hawaii Press.

Kuo, Eddie C. Y., and Aline Wong. 1979. "Some Observations on the Study of Family Change in Singapore." In *The Contemporary Family in Singapore*, Eddie C. Y. Kuo and Aline Wong, eds. Singapore: Singapore University Press, 3–14.

Lao, Chen. 1997. URL: http://china-window.com/shanghai/sstr/97/2m/2m04d3.html, *Shanghai Star*, February 4.

Lao PDR. 1997. Land Law. Vientiane: National Assembly and Prime Minister's Office.

———. 1996. Forestry Law. Vientiane: Ministry of Justice. Effective November 2. (Unofficial translation by Dirksen, Flipse, Doran, and Le.)

———. 1995. Order on Customary Rights and the Use of Forest Resources. Draft. April 4. Vientiane: Ministry of Justice and Ministry of Agriculture and Forestry.

———. 1994a. Decree No. 169. Decree of the Prime Minister on the Management and Use of Forests and Forest Land. Vientiane: Prime Minister's Office.

———. 1994b. Decree No. 186. Regarding the Allocation of Land and Forest Land for Tree Plantation and Forest Protection. Vientiane: Prime Minister's Office.

———. 1993. Decree No. 99. Regarding Land. Vientiane: Ministry of Finance.

———. 1990a. Family Law. Vientiane: People's Supreme Assembly. (Unofficial translation by Vientiane International Consultants.)

———. 1990b. Inheritance Law. Vientiane: People's Supreme Assembly. (Unofficial translation by Vientiane International Consultants.)

Lao PDR Land Titling Project. 1996. Washington, D.C.: World Bank. Unpublished.

"Law of the People's Republic of China on Land Management." 1986.

"Law of the People's Republic of China on the Protection of Rights and Interests of Women." 1992.

Le Thi Nham Tuyet. 1975. *Vietnamese Women in the Eras.* Hanoi: NXB Phu nu.

Le Tho. 1995. *Vietnamese Families: Responsibilities, Resources in the Renovation of the Country.* Hanoi: NXB Khoa hoc xa hoi.

———. 1990. *President Ho Chi Minh and the Road Towards Equality, Freedom, and Development of Vietnamese Women.* Hanoi: NXB Khoa hoc xa hoi, 24.

Le Trang Cuc. 1994. "Biodiversity Conservation and Sustainable Land Use in Da River Watershed." Presented at the Seminar Defining Highland Development Challenges in Vietnam. East-West Center, Honolulu, Hawaii, July 20–22.

Le Trang Cuc, Kathleen Gillogly, and A. Terry Rambo. *Agroecosystems of the Midlands of Northern Vietnam.* Occasional Papers of the East-West Environment and Policy Institute. Paper No. 12. East-West Center, Honolulu, Hawaii.

Leacock, William, Nene Viengvongsith, and Bouahong Phanthanousy. 1993. "Tassaeng Thong Khang, Luang Prabang: A Survey of Socio-Economic and Agricultural Aspects." Vientiane: Shifting Cultivation Alleviation Sub-Programme, Lao-Swedish Forestry Cooperation Programme. October 17. Unpublished draft report.

Lee, Peter Nan-shong. 1995. "Housing Privatization with Chinese Characteristics." In *Social Change and Social Policy in Contemporary China*, L. Wong and S. MacPherson, eds. Aldershot, U.K.: Avebury.

Lee, Soo Ann. 1979. "Population, Industrial Development, and Economic Growth." In *Public Policy and Population Change in Singapore*, Peter S. J. Chen and James T. Fawcett, eds. New York: Population Council, 229–240.

Lee-Smith, Diana. 1997. *My Home Is My Husband: A Kenyan Study of Women's Access to Land and Housing.* Ph.D. dissertation. Lund University, Sweden: Department of Architecture and Development Studies.

———. 1993. *Peasants, Plantation Dwellers, and the Urban Poor: A Study of Women and Whelter in Kenya.* Licentiate thesis. Lund University, Sweden: Department of Architecture and Development Studies.

Lefferts, Leedom. 1993. "Women Weaving and Monks: Textiles of Tai Buddhism." Paper presented at the Los Angeles County Museum, Los Angeles, April.

Legal Status of Singapore Women (booklet). 1986. Singapore: Asiapac Books and Educational Aids.

Levinson, David, ed. 1993. *Encyclopedia of World Cultures,* Volume 5: *Human Relations.* Area Files and McMillan Press.

Li Xiaojiang. 1994. "Economic Reform and the Awakening of Chinese Women's Collective Consciousness." In *Engendering China: Women, Culture, and the State*, Christina K. Gilmartin, Gail Hershatter, Lisa Rofel, and Tyrene White, eds. Cambridge: Harvard University Press.

Li Xiaojiang and Tan Shen. 1990. "Women Study in China." *Intellectual Women* (in Chinese), vols. 1–2. Zhengzhou: Henan People's Publisher.

Li Zhang (forthcoming). "The Interplay of Gender, Space, and Work in China's 'Floating Population.'"

Liemar, Lisa Marie, and Michael Price. 1987. "Wild Foods and Women Farmers: A Time Allocation Study in Northeast Thailand." Paper presented at Association for Women in Development Conference, Washington, D.C.

Liu, Shiying, chief ed. 1994. *Collection of Survey on Social Status of Chinese Women—Survey of Women's Social Status in Hubei.* China Women Publishing House.

Liu Xueqin. 1996. "Thoughts About the Commoditization of Housing." *Economic News* (April 10): 4.

Luong Xuan Hoi. 1996. "Housing for the People Who Have Low Income in the Big Cities: What Will the Policy Bring in the Future?" *Lao Dong Magazine* 124 (September 19).

LWU (Lao Women's Union). 1993. "Political Report of the Central Committee of the Lao Women's Union at the Third National Congress." December. Draft report.

Mahar, Vanessa. 1981. "Work, Consumption, and Authority Within the Household: A Moroccan Case." In *Of Marriage and the Market: Women's Subordination in International Perspective*, Kate Young, Carol Wolkowitz, and Roslyn McCullach, eds. London: CSE.

Massiah, Jocelin. 1990. "Defining Women's Work in the Commonwealth of Caribbean." In *Persistent Inequalities: Women and World Development*, Irene Tinker, ed. New York: Oxford University Press, 223–238.

McDermott, Darren. 1996. "Singapore Is Serious About Smiles, but Unpatriotic Frowns Endure." *The Wall Street Journal* (October 7): B1.

Miao Tianqing. 1996. "The Difficult Position of and the Way Out for Housing System Reform of Chinese Cities and Towns." *Journal of Shanxi Normal School* 1: 15–19.

Minh Thuy (author omits family name). 1996. "Housing and Land Price Is Still Increasing." *Vietnam Economic Times* 2(6), Special Issue on Land and Housing.

Ministry of Agriculture and Food Industry. 1995. *Report on the One Year of Implementation of Decision No. 64*. Hanoi: MAFI.

Ministry of Trade and Industry. 1990. *Economic Survey of Singapore*. Singapore.

———. 1986. *The Singapore Economy: New Directions Report of the Economic Committee*. Singapore.

Miraftab, Faranak. 1997. "Revisiting Informal-Sector Home Ownership: The Relevance of Household Composition for Housing Options of the Poor." *International Journal of Urban and Regional Research* 21(2): 302–322.

———. 1996. "Space, Gender, and Work: Home-Based Workers in Guadalajara, Mexico." In *Invisible No More: Homeworkers in Global Perspective*. Eileen Boris and Elizabeth Prugl, eds. New York: Routledge.

———. 1995. *A Misfit Between Policy and People: The Search for Housing by Female Headed Households in Guadalajara, Mexico*. Ph.D. dissertation. Department of Architecture, University of California, Berkeley.

Momsen, Janet, and Vivian Kinnaird, eds. 1993. *Different Places, Different Voices: Gender and Development in Africa, Asia, and Latin America*. London: Routledge.

Moser, C. O. N. 1995. *Gender Planning and Development: Theory, Practice, and Training*. London and New York: Routledge.

Moser, C. O. N., and Cathy McIlwaine. 1997. *Household Responses to Poverty and Vulnerability*, Volume 3: *Confronting Crisis in Commonwealth, Metro Manila, the Philippines*. Washington, D.C.: The World Bank.

Moser, Caroline O. N., and Linda Peake. 1987. *Women, Human Settlements, and Housing*. London: Tavistock.

Muzinet. 1997. "Lateline—Daily News of the Chinese World Network," URL: http://china.muzi.net/news/.

———. 1997 (June 13). "Dragonhead—Hongkong or Shanghai." URL: http://china.muzi.net/news/.

Ngaosyvathn, Mayoury. 1993. *Lao Women: Yesterday and Today*. Vientiane: State Publishing Enterprise.

Ngo Kim Chung. 1978. "About Communal Land." *Nghien cuu kinh te*, No. 6/1978.

Nguyen Duc Nghiem and Bui Thi Minh Hien. 1992. "Land Distribution in Some Communes in Quynh Coi, Thai Binh." *History Studies*, No. 1.

Nguyen Huu Dart and Phann Huu Nghi. 1992. "On Land Ownership." *Nha nuoc va Phapluat* 4: 44–48.

Nguyen, Nga My. 1996. "Some Opinions on Residents' Life Style of a Central Area of Hanoi." In *Understanding Urban Sociology*, Trinh Duy Luan, ed. Hanoi: Social Sciences Publishing House, 165.

Nguyen Senh Cue. 1993. "Land Ownership and Land Use Rights." *Cong san* 3: 30–36.

Nguyen Thi Canh. 1994. "Topic on the Urbanisation Process and the Problem of Urban Poor." Ho Chi Minh City: Institute of Economic Research.

Nguyen Trong Dieu. 1995. *Geography of Vietnam.* The Gioi Publishers.

Nguyen Van Dan. 1990. Vice Minister of Health's preface to *Medicinal Plants in Viet Nam*, World Health Organization and Institute of Materia Medica.

Nguyen Van Tiem. 1993. *Rich and Poor in the Countryside Today.* Hanoi: NXB Nong nghiep.

Nguyen Xuan Thang. 1993. "Why Land Is Under the Ownership of the Entire Population?" *Cong san* 6: 24–25.

Nha nuoc va phap luat (Journal of the Institute for the Government and Law).

Nhan dan (daily newspaper of the Communist Party of Vietnam). 1995–1996. March 27, 1996: 16; January 16, 1996: 22; August 11, 1995: 21; May 2, 1995: 19.

———. 1995. "The Land Law Has Been Seriously Broken." August 11.

Nong nghiep Viet nam. Weekly newspaper published by the Peasant Association.

Nong thon ngay nay. Newspaper published by the Peasant Association.

Nussbaum, Martha, and Jonathan Glover, eds. 1995. "Introduction," *Women, Culture, and Development: A Study of Human Capabilities.* Oxford: Clarendon Press, 1–15.

Nystron, Maria. 1994. *Focus Kitchen Design: A Study of Housing in Hanoi.* Lund University, Sweden: Lund Institute of Technology.

Obbo, Christine. 1990. "East African Women, Work, and the Articulation of Dominance." In *Persistent Inequalities: Women and World Development,* Irene Tinker, ed. New York: Oxford University Press, 210–222.

Office of Shanghai Housing System Reform. 1991. *Shanghai Housing System Reform.* Shanghai Renmin Publishing House, 214–215.

Olson, Paulette. 1998. "My Dam Is Bigger Than Yours: Emulation and Conspicuous Waste Under Global Capitalism." Forthcoming in *Thorstein Veblen in the Twenty-first Century*, D. Brown, ed. London: Edward Elgar.

O'Neill, Mark. 1996. "Shanghai in Giant Sell-Off of Public Housing." *Reuters' World Service*, April 11, available on LEXIS, World Library, Allwld.

"Opinion (for Trial Use) of the Supreme People's Court on Questions Concerning the Implementation of the General Principles of Civil Law of the People's Republic of China." 1989. *Law and Contemporary Problems* 52. Whitmore Gray and Henry Ruiheng Zheng, trans., 177–216.

Osirim, Mary Johnson. 1996. "Beyond Simple Survival: Women Microentrepreneurs in Harare and Bulawayo, Zimbabwe." In *Courtyards, Markets, City Streets: Urban Women in Africa,* K. Sheldon, ed. Boulder: Westview.

Overholt, Catherine, Mary B. Anderson, Kathleen Cloud, and James E. Austin, eds. 1985. *Gender Roles in Development Projects: A Case Book.* West Hartford, Conn.: Kumarian Press.

OXFAM UK and Ireland. 1996. "Land Allocation and Its Impacts on Rural Poor Areas." Draft Research Paper #2. OXFAM UK/I. Hanoi.

Palmer, Michael. 1995. "The Reemergence of Family Law in Post-Mao China: Marriage, Divorce and Reproduction." *China Quarterly* 141 (March): 111–134.

Pan Suiming. 1988. "Fulian Should Have Its Independent Will." Cited in Tani E. Barlow, "Politics and Protocols of Funu: (Un)Making National Woman," at 346.

Pang, Eng Fong. 1988. "Development Strategies and Labour Market Changes in Singapore." In *Labour Market Developments and Structural Change: The Experience of ASEAN and Australia*, Pang Eng Fong, ed. Singapore: Singapore University Press, 195–242.

———. 1979. "Public Policy on Population, Employment, and Immigration." In *Public Policy and Population Change in Singapore*, Peter S. J. Chen and James T. Fawcett, eds. New York: Population Council, 205–215.

Paris, Thelma R. 1990. "Incorporating Women's Concerns in Crop-Animal Farming Systems Research Methodology." IRRI Social Science Division Paper, No. 90–30. Manila: Social Science Division, International Rice Research Institute.

Peake, Linda, and Caroline O. N. Moser, eds. 1987. *Women, Human Settlements, and Housing*. London: Tavistock Publications.

Peattie, L. 1987. "Shelter, Development and the Poor." In *Shelter, Settlement and Development*, L. Rodwin, ed. Boston: Allen and Unwin.

———. 1982. "Some Second Thoughts on Sites and Services." *Habitat International* 6(12).

Pelzer, Kristin. 1994. "Research Issues—Vietnam." Paper presented at workshop Women in Socio-Economic Transitions. Bangkok: Chulalongkorn University and the University of California. June.

Pelzer-White, Christine. 1987. "State, Culture, and Gender: Continuity and Change in Women's Position in Rural Vietnam." In *Women, State, and Ideology*, Haleh Afshar, ed. London: Macmillan, 225–234.

———. 1982. "Socialist Transformation and Gender Relations: The Vietnamese Case." *Institute of Development Studies Bulletin* 13(4): 44–51.

Phimmasone, Kotsaythone, et al. *Women and Children in the Lao P.D.R. Results from the Lao Social Indicator Survey*. Vientiane: Mother and Child Health Institute, Ministry of Public Health.

Phu nu thanh pho Ho Chi Minh (Newspaper of Ho Chi Minh City Women Union).

Phu nu thu do (Newspaper of Hanoi Women Union). 1995. October 18: 27.

Planning and Finance Section of Construction Department. June 1995. *Urban Housing Area and Condition: Annual Report of Urban Construction Statistics 1994*. Beijing.

Poffenberger, Mark. 1990. *Keepers of the Forest: Land Management Alternatives in Southeast Asia*. West Hartford, Conn.: Kumarian.

Poole, Teresa. 1998. "China Scraps Pounds 1 Workers' Flats." *Independent*, May 31.

Prugl, Elizabeth, and Irene Tinker. 1997. "Microentrepreneurs and Homeworkers: Convergent Categories." *World Development* 25(9): 1471–1482 (September).

Pudney, S., and L. Wang. 1995. "Housing Reform in Urban China: Efficiency, Distribution, and the Implications for Social Security." *Economica* 62, 246: 141–159.

PuruShotam, Nirmala, and Chung Yuen Kay. 1992. "Double Trouble: The Work of Women Wage Earners in Singapore." Paper presented at Industrialisation and Women's Health: A Regional Workshop for the ASEAN Countries. Singapore, April 22–25.

Pyle, Jean L. 1997. "Women, the Family, and Economic Restructuring: The Singapore Model?" *Review of Social Economy* 55(2): 215–223.

————. 1994. "Economic Restructuring in Singapore and the Changing Roles of Women, 1957–Present." In *Women in the Age of Structural Transformation*, Nahid Aslanbeigui, Steven Pressman, and Gale Summerfield, eds. London: Routledge.

Qian, Guan Min, and Chai Wen Mei. 1987. "From Communes to the Household Contract System: The Impact of China's Rural Reform on Women's Status." In *Women Farmers and Rural Change in Asia*. Kuala Lumpur: Asian and Pacific Development Center, 353–382.

Quang, Mai, 1974. "Viet Bac: From Cradle of the Revolution to Autonomous Zone." *Vietnamese Studies* No. 41 (11th year): Ethnographical Data, vol. 3.

Rajakru, Dang. 1996. "The State, Family and Industrial Development: The Singapore Case." *Journal of Contemporary Asia* 26(4): 3–27.

Rake, C., et al. 1993. "Markets of Important Forest Products, Non Timber Forest Products, and Agricultural Products in the Provinces Hoa Binh, Son La, and Lai Chau in the North West of Vietnam." Social Forestry Development Project Song Da, Baseline Study No. 4, Hanoi. December.

Rakodi, Carole. 1991. "Women's Work or Household Strategies." *Environment and Urbanization* 3(2): 39–45.

Rambo, A. Terry, ed. 1993. *Too Many People, Too Little Land: The Human Ecology of a Wet Rice-Growing Village in the Red River Delta of Vietnam.* East-West Center, Program on Environment, Honolulu, Hawaii. Occasional Paper No. 15.

Redding, Sean. 1996. "South African Women and Migration in Umtata, Transkei, 1880–1935." In *Courtyards, Markets, City Streets: Urban Women in Africa,* K. Sheldon, ed. Boulder: Westview.

Report of the People's Republic of China on the Implementation of the Nairobi Forward-Looking Strategies for the Advancement of Women. 1994. Beijing.

Research and Planning Department, Housing and Development Board. 1995. *Profile of Residents Living in HDB Flats.* Singapore: Housing and Development Board.

Research and Statistics Department, Ministry of Labour. *Report of the Labour Force Survey of Singapore.* Singapore, various years.

Research Institute of All-China Women's Federation and Research Office of Shaanxi Provincial Women's Federation. 1991. *Statistics on Chinese Women: 1949–1989.* Beijing: China Statistical Publishing House.

Reuters. 1996. "Chinese Business News: Fees, Taxes Curbing China Housing Market Growth." September 28.

Rigg, Jonathan, and Randi Jerndal. 1996. "Plenty in the Context of Scarcity: Forest Management in Laos." In *Environmental Change in South-east Asia*, Michael Parnwell and Raymond Bryant, eds. London: Routledge, 145–162.

Rizzini, Irene, et al. 1994. "Brazil: A New Concept of Childhood." In *Urban Children in Distress*, Blanc et al.

Robertson, Claire. 1996. "Transition in Kenyan Patriarchy: Attempts to Control Nairobi Area Traders, 1920–1963." In *Courtyards, Markets, City Streets: Urban Women in Africa,* K. Sheldon, ed. Boulder: Westview.

Rodda, Annabel. 1994. *Women and the Environment.* London: Zed.

Rodriquez, Luis Valencia. 1992. "The Right of Everyone to Own Property Alone as Well as in Association with Others, Final Report Submitted by Mr. Luis Valencia Rodriquez, Independent Expert," U.N. Commission on Human Rights, 49th Session, Agenda Item 7, U.N. Doc. E/CN.4/1993/15 (December 18).

Sachar, Rajindar. 1992. "The Right to Adequate Housing: Working Paper Submitted by Mr. Rajindar Sachar, Expert Appointed by the Sub-Comm. on Prevention of Discrimination and Protection of Minorities," U.N. Commission on Human

Rights, Sub-Committee on Prevention of Discrimination and Protection of Minorities, 45th Sess., Agenda Item 8, U.N. Doc. E/CN.4/Sub.2/1992/15 (June 12).

Sagot, Monserrat. 1993. "Women, Political Activism, and the Struggle for Housing: The Case of Costa Rica." In *Women, the State, and the Family*, Esther Chow and Catheraine Berheide, eds. Albany: SUNY Press.

Salaff, Janet W. 1986. "Women, the Family, and the State: Hong Kong, Taiwan, Singapore—Newly Industrialized Countries in Asia." In *Women in the World, 1975–1985: The Women's Decade*, 2nd rev. ed., Lynn B. Iglitzin and Ruth Ross, eds. Santa Barbara, Calif.: ABC-CLIO, 162–189.

Sarin, Madhu. 1995. "Wasteland Development and the Empowerment of Women: The Sarthi Experience." In *Seed2: Support Women's Work Around the World*, Ann Leonard, ed. New York: Feminist Press.

Savanakhone and Phonekeo. 1996. "Land and Forest Allocation—Key to Sustainable Development in Laos." *Vientiane Times*, August 23–29, 1996, 10–11.

Saw, Swee-Hock. 1990. *Changes in the Fertility Policy of Singapore*. Singapore: Institute of Policy Studies.

————. 1980. *Population Control for Zero Growth in Singapore*. Singapore: Oxford University Press.

Sawio, Camillus. 1994. "Who Are the Farmers in Dar Es Salaam?" In *Cities Feeding People: An Examination of Urban Agriculture in East Africa*, Axemite Egziabher et al., eds. Ottawa: IDRC.

Schenk-Sandbergen, Lois. 1996. Personal communication.

Schlyter, Ann. 1990. "Housing and Gender: Important Aspects of Urbanization." In *Third World Urbanization: Reappraisals and New Perspectives*, Satya Datta, ed. Stockholm: Swedish Council for Research in the Humanities and Social Sciences, 235–246.

Scott, James C. 1985. *Weapons of the Weak*. New Haven: Yale University Press.

Sen, Amartya. 1990. "Gender and Coopertive Conflicts." In *Persistent Inequalities: Women and World Development*, I. Tinker, ed. New York: Oxford.

Sen, Gita, and Caren Grown. 1987. *Development, Crises, and Alternative Visions: Third World Women's Perspectives*. New York: Monthly Review Press.

Senauer, Benjamin. 1990. "The Impact of the Value of Women's Time on Food and Nutrition." In *Persistent Inequalities: Women and World Development*. I. Tinker, ed. New York: Oxford.

Shanghai Daily. 1997. "Local Residents Accumulate More Wealth." URL: http://china-window.com/shanghai/news/capit_e/data/10m/971017d5.html, October 17.

Shanghai Housing System Reform. 1991. Shanghai Renmin Publishing House.

Shanghai Municipal Statistics Bureau. 1997. *Shanghai Statistical Yearbook (Shanghai Tongji Nianjian)*. Beijing: China Statistical Publishing House.

Shanghai Statistics Bureau. 1997. *Statistic Bulletin of 1996 Shanghai Economic and Social Development* 10 (February).

Shanghai Women's Federation. 1997. *Marxist Views on Women and the National Policy of Equality of Men and Women*, 54.

Shantakumar, G. 1993. "Demographic and Socio-Economic Characteristics of Older Women: Issues and Policy Implications." In *Singapore Women: Three Decades of Change*, Aline K. Wong and Leong Wai Kum, eds. Singapore: Times Academic Press, 208–252.

Shao, Ling. 1995. "Luxurious Wind Is Blowing Over the Divine Land." Bulletin, Hong Kong (July 10).

Sheldon, Kathleen, ed. 1996. *Courtyards, Markets, City Streets: Urban Women in Africa.* Boulder: Westview.

Shiva, M. P. 1990. "Forestry Sector Review Tropical Forestry Action Plan." Vietnam: Non-Wood Forest Products, UNDP, Hanoi.

Siao, Richard, and Yuanling Chao, eds. 1994. "Provincial Laws on the Protection of Women and Children." *Chinese Law and Government* (January-February). This volume contains the translated text of sixteen of the regional regulations concerning women's rights.

Sim, Wai Chew. 1995. "Singapore Number One for Doing Business: Fortune." *Straits Times Weekly Edition* (October 28): 3.

Singapore. 1995. "Singapore Is Second." (November-December): 5.

Singapore Council of Women's Organizations. 1989. *Report on Survey of Married Women in Public Housing.* Singapore: SCWO.

Sit, Victor F. S. 1995. *Beijing: The Nature and Planning of a Chinese Capital City.* New York: John Wiley and Sons.

Smart, Alan 1995. "Hong Kong's Slums and Squatter Areas: A Developmental Perspective." In *Housing the Urban Poor: Policy and Practice in Developing Countries*, B. C. Aldrich and R. S. Sandhu, eds. London: Zed.

Smit, Jac. 1996. *Urban Agriculture: Food, Jobs, and Sustainable Cities.* New York: UNDP, Publication Series for Habitat II, vol. 1.

"Society: Marital Violence Complaints Increase in Guangzhou." 1996. *Zhongguo Xinwen She* (trans. by British Broadcasting Corp.), available on LEXIS, World Library, Allwld (April 28).

Sociology. 1994. "The Basic Situation of 1993 Shanghai Social Development." *Shanghai* 2: 10.

Son, M. 1996. Institute of Ethnology, Hanoi Vietnam. Personal communication.

Sowerwine, Jennifer, Nguyen Huy Dung, and Mark Poffenberger. 1998. "Ba Vi National Park and the Dzao." In *Stewards of Vietnam's Upland Forests*, Research Network Report #10, January.

Stamp, Patricia. 1991. "Burying Otieo: The Politics of Gender and Ethnicity in Kenya." *Signs* 14(4).

Star News. 1997. "Tallest Building Roofed." URL: http://china-window.com/shanghai/sstr/97/9m/9m02d4.html, *Shanghai Star.*

State Statistical Bureau. Various years. *China Statistical Yearbook (ZhongGuo Tongji Nianjian).* Beijing: China Statistical Publishing House.

————. 1995. The People's Republic of China: Communique Concerning the Main Data of the Sampling Survey of 1 percent of the National Population.

Statistical Data of Shanghai Women. 1994. Shanghai: China Statistics Press, 132–133.

Stearns, Lisa. 1993. "The New Chinese Women's Law." *Women's International Network News* 19 (Winter): 53.

Stockman, Norman, Norman Bonney, and Sheng Xuewen. 1995. *Women's Work in East and West: The Dual Burden of Employment and Family Life.* Armonk, N.Y.: M. E. Sharpe.

Straits Times Weekly Edition, various issues as indicated.

Stuart-Fox, Martin. 1998. "Laos in 1997: Into Asean." *Asian Survey* 8(1): 75–79.

Study of the Urban Family in Contemporary China. 1995. China Social Sciences Publishing House.

Sullivan, Margaret. 1990. *"Can Survive, La": Cottage Industries in High-rise Singapore.* Singapore: Graham Brash.

Summerfield, G. 1997. "Economic Transition in China and Vietnam: Crossing the Poverty Line Is Just the First Step for Women and Their Families." *Review of Social Economy* (Summer): 201–214.

———. 1994. "Chinese Women and the Post-Mao Economic Reforms." In *Women in the Age of Economic Transformation: Gender Impact of Reforms in Post-Socialist and Developing Countries*, N. Aslanbeigui, S. Pressman, and G. Summerfield, eds. London and New York: Routledge, 113–128.

Summerfield, G., and N. Aslanbeigui. 1992. "Feminization of Poverty in China?" *Development* 4: 57–61.

Sun, Huimin. 1990. "The Evaluation of the Quality of the Life and the Application of Time Indicators—the Living Activity and Time Distribution of Shanghai Residents." In *Papers of the Shanghai Academy of Social Sciences* (3), Shanghai Academy of Social Sciences, eds. Shanghai: Shanghai Academy of Social Sciences Press.

Sun Jinlou. 1983. "A Projecting Social Problem—an Elementary Analysis of the Causes of Housing Shortage." In *A Collection of Sociology* (Shanghai Sociology Society), 151–155.

Sung, Yun-wing. 1996. "'Dragon Head' of China's Economy?" In *Shanghai: Transformation and Modernization Under China's Open Policy*, Y. M. Yeung and Y. Sung, eds. Hong Kong: Chinese University Press.

Supreme People's Court of the People's Republic of China. 1993. "Yinfa guanyu renmin fayuan shenli lihun hanjian chuli caichan fengge wenti de ruogan juti yijian de fangzhi," Howard Yao, trans.

Tan, Augustine H. H., and Phang Sock-Yong. 1991. *The Singapore Experience in Public Housing*. Singapore: Times Academic Press.

Tan, Hsueh Yun. 1996a. "Hdb Launches New Design Plus Flats." *Straits Times Weekly Edition* (January 13): 24.

———. 1996b. "Ten-Year Plan to Breathe New Life into Ang Mo Kio." *Straits Times Weekly Edition* (July 6): 1.

Tan, Kim Song. 1995. "Singapore Once Again Second Most Competitive." *Straits Times Weekly Edition* (September 9): 1.

———. 1994. "Singapore Second Most Competitive Economy." *Straits Times Weekly Edition* (September 10): 1.

Tan, Patrick. 1996. "Qingdao Mega-Projects for Grandlink." *Straits Times Weekly Edition* (October 26): 20.

Tan, Sumiko. 1996. "'Your Vote Will Have Immediate Impact on Your Life.'" *Straits Times Weekly Edition* (December 28): 1.

———. 1994. "Singapore 'Well Placed' to Enjoy Viet Boom." *Straits Times Weekly Edition* (March 4): 1.

Tan, Tammy. 1996. "All Homes to Be Linked to Range of Services." *Straits Times Weekly Edition* (June 8): 1.

Tan, Tarn How. 1994. "Fourteen Investors Sign Up for Suzhou Township." *Straits Times Weekly Edition* (September 17): 24.

Tapp, Nicholas. 1989. *Sovereignty and Rebellion: The White Hmong of Northern Thailand*. Singapore: Oxford.

Tayanin, Damrong. 1994. *Being Kammu: My Village, My Life*. Southeast Asia Program Series No. 14. Ithaca: Southeast Asia Program, Cornell University.

Thach Lam (author omits family name). 1988. *Thirty-six Ancient Streets in Hanoi*. Ho Chi Minh City: Culture and Art Publishing House.

Thai Thi Ngoc Du. 1996. "Living Conditions of Vietnamese Women in Urban Areas." In *Culture in Development and Globalisation*, National Center for Social

Sciences and Humanities of Vietnam, ed. Hanoi (supported by Toyota Foundation).

―――. 1994. "Urban Governance and Poverty Alleviation in South Vietnam." Paper presented at the Sub-regional Workshop on Urban Governance and Poverty Alleviation in South East Asia, November 14–15. Manila.

Thai Thi Ngoc Du, Truong Thi Kim Chuyen, Ngo Thanh Loan, Vuong Tuong Van. 1995. "Working and Living Conditions of Women in Slum Areas in Ho Chi Minh City." Ho Chi Minh City: University of Ho Chi Minh City. Unpublished report.

Thanh Huong and Ngoc Dung. 1996. "Put Limits on the Use of Cultivated Land for Other Purposes." *Nong thon nguy nary*, March 13.

Thanh Mai (author omits family name). 1996. "Public Housing—Worries About It." *Hanoi Moi*, July 2.

Thorbek, Susanne. 1990. "A Female Perspective on Urbanization in the Third World." In *Third World Urbanization: Reappraisals and New Perspectives,* Satya Datta, ed. Stockholm: Swedish Council for Research in the Humanities and Social Sciences, 247–264.

Tinker, Irene. 1999. "NGOs: An Alternate Power Base for Women?" In *Gender Politics and Global Governance*, Mary K. Meyer and Elisabeth Prugl, eds. Lanham, Md.: Rowman and Littlefield.

―――. 1998. "Feeding Megacities: A Worldwide Viewpoint." *Urban Age* (Winter): 4–7.

―――. 1997a. *Street Foods: Urban Food and Employment in Developing Countries.* New York: Oxford University Press, 1997.

―――. I. 1997b. "Family Survival in an Urbanizing World." *Review of Social Economy* (Summer): 251–260.

―――. 1995. "Women in the Urban Environment: Creating Sustainable Working and Living Conditions." Paper presented at international symposium Urban Working Women and Sustainable Development. NGO Forum at the Fourth United Nations Conference on Women, Beijing. September 3.

―――. 1994. "Beyond Economics: Sheltering the Whole Woman." In *Engendering Wealth and Well-Being*, Rae Blumberg, Cathy Rakowski, Irene Tinker, and Michael Monteon, eds. Boulder: Westview, 261–283.

―――. 1993a. "Global Policies Regarding Shelter for Women: Experiences of the Un Centre for Human Settlements." In *Shelter, Women and Development: First and Third World Perspectives*, Hemalata Dandekar, ed. Ann Arbor, Mich.: George Wahr.

―――. 1993b. "Women and Shelter: Combining Women's Roles." In *Women at the Center: Gender Issues for the 1990s*, Gay Young, Vidjamali Samarasinghe, and Ken Corey, eds. West Hartford: Kumarian Press.

―――. 1991. "Women's Access to Housing and Work: And Evaluation of Unchs Programs in Indonesia, Bangladesh, and Nepal." An evaluation for UNIFEM, the United Nations Fund for Women, and HABITAT, the United Nations Centre for Human Settlements, March.

―――. 1990. "The Making of a Field: Advocates, Practitioners, and Scholars." In *Persistent Inequalities: Women and World Development*, I. Tinker, ed. New York: Oxford.

―――. 1983. "Women in Development." In *Women in Washington: Advocates for Public Policy*, I. Tinker, ed. Los Angeles: Sage Publications.

Tinker, Irene, ed. 1990. *Persistent Inequalities: Women and World Development.* New York: Oxford.

Tinker, Irene, and Gale Summerfield, eds. 1997. "Symposium: Ngo Forum, United Nations' Fourth Conference on Women, 1995." *Review of Social Economy* 55(2): 196–260.

To Dinh Lu. 1996. "Can the Land Users Have the Five Rights According to the Land Law by the End of 1996?" *Nhan dom*, January 16.

Todd, Helen. 1996. *Women at the Center: Grameen Bank Borrowers After One Decade.* Boulder: Westview.

Ton Gia Huyen. 1993. "Some Key Issues of Land Management and Land Use." *Cong san* 3: 38–39.

Tran Duc. 1991. *Cooperatives and the Golden Time of Household Economy.* Hanoi: Agric. Publishing House.

Tran Ngoc Phuong. 1994. *Housing for Low Income People in Ho Chi Minh City.*

Tran Phuong. 1969. *Land Revolution in Vietnam.* Hanoi, 12–13.

Tran Thi Lanh. 1996. Executive Director, Toward Ethnic Women, Hanoi. Personal communication.

Tran Thi Que. 1996. Executive Secretary, Socio Economic Development Center, Hanoi. Personal communication.

Tran Xuan Thu. 1995. "Questions and Answers on the Law." *Nha nuoc va Phapluat* 4: 61.

Trankell, Ing-Britt. 1993. *On the Road in Laos: An Anthropological Study of Road Construction and Rural Communities.* Uppsala Research Reports in Cultural Anthropology No. 12. Uppsala University, Department of Cultural Anthropology, Sweden.

Tremewan, Christopher. 1994. *The Political Economy of Social Control in Singapore.* London: MacMillan, esp. chap. 3, "Public Housing: The Working-Class Barracks."

Trinh Duy Luan. 1996. *Introduction to Urban Sociology.* Hanoi: Social Science Publishing House.

Trinh Duy Luan and Colleagues. 1996. Report on the workshop Improving Housing and Environment Conditions of Poor People in Urban Areas. Hanoi.

Trinh Duy Luan and Michael Leaf, eds. 1996. *Urban Housing in the Market Economy of the Third World.* Hanoi: Social Sciences Publishing House.

Trinh Duy Luan and Research Group of Sociology Institute. 1994. "Socio-Economic Features, Housing and Environment of Poor People in Hanoi: Survey in Four Quarters of Hanoi." Proceedings of a workshop.

Tripp, Aili Mari. 1996. "Urban Women's Movements and Political Liberalization in East Africa." In *Courtyards, Markets, City Streets: Urban Women in Africa,* K. Sheldon, ed. Boulder: Westview.

Tuong Lai. 1995. *Sociological Studies on Social Stratification.* Hanoi: Social Science Publishing House.

United Nations. 1996. Second United Nations Conference on Human Settlements— Habitat II, June, online, URL: http://pan.cedar.univie.ac.at/habitat/gender/gen1.html.

UN Centre for Human Settlements. 1989. *Women and Human Settlements Development.* Nairobi.

———. 1985. *Women and Human Settlements.* Nairobi.

United Nations Development Programme (UNDP). 1996. *Human Development Report 1996.* New York: Oxford University Press.

———. United Nations Fund for Population Activities and United Nations International Children's Fund. 1995. Fiftieth Anniversary in Vietnam. Hanoi: UNDP.

———. 1994. *Human Development Report.* New York: Oxford University Press.

UNICEF. 1994. *Situation Analysis of Women and Children in Vietnam.* Hanoi.

United Press International. Various reports as cited.

"Universal Declaration of Human Rights." 1948. UNGA Resolution 217 A (III) (December 10).

Usher, Ann D. 1996. "The Race for Power in Laos: The Nordic Connections." In *Environmental Change in South-east Asia*, Michael Parnwell and Raymond Bryant, eds. London: Routledge, 123–144.

Van Tien, Luong. 1991. *Country Paper Vietnam.* Contribution to the regional expert consultation on nonwood forest products in the Asia-Pacific region. RAPA. November 5–8, Bangkok.

Varghese, M. A. 1993. "Improving Health and Nutrition of Urban Slums Through Community Participation." Bombay: Women's University. A report of an IDRC-UNICEF sponsored project.

Varley, Ann. 1996. "Women Heading Households: Some More Equal Than Others?" *World Development* 24(3): 505–520.

———. 1995. "Neither Victims nor Heroines: Women, Land, and Housing in Urban Mexico." *Third World Planning Review* 17(2): 169–182.

Veblen, Thorstein. 1931 (1899). *Theory of the Leisure Class.* New York: Modern Library.

Verdery, Katherine. 1996. *What Was Socialism and What Comes Next?* Princeton Studies in Culture, Power, and History: Princeton University Press.

Vietnam Government. 1995. Civil Law. Hanoi.

———. 1993. Land Law. Hanoi.

———. 1986. Marriage and Family Law. Hanoi.

Vietnam News, August 15, 1998.

Viravong, Manivone. 1995. "Country Study: Lao People's Democratic Republic." In *Improving the Access of Women to Formal Credit and Financial Institutions: Windows of Opportunity*, Economic and Social Commission for Asia and the Pacific (ESCAP), ed. New York: United Nations, 119–135.

Vo Tran Ang. 1996. Interview in Hanoi, June 21.

Vuong Linh. 1995. "We Need Clearer Regulations on Property Issues Within Marriage." *Phu nu thanh phu Ho Chi Minh*, January 21: 15.

Wamukonya, Njeri. 1997. "Gender Biases in Agricultural Resource Control in Okavango, Namibia." Field research report, University of California, Berkeley.

Wang, Fu. 1988. "Establishment and Development of the Building Industry in New China." In *China Today: The Building Industry*, Xiao Tong, ed. China Today Series Editorial Department, 74.

Wang, Hui Ling. 1996. "Nine in Ten Hdb Residents Satisfied with Hdb Living." *Straits Times Weekly Edition* (June 22): 1.

Wang Lihong. 1996. "Too Many Vacancies, Not Enough Customers." *China Daily* (Business Weekly), Beijing: 1–2 (September 29–October 5).

Wang, Lina. 1997. "Opportunity and Challenge to China's Real Estate Industry in 1997." *Global Market Information Guide* no. 2: 25.

Wang, Shaoguang. 1995. "The Politics of Private Time: Changing Leisure Patterns in Urban China." In *Urban Spaces in Contemporary China: The Potential for Autonomy and Community in Post-Mao China*, D. S. Davis, R. Kraus, B. Naughton, and E. J. Perry, eds. Cambridge: Cambridge University Press.

Wang, Ya Ping, and Alan Murie. 1996. "The Process of Commercialisation of Urban Housing in China." *Urban Studies* 33(6): 971–989.

Wee, Kenneth K. S. 1979. "Legal Aspects of Population Policies." In *Public Policy and Population Change in Singapore*, Peter S. J. Chen and James T. Fawcett, eds. New York: Population Council, 29–46.

Wei Jinsheng et al. 1995. "Research on Rural Population Movement in China." China Population Information and Research Center. Unpublished manuscript.

Wei, Lingling. 1997. "High Demand for Housing: Overseas Capital Needed for Economical Apartments." URL: http://china-window.com/shanghai/sstr/97/8m/8m01d3.html, *Shanghai Star*, August 1.

Wen Hui Bao. 1997. "The Leaders of Shanghai Administration Center of Accumulation Fund Talk About 'The Establishment of Supplementary Accumulation Fund of Housing.'" June 26.

Wen/Kan Jun. 1997. "The Direction and Key Question of Housing Policies." *Beijing Economic News* (January 19): 4.

White, Lynn T. 1996. "Shanghai's 'Horizontal Liasons' and Population Control." In *Shanghai: Transformation and Modernization under China's Open Policy*, Y. M. Yeung and Y. Sung, eds. Hong Kong: Chinese University Press.

Wirthlin Worldwide. 1996. "Asian Values and Business Success." Report presented at an Asian business seminar, Bangkok (sponsored by Dow Jones and Co.).

Wong, Aline K. 1992. "Sex Roles, Lifecycle Stages, Social Networks, and Community Development in Singapore." In *Persons and Powers of Women in Diverse Cultures*, Shirley Ardener, ed. New York: Berg, 159–171.

———. 1981. "Planned Development, Social Stratification, and the Sexual Division of Labor in Singapore." *Signs* 7(2): 434–452.

———. 1980. "Economic Development and Women's Place: Women in Singapore." *Change International Reports*. London.

———. 1979. "The National Family Planning Programme and Changing Family Life." In *The Contemporary Family in Singapore*, Eddie C. Y. Kuo and Aline K. Wong, eds. Singapore: Singapore University Press, 211–238.

Wong, Aline K., and John Wong. 1979. "Socioeconomic Development: Review of a Decade." In *Public Policy and Population Change in Singapore*, Peter S. J. Chen and James T. Fawcett, eds. New York: Population Council, 47–69.

Wong, Aline K., and Stephen H. K. Yeh. 1985. *Housing a Nation: Twenty-five Years of Public Housing in Singapore.* Singapore: Maruzen Asia for Housing and Development Board.

World Bank. 1997. *China 2020: Development Challenges in the New Century.* Washington, D.C.

———. 1996. *World Development Report.* New York: Oxford University Press.

———. 1995. *Lao PDR Agricultural Sector Memorandum: An Agricultural Sector Strategy.* Washington, D.C.: Agriculture and Environment Operation Division, Country Department, East Asia and Pacific Region, World Bank. March 23.

———. 1993a. *China: Urban Land Management in an Emerging Market Economy.* Washington, D.C.: World Bank.

———. 1993b. *The East Asian Miracle: Economic Growth and Public Policy.* New York: Oxford University Press.

———. 1992. *China: Implementation Options for Urban Housing Reform.* Washington, D.C.: World Bank.

Xin, Bao. 1997. "'Blue Card' Strategy Lan to Win over More Home Buyers from Other Cities." URL: http://www.ocrat.com/ocrat/reaf/reafG.html, March 28.

Xinhua. 1998. "More Chinese Looking to Buy Houses." January 24.

———. 1997. "China Maintains Impressive Housing Development Momentum." August 29.

————. 1997. "China to Speed Up Housing Reform in 1998." December 24.

Xu Min. 1995. "Chinese Women and the Kitchen: Views from Four Generations." In *Women and Market Societies: Crisis and Opportunity,* B. Einhorn and E. J. Yeo, eds. Aldershot, U.K.: Edward Elgar.

Yang Lu and Wang Yukun. 1992. *Housing Reform: Theoretical Thoughts and Realistic Selection.* Tianjin Renmin Publishing House.

Yang, Shengyong. 1991. "System and Housing." In *Introduction to Housing Sociology,* Housing Sociology, Academic Committee, China Urban Housing Problems Research Society, eds. Anhui People's Publishing House.

Yates, Teresa. 1997. "Waiting for a Revolution." ICWA Letters. Hanover, N.H.: Institute for Current World Affairs, TCY-9, August.

Yeoh, Pei Lin. 1996. "Community Spirit to Count in Upgrading." *Straits Times Weekly Edition* (September 21): 1.

Yin Wenshu. 1996. "An Approach to Housing Reform Patterns of Chinese Cities and Towns." *Economics in Length and Breadth* (January): 19–23.

Zhang Hongming and Gao Liugen. 1997. "Housing Issue in Shanghai Should Make New Progress in the Period of 'The Ninth Five Year Plan.'"

Zhang, Yijun. 1997. "Speech Guides Future Progress." URL: http://china-window.com/shanghai/sstr/97/9m/9m16d2.html, *Shanghai Star,* August 1.

"Zhu Rongji on Economic, Enterprise Reform." 1996. *Hong Kong Ching Pao* (February 1): 28.

The Contributors

Tran Thi Van Anh is a researcher at the Center for Family and Women's Studies in Hanoi, Vietnam. Her work has focused on rural women and policies toward women during periods of transition.

Nahid Aslanbeigui is associate professor of economics at Monmouth University. Her main areas of research are women in development, history of economic thought, and economics education. She is coeditor of *Women in the Age of Economic Transformation* (1994), *Rethinking Economic Principles: Critical Essays on Introductory Textbooks* (1996), and *Borderlands of Economics* (1997).

Bu Xin is chair of the research committee on living environment at the Beijing Sociological Association.

Thai Thi Ngoc Du, born in 1946 in Huc, Vietnam, is professor of geography in the Department of Geography at the University of Social Sciences and Humanities of Ho Chi Minh City and head of the Women's Studies Department at the Open University of Ho Chi Minh City. She got her Ph.D. in 1971 in France, specializing in urban geography. Her research projects have been focused on urbanization, poverty and sustainable development, and women's issues.

Fei Juanhong is associate research professor of sociology at the Institute of Sociology at the Shanghai Academy of Social Sciences. She is the author of *Family, Harmony, and Crisis, Rural Women in Shanghai's Suburbs in the Reform* and *Opening Up,* and a number of journal articles on women's studies, marriage, and family.

Barbara Hopkins is assistant professor of economics and women's studies at Wright State University in Dayton, Ohio. Her research focuses on the implications for women of economic transformation from socialism to capitalism. She teaches courses on comparative economic systems, development and poverty, and the Pacific Rim.

W. Randall Ireson has worked in a variety of rural development programs in Laos, Thailand, and Vietnam since 1967. He has also taught sociology at Willamette University. He is development assistance coordinator for the American Friends Service Committee program in North Korea.

Carol Ireson-Doolittle is professor of sociology at Willamette University in Oregon. She began working in Southeast Asia more than thirty years ago and has recently published a book about Laotian women entitled *Field, Forest, and Family: Women's Work and Power in Rural Laos.* Her areas of research and teaching include gender, environment, and family.

Li Weisha is associate professor of sociology at the Hubei Academy of Social Sciences in China. She is also a member of the Standing Committee, 8th Hubei Province Committee of the Chinese People's Political Consultative Conference.

Li Zongmin received her Ph.D. in development studies from the University of Wisconsin–Madison in 1997. From 1987 to 1990, she was a research fellow at the Research Center for Rural Development of the State Council of the People's Republic of China. From 1990 to 1992, she was a Ford Foundation Visiting Scholar at the Land Tenure Center at the University of Wisconsin–Madison. Her doctoral dissertation concerns the impact of rural industrialization on intrahousehold gender division of labor and welfare in rural China and is based on fieldwork in Hebei Province.

Hoang Thi Lich is former vice director of the Center for Family and Women's Studies, National Center for Social Sciences and Humanities, Hanoi, where she is senior researcher and a gender consultant and trainer. She is author of numerous articles and publications on women's work and working and living conditions of women in households and society.

Jean Larson Pyle is codirector of the Center for Women and Work and professor of economics in the Department of Regional Economic and Social Development at the University of Massachusetts–Lowell where she specializes in the overlapping areas of labor, economic development, and policy, with particular attention to gender and diversity issues. She is author of *The State and Women in the Economy: Lessons from Sex Discrimination in the Republic of Ireland* (1990) and has consulted for the United Nations Industrial Development Organization, on gender and development issues.

Jennifer Sowerwine is a Ph.D. candidate in the Department of Environmental Science, Policy, and Management at the University of California–Berkeley. She has conducted field research in Costa Rica, Nepal, Laos, and Vietnam focusing on the tensions between growth, equity, and environmental conservation. She currently is researching the effects of rapid economic change on gender, property rights, and biodiversity among highland peoples and landscapes in northern Vietnam.

Gale Summerfield is director of the Office of Women in International Development and associate professor of human and community development at the University of Illinois at Urbana-Champaign. She also serves as director of the Equity Policy Center. She is coeditor, with Nahid Aslanbeigui and Steve Pressman, of *Women in the Age of Economic Transformation.* She is editor (with Jiaying Zhuang Howard) of *Women and Economic Transition in China.* Her current work stresses microenterprise and environmental policy.

Irene Tinker is professor emerita at the University of California–Berkeley. She has founded two action-research organizations: the International Center for Research on Women and the Equity Policy Center. She has conducted research in fifty-three countries. Tinker has been a prolific writer throughout her career; her publications include *Street Foods: Food and Employment in Developing Countries* (1997) and *Persistent Inequalities: Women and World Development* (1990).

Manivone Viravong worked at the Ministry of Agriculture in Laos for many years. She is currently a consultant to the government on socioeconomic development, and she has one of the biggest plantation farms in Laos owned by an individual. She has written many articles about women and economic development, including "Microcredit for Women in the Lao PDR" (1995).

Dia Warren lived in South China and Hong Kong from 1990 to 1993, and she researched and wrote her chapter on subsequent visits to China. She holds dual graduate degrees in law and law and diplomacy and is currently a practicing attorney in Boston.

Wei Zhangling is full professor of sociology and academic member at the Institute of Sociology at the Chinese Academy of Social Sciences in Beijing and is also president of the Family Ethics and Women's Development Research Centre.

Index

Agriculture, 95–96, 100, 107, 116; collectives/cooperatives, 16; in China, 167; in Laos, 146, 255–256; in Vietnam, 95, 98–100, 110, 122; swiddens (slash and burn), 117–129, 131. *See also* Farmers; Land policy, redistribution; Laws

Agroforestry. *See* Forest

All-China Women's Federation (Fulian, Women's Federation), 25, 174, 242

Asian Values as a development model. *See* Singapore development model

CEDAW, 165–167, 169, 177. *See* Convention on the Elimination of All Forms of Discrimination Against Women

Childcare, 92, 183, 192, 218, 262, 266

Chinese Constitution, 1982, 1992, 167–168; Civil Code, 1987, 1989, 167

Comfortable Housing Policy, 175, 182, 186, 188. *See also* Housing policy; Laws

Community: development, 65–68; participation (popular participation), 6, 66, 68, 74, 75, 175, 259, 263; providing services for women, 261–262

Confucian values. *See* Singapore development model

Convention of Human Rights, 10

Convention on the Elimination of All forms of Discrimination Against Women (CEDAW), 165–169, 177

Credit, 9, 20, 23, 60, 65–68, 72, 75, 91, 189. *See also* Savings programs

Customary law, 9, 10, 12, 17, 20, 23–26; customary rights, 16, 149, 151, 153, 159, 265, 271. *See also* Laws

Dan wei. *See* Work unit

Divorce, 19, 24, 266, 271; in China, 168–173, 176, 184, 188, 189, 205, 232, 252, 264; in Laos, 155; in Vietnam, 61, 90-91, 111–113, 136, 138

Doi moi (renovation in Vietnam). *See* Economic reforms, in Vietnam

Economic reforms (market liberalization, market reforms, transition policies) 4, 137, 271; in China, post-Mao, 179–182, 198–9, 200, 246–247; in Laos, New Economic Mechanism (NEM), 147, 156–158; in Vietnam, *Doi moi* (renovation), 55–56, 60, 62, 67, 73–74, 77–79, 96, 98–100, 122, 136–137

Education, 21, 22, 25, 55, 75, 132, 137, 140, 165, 170, 173–174, 176, 191, 260, 261–263

Employment (jobs), 22, 131, 134, 174, 182–185; in factories; in rural industry. *See also* Home-based work; Work unit

Environmental laws and regulations: China, 189–191; Laos; Vietnam. *See also* Laws

Family and family law, 60-61, 90, 101, 103, 105–106, 111–114, 168. *See* Customary law; Household

Farmers, 9, 10, 14, 16, 95–96, 99–101, 104–109, 112, 116–117, 119, 121, 123; changing time allocation by gender, 250-251. *See also* Work points

Forest (Agroforestry), 7, 18, 105, 107, 116–129; land control, 7; land use/management, 63, 113–115, 121, 131–132, 137–139, 141–142; medicinal herbs, 7, 117, 131–142; products, 133–134; protection. *See also,* Laws, Laos, forest

Fulian, 173–174. *See* All-China Women's Federation

Gender: biases/stereotypes, 19, 96, 102, 107, 131, 170, 172, 219, 221, 256–259; family labor division, 9, 86, 123–130, 220; impacts, 7, 247–249, 254, 269; relations/roles, 17, 179, 183, 186, 189–190, 218–219, 232, 241, 265–266

Grameen Bank, 14, 19, 20, 25, 68. *See also* Credit; Savings programs

Home-based work (microenterprise, informal sector), 3, 66, 70, 74–75, 86–93, 172, 190, 192, 217, 268. *See also* Employment; Street food enterprise

Household (family, marriage), 60, 74–75, 85, 90-91, 101, 110-113– 118, 122, 171; bargaining power/decisionmaking and labor division, 2, 3, 11, 14, 15, 86, 154–156, 188, 249–250, 251, 270-271; clan, 231, 232–234; composition (extended, nuclear, women-headed), 6, 11–14, 60-62, 86, 93, 103, 106, 110, 139, 159, 235–236, 243, 249, 269; definition of, 179; disputes, 158; economy, 127, 129; extended (*See* Household composition); nuclear (*See* Household composition)

Household responsibility system, 171, 252–253, 258–259, 261

House (property): ownership (private; state-owned), 80-84, 89–90, 165–169, 171–172, 176, 187– 189, 252. *See also* Work unit

Housing: amenities, lack of, 88–89, 197, 215, 216–218 (*See* also Sanitation); commercial, 198; construction, 196, 197, 198, 225–228; cost, 175, 197; discrimination against women, 9, 165, 169, 172–173, 176, 186; disputes, 3; private, 197, 211, 252–253; shortage, 170, 172, 174, 181, 195, 197, 204–5, 225, 228; space per capita, 180-181, 196, 197, 216, 234–235; state-owned, 197; traditional, 223–224; 228–229, 231. *See also* Housing rights.

Housing policy, 40-45; 200-202, 205–206, 209, 216, 220, 265; allocation systems, 3, 165, 169, 172–173, 176, 197, 209, 211, 214, 220-221, 267; commercialization, 165, 198, 199, 200, 214; commodification, 165, 175–176, 210-211, 213; employment, 199–200; family planning, 46–48, 52; family values, 45–46; political process, 38–39; reforms, 171, 174–176, 198–199, 204, 208–209, 214, 226–227; rent, 72, 82, 89, 173, 185–187, 197, 198, 199, 211; subsidies, 77, 198, 200, 210; transition to free market, 7, 177, 182, 212, 226; Yantai model, 199. *See also* Comfortable Housing Policy; Housing rights; Laws; Savings programs

Housing rights (property rights), 3, 78, 85, 89–91, 96, 111–113, 165–169,171–174, 176, 267–269; in China, 229–230, 231; in Vietnam, 59–61, 74, 78, 85, 89–91, 165–169, 171–174, 176. *See also* Land Rights; Laws

Human rights, 10, 166–167, 176, 267. *See also* Convention of human rights.

Hutong (traditional alley housing, Beijing), 190, 223–224, 228

Income inequality, 7, 77, 195, 211, 225, 269

Industrialization, impact on women: 254–255, 258

Informal sector. *See* Home-based work. *See also* Employment

Inheritance rights, 12, 18, 20, 150, 167–169, 231, 236–237, 252;

matrilineal system, Laos, 153–155; patrilineal system. *See also* Customary law; Household; Laws

Kampongs (traditional Malay housing), 10, 34

Land (property), 55, 57, 60, 64, 96, 98, 100-101, 105–107, 109–111, 132, 137–139, 141, 167–168, 170-171; commodification, 151; customary use, 10, 20, 147–148; disputes, 110, 112–113, 157; ownership, 79, 85, 89, 138–139, 148, 154, 160, 171, 176, 197; price, 84, 90, 92; private, 79, 84, 90, 167, 176; registration, 151, 158; 161; rent, 82, 89; sale, 151, 157; tenure, 16, 25, 132, 137, 140, 142, 154. *See also* Customary law; Inheritance rights

Land policy, 79, 265; allocation, 4, 98–99, 101–105, 110, 113, 138, 141, 142, 149, 151, 159, 160-1, 162, 171, 245–246; certificates, 105–109, 113, 138, 141–142; contract, 89, 91, 99–100, 166–167, 171; redistribution, 78, 246, 252; reform, 7, 77, 96, 99, 101, 168, 244–5; titling: 25, 131, 136–138, 142, 158; 159, 161, 162; transfer, 82, 84, 89–90, 101, 106–107, 113, 158, 167, 170, 172–173, 175. *See also* Land rights; Laws; Customary law

Land rights (property rights), 3, 96, 111, 113, 159, 234, 247–248, 264, 269–270. *See also* Housing Rights; Laws

Laotian Decrees. *See* Laws, Laos

Laws: China, 7, State Council Decision on Housing Reform, 182; Foreign Business, 170; Land Management, 170; Marriage law, 168, 173–174; Women's Rights (Protection) Law 1992, 173–176, 191; Laos, 156, 159; Decrees1992, 157; 1993, 157; 1994, 157–158; forest, 161; Vietnam: Land Law 1993, 6, 89–90, 101–102, 107–114, 122

Market reforms. *See* Economic reforms

Marriage. *See* Customary Law; Divorce; Household; Laws

Microenterprise. *See* Employment; Home-based work

Migration/migrants, 12, 55, 57, 63–64, 79, 92, 151, 180-181, 197, 227, 237, 269. *See also* Squatter areas/squatters, Urbanization

Mortgage, 84, 90, 105–106, 113, 175, 188. *See also* Credit, Savings programs

New Economic Mechanism (Laos). *See* Economic Reforms, in Laos

NGOs. *See* Nongovernmental organizations

NGO Forum, 1995. *See also* United Nations World Conferences for Women

Nongovernmental organizations (NGOs), 18, 21, 25, 66, 75, 107, 141, 270-271

Oxfam, United Kingdom and Ireland, 19, 138, 141

Pollution: of squatter and slum areas. *See also* Environmental laws and regulations

Popular participation. *See* Community

Property and property rights. *See* Housing; Housing rights; Land; Land rights

Public: accumulation fund (*See* Savings programs); sector reform (*See* Economic reforms)

Real estate market

Rent. *See* Housing policy, Land

Residence patterns, 7; patrilocal, 118, 127; uxorilocal, 149–150, 154 ; virilocal, 202–203, 205, 231, 236, 238

Rural. *See* Household; Land

Sanitation: Vietnam, 70, 81, 89; China: in slums. *See* also Pollution; Environmental laws and regulations

Savings programs: compulsory savings fund (public accumulation fund) 182, 188, 198, 199–200

Singapore development model (Asian Values as a development model;

Confucian values): 6, 7, 27–28, 30, 32–3, 48–50, 188, 199, 268; impact in China, 31; in Vietnam, 31; problems, 32–33; Women's Charter, 35; women as owners, 35
Slums. *See* Squatter areas
Squatter areas (and slums)/squatters, 4–6, 63–65, 67, 70, 74–75, 77, 81, 88–90, 151, 181, 190, 213–214, 269; government policy, 64, 67, 74; resettlement programs, 59, 65, 68, 72–75. *See also* Migration; Urbanization.
Street food enterprise, 12, 14, 41, 86–87. *See also* Home-based work

United Nations, Habitat II, 192, 223
United Nations World Conferences for Women: Beijing, 1995, 10; Mexico City 1975, 13. *See also* NGO Forum, 1995
Urban: food production, 146; housing, 225; renewal, 38; planning, 60, 67, 189–192. *See also* Street food enterprise; Urbanization

Urbanization, 6, 10, 22, 55–56, 59, 67, 77–78, 225, 227. *See also* Migration; Squatter areas/squatters

Vietnam Women's Union. *See* Women's Union, of Vietnam

Women's Charter. *See* Singapore, women's charter.
Women's Federation, China. *See* All-China Women's Federation
Women's Network on Economic Transition in East/Southeast Asia (WONET), 1
Women's Rights (Protection) Law, China 1992. *See* Laws, China
Women's Union: of Laos, 19, 25, 159–160, 161, 162; of Vietnam, 25, 68, 74–75, 107, 141
WONET. *See* Women's Network on Economic Transition in East/Southeast Asia
Work points, 99–100. *See also* Farmers
Work unit (Dan wei), 64, 167, 170-176, 182–185, 209–210, 215–216

About the Book

Gender disparities frequently accompany rapid socioeconomic change, as cultural traditions that protected women—even as they constrained them—collapse in the face of development reforms. This collaborative volume, involving both Asian and U.S. scholars, explores the impact of changes in women's rights to housing and land in three socialist countries that are moving toward market economies.

The authors focus on such issues as property use and ownership, efforts to recognize women's economic rights through development programming, poverty and women-headed households, and household bargaining. The final chapter surveys the impact of various development policies, highlighting successes and failures.

Irene Tinker is professor emerita of city and regional planning and of women's studies at the University of California–Berkeley. Her numerous publications include *Street Foods: Urban Food and Employment in Developing Countries*. **Gale Summerfield** is director of the office of Women in International Development, University of Illinois at Urbana-Champaign. She is editor (with Jiaying Zhuang Howard) of *Women and Economic Transition in China*.